THE
BEATLES
LITERARY
ANTHOLOGY

Edited by Mike Evans

Plexus, London

All rights reserved including the right of
reproduction in whole or in part in any form
Copyright © 2004 by Plexus Publishing Limited
Published by Plexus Publishing Limited
55a Clapham Common Southside
London SW4 9BX
Tel: 0207 622 2440
Fax: 0207 622 2441
plexus@plexusuk.demon.co.uk
www.plexusbooks.com
First Printing

British Library Cataloguing in Publication Data

The Beatles literary anthology
1. Beatles 2. Rock musicians - Great Britain - Biography
3. Rock groups - England - Liverpool
I. Evans, Mike, 1942 Oct. 30-
782.4'2'166'0922

ISBN 0 85965 315 3

Printed in Great Britain by Cromwell Press
Cover design by Rebecca Martin and Phil Gambrill
Book design by Rebecca Martin
Cover photograph by Jean-Marie Périer/At Large

CONTENTS

Once upon a time there were three little boys called John, George and Paul, by name christened . . . all of a sudden they all grew guitars and formed a noise . . . on discovering a fourth little even littler man called Stuart Sutcliffe running about them they said, quote 'Sonny get a bass guitar and you will be alright' . . . So they sat on him with comfort 'til he could play. - *John Lennon – from 'Being a Short Diversion on the Dubious Origins of Beatles', 1961*

INTRODUCTION

In 1957, the painter Richard Hamilton (who later designed the collage insert in the Beatles' *White Album*) famously defined all things Pop as 'popular, transient, expendable, low cost, mass produced, young, witty, sexy, gimmicky, glamorous and big business.' This description was particularly applicable to pop music. Yet as pop artists such as Hamilton appropriated the transient imagery of comic books and advertising, rendering them permanent, so the attention of critics and writers signalled a point at which pop music began to be taken seriously. This radical change in attitude was catalysed by the Beatles.

Before the Beatles, at the beginning of the Sixties, no one in the 'serious' press paid attention to rock'n'roll. There were no books tracing its (admittedly very short) history, and music critics never gave the popular mass-market a second thought. The weekly music press in England was divided, between the throwaway pop coverage of the *New Musical Express* and the jazz-dominated *Melody Maker*. In America, likewise, the jazz fraternity had *Downbeat* magazine, but there was no contemporary equivalent of the later *Rolling Stone*. In the space of one decade, the advent of the Beatles would change all this.

'It seemed to me that pop had come of age,' wrote critic George Melly on first hearing Paul McCartney's 'Eleanor Rigby'. As the Beatles began to transcend the traditional confines of pop music, so an ostensibly more cultured and literate audience sat up and took notice. There were other forces in play, of course. Bob Dylan's lyrics had become progressively more poetic since his first albums in the early Sixties. Indeed, by the time of the Beatles' 1966 *Revolver* album (where 'Eleanor Rigby' first appeared), John Lennon, in particular, had clearly come under his influence. Dylan, however, was first and foremost an albums artist. However significant the changes he brought to rock music, he couldn't impact upon the mainstream in the way that the overtly populist Beatles did.

Populism was the sign of the times – not only in music, but in the popular and commercial arts generally. 1960s Britain saw a democratisation of culture. Painting, fashion, photography, journalism and filmmaking all gave rise to a new generation who displaced the old elite. David Hockney, Michael Caine and David Bailey all came, like the Beatles, from modest backgrounds, These were the new movers and shakers who, in turn, informed the new opinion makers.

So it was that 'highbrow met lowbrow', as one American commentator put it. For the group's unprecedented influence on the other side of the Atlantic – not just on the US charts, but on the American psyche – ensured that of the many thousands of column inches devoted to the Beatles throughout the world, a vast number originated in the United States. And it wasn't just the music journalists who had them in their spotlight. Fashion gurus, film critics, sociologists, psychologists and political commentators all got in on the act.

During the eight short years that marked their career as a recording group, however, only a couple of biographies of the group saw publication: Michael Braun's *Love Me Do: The Beatles' Progress* – the only serious account written during the first year of Beatlemania – and the authorised (but inevitably sanitised) biography by Hunter Davies. There were also two literary efforts by John Lennon – *In His Own Write* and *A Spaniard in the Works* – which immediately made him the toast of that social group the English call 'the chattering classes'.

But, after the Beatles' break-up, the trickle of books became a flood. From the familiar story of their progress from Hamburg cellars to superstardom to in-depth musical analyses, every possible angle was covered. For every straight biography there was a score of 'I was there' recollections by friends and family, ex-colleagues, or even fans; for every realistic assessment of them as a rock'n'roll band, there was some pretentious highbrow critic trying to justify his liking for the Beatles.

Within these pages is a cross section of the very many words written about the Beatles over the years. They range from contemporary reviews to considered retrospective accounts, from thought-provoking challenges to our popular perception of John, Paul, George and Ringo to cynical put-downs by shortsighted pundits. The Beatles often courted controversy – 'We're more popular than Jesus now,' John blithely claimed – but they also stimulated debate (particularly in their candid admissions of drug use), faced the very real physical dangers of Beatlemania – and ultimately, in John's case, suffered an untimely death. (As did original bassist Stuart Sutcliffe, and manager Brian Epstein.)

The significance of the Beatles – not only in terms of their effect on popular music, but also in their impact upon social mores and attitudes – cannot be overestimated. They emerged from an austere post-war Britain, completely under the shadow of US popular culture. British youth had found a necessary escape from drab surroundings in American movies, street fashion and rock'n'roll. Less than a decade on, the Beatles had turned the tables: an affluent Britain began to dominate pop culture across the globe, and directly triggered a 'youth revolution' whose impact is still felt over 30 years later.

Mike Evans
London, 2004

JOHN LENNON 1940-1980
By Ray Connolly

As an early 1940s 'war baby', who grew up in the working-class north-west of England, journalist Connolly had a similar background to the Beatles. This extract from his 1981 biography of Lennon displays an authentic feel for 1950s teen culture.

Against her better judgement, [Aunt] Mimi bought John his first guitar. (It was once thought that Julia [John's mother] was the benevolent encourager of young talent. It is certainly a more romantic notion, and one which would have appealed to John, but it was almost certainly a reluctant Mimi who actually nurtured a growing obsession with a cheap Spanish guitar.) Ten years earlier, Elvis Presley's father had admonished his son with the advice that 'he never knew a guitar player who ever made a dime'; now Mimi was to take up the refrain: 'The guitar's all right, John. But you'll never make a living with it.'

Even if Julia did not actually buy that first guitar it was certainly she who taught John the first chords he was to play. As a girl she had sung and played banjo, and it was banjo chords that she taught John. By now he was sixteen and in his final year at Quarry Bank. All ambitious boys were already swotting for their GCEs which took place the following June, but John Lennon was busy forming his own group. Naturally enough he called it the Quarrymen, and it comprised any of the boys in his school gang who showed any musical ability and several who didn't. The personnel changed by the week as John rowed first with one and then another. 'If you'd been in my class at school I'd have had *you* in the Quarrymen,' he later told me. 'I would have made *you* join to rebel against your mother.' Anyone who liked rock and roll could join. John, of course, was the leader of the group. He didn't know any other way. From childhood he had always assumed an attitude of natural superiority.

Throughout that final year at school John wandered deeper into the world of rock music. Again it was an American culture which was being imposed from outside. It was a full year before Cliff Richard came up with 'Move It', a full year before any British act would make a proper rock and roll record, and it was nearly a year before John would meet Paul McCartney. For a year, while the embryonic Quarrymen larked about with John practising in the porch of his home, the craze grew, and the newspapers began to devote more and more space to this new phenomenon, linking it with violence and the screen rebel heroes of James Dean (who was dead before Elvis even had a hit record) and Marlon Brando. At night, instead of doing his homework, John would tune the family radio in to the weak signal of AFN Munich so that he could hear the new American records before anybody else, or he would listen to the more accessible Radio Luxembourg. (The BBC took a dim view of rock and roll music and devoted as little time to it as was humanly possible in those days.) By this time John was beginning to dress in the Teddy Boy style of the times, tight trousers and greasy hair swept back and up into a pompadour on top of his head. Poor Mimi suffered it all, but never in silence.

Nothing affected me until Elvis. I had no idea about doing music as a way of life until rock'n'roll hit me. It was 'Rock Around the Clock', I think. I enjoyed Bill Haley, but wasn't overwhelmed by him. It wasn't until 'Heartbreak Hotel' that I really got into it.
– John Lennon

John was always funny in his reflections on those adolescent days. When the exploitation film *Rock Around the Clock* was released in Britain there was much written in the papers about how it caused violence among young people. Naturally enough John had to see this for himself. Later he expressed his disappointment at the sedateness of the evening with mock mortification. 'I was most surprised. Nobody was screaming and nobody was dancing. I mean I'd read that everybody danced in the aisles. It must have all been done before I got there. I was all set to tear up the seats, too, but nobody joined in.' Writer Maureen Cleave remembers John telling her of one of the terrible moments of decision which faced him during those first few months of rock and roll. He told her: 'This boy at school had been to Holland. He said he'd got this record at home by somebody who was better than Elvis. Elvis was bigger than religion in my life. We used to go to this boy's house and listen to Elvis on 78s; we'd buy five Senior Service loose in this shop, and some chips and we'd go along. The new record was "Long Tall Sally". When I heard it, it was so great I couldn't speak. You know how you are torn. I didn't want to leave Elvis. We all looked at each other, but I didn't want to say anything against Elvis, not even in my mind. How could they be happening in my life, *both* of them. And then someone said: "It's a nigger singing." I didn't know negroes sang. So Elvis was white and Little Richard was black. "Thank you, God," I said. There was a difference between them. But I thought about it for days at school, of the labels on the records. One was yellow (Little Richard) and one was blue, and I thought of the yellow against the blue.'

These were the stories John would tell for the rest of his life with happy affection and self-deprecating earnestness. With such cosmic thoughts inside his head it was hardly surprising that his final year at school was to end in failure in all eight GCE Ordinary Levels, including art and English Language. When John got a passion about something, anything, he didn't mess about. When he didn't . . . he did.

All the time his macho view of himself was growing. He was never in any street fights or a delinquent, but he liked to dress and act tough. In many ways his life at that age was a pretence. He told Jonathan Cott of *Rolling Stone*: 'I spent the whole of my childhood with my shoulders up around the top of my head and my glasses off, because glasses were sissy, walking in complete fear but with the toughest looking little face you've ever seen. I'd get into trouble just because of the way I looked: I wanted to be this tough James Dean.'

Throughout the early part of 1957 the Quarrymen played in their homes, at street parties and weddings, usually for nothing or at the most a few shillings. When the Crickets' record, 'That'll Be the Day', was released Julia taught John more chords, and that became the first song he could play properly. 'Ain't That a Shame' was another. By now rock and roll had a galaxy of stars like Fats Domino, Ricky Nelson, the Everly Brothers, Gene Vincent and Eddie Cochran. They were all gods to John.

On 6 July 1957, not long after completing his 'O' levels, John took the Quarrymen to the local Woolton Parish Church's annual garden party where they were to play. Loyal friend Ivan Vaughan had chosen this occasion as the day John should meet a younger boy from the Liverpool Institute, a fourteen-year-old who was also obsessed with Elvis and Buddy Holly. So John Lennon, his breath smelling strongly of beer, met Paul McCartney, who had gone on his bicycle from nearby Allerton. The Quarrymen did a few variations of songs like 'Maggie May', the Del Vikings' 'Come Go with Me' and Gene Vincent's 'Be-Bop-a-Lula', the words of which John improvised because he didn't know all the lyrics. Paul thought they were quite good.

Afterwards in the Church Hall Paul showed them what he could do, including his version of the Eddie Cochran hit, 'Twenty Flight Rock'. John had to be impressed because technically Paul was a more competent guitarist than he was. He leaned over Paul's shoulder all the time to learn the chords to 'Twenty Flight Rock'. He was also impressed by the fact that Paul had begun writing his own songs, and also because he could sing. He did not, however, decide to take him into the Quarrymen immediately. He wanted him in because he was so obviously good, far better than any of the classmates who had made up the group so far. But there were two problems: John had to be the leader in everything he did, and whoever heard of a group with two lead singers? At the same time John's commercial brain was telling him that Paul, who 'looked like Elvis', had a lot of talent. A week later Paul bumped into Pete Shotton. Pete had a message. Did Paul want to join the group? He did.

The inclusion of Paul into the Quarrymen was more than simply the addition of a new guitarist. It was the spur John needed to take up writing seriously. Much has been written of how the comradeship of the Lennon and McCartney partnership soured in later years and turned into rivalry. But, in fact, although they were friends, they were always rivals, too. 'I learned a lot from Paul,' said John. 'He knew more about how to play than I did and he showed me a lot of chords. I'd been playing the guitar like a banjo so I had to learn it again. I started to write after Paul did a song he'd written.' Nothing breeds ambition like competition. Among the earliest songs John wrote were 'One After 909', which over a decade later Paul was to sing on the last Beatles album *Let It Be*, and 'Hello Little Girl', a song the Beatles eventually gave away to another Liverpool group, the Fourmost . . .

Despite the age difference (when you are fourteen years old, sixteen seems positively grown up) John and Paul became close friends and would meet at Paul's home in Forthlin Road. Paul's mother had died of cancer about a year earlier and because Paul and his younger brother Michael had largely to fend for themselves until their father came home from work the front room of their home became something of a rehearsal room for the new partnership of Lennon and McCartney. Paul had had a much more musical background than John, his father having once played in a traditional jazz band himself, and he was therefore steeped in all kinds of popular music – a facet of his character which was eventually to turn Beatle albums into musical variety shows and aggravate the life out of his co-writer.

It is difficult to imagine two more different temperaments than John Lennon and Paul McCartney. Paul was, and still is, always the hard-working, eager-beaver, charming little diplomat – the perfect PR who hid his massive ego behind a fetching smile. John was reckless, given to wild passions and obsessions, academically lazy, witty, acerbic, and straight-talking. While Paul had a very strong streak of conservatism running through him, John, despite Mimi's coaching in the social graces, was totally anti-establishment. They were as different as boys can be, and yet united by the common bond of music. Gradually the Quarrymen were taking shape, and one by one John's childhood friends

Pete and Ivan were being replaced by more ambitious musicians. And in 1958 Paul introduced another boy from the Liverpool Institute called George Harrison, who was even younger than Paul.

In John's eyes George was little more than a baby, three years younger and 'always tagging along'. In fact he was often embarrassed to be seen with George so great was the age gap. Also, at that time, George had no illusions of himself as a misunderstood intellectual. He was not academically good and when he left the Institute he took a job as a trainee electrician. In Mimi's eyes he was a really rough-looking little Ted, with a very working-class accent (his father was a bus driver) – an observation which probably worked in his favour so far as John was concerned. What worked mostly in his favour, however, was his ability on the guitar. It was the one thing he could do well, and he practised hard and long at it, with the full co-operation of his parents. Years later Brian Epstein would say that George was the most musical of the Beatles. That was probably partly to encourage him, but also because by years of practice George had a far better grasp of the complexities required to be a good virtuoso musician. When he joined the Quarrymen it was right that he played lead guitar, despite his youth. George also had something else going for him. He was nice, a naturally far more likeable person than Paul – who could be a bully, and John who, although usually funny, was often cuttingly cruel. It may have been a drag for John to have this kid tagging on to him, but at least George was a nice kid, and loyal to a fault. And unlike Paul, who always had a pretty grand idea of himself, George hero-worshipped John.

John Lennon 1940-1980, Ray Connolly, 1981

A TWIST OF LENNON
By Cynthia Lennon

The memoirs of Lennon's first wife, Cynthia, shine a revealing and intimate light on her life with John and the development of the Beatles. The title is derived from her married name being Cynthia Twist at the time of publication (1978).

Once back at college after our summer break, John and I were inseparable. John's friends at the time were few, but very close. I was in for a very testing time with them. In the beginning I think I was a bit of a joke to them; I just wasn't John's type. No way could they see it lasting. 'She's from over the water; she doesn't look anything like Brigitte.' (Bardot was John's dream girl.) 'She's not funny; what on earth does he see in her? It can't be for real. . .' Nothing was said but I knew by their faces and reactions what was going on in their heads. For my part I was sure I would never be accepted, and John too was up against a great deal of criticism from my friends. 'You must be out of your mind; he's a nut-case; you'll get nothing but trouble from that one; you're really asking for it aren't you?' There was opposition from all sides. But no one was going to interfere with our love, no matter how much truth there was in their arguments. We loved each other and that was all that mattered to us.

John and I used to have our lunch at the back of the stage in the canteen so that we could have some privacy. And it was there that we were frequently joined by two friends of John's from the school next door to the college – George and Paul. Their school uniforms hung uncomfortably on their rather thin gangly frames. Paul was an old friend of John; George a comparatively new one. I remember they were both so keen and enthusiastic, not about school, but music: guitars and the latest Chuck Berry, Bo Diddley and Buddy Holly. Paul played the guitar and George was learning frantically. They would bring in their fish and chips and their enthusiasm, and talk for as long as time allowed. At first I felt very much an outsider. I had never heard of half of the people they were ranting on about. If they had been talking about Frank Sinatra, fine, or even Tchaikovsky, great, but who the heck was Bo Diddley? I didn't have the foggiest, but I was soon to be given a crash course in rock and roll and also to learn how two students could survive on eight shillings a day. My travelling expenses came to two shillings. And John was always broke. Guitar strings were expensive and cigarettes made quite a hole in a student's allowance – and that was before the pub visits at lunchtime. Times were very hard, but great fun.

On one occasion, a crowd of us went for a lunchtime drink to our local, The Crack. We were all having a laugh and a black velvet, when we sensed there was some excitement going on outside the pub. We rushed out to see what was up only to be confronted by a beautiful shiny sports car and the easily recognisable face and figure of John Gregson, actual star of stage, screen and *Genevieve*. You could have knocked me down with a feather, but not John. He rushed off out of sight and returned carrying a dirty old boot in his hands and eagerly presented it to John Gregson saying, 'Can I have your autograph please, guv?' John was obviously thrilled to bits with his find, he wouldn't have dreamed of asking for an autograph with something so commonplace as a piece of paper but a boot, well you can't beat that for something out of the ordinary. John Gregson was highly amused. He signed on the dotted stitching and drove off into the sunset. A lovely little incident to look back on.

John and I would go to the pictures as often as we could, when we had enough money between us. We loved watching films, but the added bonus of being able to be close and warm together, for a few hours at least, was bliss. If we couldn't afford the luxury of the cinema we would visit the local Chinese coffee bar, where we became famous for making a cup of coffee last as long as two hours at a sitting. The proprietors seemed to understand the plight of the penniless student and John and I in those early days would just sit opposite each other, hold each other's hands under the formica table, and gaze avidly into each other's moon-struck eyes. The place could have collapsed about our ears for all the notice we were taking of the world about us. John would tell me a lot about himself on occasions such as these. My curiosity was insatiable. I wanted to know what made him tick; why he dressed like a down and out Teddy boy when his home and background were decidedly middle class.

John would explain that if you looked hard then there was more chance of survival when you came across a gang of tough guys. If you looked like them they were less likely to batter you than if you were dressed in arty gear and glasses. John was a self-confessed coward, but if he was really pushed he could fight as dirty as his attackers and frequently did in the old days. On the other hand, he would use every trick in the book to avoid a confrontation. If you'd ever come across a bunch of rough-necks in Liverpool, you'd find it easy enough to understand John's strategy – it was a case of the survival of the fittest.

I realised early on in our relationship that life with John was not going to be all hearts and roses. His insecurity had created an angry young man persona and I had to be prepared to take the full impact of his unreasonable rages. Everything would appear to be happiness and contentment one moment, and the next moment all hell would break loose. I would be accused of not loving enough, of being unfaithful, of looking at or talking to a member of the opposite sex for too long. John's jealousy and possessiveness were at times unbearable and I found myself a quaking, nervous wreck on many an occasion – so much so, that the thought of going into college the following day would fill me with fear and dread. I just had no idea what was in store for me. It was such a strange love I had for John. I was totally under his spell but I was really quite terrified of him for 75 per cent of the time. He tested me to the limits of my endurance. The one thought that kept me going during that time was that if I could last it out, John's faith in human nature would be restored. If he could believe in just one person, he would be well on the way to calming his troubled spirit, and I desperately wanted to see him at peace with himself and the world, for his sake and mine.

Although I had many opportunities to disentangle myself from John, I just couldn't make the break. I was faithful to him at all times. When I wasn't seeing him, I would be at home with my mother watching television, or doing college work until the early hours of the morning. My social life revolved around John and John alone. When I was out with him he would make sure that I didn't leave until the last train to Hoylake came in. I would then scramble into a carriage full of drunks and late night jokers. I was more often than not the only female on the train at that late hour, all the rest had more sense than me. It was a night-mare journey. I would find a corner seat, get out a large newspaper or a book and hide behind it, making myself as inconspicuous as was humanly possible. I wish I had been the type who could make light of a situation like that and laugh it off, but being me, painfully self-conscious, I just died with embarrassment and nerves. Those twenty minutes always seemed the longest of my life.

George and Paul often came into the college canteen in those days. George was the tender age of sixteen, Paul seventeen, John eighteen and I was nineteen. Babies really. Paul did his best to look like a student. He would wear a mac or overcoat buttoned up to the neck in order to hide the school uniform that he disliked so intensely. His hair was as long as school rules would permit and his big soulful eyes would gaze around the canteen with envy, looking forward in desperation to the day when he could leave school and blaze his own trail.

As the college term was coming to an end and examinations were imminent, we seemed to have whole days with very little to do, the theory being that if we weren't competent after two years of work then we never would be. Consequently we were given a great deal of time off to relax before the dread-ed intermediate exams. It was on such days as these that John and I would leave the college portals hand in hand for an afternoon at the cinema or a bus ride to see Aunt Mimi in Woolton, just happy being in each other's company for a while. It wouldn't be for long, though. Wandering along lost to the world, we would be brought down to earth with a bump by a piercing whistle or yell from behind us that could only mean one thing – George.

'Hi John, Hi Cyn.' He would hurriedly catch us up and then it would be, 'Where are you two off to? Can I come?' Neither of us would have the heart to tell this thin gangly kid in school uniform to push off. Poor George! He hadn't really got to the stage of serious girlfriends yet and was totally unaware of what it was all about, Alfie! So we would spend the lost afternoon as a jolly threesome, wondering what on earth we were going to do with ourselves.

I felt that I had nothing in common with this individual. He frightened me to death.
– *Cynthia Lennon, on first meeting John*

On other occasions when Paul just 'happened' to be off school too, we would take a bus, and the guitars, to the home where a friend of John's mother lived. 'Twitchy' was the irreverent nickname John had bestowed upon him. Twitchy was a waiter and worked odd hours. John had worked it all out that the house would be empty. The whole situation seemed very wrong to me. 'How on earth do we get in?' I asked, full of apprehension. John's reply didn't put my mind at rest at all. 'Oh, don't worry about a simple thing like that, he usually leaves his larder window open.' The window was slightly open and proved to be large enough for one of the errant band to squeeze through. Once in, the front door would be opened and the rush to get in broke all records. Once ensconced, illegally or otherwise, the boys would sit cross-legged on the floor, tune up their guitars and begin practising. The music would delight me, the worry and fear of what would happen if we were interrupted disappeared and I would be caught up in the harmony and joy of the music I was listening to. John, Paul and George were totally absorbed in their music. They would listen intently to their records, and then make dedicated attempts at reproducing the sound. I was really becoming hooked on the music that they made, unpolished as it was in those early days.

The session usually lasted about two hours. During this time the larder would be duly raided and tea made. Cheese butties, or anything else for that matter, would be downed, the house would be left as we had found it and we would be away before you could say Bo Diddley. It was following one such occasion that George confided in John his thoughts about my suitability as a girl-friend. 'I think she's great, John, but there is one thing wrong.' Long pause. . . 'What's that, George?' John asked. George replied with a certain amount of trepidation, 'Well, it's her teeth, she's got teeth like a horse.'

The intermediate exams were upon us before any of us had time to think a great deal about them. The atmosphere in college was serious, the carefree attitudes of the students changed dramatically to mild hysteria and near panic. Here was the crunch. Fail the exam and we would be out on our ears, with no qualifications to assist us in the big bad world. We all seemed to age over night at the unsavoury prospects of that dirty word *failure*. The usual misgivings abounded. If only we hadn't spent so much time in that bloody pub; if only we hadn't taken so much time off when we could have been working; if only. . .Oh well, it was too late to worry, we just had to do our best, such as it was.

Lennon is clearly on the road to failure
– *Quarry Bank High School Report*

Once the exams were over we were free, the weight and the worry were lifted, our futures were in the lap of the gods so we set about the happy task of enjoying ourselves once more. The summer vacation was upon us and results of our examinations wouldn't be forthcoming until late in August, so we could relax for a while. A great deal of commuting between Hoylake and Liverpool was done during the holidays and John and I spent a lot of our time with Stuart Sutcliffe. Stuart shared a flat in a very large house in Gambia Terrace, very close to college and almost next door to my beloved Junior Art School.

Stuart's part of the flat consisted of one enormous room, totally devoid of any home comforts. A double mattress lay desolately in one corner of the room underneath a large, dirty window, bare of anything remotely resembling a curtain. The floor-boards were spotted with different coloured oil paint; an easel was in evidence which seemed to dominate the room; canvasses finished or abandoned in a fit of artistic frustration were scattered around without semblance of order. Stuart's flat was the archetype of a poverty-stricken artist's studio. My first impression of this flat was one of horror. How could he live in such conditions? Chip papers filled the sooty fireplace; tubes of half-used oil paint were piled up on the mantelpiece; the walls were adorned with posters and beautiful charcoal sketches of the nude figure of the college's life model, June. I wanted desperately to get to work on the flat for him. The mothering instinct came on very strong. Stuart always looked as though he needed someone to love and care for him. He was a very slight figure, his whole demeanour was one of sensitivity and gentleness. Art to Stuart was his whole life, comfort and home luxuries were of little importance to him and as long as he had somewhere to lay his head at night and enough money to buy paints and canvasses, he was happy. His room was his castle and his independence and freedom to work on his art surmounted every other need.

On one particular visit to Stuart it emerged that he would love to be involved in music. The influence John had over Stuart was very strong and the urge to communicate with John on every level was important to him at that time. John came up with a suggestion that seemed to suit everyone. George at the time played lead guitar, Paul and John concentrated on rhythm guitar so they were really in need of a bass player in the group. Stuart, with all his enthusiasm, could possibly fill that space. But it would mean starting from scratch and learning quickly.

He was over the moon when John came up with this suggestion. The main drawback, of course, was the absence of a bass guitar. The mere thought of the price of the instrument was daunting, to say the least, to a student on a very limited government grant but Stuart was not to be put off by such trifles. He scraped enough money together to put a down payment on a new bass guitar and put himself very much in debt to acquire the instrument. But that was of little importance to him, he had what he wanted and was determined to make full use of it.

If anyone deserved success in whatever they did it was Stuart. With John's help he mastered the basic guitar chords in next to no time. Every spare moment was taken up practising, struggling to better his speed and technique, hoping for words of praise from John for his efforts, which John gave when they were really warranted. The particular problems Stuart had to contend with were coping with the size of the bass (Stuart was only tiny and the guitar was quite large to handle) and his poor blistered, bleeding fingers. The hardening of the skin on the fingers is normally a slow process but with Stuart he wanted to be able to play proficiently, yesterday! Consequently his fingers were in a terrible state as the taut strings cut painfully and relentlessly into his skin.

With the end of the summer holidays came our examination results. Gloom pervaded: I passed with flying colours but John's results were a different matter altogether. He had failed in the subject he loathed most, lettering. What now? The matter was in the hands of the head of the college and the education authorities. We could only keep our fingers crossed. As it happened luck was on our side. John was to be given the opportunity of taking the lettering exam again the following year but in the meantime he was to carry on working for the National Diploma in design. The diploma course, lasting two years, involved specialisation in a particular subject, only partly of one's own choice.

Although I have said Stuart was influenced by John, John was also influenced by Stuart in different ways. He was in awe of Stuart's paintings and they inspired John to enter the painting department for the following two years. I, on the other hand, plumped for illustration, a subject which appealed to me and was clearly suited to my particular talents.

Now John, as I found out with time, was very attractive to the opposite sex. He held a great fascination for girls and the thought of being in separate departments didn't exactly fill me with joy. But our relationship was relatively young and our feelings for each other were very strong, so I really didn't think there was much danger of losing him to anybody at that time.

The autumn term commenced with great excitement. The new courses were a challenge, and the fact that we were one step further up the ladder of our careers made us feel older and more confident for the future. We weren't the babies of the college any more. John and I spent whatever free time we had with each other, but our ups and downs, jealousies and petty rows continued interspersed with times of love and happiness.

A Twist of Lennon, Cynthia Lennon, 1978

THE ARTY TEDDY BOY
By Mike Evans

The subjects of this article – the early artistic and musical development of John Lennon, his relationship with Stuart Sutcliffe, the British art school system and the youth culture of the late 1950s – were explored by the editor in his earlier book, The Art of the Beatles *(1984).*

It was during the late 1950s, while still a grammar-school boy in North Wales, that I began to get involved with the artistic bohemia of Liverpool 8. At that point, I knew the 'full time' painters better than the students from the College of Art, although I was acquainted with Lennon's flatmate, Rod Murray and, in passing, the bunch of boisterous cronies he hung round with, though none of them by name. I do remember my art teacher at school, a genial character called David Kinmont, referring to the new breed of art student emerging at the time as 'nothing better than arty Teddy Boys'. 25 years later, while helping with my research for the *Art of the Beatles* exhibition subsequently staged at Liverpool's Walker Art Gallery, Peter Blake recalled a similarly hard-nosed crowd of students from Liverpool who graduated to London's Royal College of Art in the early 1960s. He called them 'the Liverpool toughies'.

John Lennon, regardless of his ability – or lack of it – in visual art, was an archetype: the product of a clash of cultures that first occurred in the English grammar schools, and more specifically art colleges, and manifested itself generally in the popular culture of the 1960s.

England has been, and still is, the most class-conscious of countries. Ironically, the 'levelling' of society by post-war egalitarianism only served to throw traditional class differentials into sharper focus, and to introduce new ones. The 1944 Education Act had two direct effects on matters of class as far as the generation of 'war babies' was concerned. The entry-by-merit established in the eleven-plus exam for the traditional grammar schools meant that working class children for the first time entered the mainstream of higher education in large numbers. However, the class-by-birth barriers this helped to erode were replaced by a new set of status values governed by intellectual ability. Almost regardless of their background, children from the working and lower-middle classes were categorised at eleven into the achievers and the no-hopers, those with career potential and those doomed, like their fathers, to the life of industrial and rural labour. (Another anomaly in the system was that the upper classes never had the rigidity of this academic apartheid forced upon them, fee-paying education being untouched by the changes in the State sector.)

So strong were the identity pressures associated with 'grammar' or 'secondary' education that, by the mid-1950s, when John Lennon was in his teens, the lines were fairly clearly drawn in terms of the new youth culture which was springing up all around. Grammar school culture tended to be 'posh' – even more so if the background was solidly working class. They were the 'swots', the kids more likely, in the mid-1950s, to have cottoned on to jazz. The Goons were the schoolyard cult par excellence; folk music and skiffle abounded; the Campaign for Nuclear Disarmament (CND) found its largest following. By the end of the decade, along with university fodder, the grammar schools had produced (with the help of Fleet Street) the beatniks.

Secondary schools, on the other hand, represented the mainstream proletarian teenager, who, for reasons more economic than artistic, now also had a cultural identity: an identity which was non-academic, non-literary, essentially anti-art, and centred on the style and music surrounding rock'n'roll.

The institutions of further education – universities, teacher-training colleges, art schools – were open to the grammar-school educated offspring of the masses. But whereas most establishments had specific academic criteria for entry, the art schools had a much looser system of recruitment. In the case of John Lennon, with his paucity of academic achievement, this was just as well. Despite being intellectually able, he resented and rejected the disciplines involved in passing exams, ending up with no O-Levels at all – not even in English and Art, the two subjects where his teachers admitted he showed a real talent. Throughout school, especially during the last two years, he was branded a troublemaker, the classroom joker, more interested in his embryo skiffle group and his ad hoc cartoon-sheet, *The Daily Howl*, which featured his own graphic caricatures of the teaching staff. As if in desperation to find a role for the wayward Lennon, the headmaster at Quarry Bank suggested he use the cartoons he was producing so prolifically as the basis for a portfolio to seek entry into Liverpool College of Art. It was possible to join the basic intermediate course at a local art school on the merits of artwork alone. The door was now open to 'non-academic' students who happened to show some artistic ability, the broad spectrum of would-be artists.

Since post-war National Service imposed conscription on all males at the age of eighteen, further education had been a catch-all for bright kids who wanted to avoid the call-up; most students were simply exempt. Even after conscription was abolished in the mid-1950s, college continued to attract not only the career-minded, but those still anxious to avoid a 'real job' for a year or two. What the art schools offered to those of an artistic inclination was the chance to avoid adult responsibility, and the opportunity to indulge in both the technical disciplines and the Bohemian lifestyle of the art student. For many people, the latter was indeed a greater attraction than the former.

Out of these tensions, disparate cultural pressures and influences, came a new kind of rebel. Not, on the one hand, the acceptably unconventional student, the duffle-coated radical conforming to the stereotype of the pipe-smoking jazz fan, his roots in the Angry Young Men of earlier in the decade, John Osborne's Jimmy Porter personified. And certainly not mere miscreant youth, which is all the Teds added up to in most cases: essentially conservative in their chauvinism and with limited aspirations – a revolt in style inexorably linked to a music (that of early Elvis, Buddy Holly, Little Richard) which was already just a memory on provincial jukeboxes by the closing years of the 1950s. What hit the art schools at precisely this time was a potent hybrid of these models of the teenage mal-content. From the social melting pot of the grammar schools came a mixed bag of cultural references: kids from terraced back streets more interested in pulp comics than Picasso; suburban romantics hung up on the new American Beat writers; and everywhere the all-pervasive influence of rock'n'roll and the English skiffle craze that went with it. The result was a species of which the seventeen year-old John Lennon was both typical and one of the first – the art-student-as-Teddy Boy.

With his greased-back hair, narrow-as-permissible trousers and 'slim jim' ties, Lennon already looked 'a bit of a Ted' at Quarry Bank, and he stuck out like a sore thumb at Art College. Fellow student Helen Anderson recalls, 'I liked John, we all thought he was great fun, but I never fancied him. He was greasy, a bit of a Ted, and he always smelled of chips.' Chip-shop diet notwithstanding, just a couple of years after Lennon's entry into Liverpool College of Art in 1957, the style had established itself; hence Blake's reference to the 'Liverpool toughies' who left the college a couple of years after John. Students suddenly appeared on post-graduate courses in London, at the RCA and the Slade, revelling in their working class (i.e. regional) accents, swaggering round like macho motorbikers, swearing a lot, getting into the occasional fight, terrifying some of the tutors, mesmerising most of the girls. But when he burst on to the intermediate course at Liverpool back in '57, Lennon's gritty style and coarse manner was almost unique. Almost, but not quite.

There was one other quasi-Ted among the students, a year ahead of John, who, if only for reasons of image, Lennon would inevitably have been drawn to:

Stuart Sutcliffe. As it emerged, after their introduction through graphics student and amateur journalist Bill Harry, Stuart's sense of style went much deeper than just his dress, although in 1957 that in itself certainly set him apart from his fellow students. Almost as soon as he had left Prescot Grammar School, during the summer vacation prior to his first term at Liverpool in the autumn of '56, Sutcliffe began to adapt his schoolboy 'sticky out' hair (as everyone described it) and 'swotty' glasses to look reminiscent of his recently deceased hero James Dean. By the time the young John Lennon entered the course a year later, Sutcliffe already struck a highly individual pose, with his tight drainpipe trousers, sandals, combed-back quiff and sunglasses. None of these diverse elements were, in themselves, particularly alien to art-student fashion of course, but their combination by Stuart made for a striking image that soon became the talk of the college.

Stuart was John's closest and dearest friend. They were on the same wavelength but they were opposites. Stu was a sensitive artist and he was not a rebel, as John was. He wasn't rowdy or rough. But they complimented each other beautifully. John taught Stuart how to play bass. He wasn't a musician, but John wanted Stuart to be with him. – *Cynthia Lennon*

But it was Sutcliffe's concern with style, his attitude to the visual, that sparked in John an enthusiasm that he recognised somewhere in himself. They spent hours talking, Stuart enthusing about his painter heroes (he was considered the bright new talent among college painters), about James Dean, about life in general; John raving about his rock'n'roll ambitions with a manic sense of humour that came out in gobbledegook word-play and pungent wit.

Stuart was basically intellectual rather than intuitive, John the reverse. In this respect he was more 'arty' than Lennon, who very consciously wore the mantle of the anti-intellectual Teddy Boy. But both rubbed off on each other. John admired, albeit tacitly, Stuart's ability, his self-discipline and knowledge. Sutcliffe, on the other hand, saw in Lennon the primitive, the intuitive artist he could never be, although in many ways his progress to totally abstract painting could be seen as a way of achieving the 'natural' and unrepresentational quality of music. Stuart articulated things in this way, analysed them. If John hadn't known him better, he would quickly have dismissed him as an arty pseud. Conversely, Lennon felt that if you wanted to paint in a certain way, play music in a certain way, you did it – without wasting time talking about it. It was an attitude that was to permeate much of what he did for the rest of his life.

Sutcliffe loved rock'n'roll, and in John's natural dynamism he perceived the romantic vision of the rock'n'roll musician, a vision rooted in the image as much as in any personal ambition actually to play. So when eventually John offered him a place with his skiffle-group-turned-rock-combo, he was in without hesitation.

Once Johnny and the Moondogs started gigging with Stuart Sutcliffe on bass guitar, he and John Lennon agreed that the first thing they needed was some sort of on-stage image. Although John revelled in his Ted image around the beard-and-sandals corridors of the art school, neither he nor Stuart wanted the group to ape the appearance of all the other Liverpool rock'n'roll outfits, real-life Teddy boys to a man. Not for them the mohair and lamé of pop circa '59. Right from the start they adopted a 'cooler' look. While the haircuts were definitely based on teenage America, the clothes constituted a darker, subtler look than those of other groups of the time: black polo-neck sweaters, dark blue jeans and white sneakers.

This trend in the early visual impact of the Beatles was confirmed and developed when the group made the first of several visits to the German fleshpots of Hamburg. There, the Beatles were taken up by a group of local art students. Prominent among these new camp followers were photographer Jurgen Voilmer, artist and musician Klaus Voorman, and his girlfriend, another photography student, Astrid Kirchherr.

After parting with Voorman – who nevertheless remained part of this *avant-garde* fan club – Astrid, as Stuart's girlfriend, had a significant influence on the subsequent visual development of the (then) Silver Beatles. The group had already adopted a 'black' look, and this probably helped attract the German entourage in the first place. They were the local self-styled existentialists – whose own uniform across Western Europe made much use of black sweaters, black stockings, white make-up. And leather. Soon Astrid, through Stuart, had the group in black leather jackets and trousers, winklepicker shoes and black t-shirts. A look that reflected exactly what John had always dreamed of.

Then, as if once again to throw in a contradiction, the leather-clad greasy rockers from Liverpool – first Stuart, then George, John and Paul – had their hair cut, long at the side but flat on top. A bit like Anthony Perkins, Marlon Brando, certainly not like rock'n'rollers – in fact, just like art students. After Brian Epstein 'smartened up' his boys (against Lennon's immediate instincts), the 'mop top' remained. It became even more pronounced – and the key to the Fab Four's image worldwide.

Lennon later confessed that, right through the three mad years that constituted Beatlemania on the road, inside the tight-buttoned, round-collared Pierre Cardin suits there was a Liverpool Ted struggling to get out: '. . .as soon as we made it, we made it, but the edges were knocked off. Brian puts us in suits and all that and we made it very, very big. But we sold out. . .' (Jann Wenner, *Lennon Remembers*). As their fame progressed, so the image became further distanced – anticipating young fashion generally – from the twin Fifties traditions of Teddy boys and beatniks.

The 'arty Teddy boy' syndrome wasn't just about style, but the attitude that produced that style. Even at the height of flower power, which in *Sgt. Pepper* combined the Beatles' most ludicrous image with their creative peak as recording artists, the ambitious flights of musical and lyrical fantasy were anchored by a solid bedrock of simple rock'n'roll. In the great pop tradition, no track on Pepper except for 'A Day in the Life' ran longer than a regular commercial single.

I looked up to Stu, I depended on him to tell me the truth . . . Stu would tell me if something was good, and I'd believe him. – *John Lennon*

Unlike the beatniks, the art students, the so-called intellectuals of late 1950s teenagehood, the Teds were unashamedly anti–intellectual and therefore anti-art. Lennon embraced this stance with gusto as he regaled phonies in the art-school pub, Ye Cracke. He declared more than once that '*avant-garde* is French for bull-shit'. Yet, in a way that would have been equally pretentious to a genuine Ted, he was intrigued by the nonsense humour of Edward Lear and the Goons, and subsequent notions (introduced in the main by Sutcliffe rather than by his tutors) of Surrealism and Dada – the latter itself being deliberately 'anti-art' in its con-tempt for formal values and bourgeois pretensions.

These ideas about art neatly coincided with, and helped justify and ratio-nalise, his own gut instinct, which was always in favour of inspiration rather than technique as a prime criterion for creative activity. All through his career – from his art student days when he ignored 'real' painting in favour of off-the-cuff car-toons, and championed Stuart as a bass player because he had the right 'attitude', to his 'stream of consciousness' Surrealism and eventual promotion of Yoko Ono's seemingly minimal musical talents – Lennon's inclination was to let intu-ition and inspiration rule; the rest would follow. With the partnership of the more workmanlike McCartney and the in-built discipline of writing for a work-ing group, follow it usually did. Without such constraints, Lennon's solo work, while frequently brilliant, included a proportion that was at best unmemorable, at worst incomprehensible – an accusation that could rarely be levelled at the music of the Beatles.

The audacious nature of elements of 1960s culture – poets 'performing' their work accompanied by painters and pop groups, hallucinogenic lyrics in the Top Ten, pop art itself – was in part a result of the class mix, the grammar school input into the corridors of pop-culture power. Along with Bailey, Quant, Hockney and the rest, Lennon and the Beatles personified that culture.

Right up to his death, particularly in the years when the pressures of super-stardom fell away and he could concentrate on domestic priorities and work at a natural (leisurely) pace, Lennon more and more voiced an affection for the places and lifestyle of his youth. It was a lifestyle in suburbia, tree-lined and peaceful, where even looking a bit of a Ted was rebellion in itself, and art students were the oddballs in everyone's eyes.

Out of these constraints and contradictions the most famous Working Class Hero of them all emerged – king of the Liverpool toughies, Doctor Winston O'Boogie, the ultimate arty Teddy Boy.

The Arty Teddy Boy, Mike Evans, 1987

ART INTO POP
By Simon Frith and Howard Horne

From a more sociological point of view, Frith and Howard focus on how the English art school environment of the late Fifties impacted on Lennon, Sutcliffe and other British rock 'n'rollers.

The first of Britain's art school blues musicians, John Mayall, attended junior art classes in Manchester in the 1940s, debuted as a pianist in a blues trio in 1950, and formed the first version of his Powerhouse Four when he returned to the Regional College of Art after a couple of years National Service. For the next decade (and even after his move to London and the buoyant Southern R'n'B scene in 1963) Mayall took commercial art and graphic layout jobs by day, blues gigs by night, and lived a life much like that of the original Dixielanders – he even had the same reputation as George Webb for 'purism' and an intimidating disapproval of band members who strayed away from the correct blues line. But while Mayall's stance was to be significant well into the 1960s (in his famous 1965 gesture of anti-commercialism, Eric Clapton left his art school band, the Yardbirds, to join John Mayall's Bluesbreakers) by then there were other ideological positions involved in art school students' attitudes to music-making.

John Lennon, who was at Liverpool College of Art from 1957-60, best exemplified the changes. For a start he was there as much for negative as positive reasons. He was a bright, disruptive, lower-class grammar school boy with no o-levels, no career plans, and nowhere else to go (and when he left the college three years later he had no art qualifications either). Lennon was, then, happy to go to art school simply because 'it was better than working' (and as an unqualified entrant, with few signs of artistic talent anyway, he found himself on a lettering course as dull as his school subjects). This was the period, from the mid-1950s to the mid-1960s, when art schools operated most liberally to provide further educational opportunities to working-class and middle-class school leavers who had neither academic nor occupational qualifications but whose 'awkwardness' seemed to have some sort of creative potential. In 1959, for example, Keith Richards, council estate yob and truant, was expelled from secondary school and wangled a place at Sidcup College of Art, while Chris Dreja, later of the Yardbirds, then of the Surbiton middle class, found himself placed in his secondary mod's 'pre-art school set-up called the "art-stream"'. Dreja had failed the eleven-plus and already, as a thirteen-year-old, was obviously 'anti-social' but, as he remembers, 'if you took certain aptitude tests or your hair was too long and you didn't fit in anywhere else' you were defined as an art school type. Dreja joined the art stream experiment in its third year; two years above him were Eric Clapton 'plus a whole collection of other buffoons and social drop-outs'. (1)

For such misfits and rebels, art college was as much an ideological battleground as school had been, and fellow students were as despised for their sloppy bohemian pose as fellow school pupils had been for their stupidity and/or eagerness to please. Lennon and Richards alike thus played up their supposed working classness, dressing up as teddy boys (or what their peers thought were teddy boys), using rock'n'roll as a sign of their contemptuous vulgarity.

'I think it is shit music,' John Lennon sneered about jazz, 'even more stupid than rock and roll, followed by students in Marks and Spencer pullovers. Jazz never gets anywhere, never does anything, it's always the same and all they do is drink pints of beer.' Fellow student Michael Isaacson, who ran the college music club 'and provided a staple diet of jazz, notably the trendy sounds of Miles Davis and the Modern Jazz Quartet,' remembers Lennon's response: 'What a lot of fucking shit you play. Why don't you play something proper – like Little Richard, Chuck Berry, Elvis Presley?'

> Isaacson's retort was a challenge: 'What do *you* know about it? Most
> of the people here like this. If you really want to do something,
> bring your group to the art school dance and prove yourselves. I'll
> put you on and give you a break.' The group did play, and Isaacson
> says they were a shambles, with a poor sound, and deservedly got a
> thin reception. (2)

Even as they were being awkward and rude, taking their own musical interests far more seriously than their fellow students' artistic skills, using rock'n'roll as a way of puncturing bohemian pomposity, students like Lennon were finding unexpected opportunities in art school life and were being changed by them. At the very least colleges offered even the idlest students material benefits. They provided stages and audiences for first, faltering performances, and while reception may have been 'thin', college audiences have always put less value on 'professionalism', been more open to experiment and surprise than any other group of rock and pop fans. Entertainment doesn't necessarily define an art school night out; bad performances can easily be transformed, by the right sort of self-consciousness, into good performance art (or ordinary Dada).

31

In the late 1950s experiments were mostly less drastic but equally necessary – they gave musicians a chance to make music without having to please anyone, without having to fit either the showbiz routines which had already changed the approach of rock'n'rollers like Cliff Richard or the rapidly hardening formulas of jazz, folk and skiffle clubs. Colleges provided rehearsal space and time – lunch sessions seem to have been routine in all art colleges, and even Jimmy Page, who arrived at art school as a well-established rock and roll guitarist, found college life valuable simply for its lack of formal demands – 'he immersed himself in blues studies, collecting old records, practising hours every day.' (3)

Stuart also dreamt up a new name for the group. Buddy Holly had his Crickets, and, on a forthcoming month–long tour of Britain, Gene Vincent was going to be backed by the Beat Boys. How about 'The Beetles'? One of the motorbike gangs in *The Wild One* **was called that too. A brainstorming session with John warped it eventually to 'The Beatles' – you know, like in 'beat music'. –** *Pauline Sutcliffe,* **Backbeat**

For less worldly, less experienced students, the most valuable college resource was other students, who provided ideas, records, equipment, moral support, even money. It was in college that Keith Richards first heard American blues, got an electric guitar (in a swap for some records), and played in an R'n'B band. It was from a college friend, Andy 'Thunderclap' Newman, that Pete Townshend learnt the creative use of tape recording. It was at a college gig that Ray Davies met Alexis Korner and so got access to the London R'n'B scene. It was thanks to his college contacts that John Lennon improved the early Beatles sound – they became the first of many groups to subsidise their equipment costs illicitly, from student union funds!

In a sense all we're describing here is a familiar aspect of student life – art colleges were special in the late 1950s and early 1960s only because universities and technical colleges then catered for a much narrower range of student interests, demanded much more systematic academic work, and weren't yet into the entertainment business. But art school friendships also involve attitudes and influences that are not normal in other educational settings even now – they offer a way for students to apply the tenets of Romanticism (all art students are, after all, in one way or another, 'creative') to everyday life. For Pete Townshend, for example, friendship with Tom Wright didn't just mean access to 'a massive collection of American blues, R & B and jazz albums'. Wright also gave Townshend 'his first taste of marijuana', and, as Dave Marsh comments:

> At the time, one of the major functions of pot smoking was to
> throw Townshend together with a group of very unconventional
> students, leading him to question the relative social stability in which
> he'd been raised and supporting his ego by marking him as
> eccentric rather than just weird. (4)

Eric Burdon remembers meeting John Steel (who became the Animals' drummer) in his very first class at Newcastle College of Art ('I heard someone yell from the back of the room: "Is anyone here interested in jazz?"') and the two of them were soon part of the college clique who dominated lunchtime jam sessions and the studio record player, spending the rest of their time in 'frantic' record exchanging, film-going and discussions of white American beat style and black American beat music. For John Lennon, by far the most significant aspect of art school life was his friendship with students like Bill Harry and, in particular, Stuart Sutcliffe – 'they would sit for hours in Ye Cracke,' the student pub, 'discussing Henry Miller and Kerouac and the "beat" poets, Corso and Ferlinghetti.' Lennon had always regarded himself as a genius; Sutcliffe taught him, by both precept and example, what it meant to be an 'artist':

> From Stu, he learned of the French Impressionists, whose
> rebellion against accepted values made that of Rock and Roll
> seem marginal. Van Gogh, even more than Elvis Presley, now
> became the hero against whom John Lennon measured the world. (5)

Through Sutcliffe, Lennon (and the Beatles) became, first, part of the Liverpool 8 art scene, the bohemian cafés, pubs, clubs and pads (the flat Sutcliffe and Lennon shared in Gambier Terrace was even featured in the *People* as an example of 'beatnik horror'), and then, part of the Hamburg art scene (so that, eventually, Lennon moved from wearing a rock hairstyle to shock the art school world to wearing an art school hairstyle to shock the pop world). (6)

The changes in Liverpool music in this period weren't caused by the Beatles (or by art schools). The Cavern, which had started as a trad jazz hangout, had already moved into modern jazz and skiffle, and became a 'beat club' in 1960 out of commercial necessity (just as the jazz group the Bluegenes became a beat group, the Swinging Blue Jeans). The Beatles' importance (or, rather, the importance of Lennon and Sutcliffe) was to keep a sense of Bohemia alive in the club, even as it drew a younger, lower class, more casually hedonistic crowd, and to apply an artistic attitude to these youths' concerns for style and rock'n'roll.

Lennon had, indeed, first been drawn to Sutcliffe by the way he looked:
For Stu, in 1959, resembled neither Teddy Boy nor jazz cellar habitué. He had evolved his own style of skin-tight jeans, pink shirts with pinned collars and pointed boots with high, elasticated sides. His dress, in fact, was disapproved of by the Art College far more than John's, but was tolerated because of his brilliance as a student. (7)

1) John Platt, Chris Dreja and Jim McCarty (1983) *Yardbirds*, Sidgwick & Jackson, London, p.8. John Lennon quote from Hunter Davies (1981) *The Beatles*, Panther, London, p.64.

2) Davies, op. cit. p.77 and Ray Coleman (1985) *John Lennon*, Futura, London pp.62-3.

3) Stephen Davis (1985) *Hammer of the Gods*, Sidgwick & Jackson, London, p.18.

4) Dave Marsh (1983) *Before I Get Old*, St Martin's Press, New York, pp.50-1.

5) Philip Norman (1981) *Shout!*, Elm Tree, London, p.52. And see Eric Burdon (1986) *I Used To Be an Animal but I'm Alright Now*, Faber & Faber, London, pp.17-19.

6) The best account of the Beatles' art school influences is Mike Evans (1984) *The Art of the Beatles*, Anthony Blond, London, ch. 1.

7) Norman, op. cit., p.52.

Art Into Pop, Simon Frith and Howard Horne, 1987

JOHN LENNON 1940-1980 (2)
By Ray Connolly

This account of the Beatles' very early days contrasts the rough-and-ready rock'n'roll of their Hamburg period with the sharply manufactured (but dull) professionalism of the era's major pop stars.

The financial rewards for being in the Quarrymen at that time were not exactly bewitching and they rarely earned more than a couple of pounds a night. The basic trouble with the group was that they had three guitarists, no proper bass player since Stu was so hopeless, no drummer and no proper equipment. George Harrison could undoubtedly have made a better career for himself by joining one of the more professional groups of the time who were aware of his prowess, but he didn't. Of course, they were all still very young, just two schoolboys and two college students. Still, they did get gigs, places like the Finch Lane bus depot party (George's father worked there) and eventually they even got selected to appear in one of the heats to a Carroll Levis *TV Discoveries* show which took place in Manchester. It was at this point that the name Quarrymen finally disappeared, to be replaced for a short time by Johnny and the Moondogs. The change of name did not help their fortune. The Moondogs did not go on to become one of Mr Levis's discoveries. They went back to Liverpool and changed their name again. This time they became the Beatles, after a short aberration when they took the rather grandiose showbiz title of the Silver Beatles.

The first regular gigs that the Beatles were to get came ironically through the one Beatle who could not play, Stu. Because of his friendship with a local Liverpool hustler Allan Williams the four began to appear in the basement of Williams's coffee bar known as the Jacaranda, a meeting place for itinerant scrubbers, students and all kinds of rag, tag and bobtail people from Liverpool 8. Because the Beatles were still at college or school most of the gigs were in the lunch hour, and the line-up was still very basic. They were still without a drummer and Stu's bass playing had hardly improved. But in their black Marks and Spencer polo-neck sweaters, black jeans and white gym shoes they at least were beginning to look like a group, and what they lacked in professionalism they made up for in energy and enthusiasm, playing in front of borrowed amplifiers and speakers, and trying to cover up for Stu on bass. Other groups also played at

35

the Jacaranda, minor local stars like Rory Storm and the Hurricanes, who had a drummer called Ringo Starr, and Cass and the Casanovas.

By 1959 a great deal had happened in the rock and roll world which was to affect the Beatles. Buddy Holly and Eddie Cochran were both dead, Chuck Berry was in jail. Elvis was being musically emasculated in the US Army, and the first generation of British rock and rollers were enjoying their first flush of success. Like all true connoisseurs of rock music the Beatles found their more successful contemporaries cringingly embarrassing: after one good record with 'Move It', Cliff Richard was becoming increasingly wet, Tommy Steele was always a hyped-up joke for the media (a good family entertainer, but never a rocker), Wee Willie Harris was an even worse joke, and, while Marty Wilde and Billy Fury undoubtedly had talent, it was a derivative talent, seemingly based on whatever happened to be doing well in the American charts. Even American rock and roll was going soft, it seemed, with newcomers like Bobby Vee, Fabian, Bobbie Vinton and Frankie Avalon singing teenage laments about high school proms and graduation rings. This was not the music that had first attracted John Lennon and Paul McCartney. When Elvis had started it had all been straight from the gut lust, a sound produced apparently by mainlining virility and passion. He had taken black rhythm and blues music and bleached it into a steaming poor white rock driven along by jangling guitars and an eruption of nervous energy. Chuck Berry and Buddy Holly had adopted that sound, and given it a new literacy, observations on the American way of auto-life in the case of Chuck Berry, and whimsical, clever, sad little love songs from Buddy Holly. But most of the newer sounds were simply pale shadows of that music, augmented and softened now with orchestral backing or pizzicato strings. The Beatles hated it.

They may not exactly have hated Billy Fury, but then neither did they love him either. He was from Liverpool himself but had become a very big star in the moody Elvis mould while they had been beavering along at school. But it was Billy Fury who first suggested that they be given a decent break. The incident occurred when impresario Larry Parnes, Fury's manager, was looking for a group to accompany Fury on a tour. At Allan Williams's suggestion Parnes and Fury came to Liverpool to audition some of the local groups. The audition took place in Williams's new club the Blue Angel.

As always the Beatles were short of a drummer for the audition (a drum kit was very expensive, so drummers were always in short supply) but they borrowed somebody and played along with the other groups for Parnes and Fury. Fury wanted the Beatles, but Parnes was worried about the bass player. Stu had played with his back to Parnes during the whole audition because he actually couldn't play, but Parnes hadn't been fooled. He asked if the group would play again without the boy on bass. 'No,' said John, with a loyalty which was not to turn into a lifelong habit. Either Parnes wanted them with Stu, or not at all.

Parnes chose to live without them on that occasion, but a few months later he booked them for a tour with one of his less prestigious protégés, a youth named Johnny Gentle. (All of Parnes's boys had names like Wilde, Fury or Gentle.) Again they found themselves a fill-in drummer and set off on their first tour. It was not a success. Although they took Stu (who was not being paid) along with them, they used to pull the lead out of his amp so bad was his playing, and although he was John's friend this did not prevent him from becoming the butt of a great deal of the more vicious Lennon humour. It is worth remembering that not everyone liked John Lennon. To many people he was a mean, vicious and cruel man who made fun of authority and scoffed at weakness. He could behave like a complete bastard, and frequently did – as he was openly to admit many years later.

In the summer of 1960 Paul left school with one 'A' level (in Art) and to no one's surprise John was kicked out of art college. Allan Williams, their friend and de facto manager, got them a booking in Hamburg. From now on they were no longer part-time students and part-time musicians: all three, plus Stu, and a new drummer they had picked up called Pete Best, were to become full-time musicians. The Beatle sound was about to be conceived.

So you see lads, I'm very annoyed (you can say that again) you should welsh out of your agreed contract. If you decide not to pay I promise that I shall have you out of Germany inside two weeks through several ways and don't you think I'm bluffing. – *letter to the Beatles from their original manager, Allan Williams*

When the Beatles finally emerged to national and then international prominence there was a genuine surprise in the pop world at their technical abilities and apparently limitless repertoire. How could four unknown men play so well, write so originally, sing in such close harmony and be so totally self-confident and professional? The answer lay basically in Hamburg. Unlike most British rock stars, the Beatles had years of playing and writing together before they became famous. They had masses of opportunities to make their mistakes and learn from them before being catapulted into the public gaze. Had they won the Carroll Levis *Discoveries* show they would most probably have withered and died before very long; had Larry Parnes recognised the budding talent they would have been robbed of their opportunities to experiment, and found themselves with some butch name and mohair suits long before they were ready for success. As it was, the world took an awful long time to recognise the Beatles, and when it did they had paid more than their dues. They were good and they knew it.

In Liverpool they had already built up a small following before going to Hamburg, but it was in the long tortuous hours of playing on stage in the small sleazy India Club in Hamburg that they were to begin to graduate from being just a good rock and roll band, to being the best group in the world. Billy Fury, Marty Wilde, Cliff Richard and Adam Faith all had it much easier. They got to the top very quickly, without having time to really learn their trade, and it was only Cliff Richard among the dozens of early British rock stars who was to make any lasting impression. Phil Spector used to say that you can't hide talent; but sometimes talent needs hiding while it is being nursed. In Liverpool the longest gig the Beatles had ever played was an hour. In Hamburg they were expected to go out and entertain for as long as eight hours at a stretch. No wonder they got good. They were given the opportunity to fail, to rehearse and improvise before an audience. And when it came to rock and roll they recognised and were grateful for their opportunities.

Domestic arrangements on that first visit to Hamburg were primitive, all five boys sleeping in one room behind a cinema screen. They did everything together. Everything. Apart from the girls, there was drink and there were pep pills. At first they started on Preludin, slimming pills, because they were told that that was the way to stay awake during their marathon playing stints; and then they graduated to whatever else was available, usually purple hearts, which, combined with the alcohol they were consuming, made them even loonier.

Before long they moved to another, larger club called the Kaiserkeller, and more marathon sessions, in which they had to play very loudly to get their drunken unruly audiences to pay any attention at all. None of the Beatles had much knowledge of the German language and John never even bothered to try and learn. They were rough bars, where the waiters carried flick knives, and sailors would get drunk and brawl while the Beatles played deafeningly on. When the Beatles weren't playing, Rory Storm and the Hurricanes were, driven along by Ringo's steady drumming. Of course there were still arguments in the group, particularly between Paul and Stu. Paul had been John's special friend until Stu had come along. Paul probably resented him. And Stu was still having trouble with his bass guitar.

The Beatles stayed in Hamburg for five months on that first occasion. Of course the local rockers liked them, but they were now taken up by a new force of fans from the local art college including Klaus Voorman and his girlfriend

Astrid Kircherr, the first in the never-ending line of self-considered intellectuals who were to become Beatle fans. Klaus was also a musician and was eventually to turn up in England in the mid-sixties to illustrate the cover to the *Revolver* album and play bass with John on several solo albums including *Imagine*. Over the next few months Astrid set about photographing them, moody black and white pictures, encouraging them to wear black leather, and eventually to comb their hair forward.

Then just before Christmas 1960 they ran into trouble. George was deported because at seventeen he was under age, and Paul and Pete Best were thrown into jail after accidentally starting a fire in the room in which they lived.

One by one the Beatles drifted back to Liverpool. The great adventure had ended in failure. They were all broke. Only Stu had done well: he had fallen in love with the enigmatic Astrid. John went home to Mimi and got his customary scolding, and dropped out of sight for a while. He wasn't even sure whether he wanted to continue with the Beatles, he was to say later. John may have been the exhibitionist on stage, he may have talked more than virtually anybody in the world but, even then, he was always prone to states of reclusivity.

The need to work brought him out of it. At first they played a few gigs at Pete Best's mother's club, the Casbah, and then just after Christmas, 1960, they appeared at Litherland Town Hall. It was then that they first realised that something had changed while they had been in Hamburg. Suddenly they had fans. They were unlike anything or anybody else. John would say later that they were the first punks. A few weeks later they began making regular appearances at the Cavern club in the city centre, mainly during the lunch hour since evenings were reserved for trad jazz. Their fans became more numerous. Their fame was spreading like wildfire around Liverpool. They looked and sounded different, and alongside the thin, over-rehearsed rock groups of the day, who usually played variations of the Shadows' sound, their music was positively brutal. Altogether they were to make over 250 appearances at the Cavern.

Later in the year they returned to Hamburg, and this time they even made a record, with John singing 'My Bonnie Lies Over the Ocean' for Bert Kaempfert's company. Later, when it was released in America at the height of Beatlemania, it was a huge success, but John always hated it. It was on this trip that Stu eventually decided that he was never going to be happy as a musician, and left to join the local art college. Paul finally took over the bass guitar. For a year John and Stu wrote to each other, long letters of affection. Then in April 1962 Stu died of a brain haemorrhage. He had never been cut out to be a musician, but he was certainly an artist of some promise, and certainly more intellectually able than the other Beatles. Although John had teased him mercilessly about his bad playing, and had not been particularly distressed when he voluntarily left the group, Stu's death hit John badly. Stu had been an intellectual soul–mate.

Altogether the Beatles made five trips to Hamburg and each time they made a bigger impression. Each time Cynthia stayed at home – the steady girlfriend, while John wallowed in excesses of sex, pills and drink. Cynthia was the archetypal rock and roll widow. Whenever they were in Liverpool the Beatles appeared at the Cavern or local dance halls. Very, very slowly their earnings were increasing, but still no record company had come along to whisk them away to fame and fortune. Part of the trouble was that they no longer had a manager, due to a disagreement with Allan Williams, and there was no one to realise their abilities. All the record companies were based in London and in those days Liverpool was a very long way away.

Then in October 1961 Brian Epstein, then 27, and the manager of one of his family's Liverpool music shops, was asked for a copy of 'My Bonnie'. Later in the day he was asked again. He had never heard of the Beatles, but an acquaintance had. He was told he could see them at the Cavern where they were performing. The club was dank with sweat, excitement and poor draining, the music was deafening, and the four boys on stage looked extremely rough. But they had presence, they generated excitement, and they were funny. After the show he asked if he could be their manager. They agreed. They had nothing to lose. To them Epstein was a man of some sophistication.

Much has been made of Epstein's homosexuality in deciding to manage the Beatles. But probably not even he ever really knew what were his true motives. He had been to RADA, without much success, and clearly was attracted by the bright lights. Perhaps he really did think that the Beatles would be 'bigger than Elvis', as he claimed a year later. But that was more probably hindsight. In all likelihood he was simply a fairly well–off young man, attracted to the four unkempt individuals who had no respect for anything, least of all him, and who, unlike him, had not had so much of their personalities repressed by guilt, family, religion and school.

John Lennon 1940-1980, Ray Connolly, 1981

A CELLARFUL OF NOISE
By Brian Epstein

Brian Epstein's account of his early experiences managing the Beatles was published in 1964, at the height of Beatlemania. Despite his natural restraint, Epstein's sense of amazement shines through – such as in this recollection of his momentous first encounter with 'the boys'.

The name 'Beatle' meant nothing to me, though I vaguely recalled seeing it on a poster advertising a university dance at New Brighton Tower and I remembered thinking it was an odd and purposeless spelling.

Raymond Jones was one of any average dozen customers who called in daily for unknown discs and there seems now no valid reason why, beyond my normal efforts to satisfy a customer, I should have gone to such lengths to trace the actual recording artistes. But I did and I wonder sometimes whether there is not something mystically magnetic about the name 'Beatle'?

Now they are world famous, the Beatles defy analysis as to the specific ingredients of their success, but I do wonder whether they would have been quite as big if they had been called, for example, the Liverpool Four, or something equally prosaic.

One interesting feature of the Beatles' entry into my life was that without being conscious of it, I had seen them many times in the store.

I had been bothered a little by the frequent visits of a group of scruffy lads in leather and jeans who hung around the store in the afternoons, chatting to the girls and lounging on the counters listening to records. They were pleasant enough boys, untidy and a little wild and they needed haircuts.

I mentioned to the girls in the shop that I thought the youth of Liverpool might while their afternoons away somewhere else, but they assured me that the boys were well behaved, and amusing and they occasionally bought records. Also, said the girls, they seemed to know good discs from bad.

Though I didn't know it, the four lads were the Beatles, filling in part of the long afternoon between the lunchtime and evening shows in the best cellars.

On October 28 Raymond Jones left the store after I had taken a note of his request. I wrote on a pad: '"My Bonnie". The Beatles. Check on Monday.'

But before I had had time to check on Monday, two girls came into the store and they too asked for a disc by this curiously-spelled group. And this, contrary to legend, was the sum total of demand for the Beatles' disc at this time in Liverpool. It is untrue that there was a milling fighting crowd around NEMS waiting for the disc to arrive.

That afternoon I telephoned a few of the agents who imported discs, told them what I was looking for and found that no one had heard of the thing, let alone imported it. I might have stopped bothering there and then if I hadn't made it a rigid rule never to turn any customer away.

Nothing could come close to what he gave them – which was absolute love – and that's irreplaceable. And they needed that in those days. They needed a man with wisdom and a little bit of money. He also had grace and charm, which impressed a lot of people worldwide. I think there is no doubt that had they not had a manager of Brian Epstein's determination – I don't think that they would have emerged from Liverpool. – Ray Coleman

And I was sure there was something very significant in three queries for one unknown disc in two days.

I talked to contacts in Liverpool and found, what I hadn't realised, that the Beatles were in fact a Liverpool group, that they had just returned from playing in clubs in the seamy, seedy end of Hamburg where they were well known, successful and fairly impoverished. A girl I know said: 'The Beatles? They're the greatest. They're at the Cavern this week'. . .The Cavern. Formerly a jazz club which had been a huge success in the mid-1950s, it was now owned by Raymond McFall, an ex-accountant who was filling some of his jazz programmes with raw 'Made in Liverpool' beat music played, usually, on loudly amplified guitars and drums. The Cavern was a disused warehouse beneath Mathew Street, Liverpool and I remember that I was apprehensive at the thought of having to march in there among a lot of teenagers who were dressed as if they belonged, talking teenage talk and listening to music only they understood. Also, I was not a member.

So I asked a girl to have a word with the Cavern, to say that I would like to pop in on November 9th at lunchtime and to ensure that I wasn't stopped at the door. I have never enjoyed scenes on doors with bouncers and people asking for 'your membership card, sir,' or that sort of thing.

I arrived at the greasy steps leading to the vast cellar and descended gingerly past a surging crowd of beat fans to a desk where a large man sat examining membership cards. He knew my name and he nodded to an opening in the wall which led into the central of the three tunnels which make up the rambling Cavern.

Inside the club it was as black as a deep grave, dank and damp and smelly and I regretted my decision to come. There were sometime 200 young people there jiving, chatting or eating a 'Cavern lunch' – soup, roll, cokes and things. Over all the speakers were loudly-amplified current hit discs, then mainly American, and I remember considering the possibility of some 'tie' between NEMS and the Cavern in connection with the Top Twenty.

I started to talk to one of the girls. 'Hey,' she hissed. 'The Beatles're going on now.' And there on a platform at the end of the cellar's middle tunnel stood the four boys. Then I eased myself towards the stage, past rapt young faces and jigging bodies and for the first time I saw the Beatles properly.

They were not very tidy and not very clean. But they were tidier and cleaner than anyone else who performed at that lunchtime session or, for that matter, at most of the sessions I later attended. I had never seen anything like the Beatles on any stage. They smoked as they played and they ate and talked and pretended to hit each other. They turned their backs on the audience and shouted at them and laughed at private jokes.

But they gave a captivating and honest show and they had very considerable magnetism. I loved their ad libs and I was fascinated by this, to me, new music with it's pounding bass beat and it's vast engulfing sound. There was quite clearly an excitement in the otherwise unpleasing dungeon which was quite removed from any of the formal entertainments provided at places like the Liverpool Empire or the London Palladium, though I learned later that the response to the Beatles was falling off a little in Liverpool – they, like me, were becoming bored because they could see no great progress in their lives.

I hadn't appreciated it but I was something of a figure in the Liverpool Pop Scene as a Director of NEMS, and I was surprised when after the Beatles had finished, Bob Wooler, the Cavern Disc jockey, who later became a great friend of mine, announced over the loudspeaker that Mr Epstein of NEMS was in the Cavern and would the kids give me a welcome.

This sort of announcement then, as now, embarrassed me and I was a little diffident when I reached the stage to try to talk to the Beatles about 'My Bonnie'.

George was the first to talk to me. A thin pale lad with a lot of hair and a very pleasant smile. He shook hands and said 'Hello there. What brings Mr

Epstein here?' and I explained that I'd had queries about their German disc.

He called the others over – John, Paul and Peter Best – and said 'this man would like to hear our disc.'

Paul looked pleased and went into the tiny band-room next to the stage to get it played. I thought it was good, but nothing very special. I stayed in the Cavern and heard the second half of the programme and found myself liking the Beatles more and more. There was some indefinable charm there. They were extremely amusing and in a rough 'take it or leave way' very attractive.

Never in my life had I thought of managing an artiste or representing one, or being in any way involved in behind the scenes presentation, and I will never know what made me say to this eccentric group of boys that I thought a further meeting might be helpful to them and to me.

But something must have sparked between us, because I arranged a meeting at the Whitechapel store at 4.30 p.m. on December 3rd, 1961, 'just for a chat,' I explained, without mentioning management because nothing as precise as that had yet formed in my mind.

A Cellarful of Noise, Brian Epstein, 1964

BEATLE! THE PETE BEST STORY
By Pete Best and Patrick Doncaster

The ousting of Pete Best from the Beatles in favour of Ringo Starr is among the most famous sackings in rock history. In his 1985 autobiography, Best describes the way in which his joy, following the successful audition with George Martin at EMI, was almost immediately soured by the duplicity of his band mates.

It was a Wednesday at the beginning of December, an early-closing day when NEMS shut for the afternoon. We had a few pints in the Grapes in Mathew Street first, then strolled on to see him afterwards, taking our time and arriving later than he expected us.

Brian opened up to let us in and we just stared vacantly at him. We had eyed each other so many times before at NEMS, where we used to crowd into the booths, cadging a listen to the latest discs by the Shirelles, Bobby Vee, Marvin Gaye and others. Whenever he discovered us, bunched together playing record after record, one of us would quickly grab a disc, crying, 'That's the one. Who's buying?' He would just glare at us, knowing we had no intention of making a purchase.

Now we stood there in very different circumstances – sheepish and untidy and late, but Epstein made an effort to put us at our ease. He was obviously shy, but he smiled and welcomed us inside. Upstairs in his office he said, tongue-in-cheek: 'I used to dread you people coming in, completely disrupting the place.' Then he went on to explain the purpose of the visit. 'I'm the manager of this store,' he said, 'and I think I can do something for you.'

'Can you buy us into the charts, Brian?' Lennon asked mischievously. Brian played along. 'No,' he smiled, 'but I think I can do a lot for you.' He had apparently checked up on us contractually and found that we managed our own affairs, for he went on to say that he would like to manage us. 'I'll be quite honest,' he admitted, 'I've never been engaged in this kind of thing before.'

There were some moments of silence, then Lennon said to me: 'What do you think?'

'We'll have to talk it over,' I said. I didn't consider myself to be manager of the Beatles, although I dealt with all our business matters. I was *acting* manager and it wouldn't break my heart to shed the administrative load, but Brian's offer wasn't one to decide all in a few moments. Lennon seemed to be in agreement.

'We'll let you know,' he told Epstein and we said our goodbyes and left, promising to be in touch.

Certainly there were several things in his favour, most of them connected with the fact that Eppy – as he would be known to us from now on – was well-heeled.

'See the suit he'd got on?' said George, impressed.

'And the shiny shoes?' someone else put in. But we all agreed he was a bit 'antwakky', a bit of Liverpool dialect that meant Mr Epstein was pretty out of step as far as we were concerned. Even so, we concluded he was a neat gentleman indeed, he even carried a briefcase with him into the Cavern. But it was the general opinion of the Beatles that we could change him – he wouldn't change us . . .

They needed a good solid beat and I said to Brian, 'Look, it doesn't matter what you do with the boys, but on record nobody need know. I'm gonna use a hot drummer,' and I used the guy who was the best session drummer of the period. Brian said, 'Okay, fine.' Now it was pretty tough for him and I felt guilty, because I felt maybe I was the catalyst that had changed his life, so I'm sorry about that, Pete.
– *George Martin*

The news that he had taken us under his wing spread round Liverpool like a prairie fire. The name meant something to a lot of people and clearly he commanded respect. 'You're going places now,' was a frequent comment. We signed the deal confirming Brian as manager in the sitting room at Hayman's Green above the Casbah, which would still remain the group headquarters. As three of us were still under 21, the contract had to be witnessed. Performing this duty was Alistair Taylor, who then worked in Brian's store but later would rise in the NEMS empire to be general manager.

Our signatures were scrawled across the Queen's head on sixpenny stamps. John Winston Lennon (in 1969 he would change it to John Ono Lennon in an official rooftop ceremony at the Apple Corps headquarters in London) . . . James Paul McCartney . . . Peter Randolph Best (so the contract described me, transposing my Christian names, although I signed it R. P. Best) . . . and plain George Harrison. I never have seen mention of a middle name for George.

Only one stamp failed to accommodate a signature – the first and most important on the document: the one reserved for Brian Epstein. Nevertheless, he would say in his book later, 'I abided by the terms and no one worried.' Certainly no one worried on that day, but we did wonder later if Brian had been scared to sign for some reason, perhaps in case anything went embarrassingly wrong and he would be held responsible . . .

He could be our ticket to the Big Time, which is why we went along – under some protest – with his suggestions that we smarten up; that we should discard our 'German' look for neat suits. He claimed that no one in the world of entertainment outside our present environment would tolerate our slovenly look, our chatting to the birds near the stage, our eating and drinking on the stand, our playful butting and jostling and generally enjoying ourselves. Discipline was what we needed most; perhaps Brian's brief term in the Army had inspired him, along with his own fastidious tastes. Lennon was more reluctant to change than the rest of us and told Brian so in his best caustic manner. But in the end we all conformed.

Our first stage suits were shiny dark blue mohair which had been purchased for our first night club date in Liverpool's Cabaret Club, an engagement arranged by Epstein. This was an up-market venue and not the kind of place we had been used to. Lennon was in rebellious mood, already having voiced the opinion that our new manager was trying to turn us into Little Lord Fauntleroys.

When John saw the club's multi-coloured check flooring he could contain himself no longer: 'How the hell can you expect us to perform in shiny bloody suits on a floor like that?' he stormed at Eppy. 'With all the lights and reflection we'll look like bloody rainbows!'

Brian blushed the way he always would, clenching his fists until his knuckles showed white.

'You just manage us – don't try to redesign us!' John went on relentlessly. 'People want to see the Beatles! This isn't the Beatles!' Which was true: we were at home in our leathers; we liked to be casual. Suits and collars and ties were for people who worked in offices.

Lennon's outburst made no difference. When hurt, Brian retired from such scenes as this in silence, and we went on wearing our suits – four up-market looking lads playing for up-market people. And we would go on wearing suits – and ties.

At this time Brian had another worry – that we shouldn't become involved with drugs of any kind. There were many stories of jazz and pop musicians being charged with drug offences and they caused him concern. This was not for the Beatles, he said firmly. This was no way to the top and, in one of his impassioned pep talks, he implored us to steer clear.

My friendship with Epstein continued during this period of change as he became more absorbed in the business. He even took me out to his family home in the smart suburb of Childwall to meet his father Harry and his mother Queenie. I was there for about half an hour and found it all very pleasant, without detecting any hint that his interest in me might be anything other than businesslike. But it did happen.

We were having drinks after a lunchtime Cavern session when he asked me if I would mind if he called for me and took me for a drive that evening. It was a night when the Beatles were without an engagement, so we set off in Brian's smart Ford Zodiac, talking mainly about business, as we frequently did in his office.

Blackpool lay ahead as he said: 'I have a very fond admiration of you.' 'Me or the group?' I asked him, a bit confused. He made it clear that he meant me personally.

We had reached the outskirts of the resort when he came to the point. 'Pete,' he said, 'would you find it embarrassing if I ask you to stay in a hotel overnight? I'd like to spend the night with you.'

It didn't sound terribly shocking at the time, the way the question had been put and I admit that I didn't immediately realise that I was being propositioned. I hadn't experienced anything like this before. I told him that I would much prefer to go home, which we did. There was no argument, no scene.

In retrospect it was obvious that he had wanted to start a relationship, but there had been nothing nasty about it, nothing obscene, nothing dirty. It was a very gentle approach. He never again asked me to go for a drive with him and never returned to the subject of a relationship. We both carefully forgot about the journey to Blackpool and the conversation of that night.

Epstein immersed himself in the problem of trying to find a major record company that might be interested in his new charges, and astonished us by the pace at which he worked. Just before Christmas 1961, Brian, using his contacts and his muscle as a major record retailer in the north-west, had intrigued the Decca company sufficiently to induce them to send a scout from London to take a look at these Beatles who were the rage of Merseyside.

The Decca scout was a young chap named Mike Smith, who had been lending an ear to talent on behalf of his boss, Dick Rowe, head of the all-important Artists and Repertoire (A&R) department of the recording giant, which marketed a host of American as well as home-produced hits. During his long career, Dick had been associated with a string of household names, ranging from big bands to star singers.

Mike Smith braved the rigours of the Cavern to listen to us and liked what he had heard. After his return to London word came quickly that Decca wanted us to audition for them. The date was set for 1 January 1962. It was some way to start a New Year.

Brian Epstein already had his selling line: 'I've got four boys who are going to be bigger than Elvis!' He would say it to recording companies, to press men, to anybody showing some interest in the new, cleaned-up version of the Beatles. It must have sounded laughable at the time. Elvis was sitting firmly on his throne, having succeeded Bill Haley years back as the King of Rock'n'Roll. The world lay before him and from where we were sat he appeared to be immovable.

We had often discussed our ambitions and we knew the first objective was to record for a major label and top the charts. Elvis was light years away in our reckoning. Yet all four of us were convinced that one day the Beatles would be famous. We felt that we had a certain charisma, a special relationship with audiences, though we never tried to guess just how far success might take us. We saw no further than a Number One record. We had a sort of chant that John used to lead: 'Where are we going, lads?' he would yell. 'To the toppermost of the poppermost!' was our shouted reply.

On New Year's Eve, 1961, however, there were no thoughts of being bigger than anyone as we headed for London. We travelled down without Brian, who was due to meet us at the Decca studios next morning. It was bitterly cold and it was snowing; Neil Aspinall drove us down by van and the journey took up most of the day. In the Midlands he lost his way in the snow, and the revellers were already about in London's West End by the time we booked into the Royal Hotel near Russell Square. Instead of an early-to-bed night we decided to join the New Year festivities in Trafalgar Square and watch all those daft lads jump into the fountain and dance in the spray as we had seen in previous years on television.

We had a few beers in a pub near Charing Cross while Neil parked the van. When he joined us he was full of excitement. Two fellows had approached him and asked if they could climb into the van for a few minutes. It was some seconds before he realised they were junkies looking for somewhere to give themselves a fix, but once he had they were told to 'bugger off'.

In the square we joined in the singing of 'Auld Lang Syne', kissed a few willing lips but we didn't exactly let ourselves rip, and we didn't even dip as much as a finger into the icy waters of the fountains, where the usual bravehearts were trying to catch pneumonia. The implications of the audition were uppermost in our minds; at last the Big Time was beckoning. Decca was a name known throughout the world and we had to be ready to take them by storm in the morning.

It certainly wasn't a good start to New Year's Day, however. We were due to meet Eppy at the studios at 10.30 a.m. but didn't arrive until around eleven. I can't remember whether we overslept or were held up in London's traffic – 1 January was not a public holiday at that time so it was business as usual in the city. Brian was really angry. He always made a point of being punctual himself and couldn't abide other people being late. He had also been understandably worried. 'I had visions of you being smashed up in the van,' he said, obviously relieved at seeing us in one piece.

Mike Smith, who was to conduct the audition, welcomed us in the studio and we tried to put a bold face on the drama that was about to unfold. 'Happy New Year, Mike,' George said, 'didn't see you in the fountain last night!' But most of us were already suffering from nerves.

For the first time in our lives we were in a top-flight studio and felt the thrill of it, contrasting its sophistication with the barren school hall in Hamburg in which we cut 'My Bonnie'. In the midst of Decca's electronic splendour our amps must have appeared rather shabby, for they insisted that we took advantage of their equipment instead. Our nervousness showed during some of the takes, mostly during the solo voices, but we ploughed on from midday until well into the afternoon, giving of our best.

Eppy and Mike Smith chose a mixture of songs that they calculated would have the Decca bigwigs standing on their heads. Among them were 'The Sheik of Araby', 'Till There Was You', 'Take Good Care of My Baby', 'Money', 'Memphis Tennessee', 'Three Cool Cats' and 'September in the Rain'. I believe there were two Lennon-McCartney efforts – 'Like Dreamers Do' and a new composition of Paul's called 'Love of the Loved'. Thinking back, it was a strange dish to set before the recording kings, with the emphasis on standards which, I remember, was mainly at Brian's insistence. Really we were doing little that was different.

Only one sour note marred the proceedings. At one stage Brian began to voice some criticism either of John's singing or his guitar playing, I'm not sure which. Lennon burst into one of his bouts of violent, uncontrollable temper, during which his face would alternate from white to red.

'You've got nothing to do with the music!' he raged at Eppy. 'You go back and count your money, you Jewish git!'

Brian looked like he had cracked down the middle; he blushed profusely, seething inside but remaining silent. Everything stopped. Mike Smith, the sound engineers and the rest of us all looked at each other in amazement. Then Epstein walked out and didn't return for nearly twenty minutes.

We could hardly wait to hear the play-backs and when we did listen to the results we were well pleased. Mike Smith and Eppy, now recovered from John's outburst, also seemed to be extremely happy with the way the session had gone. All that was left was the verdict from on high, but that wouldn't be given immediately. Eppy was optimistic enough to treat us all to a spanking dinner before the drive home; we went to a restaurant at Swiss Cottage recommended by Mike Smith. Everybody was in high spirits, convinced that the audition had been a great success and that stardom was lurking just around the corner, and no one was more jubilant than Brian. He had driven down to London on his own, but he had company on the return journey, as Paul and George opted for the comfort of his Zodiac while John and I joined Neil in the van.

Then came the long wait. We felt certain that we would hear the good news from Decca within a few days, but they dragged past into a week, then another week and another until they stretched into months. All the initial enthusiasm wore thin and our hopes began to fade a little more with each week of silence. Brian had lost his ready smile and badgered Decca for a decision.

It wasn't until March that he learned from top man Dick Rowe we had been given the thumbs down. According to Eppy, Dick had told him 'groups of guitarists are on the way out', to which Brian trotted out his slogan that one day we were going to be bigger than Elvis, which he still fervently believed.

. . . When somebody remarked to John Lennon that Dick Rowe must be kicking himself, John retorted, 'I hope he kicks himself to death.' But then he always was the sensitive kind. – *David Hepworth*, Front Line, BBC Radio Four

Brian returned from London with the sad news late at night and at Lime Street Station apparently rang one of the other Beatles to gather the rest of the group to meet him. I wasn't invited and, puzzlingly, the news of the Decca turndown was kept from me for days to come. When I did eventually learn our fate their lame excuse was that they had all thought I would take the result extremely badly. I had to laugh in my bewilderment.

What kind of a guy did they take me for? I had roared and rampaged through Hamburg with them, gone mugging with John and waded into all sorts of thugs with him. What had changed to make any one of them think I might be broken up by this particular kick in the pants? My reaction was as normal as their own. It wasn't the end of the world for the Beatles.

As for Dick Rowe, he became The Man Who Turned Down The Beatles for ever more – the title he chose when he decided to write his autobiography recently. 'More people know me for that reason rather than for any successes I have had – because of Brian Epstein's vindictiveness,' he told Patrick Doncaster in a 1980 interview for the *Daily Mirror*. He was the only record company boss actually named in Brian's own book as rejecting the Beatles, although at least four other major companies would also turn us down after listening to our demo tapes . . .

While we awaited George's arrival a song was born that would have far-reaching consequences for us all. The title started out as 'Love, Love Me Do' but was quickly abbreviated by popular agreement by lopping off the first 'love'. The number was conceived in the course of one afternoon in the flat opposite the club; it was a Lennon-McCartney original.

When we gave it a first work-out during two days of rehearsal at the club prior to opening night, somehow it didn't sound right. We would all take part in discussions on how a number should be arranged and we knew that there was something missing from the way 'Love Me Do' originally emerged.

Influenced by Bruce Channel's hit 'Hey! Baby', which was dominated by harmonica, John began playing around with a new harmonica intro for 'Love Me Do', finally finding the answer in a blues-like wail. It gave the song a hint of sadness, noted by listeners when they heard it later in the year; it was understandable since we were still numbed by Stu's death. Be that as it may, the harmonica strengthened the number considerably, probably helping it on its way to the charts when it became the Beatles' British debut disc . . .

While we were enjoying the freedom of St Pauli [Hamburg], back home in England Brian Epstein had reached a crossroads in his brief life as our manager. There were few more doors left on which to knock in his search to find someone to record us. His family was becoming edgy, concerned that he was wasting his energy on the Beatles when they could be far better deployed in the family business. Desperate, Brian sought parental approval for one more last-ditch assault on London where possibly, he thought, some 'cheapo' minor label might be interested in the Beatles.

His first move after arriving in London was to visit the HMV store in Oxford Street where, he had learned, tapes could be transferred onto disc for a fee of a few pounds. He felt this would make for easier handling and listening. During the course of this operation an engineer showed enough interest in the original songs on the tapes to pass the word on upstairs, where EMI housed its music publishing department. Intrigued by the Beatles, Syd Coleman, the publishing boss, called George Martin's office at Parlophone, the only label in the EMI group which had not already turned us away. The result was an appointment for Eppy to meet Martin, Parlophone's chief, the following day. When he heard our demos, George Martin, who would later confess that was looking for 'something like a Cliff Richard and the Shadows sound', thought maybe we might fill the bill.

The news came to us in the Grosse Freiheit in a telegram from Brian which

George Harrison opened and read out: 'Congratulations boys. EMI request recording session. Please rehearse new material.'

It was another 'morning after the night before', but we managed to smile, then laugh and thump each other on the back by way of celebration. This could be it at long last, one more chance – possibly our last – to crack the Big Time; to show what we could really do. 'Where are we going, lads?' we shouted. 'To the toppermost of the poppermost.' Wheels were already beginning to turn in the fertile minds of Lennon and McCartney at the mere mention of 'new material' but there was still a long road to travel. George Martin was only promising to lend an ear, just as Decca had done.

Brian flew out to Hamburg to celebrate this new milestone in the Beatles' chequered history. He spent a whole night crawling round the Hamburg clubs with Lennon on a king-size drinking spree.

The first time I heard the Beatles, I must have been eleven years old. I was with some friends at Wallsend swimming baths . . . Suddenly, the echoing chamber beneath the town hall was filled with an eerie wail. It was 'Love Me Do'. A lonely harmonica sent an icy message up my spine and into my brain . . . I knew then I wanted to play that lonely harmonica . . . – *Sting*

'Look at this,' John said triumphantly next day, opening his fist to display 100 marks. 'I got Eppy stoned and while he was crying in his beer I conned him out of a hundred.' It was the kind of thing John could do without ever thinking about it again.

It was on 6 June 1962, the anniversary of D-Day, that the Beatles, freshly returned from our Hamburg triumph at the Star Club, invaded Number Three Studio at Abbey Road, EMI's celebrated London recording citadel. It would prove to be an historic day for everyone involved – even me, in a way. For the Beatles it was a last-ditch attempt to break into the record business. For George Martin, who probably viewed it initially as just another try-out, it would prove to be a turning point in his life.

George Martin was a gentle man who had been in the Fleet Air Arm during the war. Now, at the age of 36, he was chief of a record label that had attracted most attention – and praise – for its comedy output, guiding the disc destinies of Peter Sellers, the Goons and Peter Ustinov. George, who had studied oboe at the Guildhall School of Music, was also a jazz aficionado and had recorded such stalwarts as Humphrey Lyttelton and Johnny Dankworth. His pop production was small, although, like [Hamburg club owner] Bruno Koschmieder and others hungry for talent, he had made several excursions to the Soho coffee bars in the late fifties. He had seen Tommy Steele singing there with the Vipers skiffle group – but signed the Vipers, turning Tommy Steele down, thus leaving the field wide open for Decca very soon afterwards.

Now, a few years later as he gazed upon the Beatles for the first time in Number Three Studio, he noted with some interest that they were clean and tidy, so he has said since. We in turn found him to be a neat, slim, well-spoken type with none of the bounce or swagger or 'Hi-baby' schmaltz of Tin Pan Alley. The other Beatles had a few cheerful exchanges with him but, intent on the task ahead, I quietly got on with setting up my kit so I never entered into any conversation with him.

His extremely professional ear listened intently to a selection of our regular oldies, plus a handful of Lennon-McCartney originals that included the now finalised version of 'Love Me Do', which we had tried out on our Hamburg audiences with much success. Mr Martin, however, showed little apparent excitement afterwards as he talked earnestly with Brian while we packed up our gear. Eppy seemed to be optimistic enough, even though George Martin had not promised anything definite, and we all went home to Liverpool to await the verdict. Again, it would be a long time coming . . .

It was still only around mid-June when a strange conversation took place in my home during a visit by Joe Flannery, manager of a group called Lee Curtis and the All-Stars and a childhood friend of Epstein's. Out of the blue he said: 'When are you going to join us, Pete?'

I smiled. This was obviously some kind of gag he was pulling. 'You must be joking,' I said. 'Why would I want to quit the Beatles when we're just about to get our big break on Parlophone?'

'Maybe I've jumped the gun,' he said seriously, mumbling something about it obviously being a rumour going the rounds, and we left the subject there.

Why should anyone start a rumour like that? I had no intention of leaving, not after two years as a Beatle, not having travelled this far. But Joe's words nagged at me. Had there been some secret dealing with old pal Epstein? Some talk of switching me or dropping me?

The next weekend we played the Plaza Ballroom at St Helens and at the end of the evening I decided to tackle Brian, repeating the conversation that had taken place with Flannery. Eppy became very quiet, blushed as he always did and started to stammer.

'Look, Brian,' I said, are there any plans to replace me in the Beatles?'

'I'm telling you as manager,' he said convincingly, 'there are no plans to replace you, Pete.'

That was good enough for me. The rumour had been quashed for good and all and I thought no more about it as we continued our busy schedule, laughing and clowning, drinking together, travelling together.

There had even been a warning from Brian that my relationship with Kathy 'might be bad for the business'. On the face of it, nothing had changed.

At the end of July, George Martin at last decided to sign the group and record them in September, but, as in the case of the Decca audition, the news was kept from me. John, Paul and George knew the verdict straight away but said absolutely nothing to me, not even a hint. I would learn it the hard way.

Some two weeks after the Parlophone decision, on the night of Wednesday 15 August, we played at the Cavern and, in the normal way, talked later about arrangements for the following night, when we were due to appear at the Riverpark Ballroom in Chester. The regular drill was that Neil Aspinall and I would collect the other Beatles in his van and drive it to the venue.

As Lennon was leaving, I called: 'Pick you up tomorrow, John.'

'No,' he said, 'I've got other arrangements.' At the time this didn't strike me as being odd, even though it didn't conform to the usual pattern. John was going through a trying domestic period; in eight days' time he was due to marry Cynthia, who was already pregnant.

Before I left the Cavern that night, Brian told me that he would like to see me the following morning at his office in Whitechapel at 10 a.m. Again there was nothing particularly worrying about this, as we had frequently met there to discuss the business of the Beatles, while my home was still the group headquarters for kit and transport.

Next day Neil drove me into town and dropped me off at Whitechapel. I found Brian in a very uneasy mood when I joined him in his upstairs office. He came out with a lot of pleasantries and talked anything but business, which was unlike him. These were obviously delaying tactics and something important, I knew, was on his mind. Then he mustered enough courage to drop the bombshell

'The boys want you out and Ringo in . . .'

I was stunned and found words difficult. Only one word echoed through my mind. Why, why, why?

'They don't think you're a good enough drummer, Pete,' Brian went on. 'And George Martin doesn't think you're a good enough drummer.'

'I consider myself as good, if not better, than Ringo,' I could hear myself saying. Then I asked: 'Does Ringo know about this yet?'

'He's joining on Saturday,' Eppy said.

So everything was all neatly packaged. A conspiracy had clearly been going on for some time behind my back, but not one of the other Beatles could find the courage to tell me. The stab in the back had been left to Brian, and it had been left to almost the last minute. Even Ringo had been a party to it, someone else I had considered to be a pal until this momentous day. He and I had kept our friendship rolling whenever possible since that first trip to Hamburg. We would often meet at lunchtime at the Cavern, where musicians tended to congregate whether they were appearing there or not. We would meet at other venues on the same bill and, of course, at my home if Rory Storm was playing the Casbah.

Epstein went on to what for him was simply next business at this shattering meeting. 'There are still a couple of venues left before Ringo joins – will you play?'

It makes me happy in view of the fact that they've actually given me an acknowledgement – I'm on ten tracks, a little bit of recognition, which for so many years was denied. Financially, it's going to be rewarding as well, because this time around there are royalties.
– Pete Best, on the 1996 release of The Beatles Anthology 1

'Yes,' I nodded, not really knowing what I was saying, for my mind was in a turmoil. How could this happen to me? Why had it taken two years for John Lennon, Paul McCartney and George Harrison to decide that my drumming was not of a high enough standard for them? Dazed, I made my way out of Brian's office. Downstairs, Neil was waiting for me. 'What's happened?' he asked as soon as he saw me, 'you look as if you've seen a ghost.'

'They've kicked me out!' I said.

Neil could scarcely believe it either. We headed for the Grapes to sink a couple of pints. 'All I want to do is try to get my thoughts together,' I told him. He was really upset and as disgusted as I was at this sudden, stupefying blow. He began to talk about quitting his job as road manager.

'There's no need for that,' I told him. 'Don't be a fool – the Beatles are going places.'

Beatle! The Pete Best Story, Pete Best and Patrick Doncaster, 1985

WHY THE BEATLES CREATE ALL THAT FRENZY

By Maureen Cleave

Maureen Cleave's 1963 Evening Standard *article was among the earliest pieces about the Beatles to appear outside of Liverpool. Struck by the band's unique image, as much as their music, Cleave was to subsequently become friends with John and Cynthia.*

The Beatles are the darlings of Merseyside. The little girls of Merseyside are so fiercely possessive about their Beatles that they forced Granada to put them on television, and they wouldn't buy their first record in case they should become famous and go away to London and leave them.

Fortunately others did buy it, and now they are buying the second one, 'Please Please Me', at the rate of 50,000 a week.

They are a vocal-instrumental group, three guitars and drums, and they don't sound a bit like the Shadows, or anybody else for that matter.

But I think it's their *looks* that really get people going, that start the girls queuing outside the Liverpool Grafton at 5.30 for 8pm. Their average age is twenty and they have what their manager likes to call 'exceptional taste in clothes'. They look scruffy, but scruffy on purpose.

They wear bell-bottom suits of a rich Burgundy colour with black velvet collars. Boots of course. Shoes seem to have died out altogether. Their shirts are pink and their hairstyles are French. Liverpool lads of twelve and upwards now have small bouffant Beatle heads with the fringe brushed forwards.

On the stage, there's none of this humble bowing of the head, or self-effacing trips over the microphone leads. They stand there, bursting with self-confidence and professional polish – as well they might, for they have been at this game since 1958. They know exactly what they can get away with, and their inter-song patter is in the Max Miller-music hall tradition, with slightly bawdy schoolboy overtones.

John Lennon has an upper lip which is brutal in a devastating way. George Harrison is handsome, whimsical and untidy. Paul McCartney has a round baby face, while Ringo Starr is ugly but cute. (He's called Ringo because he wears two on each hand.)

'Their physical appearance,' said my friend, who is a Liverpool housewife, 'inspires frenzy. They look beat-up and depraved in the nicest possible way.'

They are very friendly and charming. They like each other and everybody else, and are seen around a good deal. They also write their own songs.

They are considered intelligent, three of them went to grammar school, and John Lennon had more education at the Liverpool College of Art.

'It helps being intelligent, I suppose,' he said, 'though, mind you, I've met people in this business who aren't as thick as they look. On second thoughts, I'd rather be thick and rich, than bright and otherwise.

'We all want to get rich so we can retire. We don't want to go straight or get to be all-round entertainers.

'We'd like to have a bash at acting; not that we can do it but we'd like to see ourselves up there.

Watching from the wings, I was transfixed by this group performing their second single, 'Please Please Me'. It was a pop epiphany. The Beatles didn't look that different from the other acts – they were all wearing suits and ties – but they exuded an attitude that was blunt and honest as they mimed to the sound-track of their single. The sound was familiar but . . . it took it to another level and injected the pentecostal joy back into rock'n'roll. – *Andrew Loog Oldham*

'People try to pin labels on to us. Now they say we're rhythm and blues, but ever since I read two years ago that calypso was taking England by storm, I've never believed a word I read. For us, this is just good fun.

'We don't really bother about what we do on the stage, or on television for that matter. We practise what we call "grinnings at nothings". One-two-three, and we all grin at nothing. When we go on tour with Helen Shapiro next week, I don't know how we'll manage. I thought I might lie down on the floor, like Al Jolson.'

Paul McCartney said John was self-confident because he was too blind to see all the nasty little faces in the audience not enjoying it.

'He can't see a thing,' said Paul. 'Can't tell how they're taking it. He develops these catch-phrases. You know what his latest one is? "Thank you, folks, you're *too* kind." Imagine that – "Thank you, folks, you're *too* kind," twenty times over. After a bit, the audience joins in. It drives us daft and we get him to change it.

'Actually, John has a great laugh about being blind. Our humour is based on anything other people don't laugh at – death, for instance, or disease. It sounds dreadful if you write it down, but it's the cruel stuff, the *cruellies*, that make us laugh. Not that we're unkind, or anything. We're just silly.'

You can dance to the Beatles, but my Liverpool housewife says most people prefer to listen.

'They like to sit and throb,' she said, 'or stand and throb, and the walls stream with sweat. It's lovely.'

It takes you back, doesn't it? To the early days of rock'n'roll.

Evening Standard, 2 February 1963

THE SOUND OF THE CITY
By Charlie Gillett

Much-respected music critic Gillett wrote the first in-depth analysis of rock'n'roll's complex history. As such, it placed the early Beatles in the context of their musical roots and influences.

Until the Beatles made their first record in the fall of 1962, it had been very difficult for any group based outside London to gain access to the record companies. It had almost always been necessary for ambitious musicians, singers, and groups to move to London and hope to attract the attention of somebody who mattered.

Without the reputations that came through records, groups outside London had to depend on the support of people who knew them through direct hearing, which meant that a group famous in Newcastle could be unknown 30 miles away on Teeside, and that groups in south Lancashire had little demand in Yorkshire. Accordingly, Bristol, Birmingham, Glasgow, and other cities each had their own local groups.

The equivalent situation in the United States would have meant that each city's groups had their own distinctive styles and that enterprising local businessmen in some of the cities would have formed record companies to exploit the inflexibility of the majors (the London-based companies), who usually rejected the few groups they did agree to audition, on the grounds that they were too noisy and lacked the control and technical proficiency expected of singers and musicians who made records. But in Britain there was little opportunity for such enterprise because there were no local radio stations to reach the local audiences. So with few exceptions, the groups remained unrecorded until the Beatles' manager, Brian Epstein, with more persistence than most, and a better group to promote, finally persuaded EMI to record the group in the fall of 1962.

The success of 'Love Me Do', which made the lower reaches of the top twenty, and 'Please Please Me', which made second place, enabled Epstein to place several other south Lancashire groups he represented on EMI's roster, and a large proportion of them were successful. But apart from the Beatles, the south Lancashire groups had much less ability or individuality than their success suggested. Their important quality was a freshness which contrasted with the relatively characterless singers that audiences were accustomed to. But as singers, musicians, arrangers, and composers they were not only amateurs compared with the Americans they copied, but had little to say or express about their experience and feelings. They were pop music singers who lacked the kind of assurance that, for example, would allow one of them to improvise from an agreed arrangement without panicking the others.

The Beatles were different in several respects from the other groups with whom they were bracketed as part of 'the Mersey Sound', both as musicians with a thorough understanding of the culture from which they drew their style, and as people who were unlike entertainers previously familiar to audiences and journalists.

The group's vocal style was a derivative of two American styles which had not previously been put together, the hard rock and roll style of singers like Little Richard and Larry Williams, and the soft gospel call-and-response style of the Shirelles, the Drifters, and the rest of the singers produced by Leiber and Stoller, Luther Dixon, and Berry Gordy. Instrumentally the Beatles were at first less inventive, producing a harsh rhythm and shrill sound comparable to some of the better American 'twist' records, including Bruce Channel's 'Hey! Baby' and Buster Brown's 'Fannie Mae'.

Although the twist had been fairly successful (without the impact it had in America), the gospel-harmony groups had very little success in Britain, and the result for the British audience was a sound with a familiar rhythm and a novel vocal style. The way the Beatles echoed one another's phrases, dragged out words across several beats, shouted 'yeah', and went into falsetto cries, was received in Britain as their own invention; it seemed that Britain had finally discovered an original, indigenous rock and roll style.

The Beatles made no pretence that this was so and stressed how much they owed to Chuck Berry, the Miracles, and Buddy Holly and the Crickets. In an interview with the *New Musical Express* (February, 1963) during the first flush of their popularity, they listed as their favourite singers Chuck Jackson and Ben E. King (given by both Lennon and McCartney), the Shirelles and Miracles (Lennon), Larry Williams (McCartney), and Little Richard (McCartney and Harrison). Harrison also mentioned Eartha Kitt, who was not evidently much of an inspiration to the sounds he made; Ringo Starr's choice of Brook Benton and Lightnin' Hopkins similarly had little bearing on his style (which more likely drew on Carl Perkins).

On their singles and albums through 1963, the Beatles continued to draw from their American influences, trying to realise their ambition to record a great raving dance song but invariably sounding better when they sang at a medium tempo, hitting the harmonies Lennon was interested in and doing so with precisely the confidence in themselves that the other British groups lacked, a confidence that enabled them to take risks, be unorthodox, and shrug off disasters.

Some of the records they made in this period were good. Their LP tracks 'You Really Got a Hold on Me' and 'Baby It's You' transformed the innocence of the interpretations by the Miracles and the Shirelles into much stronger songs and created a sense of greater resilience behind the tender messages. In contrast to the expressiveness of these and other LP songs, the group's singles were more obviously concerned with effect, 'Please Please Me', 'From Me To You', and 'She Loves You' successively using more devices calculated to excite and offering less complexity in their arrangements.

But for the audience at the time, it was the simplicity of the Beatles' arrangements that endeared them to their listeners. The first LP sleeve notes mentioned that only one track had any kind of double-tracking or other such studio tricks. The British audience valued authenticity, and despised the lush contrivances of contemporary American records. The Beatles re-established the singer's autonomy in the studio. They were able to do so because they played their own instruments, and were therefore less subject to their producer than a studio group would have been. They came to their recording sessions with their own songs, many of which they had tried before live audiences on their tours. They listened attentively to the records that sold well in the United States and borrowed anything that seemed to fit what they were already doing. The Four Seasons, the Beach Boys, Phil Spector's sound were all saluted in their sounds, and the early rock'n'roll singers continued to provide inspiration, though their performances were never transcended by the Beatles' versions of the songs.

Musically, the Beatles were exciting, inventive, and competent; lyrically, they were brilliant, able to work in precisely the right kind of simple images and memorable phrases that distinguished rhythm and blues from other kinds of popular music. They were also facile, so that some songs were words to sing and did not represent feelings the singers wanted to express – for example, 'It Won't Be Long' and 'All I've Got To Do' on their second LP (called *With the Beatles* in England and *Meet the Beatles* in the United States). They had enough ability to endure as institutional hitmakers alongside Cliff Richard and the Shadows. But there was something else about them, and it was this that transformed the nature of the world's popular music as decisively as rock and roll had done nine years before – their character as people.

The Beatles provided in meat and bone and a sharp glance across a room the spirit that several authors and playwrights had been trying to depict in fictional characters and the film industry subsequently tried to represent with actors. John

Osborne drew Jimmy Porter in *Look Back in Anger,* and Richard Burton played Porter in the film. Alan Sillitoe created Arthur Seaton in *Saturday Night and Sunday Morning* and Colin Smith in *The Loneliness of the Long Distance Runner,* who were played by Albert Finney and Tom Courtenay with much more authenticity than Burton had brought to Porter. But the characters as such still carried too much structured statement to be convincing. The authors had social messages to get across, and the characters inevitably came second, functioning as conduits for the writers' ideologies. In themselves, though, the films seemed much more real than the traditional product of British studios. They presented life in the working class as being more real, interesting, and honest than in the middle class, a belief that middle-class socialists had had for some time but a novel theme for films.

The Beatles unwittingly exploded this image of working-class youth. In their first two years of fame, they did not make long structured criticisms of established society, but spoke briefly, obscurely, epigrammatically, in the same spirit that they wrote their best songs. Their social message was rarely expressed, but hung about their heads as an aura of impatience with convention and evident satisfaction with wealth and fame, and was expressed in their carefully chosen styles of bizarre clothes. Where authors had shown working-class youth as caged within a harsh physical world, resentful toward those they believed had made it that way, but resigned to their place in such a world, the Beatles presented working-class youth loose and free, glad to be out, unafraid to snub pretension, easily able to settle in comfortably where a rest could be found.

They are working class and their roots and attitudes are firmly of the north of England. Because of their success, they can act as spokesmen for the new, noisy, anti-establishment generation which is become a force in British life. The Beatles are part of a strong-flowing reaction against the soft, middle class south of England, which has controlled popular culture for so long. – *Frederick Lewis,* New York Times *1963*

This image also turned out to be illusory, or at best only temporarily true. The Beatles ultimately settled for what they first pulled faces at, the luxuries of the wealthy, but not before they had significantly shifted the taste of audiences throughout the world. In contrast to the pained narcissism of most singers, the

Beatles lightly mocked themselves as they sang, amused at the frenzy they aroused in their audiences. They were one of the few popular music acts to have more or less equal support from male and female admirers, and one of the few who were as interesting musically as they were visually.

In the United States, their success was not immediate. Their first four records were released in 1963 with little promotion or reaction. Capitol, who had first option for the American release of EMI's product, allowed other companies, including Vee Jay and Swan, to take up the group's records. The rest of the world took the British group more seriously, and at the end of 1963 Capitol conceded to the pressure of EMI, the Beatles' manager, and, in effect, world opinion, and itself put heavy promotion behind the next Beatles record, 'I Want to Hold Your Hand'. It went quickly to the top of the national charts, followed by several earlier Vee Jay releases and Swan's 'She Loves You', so that in one week in March the Beatles had the top five records in the country, an unprecedented phenomenon. As in Britain, the extent of the group's impact was more visual and social than musical, and depended on the intensive coverage in the press and on television. America was no more accustomed than had been Britain to singers who were witty and intelligent and derisive of social conventions, who built out of this character a new kind of sex appeal, and who attracted the attention of both music critics and social critics.

And among the people who were most surprised by all the fuss were the Beatles themselves. For, as they kept telling anyone who would listen, there was nothing particularly new or startling in any of their records. For reasons that defied discovery, a large proportion of the Western world was determined to imbue the Beatles with all the qualities that could possibly be ascribed to any and all kinds of popular music. With stamina and versatility that were themselves worthy of admiration, the Beatles did their best to keep up with expectations.

The Sound of the City, Charlie Gillett, 1970

TWIST AND SHOUT
By Phil Johnson

'Twist and Shout' is one of the Beatles' most celebrated cover versions. The Beatles' early covers both exposed and popularised (mainly black) music that might otherwise have remained obscure.

It's a rock'n'roll *Boy's Own* story: on Monday, 11 February 1963, the Beatles are at Abbey Road studios, coming to the end of a twelve-hour shift spent recording the whole of their first album. John Lennon strips to the waist before going for a take on a last number which has only just been agreed.

Taking a swig of milk, a last Zubes cough sweet from the glass jar on top of the piano to ease his throat, and a final counteractive puff on a Peter Stuyvesant, he sits out the intro to a song then best known as a hit for the Isley Brothers. Then he begins: 'Well shake it up baby, twist and shout.' His voice is nearly gone, a wild, hoarse roar, thick with mucus, lisping at the consonants. By the time he gets over the penultimate bridge of harmonies – the soon-to-be-famous *aaah, aaaahh, aaaaahhh, aaaaaahhhh* – Lennon is screaming. Although George Martin coaxes him into a second take, his voice has gone and it's the first take that makes it on to wax. It's long past the studio's bedtime and when the Beatles ask to hear a playback of the song, Brian Epstein has to agree to take the second engineer home in his Ford Anglia, in case he has missed the last bus.

Just as 'Twist and Shout' closed *Please Please Me* (Parlophone 1963), it also closed the Beatles' concerts, and for years it was their most popular live number. In its many subsequent interpretations, the song has remained a closing number, held back for encores, notably by Bruce Springsteen, Peter Gabriel and Sting on their Amnesty International tour of 1988 – to summon up the essence of uncomplicated good-time pop and soul. At its worst, in cynical versions by Lindisfarne or Black Lace, it's the musical equivalent of a Party Four can of bitter, but for all that, it remains 'Twist and Shout'. Like 'Louie Louie', it is strong enough to survive the abuse to which it has been subjected.

On the Beatles' recording Lennon's laryngitis came across as the nearest a white English boy had yet got to soul. 'Twist and Shout', like 'Money (That's What I Want)' on the follow-up album *With the Beatles*, was Lennon in extremis, so out of control, so cheeky-rough (as opposed to Paul's cheeky-nice) and so sexy that at the time it seemed to mark a peculiarly English catharsis; to be able to see and hear a white man scream was, in 1963, quite new. When 'Twist and Shout' was released on an EP in July, with its cover shot of the Fab Four caught in a mid-air jump, the song and the photo became the group's most powerful icons yet. In the playground at primary school we practised the jump, sang the *aaaahh*monies and trilled Paul's trademark 'oooh'. 'Twist and Shout' also became important in retrospect, as proof that the Beatles could indeed rock, and weren't just boring latter-day Schuberts, as the critic Tony Palmer would have them.

Like the rest of the songs on the album, 'Twist and Shout' had been in the Beatles' stage act for at least a year. You can hear an early version recorded live at Hamburg's Star Club in 1962 and it's faster and even more raucous than the studio track (*Live at the Star Club, Hamburg*, Bellaphon). Lennon is only slightly less hoarse, so maybe the legend of the cold has been talked up a bit for posterity. Or maybe he caught a lot of colds.

Credited to the pseudonyms Russell and Medley, the song was actually written by Bert Berns, the songwriter-producer who understudied Leiber and Stoller at Atlantic Records. The very first version of 'Twist and Shout' was by the Top Notes, produced for Atlantic by Jerry Wexler and Phil Spector in 1961. While it's customary to prefer the original to a copy, the Top Notes' version is unbelievably bad – the Coasters crossed with Duane Eddy – and almost unrecognisable as the classic it was to become. 'It was horrible,' Wexler later remarked, while Berns, who had watched the session from the control booth, told Wexler and Spector: 'Man, you fucked it up.'

Berns took the song to the Isley Brothers and it is their version that becomes the *de facto* original, providing the model for the Beatles, 'ooohs', 'aaahs' and all (*20 Golden Pieces*: Isley Brothers, Wand Records 1963). Though it became a big hit, it's hard to rate the Isleys' version over the Beatles'. The vocals are soulful, but the arrangement is poppy and the middle-eight (which the Beatles did as a foot-tapping Shadows-ish guitar break) is a horn arrangement with a Mexican feel that sounds rather lame today.

The Mexican elements are important. Listen to any version of 'La Bamba' and then start singing the words to 'Twist and Shout'. You'll find that they fit remarkably well. 'La Bamba' was a hit for Richie Valens in 1958, but the melody is based on an ancient Mexican fishermen's song whose words reputedly changed according to how many fish were caught that day. Berns may well have borrowed the chord sequence from Valens, slowed it down and made it into just the kind of Latin-based call-and-response tune that was then all the rage in R&B.

After the Beatles came the deluge. Fellow beat group Brian Poole and the Tremeloes took the song to No. 4 in Britain in July 1963 with an awful version, treacle-thick with echo (*Twist and Shout with Brian Poole and the Tremeloes*, Decca); the Searchers tried it, and so, unable to resist a song with 'twist' in the title, did Chubby Checker.

The Shangri-Las did it as unconscious surrealism, all booming sound-effects (engines? rain?) with the girls' voices coming from an echoey distance in a Spectorish wall of sound (*Leader of the Pack*, Red Bird Records 1965). A live version by a still-obscure Jimi Hendrix, who had once played guitar with the Isleys, sounds terrible but is full of morbid interest (*20 Golden Pieces of Jimi Hendrix, Vol. One*, Bulldog 1979). Picking up the chunka-chunka ska-like rhythm-guitar figure on the Isleys' version, it offers potential dissertation material: did Hendrix invent reggae?

The first gig the Beatles ever did after changing their name from John Lennon and the Silver Beatles to the Beatles was at that [local Coventry] club. John Lennon freaked out at the records I was playing, songs like 'You Really Got a Hold on Me', by the Miracles, and 'Mr Moonlight', by Dr Feelgood and the Interns. – *Pete Waterman*

For the next truly entertaining version we have to wait until 1969, when the song is sufficiently established even for Tom Jones's Las Vegas show (*Tom Jones Live in Las Vegas*, Parrot). Jones's opening enquiry, 'Do you feel all right?', is delivered with all the leery menace of 'Did you spill my pint?' The effect is much more British working-men's club than Vegas lounge and Jones is in glorious voice, tearing into quotes from 'Land of a Thousand Dances' and Stevie Wonder's 'Uptight' before the song succumbs to audience screams and the inevitable reprise of 'It's Not Unusual'.

When punk came along, there was a revival of interest in old beat stompers. In 1976, as part of the 100 Club's Punk Festival, a band of Siouxsie Sioux, Sid Vicious, Marco Pirroni and Steve Severin performed a medley of 'Twist and Shout', the Lord's Prayer and 'Knocking on Heaven's Door'. An A&R rep from Island Records was reported as saying: 'God, it was awful.'

A live version by the Who, recorded on an American tour (*Who's Last*, MCA 1985), sounds like a closer not only for the show but for the song itself. It ends in a frenzy of guitar feedback, finally dissolving in a razor-slash of angry chords that continue to buzz resentfully until the fade. The song seemed doomed to be history repeated as farce, with Lindisfarne's ghastly version on *C'Mon Everybody: The Greatest Party Hits Album Ever* (Stylus 1987) and a less than crucial rap by Salt 'n' Pepa (*A Blitz of Salt 'n' Pepa Hits*, ffrr 1991).

As I write, 'Twist and Shout' is back in the charts, as a reggae number by Chaka Demus and Pliers (*Tease Me*, Mango 1994). It has come full circle. 'I heard the Isleys' version in an elevator in New York,' Chaka Demus's producer, Sly Dunbar, told me, 'and I reflected on "Tease Me" and saw that it was the same tempo. If you divide rock'n'roll tempo by two, you get ska, and if you divide ska by two you get reggae.'

It's a joyful sound, bubbling with life, and they even do the 'aaaahhs' and the 'ooohs'. But, ultimately, this is 'Twist and Shout' as post-modernism; the original innocence has gone, drained away through a sink of all the other versions. Still, it went to No. 1.

Lives of the Great Songs, edited by Tim De Lisle, 1994

BIG TIME
By Stanley Reynolds

Reynolds was a Boston-born journalist who settled in Liverpool in the early 1960s. He saw the rise of the Beatles at first hand, as described here in one of his regular pieces for the Manchester Guardian.

Written across the front of St George's Hall, Liverpool (a building dear to the heart of John Betjeman) are huge chalked letters saying 'I Love the Beatles.' There is hardly anything cryptic about this declaration to anyone who has ever viewed *Juke Box Jury*, listened to *Pick of the Pops*, or fathered a teenage daughter, for in the last six months the Beatles have become the most popular vocal-instrumental group in Britain and as everyone with any pretension towards mass culture should know, the Beatles are from Liverpool.

In fact, there is a connection between Liverpool and the four young musicians that seems to go deeper than pride for hometown boys; something, perhaps, deep in the mysterious well of English, and especially Northern working-class sentimentality. When Liverpool, and the North in general, was a forgotten second class citizen, this rock group suddenly made Liverpool fashionable in the entertainment world. After their first two records it became necessary for people in the business in London to learn a few words of Scouse.

And their third record, 'From Me To You', was the top selling record, with 500,000 copies sold, for six weeks; another song written by them but sung by another Liverpool boy is current top; and still another of their songs sung by yet another Liverpool singer was number one on the sales charts for several weeks.

Unlike earlier Liverpool entertainers, who seemed to either Londonise themselves or specialise in being Scouser yokels, the Beatles have come up with a different, and heavily Northern flavoured, sound of their own. It is amusing without becoming a joke. Bowing to romantic pseudo-sociology one might say that they are representative of the war babies who were unable to get jobs in the England of HP fridges and Whipsies. They have certainly set off a chain reaction in Liverpool, where there are now about 200 rock groups. London talent scouts are said to cruise Merseyside's clubland like sharks in a swimming pool. What Lord Hailsham tried to do for the North-east, the

Beatles have apparently been able to do for Liverpool.

In order to become the second city of the British musical industry it seems that Liverpool now only needs its own recording studio. But even with having to go to London to record, Liverpool has won the title of 'the Nashville of Britain', and if one looks at the percentage of Liverpool records in the sales charts, the city does indeed rank with the American pop music capital.

But if the Beatles have overnight made Liverpool something that the London music world has to reckon with, the Beatles' own success has not been overnight. When they first played at the Cavern Club in Liverpool, now a sort of D'Oyly Carte of what the cognoscenti call the Liverpool Scene, they received a note from the management saying: 'If you play another rock number you'll have to leave.' (Another early Liverpool rock artist, Rory Storm, was actually fined ten shillings by the former Cavern management for playing rock.) So the Beatles went to Germany – thus setting a career pattern for other Northern groups, for Hamburg now rocks with Merseyside music – but they then experienced the same difficulty as they had had at the Cavern. Then Paul McCartney, who with John Lennon writes the Beatles' songs, decided on a typically Liverpudlian approach. 'There was a big German pop singer at the time named Peter Krause,' he said. 'Everyone wanted us to sing like him. One night I stepped to the mike and said in fractured German, "Und nun wir mochen Peter Krause's latest single spieled. A grosser hit." Then we played just what we wanted.'

So life was never better than / In nineteen sixty-three / (Though just too late for me) – / Between the end of the Chatterley ban / And the Beatles' first LP.
– *Philip Larkin, 'Annus Mirabilis'*

After a time the Beatles' own sound caught on and they became best-sellers in Germany with a recording called 'My Bonny'; this was before they had been discovered in England. They experienced difficulty in breaking into England because they were strongly influenced by American singers such as Chuck Berry, and the Shirelles, who are not well known here. Berry, a coloured man who is now doing his singing in a prison cell, was the original rhythm and blues singer, as opposed to ordinary rock. The Beatles are in the rhythm and blues tradition, which is very Negro and earthy, and related to folk music. Four years ago, when they started singing together, England was going through a trad and skiffle craze.

Three of the four Beatles – Paul McCartney, George Harrison and John

Lennon – are grammar school boys. The fourth, Ringo Starr, aged 22, who is the drummer and a kind of talking Harpo Marx figure, claims, in true Liverpool fashion, that he 'was educated at Butlins'.

It was in Europe that they started forming the Beatle image: the brushed straight down over the forehead haircuts, strangely reminiscent of the left-wing angry young men of Berlin in the 1930s; the publicity pictures in dark suits, looking stern and stiff like old-time Wild West badmen, and usually taken on a bomb site or a scrap yard, was the idea of a German photographer.

The Cinderella aspect of the story started when Mr Brian Epstein, the director of a chain of Liverpool music shops, found that customers were asking for records by the Beatles. He traced them back to Hamburg, only to find that they were back playing at the Cavern only 100 yards away from his office. Mr Epstein, still only 28, signed them up and has been managing them, and half a dozen other Liverpool recording groups, ever since. (There are fourteen other Liverpool groups, under separate management, also making records now.)

Mr Epstein, an oddly shy former student at RADA, has been lucky. Each of the top Liverpool groups has its own style, and Liverpool, with a folk music tradition perhaps as old and original as the American Negro's, does not lend itself to imitation.

A visitor to the Cavern will sense this right off. There is something essentially Liverpudlian about Matthew Street, in the centre of the markets and warehouses, where a dray horse with a flowered bonnet stands by the Cavern entrance oblivious to the beatniks and the noise. And inside the club, down CND symbol-smeared walls to a dark and bronchial cave, the dancers have originated the Cavern Stomp, because they did not have room enough to twist. In the dressing room off stage a steady flow of rock artists come to talk with Mr Bob Whooler, the Cavern's full-time disc-jockey whose visiting card tells you, with Dickensian charm, that he is 'a rhythm and blues consultant'.

That is the Cavern, duffel coats and feigned boredom. On tour it is like a Hollywood success story. At the Odeon, Manchester, in the Beatles dressing room, the four boys were asking a reporter from a disc magazine to please see if she could do something to stop girls from sending them jelly babies. She had once said they liked them. 'We've got two ton of them now,' John Lennon said. 'Tell them to send us E-type Jaguars or button-down shirts.' Someone came in and said two girls had won them in a contest. 'Just who are these girls who won us?' John Lennon asked. 'I mean, how long have they won us for?'

Outside the street was crowded with girls who could not get into the theatre. They threw stones at the window to draw the Beatles' attention.

Someone pointed out that Caruso under similar circumstances once sang to such a street audience, so Paul McCartney stuck his head out of the window but only to wave a 'Beatle doll'. Someone asked if they had bought any cars and the curious Puritanism of the North showed in their faces. No, they said, no taste for champagne and no cars; they were putting their money in the bank. Pale from night work and needing a lot of make-up even after a holiday in the Canary Islands, it seemed an unlucky task to be the symbol of modern Northern youth. But if you had left the theatre then, going out by a side door, and had come face to face with the mob of teenagers who rushed forward, their smiles, like Ezra Pound said, all teeth, only to be then recognised as nobody; then under the crushing contemptuous glares, you would have realised the importance of being Ringo Starr.

The Guardian, 3 June 1963

THE LOVE YOU MAKE
By Peter Brown

Former Brian Epstein aide Brown published his 'spill the beans' memoir in 1983. It included a paternity suit against Paul, alleging a liaison that would have taken place after the Beatles' 1963 relocation to London and the beginning of the relationship with his girl-friend of five years, actress Jane Asher.

By now it was no secret that Paul McCartney was going out with Richard Asher's daughter, although the press blithely ignored the fact that Paul was ensconced in the Ashers' guest bedroom. The press also was ignoring the rumours that Paul's amorous adventures had already caused him a great deal of trouble. One of the club owners on the Grosse Freiheit in Hamburg was claiming that Paul had made his daughter pregnant and that Paul was the father of a young child. The mother, a pretty girl with long, straight hair named Erika Hubers, was a waitress in one of the clubs. Paul had allegedly dated Erika during one of his Hamburg stints. Erika claimed that Paul had known she was pregnant and had encouraged her to have an abortion. She refused, and a daughter named Bettina was born on the day Paul left Hamburg. Legal documents to the effect were drawn up in Hamburg and delivered to Liverpool, where the matter was quickly turned over to David Jacobs in London. Paul denied any responsibility and the documents were sent back to Hamburg unanswered. Jacobs contended that the German tribunal had the right to deal with the matter if they wished, and if the mother continued to press charges the matter could proceed there. Jacobs preferred the slow bureaucracy of the German courts. In England the matter was likely to be given prompt attention and tremendous publicity. The case, howev-er, would not go away, and the girl's family threatened to file papers in England. In 1966 a settlement was reached. However, in 1981 Bettina Hubers started to pursue the case again, while Paul continues to deny his paternity.

But that was hardly the end to the complications of Paul's love life. In the spring of 1964, during the shooting of *A Hard Day's Night*, an even more deli-cate situation of the same nature arose. A young girl in Liverpool had given birth to a baby boy she claimed was Paul McCartney's son. Paul denied being the father, and the young girl was referred to an acquaintance of David Jacobs in

Liverpool, a man named D. H. Green. She and her mother visited Green's office in late March. Green told Jacobs that he found them quite decent and reasonable. He felt that the girl had no intention of trying to hurt Paul and that her only concern seemed to be getting enough money to buy a pram for the infant.

Jacobs was in the midst of negotiating a small settlement for this purpose when the girl's mother confessed her plight to a friend. He knew how much the child was worth and intended to see the mother was properly looked after. He eventually made contact by telephone with David Jacobs in London.

We had that image, but man, our tours were something else . . . you know, the Beatles tours were like *Fellini's Satyricon*. – *John Lennon*

Jacobs' greatest concern was that even if they gave the girl a large settlement it would in no way ensure that the newspapers would not get hold of the story, or that more wouldn't be demanded later. Jacobs' advice to Brian and Paul was that the less money they paid, the less culpable they would appear if the story did come out. Brian agreed that the best they could do was pay the girl a small sum and hope that the matter would be kept quiet.

Jacobs drew up the agreement. For the mother, with the stipulation that Paul should continue to deny being the father of the child, and that this payment did not in any way represent an admission, there was a four-figure sum. The deed stated that in the eventuality of a prosecution and trial that proved to the satisfaction of the court that the child was indeed Paul McCartney's, the maximum payment the court could order for the maintenance and education of the child was £2.10s a week until he was 21. In consideration for the money paid to her, she was never to make any claim against Paul in the future or allege that he was the father or disclose the terms of the agreement; otherwise she would be liable to return the payment.

By this time, however, the newspapers had heard hundreds of all sorts of crank rumours and accusations about all four of the Beatles. Cynthia Lennon later summed it up: 'It appeared from the evidence on the solicitor's desk at this time that Paul had been a bit of a town bull in Liverpool. Claims for paternity suits rolled in. He found himself in great demand in more ways than one. Whether the claims were true is anybody's guess.'

The Love You Make, Peter Brown, 1983

LOVE ME DO: THE BEATLES' PROGRESS
By Michael Braun

Published in 1964, whilst Beatlemania was at its peak, Love Me Do *represented the first 'serious' book about the Beatles — as opposed to picture books and souvenir publications aimed at the committed fan.*

For as long as anyone can remember, the weather has been the main topic of conversation in Britain, but last year it had some very unexpected competition. Just as the Profumo-Keeler-Ward balloon was fizzling out, everyone became aware of four young men from Liverpool. At first people just stared at their haircuts; a few even listened to their music. Then gradually, as autumn turned to winter, all that could be heard from John o'Groat's in the north, to Land's End in the south, was Beatles, Beatles, Beatles. The island that had bravely withstood invasion from the outside for nearly 1,000 years had been conquered from within.

Britain's teenagers had been the first to realise that Beatles weren't bugs. The purchase of pop records accounts for a good portion of the £1,000 million they are supposed to spend a year, and the Beatles' first record, 'Love Me Do', had entered the national pop charts and their second, 'Please Please Me', had become number one. They made frequent appearances on several television shows which are devoted entirely to playing pop music and which command huge audiences.

They were also heavily featured in the newspapers that report on pop music and conduct the pop charts and are read largely by teenagers. One of the papers, the *New Musical Express*, claims to have a larger readership than any other musical paper in the world. While those old enough to vote still hadn't heard of the Beatles, 12,000 lined up all night for tickets to a concert, and 20,000 mobbed them at London Airport, delaying the departure of the Queen and the Prime Minister.

Then in October the government went through a week of crisis following the resignation of Harold Macmillan. As rumours and politicians swirled through London the Beatles were besieged by a mob of the faithful while they rehearsed at the Palladium. Reports differ as to the size of the crowd, but the story provided a respite from weightier affairs of state and during the next few days Britain's adults became aware that 'Beatles' was not a misprint.

As a result of the publicity over the storming of the Palladium, the Beatles were invited to appear at the Royal Variety Performance. The programme starred Marlene Dietrich and most of Britain's top entertainers. On the day of the show the Prince of Wales theatre in Picadilly Circus was blockaded by a horde of teenage girls screaming for the Beatles. Miss Dietrich had trouble entering the stage door, and when the Queen Mother accompanied by Princess Margaret and Lord Snowdon arrived they were greeted by shouts of 'We want the Beatles.'

On stage, the Beatles sang several songs to a respectful, though undemonstrative, adult audience. Before the last number, one of the group, John Lennon, stepped to the front of the stage. 'On this next number,' he said, 'I want you all to join in. Would those in the cheap seats clap their hands? The rest of you can rattle your jewellery.'

They are so fresh and vital. I simply adore them. – *HRH Elizabeth, the Queen Mother*

Afterwards, in the royal lounge, the Beatles were presented to the Queen Mother. She told them she had enjoyed the show and asked them where they would be performing next. At Slough, they told her. 'Ah,' she said with obvious delight, 'that's near us.' Beatlemania had received the royal imprimatur.

From then on there was no restraining the press. For the past several years Britain's national newspapers have been engaged in a fierce struggle to attract the younger generation of readers. The popular papers reprint the pop music charts and patriotically bemoan the fact that the top-selling records have always been made by Americans or by singers such as Cliff Richard and Billy Fury who have studied Elvis, Avalon, and Anka and mastered American accent and presentation.

At first, the Beatles also sounded American. There was something of the Everly Brothers' instrumentation plus the style and presentation of the Miracles and Little Richard. But this time the beat wasn't coming from Nashville or Harlem. As one fourteen-year-old girl told the *Observer*, 'You usually think of film stars, pop singers, and so forth as living in glamorous places, Hollywood and so on. But the Beatles aren't like that. It's *Liverpool* – where *Z-Cars* comes from.'

In short, four local lads with funny but acceptable haircuts; who sang funky but were clean, adorable, and cheeky – but not too cheeky; just perfect for British idols. The press took a brief look and a briefer listen and with a whoop of pure joy from their circulation departments gave birth to the 'Mersey Sound'.

Since most people in Britain read at least one of the many daily and Sunday newspapers that circulate from one end of the country to another, within a week everyone was talking about the Beatles. The popular papers vied with one another to run versions of headlines incorporating the words 'Beatles', or 'Yeah, Yeah, Yeah'; the serious Sundays ran long analyses (the *Observer* printed a picture of a guitar-shaped Cycladic fertility goddess from Amorgos that it said 'dates the potency of the guitar as a sex symbol to about 4,800 years before the Beatle era'). Their shaggy haircuts became a cartoonist's standby.

As an American living in England I was curious to find out what was happening in this country I had always thought of in terms of sonnets and thatched roofs. I was helped somewhat by the papers. On the one hand the *Daily Mirror*, which has the biggest circulation in the world, said:

'YEAH! YEAH! YEAH! *You have to be a real sour square not to love the nutty, noisy, happy, handsome Beatles. If they don't sweep your blues away –* brother, you're a lost cause. *If they don't put a beat in your feet –* sister, you're not living. *How refreshing to see these rumbustious young Beatles take a middle-aged Royal Variety Performance by the scruff of their necks and have them beatling like teenagers. Fact is that Beatle People are everywhere. From Wapping to Windsor. Aged seven to 70. And it's plain to see why these four energetic, cheeky lads from Liverpool go down so big. They're young, new. They're high spirited, cheerful. What a change from the self-pitying moaners crooning their love-lorn tunes from the tortured shallows of lukewarm hearts. The Beatles are whacky. They wear their hair like a mop – but it's WASHED, it's super clean. So is their fresh young act. They don't have to rely on off-colour jokes about homos for their fun. Youngsters like the Beatles – and Cliff Richard and the Shadows – are doing a good turn for show business – and the rest of us – with their new sounds, new looks.* GOOD LUCK, BEATLES!

The *Sunday Times* took a more analytical approach:

Sexual emancipation is a factor in the phenomenon, though at a superficial level this may not be so important. 'You don't have to be a genius,' said a consultant in a London hospital, 'to see parallels between sexual excitement and the mounting crescendo of delighted screams through a stimulating number like "Twist and Shout", but, at the level it is presented and taken, I think it is the bubbly, uninhibited gaiety of the group that generates enthusiasm. There is none of Presley's overt sexual attack, nor for that matter any of the "smoochy" adult sensuality of Sinatra.'

I had seen the Beatles perform; I had listened to their records. They were enjoyable but no more enjoyable than scores of other pop quartets that had flickered briefly into my consciousness. What was fascinating about the Beatles (at least to me) was the things they said:

'None of us has quite grasped what it is all about yet. It's washing over our heads like a huge tidal wave. But we're young. Youth is on our side. And it's youth that matters right now. I don't care about politics. JUST PEOPLE.*'* – Ringo Starr, 23, Drummer (Ambition: 'to be happy')

'I wouldn't do all this if I didn't like it. I wouldn't do anything I didn't want to, would I?' – George Harrison, 21, Lead Guitarist (Ambition: 'to design a guitar')

'Security is the only thing I want. Money to do nothing with, money to have in case you wanted to do something.' – Paul McCartney, 22, Bass Guitarist (Ambition: 'to be successful')

'People say we're loaded with money, but by comparison with those who are supposed to talk the Queen's English that's ridiculous. We're only earning. They've got capital behind them and they're earning on top of that. The more people you meet, the more you realise it's all a class thing.' – John Lennon, 23, Rhythm Guitarist (Ambition: 'to write a musical')

'Why do you wear all those rings on your fingers?'

'Because I can't get them through my nose.' – Ringo

'It's disturbing that people should go around blowing us up, but if an atom bomb should explode I'd say, "Oh, well." No point in saying anything else, is there? People are so crackers. I know the bomb is ethically wrong, but I won't go around crying. I suppose I could do something like wearing those "Ban the Bomb" things, but it's something like religion that I don't think about; it doesn't fit in with my life.' – Paul

'I don't suppose I think much about the future. I don't really give a damn. Though now we've made it, it would be a pity to get bombed. It's selfish but I don't care too much about humanity – I'm an escapist. Everybody's always drumming on about the future but I'm not letting it interfere with my laughs if you see what I mean. Perhaps I worried more when I was working it out about God.' – John

'Don't for heaven's sake say we're the new youth, because that's a load of old rubbish.' – Paul

'Naturally, I'm part of my generation. I like the way people bring things out in the open. I'd hate it if when you spoke about sex everybody curled away.' – George

'Do you wear wigs?'

'If we do they must be the only ones with real dandruff.' – John

'At school we had a great hip English master and instead of keeping us to the drag stuff like Return of the Native, *he would let us read* Tennessee Williams, *and* Lady Chatterley's Lover, *and* The Miller's Tale.*'* – Paul

'I get spasms of being intellectual. I read a bit about politics but I don't think I'd vote for anyone; no message from any of those phoney politicians is coming through to me.' – John

'We've always had laughs. Sometimes we find ourselves hysterical, especially when we're tired. We laugh at soft remarks that the majority of people don't get.' – George

'The thing I'm afraid of is growing old. I hate that. You get old and you've missed it somehow. The old always resent the young and vice versa.' – John

'I'd like to end up sort of unforgettable.' – Ringo

'Ours is a today image.' – John

Love Me Do: The Beatles' Progress, Michael Braun, 1964

A SECRET HISTORY
By Alistair Taylor

Taylor was an assistant to the Beatles from the early days of Beatlemania. He published these reminiscences in 2001.

Brian said the boys demanded that I come with him to their very next concert for a reunion. That was at the East Ham Granada. And it turned out to be a very explosive evening for me. Beatlemania was now in full flight and it was a frightening experience. The cinema was besieged by thousands of screaming, chanting youngsters. The noise was exhilarating but the pushing and shoving tested the resources of the Metropolitan Police Force to the limit.

In the dressing room, it was the usual casual chaos with Neil Aspinall struggling to control the inevitable hangers on and to protect the boys from their own astonishing popularity. Scriptwriter Alun Owen was there that night to discuss a film to be made the following summer and George Martin arrived with great news. He held up his hand for silence and announced, 'Listen, everybody. I've got something important to tell you all. I have just heard the news from EMI that the advance sales of "I Want to Hold Your Hand" have topped the million mark.'

That was the first time it had ever happened. Cheers and champagne ran round the dressing room but, as they died down, there was a mocking remark from John: 'Yeah, great. But that means it'll only be at number one for about a week.' I don't think he was joking.

The Beatles' actual performance that night was drowned out as usual by the hysteria from the audience. The boys gave it their impressive all and the crowd went collectively insane. It was a breath-taking experience from the wings. At one point, I was convinced my ears were going to burst.

The boys always closed their set with 'Twist and Shout' and I had only just heard the familiar final chords when George shouted, 'Come on, Al,' and I joined in the dash to beat the fans. They grabbed me and almost bodily propelled me along corridors and down passages to the stage door which was opened for us as we sprinted. Outside, the gleaming Austin Princess limousine was there with the engine running and the doors open. In front was a police car with blue light already flashing and behind was a motorcycle escort.

I took all this in in the flash that it took us to cross the pavement and leap into the car. Then Ringo got his foot stuck in the closing door and everyone started yelling at him. When I looked straight ahead I realised why as hordes of fans looked on the point of breaking through the thin blue line of straining policemen. Even I started yelling at Ringo to get his foot in so we could shut the door and escape. It was only a few seconds but it seemed like ages before he freed his foot, and we sped off to the Beatles' flat in Green Street. We shot past the marauding fans just in time and hurtled through London, helped through inconvenient red traffic lights by our police escort.

We are all chaotic and mixed up inside. We are anxious to have a greater freedom to live. We have a greater feeling of the need to express ourselves . . . in the past we have been controlled automatons . . . but you cannot hold nature back forever. All the parts in use had to seek an outlet and rhythm is one of those outlets . . . then along came the Beatles with their fresh beat and fresh innocence. – *An unidentified psychiatrist, quoted in the* Daily Mirror *1963*

We had a marvellous night when we arrived. There were just the four Beatles, Neil and myself. The Beatles rolled a joint or three and I clung to my scotch and Coke and they laughed about the early days. They took the mickey out of me for being straight, but that's me. I'm always happier in my suit than in the latest fashion item and always happier with alcohol than drugs. The boys took the piss, certainly, but in that friendly English way that let me enjoy the process. It was great to be back in the fold. It was like being a member of the best gang in the world being on the fringe of the Beatles. Apparently, you could do anything, go anywhere, and be anybody.

I realised early on in my return, however, how terribly trapped Beatlemania had made them. They couldn't go anywhere without being mobbed. There were fans camped outside their homes day and night and everything they said or did was monitored. I'd have taken drugs or any damn thing if I had to live with that pressure. Often they would almost retreat into just the four of them. They were lucky they had each other with whom to share that bizarre experience of genuine superstardom.

A Secret History, Alistair Taylor, 2001

SHOUT! THE TRUE STORY
OF THE BEATLES
By Philip Norman

Journalist Norman's much-acclaimed Shout! *was published in 1981. As well as revealing aspects of the Beatles' personal biographies that hadn't been detailed before, it shed new
light on their business affairs.*

It had become clear at an early stage, to various sharp-eyed people, that the
Beatles were capable of selling far more than gramophone records by the million.
Beatlemania demonstrated as never before to what extent young people in
Britain were a 'market', gigantic and ripe for exploitation. From October 1963
onward, Brian Epstein carried in his wake a little trail of businessmen, coaxing,
cajoling, sometimes begging to be authorised to produce goods in the Beatles'
image.

'Merchandising' as a concept was largely unknown in mid-20th century
Britain, even though the Victorians had been adept at it. Walt Disney, that peer-
less weaver of dreams into plastic, was imitated on a small scale by British toy
manufacturers, producing replicas of television puppets. Pop singers until now
had lasted too short a time in public esteem to sell any but the most ephemeral
goods.

No precedent existed, therefore, to warn Brian that there were billions at
stake. He saw the merchandising purely as public relations – a way to increase
audience goodwill and keep the Fan Club happy. He worried about the Fan
Club, and keeping it happy.

The first Beatle products catered simply for the desire, as strong in girls as in
boys, to impersonate their idols. In Bethnal Green, East London, a factory was
producing Beatle 'wigs' at the rate of several thousand each week. The hairstyle
which Astrid's scissors had shaped for Stu Sutcliffe became a best-selling novel-
ty, a black, fibrous mop, hovering just outside seriousness, 30 shillings apiece. A
Midlands clothing firm marketed collarless corduroy 'Beatle jackets' like the one
Astrid had made for Stu; the one which the Beatles at the time despised as
'Mum's jacket'. Girls, too, wore the jackets, the tab–collar shirts, even the elas-
tic-sided, Cuban heel 'Beatle boots', obtainable by mail order at '75s 11d,

including post and packing.'

Christmas 1963 signalled a fresh avalanche of Beatle products into the shops. There were Beatle guitars, of plastic, authentically 'autographed', and miniature Beatle drums. There were Beatle lockets, each with a tiny quadruple photograph compressed inside. There were red and blue Beatle kitchen aprons, bespeckled with guitar-playing bugs. The four faces and four signatures, engraved, printed or transferred, however indistinctly, appeared on belts, badges, handkerchieves, jigsaw puzzles, rubber airbeds, disc racks, bedspreads, 'ottomans', shoulder bags, pencils, buttons and trays. There was a brand of confectionery known as 'Ringo Roll', and of Beatle chewing gum, each sixpenny packet warranted to contain seven photographs. A Northern bakery chain announced guitar-shaped 'Beatle cakes' ('Party priced at 5s') and fivepenny individual Beatle 'fancies'.

When I grew my hair long in 1954, people ran away from me on the subway in fright. Ten years later, when I first saw the Beatles with long hair, I thought somebody had stolen my picture and shown it to them. I remember calling up *Variety* and accusing the Beatles of stealing my look. The woman there said, 'Look, sir, let me tell you something. Their hair is like the Three Stooges, not yours!' – *Tiny Tim*

Brian, in the beginning, personally examined the products of each prospective licensee. In no case, he ruled, would the Beatles directly endorse any article. Nor would they lend their name to anything distasteful, inappropriate or overtly exploitative of their fans. And, indeed, parents who had scolded their children for buying 'trash' were frequently surprised by the goods' quality and value. The Beatle jacket was smart, durable and well-lined. The 'official' Beatle sweater ('Designed for Beatle people by a leading British manufacturer') was 100 per cent botany wool, hardly extortionate at 35s.

Soon, however, unauthorised Beatle goods began to appear. Though NEMS Enterprises held copyright on the name 'Beatles', infringement could be avoided simply by spelling it 'Beetles'. The vaguest representation of insects, of guitars or little mop-headed men, had the power to sell anything, however cheap, however nasty. Even to spot the culprits, let alone bring lawsuits against them, meant a countrywide invigilation such as no British copyright-holder had ever been obliged to undertake. NEMS Enterprises certainly could not undertake it. And so, after one or two minor prosecutions, the pirates settled down, unhampered, to their bonanza.

By late 1963, the merchandising had got into a tangle which Brian Epstein had not the time nor the will to contemplate. He therefore handed the whole matter over to his solicitor, David Jacobs. It became Jacobs's job, not only to prosecute infringements, where visible, but also, at his independent discretion, to issue new manufacturing licenses. Prospective licensees were referred from NEMS Enterprises to Jacobs's offices in Pall Mall. Since David Jacobs, too, was deeply preoccupied, with social as well as legal matters, the task of appraising designs, production strategy and probable income was delegated to the chief clerk in his chambers, Edward Marke.

This arrangement quickly proved inconvenient. Among the cases currently being handled by M. A. Jacobs Ltd. were several claims for damages by the relatives of passengers lost aboard a cruise ship, the Lakonia. The waiting-room where these bereaved litigants sat also served as a dumping ground for cascades of Beatle guitars, plastic windmills and crayoning sets. Mr Marke, though a conscientious legal functionary, knew little of the manufacturing business. So David Jacobs, in his turn, looked round for someone to take on this tiresome business of making millions.

His choice was Nicky Byrne, a man he had met, and been rather impressed by, at a cocktail party. Byrne, indeed, was rather a celebrated figure at parties, of which he himself gave a great many at his fashionable Chelsea garage-cum-flat. Small, impishly-dapper, formidably persuasive, he had been variously a country squire's son, a Horse Guard trooper and an amateur racing driver. His true avocation, however, was membership of the 'Chelsea Set', that sub-culture of debutantes, bohemians, heiresses and charming cads which, since the mid-Fifties, had flourished along and around the King's Road.

Nicky Byrne was not a totally implausible choice, having in his extremely varied life touched the worlds of show business and popular retailing. In the Fifties, he had run the Condor Club, in Soho, where Tommy Steele was discovered. His wife, Kiki – from whom he had recently parted – was a well-known fashion designer with her own successful Chelsea boutique.

The offer from Jacobs was that Byrne should administer the Beatles' merchandising operation in Europe and throughout the world. He was not, he maintains, very eager to accept. 'Brian Epstein had a very bad name in the business world at that time. Nobody knew who was licensed to make Beatle goods and who wasn't. I got in touch with Kiki, my ex-wife, to see what she thought about it. I mentioned this schmutter firm in Soho that was meant to be turning out Beatle gear. Kiki said, "Hold on a minute." She'd had a letter from a firm in the Midlands, asking her to design exactly the same thing for them.'

Nicky Byrne was eventually persuaded. He agreed to form a company named Stramsact to take over the assigning of Beatle merchandise rights. A subsidiary called Seltaeb – Beatles spelt backwards – would handle American rights, if any, when the Beatles went to New York in February to appear on *The Ed Sullivan Show*.

Five partners, all much younger than Nicky Bryne, constituted both Stramsact and Seltaeb. One of them, 26-year-old John Fenton, had already been doing some merchandising deals of his own via David Jacobs. Two others, Mark Warman and Simon Miller-Munday, aged 20 and 22 respectively, were simply friends of Nicky's who had been nice to him during his break-up with Kiki.

Nicky Byrne's most picturesque recruit, after himself, was 23-year-old Lord Peregrine Eliot, heir to the Earl of St Germans and owner of a 6,000 acre estate in Cornwall. Lord Peregrine's qualification was that he had shared a flat with Simon Miller-Munday. Although extremely rich, he was eager to earn funds to recarpet his ancestral home, Port Eliot. For £1,000 cash, His Lordship received twenty per cent of the company.

The Beatles actually sing part of this song ['All I Want for Christmas is a Beatle'] in one of their Christmas fan club messages (strangely, it sounds like they are singing 'All I want for Christmas is a bottle'). – *Liner Notes,* Flabby Road – 26 of the all time great Beatle Novelty Songs

Only Malcolm Evans, the sixth partner, a junior studio manager with Rediffusion TV, had any definite professional ability of any kind. Evans had met the others at a Nicky Byrne party, the high spot of which was the pushing of a grand piano through the Chelsea streets. 'Nicky had got the entire Count Basie Orchestra to play at his party,' Evans says. 'I remember that they were accompanied on the bagpipes by a full-dress pipe major from the barracks over the road.'

The contract between Stramsact-Seltaeb and NEMS Enterprises was left to David Jacobs to draw up, approve, even sign on Brian's and the Beatles' behalf. 'I was at my solicitor's, just round the corner,' Nicky Byrne says. 'He told me, "Write in what percentage you think you should take on the deal." So I put down the first figure that came into my head – 90 per cent.

'To my amazement, David Jacobs didn't even question it. He didn't think of it as 90 per cent to us, but as ten per cent to the Beatles. He said, "Well, ten per cent is better than nothing.'"

Christmas, far from diverting the mania, actually seemed to increase it. The Beatles *became* Christmas in their fancy dress, playing in the NEMS Christmas Show at Finsbury Park Astoria. One of the sketches was a Victorian melodrama in which George, as 'heroine', was tied on a railway line by 'Sir Jasper' (John) and rescued by 'Fearless Paul the Signalman'. They had acted such plays and farces for years among themselves. Mal Evans, their second road manager, stood by, laughing, as all did, at the good-humoured knockabout fun; Mal had just received a savage tongue-lashing from John for having lost his twelve-string 'Jumbo' guitar.

Beatle records made the December Top Twenty literally impassable. As well as 'I Want To Hold Your Hand' at Number One, it contained six songs from the *With the Beatles* LP – indeed, the album itself, with almost a million copies sold, qualified for entrance to the singles chart at Number Fourteen, while the customary seasonal 'gimmick' record was Dora Bryan's 'All I Want For Christmas Is a Beatle'.

Shout! The True Story of the Beatles, Philip Norman, 1981

BUILDING THE BEATLE
IMAGE
By Vance Packard

Sociologist and best-selling author Packard came to prominence in 1957 with his exposé of the advertising industry, The Hidden Persuaders. *He was well placed to take this slightly cynical view of Beatlemania and its merchandising.*

What causes an international craze like the current Beatlemania? Press agentry can only swell a craze. To get one started you need to bring into fusion five vital ingredients. This is true whether the craze involves Davy Crockett, Liberace or Elvis Presley.

Only three years ago it is doubtful that any observer of pop culture would have picked the Beatles to inspire madness on both sides of the Atlantic. In 1961 the Beatles affected a beatnik look. They wore black T-shirts, black leather jackets, blue jeans and dishevelled hair. In one picture taken of them that year they scowled at the camera as good beatniks should.

Then along came Brian Epstein, an aristocratic-looking young Englishman who ran a record shop and soon became their manager. First he made them scrub, comb their hair and get into civilised clothing. Then little by little, by a combination of hunch, luck and design, he began exploiting the five ingredients that will create a craze.

First, the Beatles needed a symbol that would make them stand out in people's minds, a symbol such as the coonskin cap that Walt Disney gave to his Davy Crockett creation. For a symbol it was decided to exploit their already overlong hair. The Beatles let it grow longer and bushier, combed it forward – and then had it immaculately trimmed. The result was not only eye-catching but evocative. Such hairdos were common in the Middle Ages and the new coiffure suggested the ancient roots of England.

A second ingredient necessary for a craze is to fill some important subconscious need of teen-agers. Youngsters see themselves as a subjugated people constantly exposed to arbitrary edicts from adult authorities. The entertainment world has developed many strategies to offer youngsters a sense of escape from adult domination. Television producers of children's shows sometimes make adult figures either stupid or villainous. The press agents for some teen stars pub-licise the stars' defiance of their parents. Teenage crooners relate with amiable condescension their support of their parents.

Rock'n'roll music, of course, annoys most parents, which is one of the main reasons why millions of youngsters love it. But the Beatles couldn't possibly hope to outdo Elvis Presley in appalling parents. Instead of open opposition, the Beatles practice an amiable impudence and a generalised disrespect for just about everybody. They succeeded, happily, in getting themselves denounced in some pretty high adult places. The Lord Privy Seal indicated his annoyance. And Field Marshal Lord Montgomery growled that the Army would take care of those mop-top haircuts if the Beatles were ever conscripted.

But the Beatles – under Mr Epstein's tutelage – also have put stress on filling other subconscious needs of teenagers. As restyled, they are no longer rough-necks but rather lovable, almost cuddly, imps. With their collarless jackets and boyish grins, they have succeeded in bringing out the mothering instinct in many adolescent girls.

The subconscious need that they fill most expertly is in taking adolescent girls clear out of this world. The youngsters in the darkened audiences can let go all inhibitions in a quite primitive sense when the Beatles cut loose. They can retreat from rationality and individuality. Mob pathology takes over, and they are momentarily freed of all of civilisation's restraints.

I have to say the most important mark the Beatles left on this society and for future generations is the popularisation of the Beatle wig. I still have several and wear them proudly. – *David Letterman*

The Beatles have become peculiarly adept at giving girls this release. Their relaxed, confident manner, their wild appearance, their whooping and jumping, their electrified rock-'n'-roll pulsing out into the darkness makes the girls want to jump – and then scream. The more susceptible soon faint or develop twitch-ing hysteria. (One reason why Russia's totalitarian leaders frown on rock'n'roll and jazz is that these forms offer people release from controlled behaviour.)

A third ingredient needed to get a craze started – as Brian Epstein obviously knew – is an exciting sense of freshness. In an informal poll conducted through my offspring, who are at high school and college, I find that the fact that the Beatles are somehow 'different' – something new in the musical world – made the deepest impression. Teenagers feel they are helping create something new that is peculiarly their own. And as my fifteen-year-old expert (feminine) explained, 'We were kind of at a lag with popular singers.'

The delivery, if not the music, is refreshingly different with the Beatles. Surliness is out, exuberance is in. Sloppiness is out, cleanliness is in. Self-pity is out, whooping with joy is in. Pomposity is out, humour is in.

A fourth ingredient needed to keep a craze rolling once it shows signs of starting is a carrying device, such as a theme song. The carrying device of the Beatles is found in their name. It playfully suggests beatnik, but it also suggests 'beat' and the beat is the most conspicuous feature of the Beatles' music. It is laid on heavily with both drums and bass guitar. When the screaming starts, the beat still gets through.

Finally, a craze can succeed only if it meets the mood of the times. England, after centuries of cherishing the subdued, proper form of life, is bursting out of its inhibitions. There has been a growth of open sexuality, plain speaking and living it up. The Beatles came along at just the right time to help the bursting-out process.

What is the future of the Beatle craze in America? At this point it is hard to say. But the Beatles are so dependent upon their visual appeal that there is a question whether they can sustain the craze in their American territory from across the Atlantic. Another problem is that they are not really offensive enough to grown-ups to inspire youngsters to cling to them.

Frankly, if I were in the business of manufacturing mophead Beatle wigs, I would worry. Crazes tend to die a horribly abrupt death. It was not so long ago, after all, that a good many unwary businessmen got caught with warehouses full of coonskin caps when the Crockett craze stopped almost without warning.

Saturday Evening Post, 1964

LOVE ME DO: THE BEATLES' PROGRESS (2)

By Michael Braun

This second extract from Love Me Do *continues in the style of fairly candid, on-the-road close-ups. By the time its description of the Beatles' US debut on* The Ed Sullivan Show *was published, they literally had the world at their feet.*

An audience consisting mainly of teenage girls had been invited to watch the rehearsal for that evening's show as well as the taping of two additional songs for the programme in three weeks' time. They were reasonably quiet until Ringo's drums were rolled on stage. Then they began to scream. Before the Beatles appeared, Sullivan came on stage and asked the audience to give their attention to all the other fine performers besides the Beatles who were appearing, because if they didn't he would call in a barber. Then he said, 'Our city – indeed, the country – has never seen anything like these four young men from Liverpool. Ladies and gentlemen, the Beatles!'

What happened to the audience next led a writer in the *New York Herald-Tribune* the following day to compare it with 'that terrible screech the BMT Astoria train makes as it turns east near 59th Street and Seventh Avenue'.

While the Beatles rehearsed, Cynthia Lennon stood in the back of the theatre talking to Maureen Cleave. Cynthia wanted to go shopping but was afraid to go out alone. 'The fans here seem a bit wackier than in England,' she said. A fan who happened to be standing near by overheard, and ten minutes later came back with a huge parcel.

'There's no need for you to go shopping now,' she said as she presented her with a present for their six-month-old son – a 'Barracuda Atomic Sub'.

When the rehearsal and taping ended, Sullivan stood on the stage. 'It warms me to hear such enthusiasm,' he said.

'I'm going to be sick,' said a cameraman in the background.

Someone asked Sullivan about the comment of his musical director Ray Bloch that had appeared in the *New York Times* that morning. Bloch had told the *Times*: 'The only thing that's different is the hair, as far as I can see. I give them a year.'

Sullivan called Bloch over.

'Now, Ray,' he said, 'you can't say things like that.'

'They asked me how long I thought the Beatles would be making this kind of money,' replied Bloch, an elegant little man in a goatee, 'and I said about a year. Of course, I meant that they would then make a movie and make *more* money.'

On the other side of the stage a young man carrying a stenographic pad walked over to a CBS press aide. He worked for *Time* magazine and had been sent to New York from Washington. 'I don't know if this story is going in "Music" or "Show Business",' he said.

'It should go in "National Affairs",' said the CBS man.

Sullivan was talking about the Beatles. 'I remember the first time I saw them. I was at London Airport and there were mobs. There must have been 50,000 girls there and I later found out they had prevented Lord Home and Queen Elizabeth from taking off. I said to Mrs Sullivan, "Here is something." It was just like years ago when I was travelling in the South and I used to hear the name of Presley at fairs. Of course, he was all wriggling and sex. These boys are good musicians. When I finally saw them play in England, and the reaction, I said to Mrs Sullivan, "These boys have something."'

The *Time* man asked the press aide whether it was true that the Beatles had been invited to the White House.

'I understand the young girl is a big fan,' said the CBS man, 'but the Secret Service won't let her go to the Coliseum. I'm going to try and set up a performance at home.'

An hour before the Ed Sullivan programme was to begin, an instrumental trio wandered up and down the aisles serenading the largely teenage audience with soothing music. The fact that the only way back stage was through the men's room somewhat encouraged the girls to stay in their seats.

The troupe of boys from *Oliver* who were also to appear on the show arrived at the theatre. Someone asked them if they were Beatles.

'No,' replied a five-year-old with a Beatle cut and the broadest New York accent, 'we're roaches.'

Upstairs, the Beatles are having their pictures taken with Sullivan. A CBS press man is waving a pair of shears and a comb. 'C'mon, fellas,' he is saying, 'it's just a gimmick photo.'

Just before the programme is to begin, columnist Earl Wilson meets Sullivan backstage.

Wilson: 'Is it true, Ed? Are you going to wear it?'

Sullivan: 'I've already worn it.'

Wilson: 'How did you look?'

Sullivan: 'It's a wig like any other. By the way, your hair looks great.'

The next day the photograph with Wilson's column shows him wearing a bald wig.

The Beatles' recording manager, George Martin, is in the audience. He plans to record their concert at Carnegie Hall. Someone asks him why, since all the songs have been recorded before.

> **I saw the Beatles in England in 1963 at a command performance. They were not unknown, as Ed Sullivan used to claim. I heard his press agent on the air not long ago talking about how nobody knew who the Beatles were and they couldn't get any publicity. Well, that's all bullshit . . . I bought a film from the BBC and showed it on January third, 1964 . . . a month before Sullivan brought them here.**
> *– Jack Parr, original host of* The Tonight Show

'I don't know,' he says. 'It's just a bit of history, I guess.'

Sullivan is on stage doing a warm-up. 'Listen, kids,' he says, 'there are other talented performers on this show,' (groans) 'so clap for them too.' (Perfunctory clapping.) 'We'll be going on in eight minutes.' (Groans.)

He walks off stage and reappears in a Beatle wig, and, to show the spirit of history that pervades, thanks Randy Parr for the wig. Miss Parr, it turns out, has persuaded her father to end his long feud with Sullivan in order to obtain a ticket for her to see the show.

The programme opens with an announcement of a congratulatory telegram from Elvis Presley and his manager Colonel Parker. Elvis says he is reciprocating the Beatles' telegram when he visited England in 1962, a visit unknown to all but Elvis. When the boys come on stage (screams), their names are superimposed on the screen. Under John's it reads, 'Sorry, girls, he's married.' In 'She Loves You' the screams for George and Paul's head-shaking are a split second late, but this, after all, is the first time they've been seen and the girls need time to coordinate their screams.

Backstage, Maureen Cleave wants to go up to their dressing room but [Beatles press agent and PA Brian] Sommerville tells her, 'My dear, they're changing their trousers.'

The door opens, and trumpeter Dizzy Gillespie walks in. 'What a mob!' he says as he is introduced to Sommerville by Alfred Aronowitz of the *Saturday Evening Post*.

'How do you do?' says Sommerville.

'Can I see 'em, man?' asks Gillespie.

Sommerville hesitates, and Aronowitz asks, 'Do you know who this is?'

'I've heard the name,' says Sommerville.

Just then George walks over. 'How do you do?' he says to Gillespie, and to Sommerville, 'I've lost me shoe.'

'I haven't come to hear you, man,' says Gillespie, 'I just want to get a good look at you.' He then asks George for his autograph and after receiving it tells him that he's 'going to sell it for two Count Basie records'.

During this exchange, Carol James, a Washington disc jockey, who had been the first to play a Beatle record in America, takes out a portable tape-recorder and begins to record the conversation. A CBS guard comes over, says that tape-recorders are forbidden in the studio, and throws James out.

As soon as James has been ejected George takes the ear plug from his transistor radio, holds it to Gillespie's mouth, and begins his own interview.

'Are you interested in Anglo-American relations?' he asks.

'Yes,' says Dizzy. 'I've got quite a few.'

The other three Beatles came downstairs with transistor radios, bearing the words Pepsi-Cola on them, plugged into their ears. They raced back to the Plaza, and, as they entered the door, a young man said to his date, 'They'll never believe it, never. . .We were so close.'

Love Me Do: The Beatles' Progress, Michael Braun, 1964

WHY WE LOVED THE BEATLES
By Paul Theroux

Travel writer and novelist Theroux penned this sharp reflection of the Beatles' arrival in the USA, 1964, for a Rolling Stone *commemorative edition, twenty years later.*

We had been used to another sort of English person – meddlers, bumblers, know-it-alls, creeps, posturing pieces of wood like David Niven, sagacious old egomaniacs like Alistair Cooke or examples of metal fatigue like Joan Collins – professional limeys haw-hawing all over Hollywood, boasting about what frightful snobs they were. And among the last English entertainers on *The Ed Sullivan Show* was an elderly fart who called himself 'Mister Pastry' and who was almost certainly insane.

Considering the precedent, how could the Beatles possibly have failed? They seemed like much nicer images of ourselves; how were we to know they had been Americanised long before they arrived in New York? They were also tough and cynical lads, out for what they could get, even willing to dress identically (only the Ritz Brothers and candy-assed quadruplets pulled shit like that!). They allowed themselves to be manipulated in order to succeed. The Beatles' style and outlook were so strongly influenced by American pop culture that had they been unable to prove themselves here, they would have regarded themselves as failures.

Since the Second World War, Europe has been full of people who are sort of secret Americans – Europeans with a powerful fantasy life, walking around muttering, 'Ay, baby, I like you beeg teets. I am a hot-rod keed, and I want a piece de action.' Nearly always, they wind up in America. They're the feverishly vindictive little wimps who tell you, 'My guntry is all gommuneest,' and then pinch your bum. New Americans. I think of the Beatles as an exuberant and freakish variety of this often misery-minded and right-wing type. The Beatles were working-class Liverpudlians, spiritual refugees from a neglected corner of a provincial town. Their fantasy life (dollars, hot rods, reefers, groupies) was fuelled by America. If they had been Londoners or middle class – Mick Jagger was both – they would have put on the kind of snotty metropolitan contempt that smug, big-city Europeans pretend they have for the States. But they didn't. The Beatles revelled in just being in America: we were their liberation.

One of the best and most reliable escape routes from the English class system is across the Atlantic – flight to America. The Beatles had an understandable mistrust for English institutions. What had the system ever done for them? And they knew it was impossible for an English person to rid himself of his class identity without leaving England. America was a happy alternative to messy families and cultural narrowness and a national attitude that somewhat despises entertainers. They knew how few rewards there were in Britain for even very talented people; any plausible crook can get a knighthood. America was not only fat, pleasant vulgarity, but also freedom, money, sunshine and limitless optimism. There has never been much of that in Britain.

I remember the precise moment, the precise night, that I went to this place in New York City called the Dom and they turned on 'I Want To Hold Your Hand', and I heard that high, yodelling alto sound of the OOOH that went right through my skull, and I realised it was going to go through the skull of Western civilisation. – *Allen Ginsberg*

Untypical for English popular musicians, their influences did not come from the English music hall or from fruity-voiced folk singers – the sackbut-and-crumhorn brigade. The Beatles had begun by imitating Elvis Presley, Chuck Berry and Buddy Holly. Mimicry gave them a useful direction, then they went on their own calculating way. But having trusted from the beginning the magic of American pop music, they needed American approval. *The Ed Sullivan Show* was the high water-mark of American mass culture, the most noticed variety show in the country, and they knew it contributed to the making of Elvis.

The Beatles' unaffected pleasure in performance surprised everyone. When they said 'Love Me Do', they meant it, and so we did. They seemed oddly grateful and anxious to please – none of that insecurity and snobbery we had associated with Great Britain, but instead the gusto of four working-class lads who were so unspeakably relieved to have been sprung from the prison of decrepit senile Europe that they married us and moved in.

Rolling Stone, 16 February 1984

WAITING FOR THE BEATLES
By Carol Bedford

This evocative piece gives us some idea of what it was like to be an American fan at the height of Beatlemania, when the boys finally hit Main Street, USA.

The night the Beatles flew in, the atmosphere in the city had increased to fever pitch. My brother Billy said he would be happy to take me to the airport to see their plane land. We set off several hours before the plane was due as I wanted a good vantage point. When we arrived we were both surprised to see hundreds of girls already there. All the girls were standing on one side of a fence topped with barbed wire, while the police were on the other side of the fence to make sure that no one got over it. I found a place in front of the fence. A reporter was standing next to me and started asking me questions.

'Are you going to scream when they land?'

'No, that's childish. I'm twelve years old. I'm too old to be so silly.'

The plane landed at eight o'clock. It was a pitch black night, but the entire airport was lit up with the landing lights and the reporters' flash bulbs. When the plane landed and the doors opened, the first one out was George. He poked his head out and then went back inside the plane. A few minutes later he reappeared and walked down the steps with John, Paul and Ringo behind him.

That split second when George poked his head out, every girl in the area screamed her head off. I can't explain what came over me. I found myself not only screaming at the top of my voice, but hitching my tight, wool skirt up to my waist and scaling the seven or eight foot fence to the point where I cut my hands on the barbed wire at the top. The reporter who had been told that I would not scream stood to one side in total shock. Billy was trying to pull my skirt down over my hips and a policeman on the other side of the fence was hitting my hands with a night-stick.

The only way Billy could get me down and avoid possible arrest was to shout, 'Let's go to the hotel! I'll drive you to the hotel if you come down!' By this time, the Beatles had reached their car and were getting in it so I immediately got down and raced with Billy to our car. There were hundreds of girls – girls with their boyfriends, girls with their mothers, girls with their friends – all racing for their cars to try and follow the Beatles.

On the way to our car, we ran into Jim, a friend of Billy's, who asked, 'Can I catch a ride to the hotel?' Billy said, 'Yeah. It's the funniest thing I've ever seen in my life; all these girls are going hysterical. I can't miss the scene at the hotel.'

We charged to the car. Billy was driving, I was in the front seat and Jim was in the back. Billy took off from the airport parking lot like a bat out of hell. He was speeding along the road at such a rate that I could not bear to look at the road in front of us. I turned to face Jim in the back seat. I then saw the police cars following us. They were bearing down on us very quickly. They had their sirens going, so naturally I assumed they were after us for speeding. I turned to Billy. 'Oh, my God. Now we're going to get a ticket.' Jim turned around and burst out laughing. 'They're not following us,' he explained. 'They're leading the car that the Beatles are in! We beat the Beatles out of the airport!'

When we reached the hotel, we parked the car quickly and raced to the front. It was jam-packed with bodies. These girls had skipped the airport scene in the hope of seeing the Beatles enter the hotel.

We inched our way through the girls to the front of the hotel. The entire ground floor was faced with glass panelling and was not made to withstand the onslaught of Beatlemania. Girls were pressed hard against the glass trying to get into the hotel. The hotel staff had shut and barricaded the doors to prevent this – but the glass had no place to move to under this pressure so it shattered. One girl was pushed through the glass and cut very badly. The hotel authorities desperately tried to push the sea of girls back so they could reach the injured girl. (Later, we heard that the girl received a phone call from the Beatles while she was in hospital. They were very upset about her misfortune. She was very pleased to talk to the Beatles, but she would miss the concert.)

Billy was frightened when the glass broke and the girls continued to push. He told me to come with him away from the glass. This didn't work so he changed tactic and pointed out that it was highly unlikely that the Beatles would walk in the front of the hotel. This made sense. Not only were there about 500 girls outside the hotel but there were another 200 inside, lining the balcony. A large portion of these girls had booked rooms at the hotel in order to try and see the Beatles.

I followed Billy as he walked around to the back of the hotel. The Beatles had just gone in and up a laundry chute in order to get to their rooms. The girls were crying hysterically. One girl had grass in her hand screaming 'Ringo! Ringo walked on this grass!' The next night was the concert. Billy and I went to our seats in the balcony. There was a girl with her father next to our seats; Billy sat by the father leaving us girls to ourselves. There were Beatle look-alikes that the auditorium had hired. These four guys were nearly mauled to death because they looked enough like the Beatles to be attacked by 300 over-anxious girls. The police had to be brought in to save the men's lives. Police were scattered throughout the auditorium. They were standing three-deep in front of the stage and were positioned every few feet on the ground floor and balconies.

The lights went out, and girls screamed. But it was only the support band. People started milling around again; it was only the Beatles that people had come to see.

Then the lights went out a second time and the Beatles came on. They were wearing navy blue suits with collarless jackets. Flash bulbs were going off at such a rate that you could barely see the stage. Girls were immediately on their feet, including myself. I lost control completely. My hands were stretched over my head or I reached out in front, as if I could touch them.

They started with 'I Saw Her Standing There'. Girls on the ground floor raced for the stage. Police were trying to push them back and, failing that, at least keep them from climbing onto the stage. One girl made it. She grabbed John who was forced to stop playing his guitar. He called for help as the girl was kissing his face and grabbing his hair. A policeman came to John's rescue. John couldn't stop laughing. Paul got into the mood and fell on one knee in proposing style at John's feet. Lennon continued to laugh. The girls went wild – more charged the stage.

Elvis was no longer rocking, and they did the same thing as Elvis had done: They unlocked the music scene. No one was playing that raw stuff he played. I think that when their success came, the Beatles were a bit disappointed in the scheme of things because they became so big so fast. They wanted to conquer America, but we gave it to them on a silver platter. – *Roy Orbison*

The next song was a slow number, 'This Boy', in an attempt to calm the fans. But this had no effect. During this song, a policeman nearly lost his life. He was blocking my view of Ringo and I raced to push him over the balcony. Billy just managed to restrain me. The cop lost his hat though.

The Beatles were on stage for only 25 minutes. I'm not sure if this was because they were scared to death or if it was due to the fact that 25 minutes was about the limit of hysteria that any of us could handle. You could hear very little of the music above the screams. People would stay quiet just long enough to recognise the song – was it 'Long Tall Sally' or 'She Loves You'? – and the screaming would start again and remain for the rest of the song. And the flash bulbs never stopped going on-off, on-off.

When the Beatles bowed, we knew they were going. Despite the fact that we were all hoarse from screaming our heads off for the last half-hour, we all managed to scream even louder as they left the stage.

After the concert, everyone moved as if in slow motion. We were exhausted, but satisfied. I went out of the auditorium with Billy and, in a state of shock, walked straight into an on-coming car. By luck the driver was watching what he was doing far more than I was. Billy nearly fainted.

We got into the car and were on our way home when the car radio announced that the Beatles' plane was taking off. Right over my head there was an aircraft. Despite the fact that Billy was driving at 65 mph on the highway, I opened the door to get out and have a better look. Billy acted quickly and prevented disaster; he stopped the car on the shoulder of the road so I could get out. I cried in Billy's arms. 'They're gone. Oh God. They're gone.'

(A couple of years later, Billy was poking fun at me for my insane behaviour at the concert. His fiancee did not respond with the expected laughter. She then told him that she too had attended this concert. When the Beatles were trying to leave the concert area, she had thrown herself on the front of their car and had cut herself on the windscreen. She pulled up her sweater to reveal the scar. Paul had noticed she was injured and frantically waved to a policeman in order to get his help. The policeman dragged her from the car so the Beatles could continue on their way to the airport. At hearing this tale, it was Billy who failed to laugh.)

Waiting for the Beatles: An Apple Scruff's Story, Carol Bedford, 1984

BEATLES DOWN UNDER: 1964
By Glenn A. Baker

The sheer madness of the Beatles' 1964 tour of Australia and New Zealand is well cap-
tured in this journal. Despite stand-in drummer Jimmy Nicol replacing Ringo for the early
dates, the scenes of Beatlemania were even more spectacular than those across the USA.
In Sydney alone, an estimated half of the city's two million population flooded the streets
to greet the group.

As the convoy inched down the road towards the Anzac Highway, the red-faced Beatles witnessed a degree of adulation that was new, even to them. Wildly waving and squealing fans of all ages lined the road up to six deep, standing on parked cars and swinging out of trees. Progress ceased at regular intervals as police battled to clear a way through the surging, spilling mass. Police estimates of the motorcade route crowd was 200,000 plus.

EMI National Promotions Manager Kevin Ritchie, travelling in the car with [Beatles publicist and personal asistant Derek] Taylor and Ravenscroft, described the scene: 'They were very emotional; 12,000 miles away from home and this was happening. We all felt like members of the royal family as we waved to the crowd – all the mums, dads, kids, babies, and even cripples who had been placed in the front line. Declared or not, I would say that the whole of Adelaide had a public holiday on that Friday, there couldn't have been anybody in any sort of industry or school that day. The whole city had come to a complete halt to welcome the Beatles.' Ravenscroft adds: 'Nobody wanted to be left out, there were even blind people waving their white sticks at us.'

At the Town Hall, scenes of unprecedented, unexplainable and quite unbelievable madness were unfolding. Not even London during the blitz had seen such a cacophonic panorama. The barriers were crowded and beginning to give way at 10 a.m. as thousands of sons, daughters, mothers, fathers, grandmothers, grandfathers, uncles, aunts and spotted dogs battled each other for prime positions. The agile perched precariously on tree branches, building ledges, telephone poles, traffic lights, truck tops and roofs. The police found themselves unable to wade through the seething walls of humanity to order the climbers down.

By 12.30 p.m. all streets intersecting King William Street were closed off by police, as the inner city numbers climbed to around 30,000. Casualties were surprisingly light. A 60-year-old woman fainted, four girls were trampled, a boy ran into the side of a moving bus, and a girl burned her leg on the exhaust pipe of a police motorbike.

Though it appeared that every upstanding citizen of Adelaide was smitten hopelessly with Beatlemania, such was not the case. Conservative educationalists, employing supression tactics that would not have been out of place on the Gulag Archipelago, managed to remove many thousands of potential welcomers from the front lines.

Copenhagen has been reduced to a city of turmoil and the same exciting scenes recurred in Amsterdam. Beatlemania is coming. So watch out Australia! – Sydney Sun Herald, 7 June 1964

Adelaide Girls High School students suffered the worst. In (more than twenty) letters delivered to the *News* they pointed out that, although only two streets away from the motorcade passage, they were confined to a small central yard. 'I am a prisoner at Adelaide Girls High Prison,' one letter read. 'They barred the gates and guarded them with prefects. All that was missing was loaded rifles. Inside the school we had demonstrations and even fights. Some colleges came from the other side of town but we girls were not allowed to go 220 yards in our lunch hour. Yet we had to walk more than a mile and stand in sweltering heat for over two hours to see the Queen.'

At Walford Church of England Grammer School in Unley 200 senior students staged a sit down strike when teachers confiscated their transistor radios during the arrival description. They sat on the asphalt playground chanting, 'We want the Beatles,' until teachers persuaded them to return to classes. Headmistress Miss N. Morrison curtly explained to a reporter that 'transistors are banned from the school'.

Brighton High School students slow-clapped during assembly and inserted 'yeah yeah yeah' into the school hymn. Four students from Port Adelaide Technical High School rang the Education Department three times requesting permission to see the Beatles parade. 'They put the phone down in our ears the third time,' said one incredulously.

Of course, not every school became an instant internment centre. Quite a few headmasters took advantage of the very obscure Arbor Day to grant their students a half day holiday (to the best of educated opinion, there is no other known instance of Australians celebrating the tree planting day in such a manner).

Plympton High School headmaster Mr. J. G. Goldsworthy sent circulars to parents inviting them to give written permission for their children to leave school grounds to see the Beatles and got a response of 95 per cent. 'I have no objections at all to these four young gentlemen,' he said. 'The highway is only a hundred yards from the school and the procession does fall completely within the school lunchbreak.' Adelaide Boys High students were allowed to line both sides of Anzac Highway and girls from Vermont Technical High School were permitted to walk a mile to the route.

Inspector Wilson of the Traffic Division criticised the lack of control of schoolchildren grouped along the highway, suggesting that teachers should have exercised more control. What he didn't realise was that far more control than was reasonable was being wielded just streets away.

From Anzac Highway, the motorcade wound through West Terrace, North Terrace and King William Street, the estimated 40-minute journey taking a little over an hour and clocking in at a mean nine mph. From North Terrace the bursting crowds caused nightmarish headaches. Police on foot, motorbikes and horses formed a ring around the car and struggled to clear a driveable space before it. Inch by inch the beseiged vehicle moved toward the beckoning iron gates of the Town Hall.

'Outside the Town Hall, the kids were physically lifting the cars off the road,' says Ernie Sigley. Adelaide is the most English city in Australia, particularly around the migrant area of Elizabeth, but it does have a reputation as 'the city of churches', a bastion of Victorian decorum. Such an outpouring of unrestrained fervour was, therefore, all the more unbelievable. But it was happening, as newsreels, newspapers and the Beatles themselves would later attest.

Ten council employees were required to edge open the gates and allow the battered car entry. Once safe inside, the four were escorted to the Lord Mayor's chambers for their first civic reception in Australia.

Out on the balcony it was as much Bob Francis' moment of glory as the Beatles'. He scurried about, back and forth, positioning each moptop and pointlessly urging the crowd of 30,000 to quieten down. With a reasonable PA set up, he was able to briefly interview each of the obviously shell-shocked Beatles. George yelled, 'Hello! Hello! It's marvellous, it's fabulous, the best reception ever.' Jimmy got a medium response when introduced, with some booing evident. Carried away by the moment he gushed, 'Oh this is the best I've ever seen anywhere in the world!' John had real difficulty putting his words together. His voice wavered emotionally as he declared, 'Yes it's definitely the best we've ever been to, it's great [a huge swell of vocal approval], it's marvellous.' Told there were only a million people in the State, he butted in with, 'and they're all here aren't they?' For Paul, it might just as well have been another concert stage in yet another nameless city. Slickly he spruiked, 'Hello everybody. How are you, alright? Thank you very much. It's marvellous. . .this is fantastic, thank you.'

Inside the Town Hall, the Beatles faced 90 friends of friends. In the sombre Queen Adelaide room, normally reserved for visiting dignitaries, they spent 25 minutes chatting to Mayor Irwin and his wife and were presented with (still more) toy koala bears. Welcoming them, the good Mayor said, 'We are delighted to have you in Adelaide and for having turned on a better day for you than they did in Sydney.' Sipping orange juice and Cokes, the group responded to cries of 'speech' by shoving John forward to state once more, 'We are pleased to be here. It's the best welcome we've ever had.'

After the Mayor had got Paul to autograph an Oliphant cartoon from the *Advertiser*, the four were smuggled out through a back entrance of the Land Titles Office into a waiting car on Flinders Street and off to the squat two-storey South Australian Hotel on North Terrace. It was twenty minutes before the street throng woke up to the deception. Meanwhile, police chiefs were beating their chests loudly. Mounted Police Inspector J. F. Crawley said it was the proudest day of his life. Deputy Commissioner Mr G. M. Leane said, 'I am proud of the way in which the police and crowds conducted themselves. It was a credit to Adelaide.'

Sunday June 14 saw Beatle madness on three fronts. By dawn, boisterous crowds were assembling in Melbourne, Sydney and Adelaide, all planning to catch sight of one or more moptops.

As the indefatigable citizens of Adelaide were mounting one final burst of affection for the departing heroes and a goodly portion of' Melbourne's population was taking up vantage points from Essendon to the city, 5,000 Sydney Beatle fans were back out at Mascot terminal waiting for Ringo.

Having finally been discharged from hospital, Ringo had set out with Brian Epstein for San Francisco on Saturday morning, after discovering that a route via the US would get them to Australia almost 24 hours earlier than planned. An hour before departure, when Brian asked Ringo for his passport, he winked and said, 'I haven't got it.' After briefly pondering and rejecting the possibility of a joke, Epstein organised a car to pick it up from Ringo's home. However the car was just not fast enough and officials had to arrange a special clearance for Mr Starkey to travel without it. 'After all, a Beatle's a Beatle all over the world isn't he?' commented an official. On the steps of the plane Brian asked Ringo if he would like to meet Vivien Leigh. 'Who's Vivien Leigh?' he retorted. The actress certainly knew who Ringo was and pumped his hand furiously.

The change of planes in the gay city on the bay caused a riot, with 300 fans at the airport and five hospital cases. Ringo agreed to meet the San Francisco media in a brief press airport conference but this broke down into a wild melee when TV cameramen rushed the startled drummer demanding autographs for their daughters.

Reunited with his passport, Ringo boarded a Qantas jet to Sydney on Saturday afternoon. As he left, more than 100 fans were milling at Mascot. Airport manager Mr. G. Inglis had announced that arrangements would be similar to the previous Thursday so the hapless devotees were once more thrust out into the cold at 11 p.m., guarded by twenty Commonwealth policemen. One of the first to arrive was sixteen-year-old Fairfield schoolgirl Mary Jackson who told a reporter she would wait all day if necessary. 'I got wet waiting for the Beatles on Thursday,' she said, 'so it would take a lot to stop me waiting for Ringo. I don't mind having to stay up all night. Every minute will be worth it if I see him.'

'DEAR Ringo, I hope you like this PAINTING I DID of you. You are my favorite musician in the universe (really!) . . . Your biggest fan, Marge Bouvier' [aka Marge Simpson]

Most of those waiting did see Ringo as he disembarked, stepped into a Holden and passed through customs with the other passengers. Twenty-year-old Edward Beard of Brighton-Le-Sands got sufficiently carried away to sprint towards the landing aircraft and paid a heavy price for his impulsive act. Arrested by Commonwealth Police, he was charged with trespassing, resisting arrest and using indecent language. In Redfern Court on the following Tuesday, a Sgt. Headland told Mr. J. A. Letts S.M., 'He was stopped by a Qantas security guard but broke free. I grabbed him but he broke away and had to be held by two other police. He kept yelling, "I'm not going to be taken by you mug coppers." At Mascot police station he resisted being placed in the cells and used indecent language.' After being told by the Crown Solicitor that the Civil Aviation Department wanted the matter treated seriously, the Sitting Magistrate fined Beard £23 with £7.7s costs and placed him on a £50 good behaviour bond, adding to good measure, 'It is difficult to understand this type of conduct by young people.' Outside the courtroom, Beard said, 'I won't be going to the

Beatles concert now. Tickets cost money.' However his biggest regret was, 'I was only a few feet from the plane door when they grabbed me. They took me away and I didn't get to see Ringo at all. Now I don't think it was worth it.'

Inside the Sydney domestic terminal, Ringo faced his first Sydney press gathering, with most questions coming from 2SM's Garvin Rutherford. Ringo declared that he had switched from Scotch to Bourbon, itemised every piece of his personal jewellery and assured all present that he was still very much in possession of his tonsils. Some of his captured quotes included, 'I've heard that you've got a bridge or something here. No one ever tells me anything, they just knock on my door and drag me out of bed to look at rivers and things. At the moment I love it all, I think we all do, I mean wouldn't you if you got off a plane to all this?' To the endless and idiotic question 'Do you ever have your hair cut?' he curtly replied, 'Of course, it'd be down by my ankles if I didn't.'

After about 90 minutes in Sydney, Ringo and Brian flew on to Melbourne, encountering the beginnings of the crowd that would greet the others later in the day. The operation was reasonably smooth until the car pulled up in front of the front doors of the Southern Cross Hotel in Swanston Street. The crowd by that point was around 3,000 and, in retrospect, it would have been far wiser to have taken Ringo in by the laneway garage entrance.

Dick Lean, who met the pair at Essendon Airport, recalls the moment vividly. 'Mick Patterson, the police inspector, decided to put Ringo on his very broad shoulders and make a dash for the entrance. It seemed like a good idea until our PR lady Elanor Knox began bowing and waving to the crowd, then tripped and fell down right in front of this piggy back. Well Mick stepped on her and down came Ringo, right into the grasping claws of hundreds of kids. When we finally pulled him out and got him inside he was as white as a sheet and the first words he said were, "Give us a drink, that was the roughest ride I've ever had." Then he went straight to his suite to lie down.'

As a shaken Ringo Starr was resting safely inside his hotel room, the remainder of the group were heading towards Melbourne in an Ansett ANA Fokker Friendship, and it was a case of out of the frying pan into the fire. The Fab Four, although they didn't know it, were about to ignite an explosion of human emotions which would certainly equal, if not eclipse, that which had occurred in the South Australian capital.

Alarmed at the events in Adelaide, the Victorian police force had made a last-minute decision to call in the army and navy to assist with crowd control. Initially seen as a chronic case of over-reaction, the move proved to be a wise one.

After taking a breather for lunch, the crowd that had welcomed Ringo began to swell appreciably until 10,000 were thronging Exhibition Street at 2 p.m., two hours before the rest of the group were due. By three o'clock the first barriers were knocked down, as the crowd pushed towards the hotel chanting, 'Ringo, Ringo' and 'We want the Beatles.' Half an hour later, the combined unit of police, army and navy, forming a human barricade at the front of the Southern Cross, began to lose control.

At this point the first casualties began to occur, requiring mounted police to retrieve unconscious girls from the midst of the mass and carry them to a first aid station established in the Australia-American Centre, across the road from the hotel. The faintings were jointly attributable to nervous exhaustion, hysteria and hunger, as many of the girls had first taken up vantage spots early on Saturday morning.

Out at Essendon Airport, 5,000 fans were on hand to shriek to the heavens as Paul McCartney bounded down the aircraft steps onto the tarmac, madly waving to the horde before him. At least another 20,000 packed the mile motorcade route to the city, offering a welcome even more raucous than their Adelaide counterparts. The procession of vehicles was stopped repeatedly as crowds spilled onto the road.

As the procession inched closer to the city at around 4 p.m., the madness heightened and even the police became flustered. The carefully planned exercise was thrown into chaos by a young constable on point duty at the corner of Elizabeth and Victor Streets who let the entire convoy across the intersection with the sole exception of the car carrying Brodziak and Derek Taylor. Meanwhile, the twelve police motorcycles at the front of the parade made radio contact with the hotel nerve centre and were told to abandon plans to send the four musicians in through the front door. Instead they were to create a diversion, along with a special dummy police car, by pulling up at the front door with sirens blaring – allowing the actual Beatles' car to sneak into a laneway garage entrance. The car left at the intersection did not disgorge its passengers for another half hour at least.

Unaware of the eleventh hour change of procedure, the 20,000 strong crowd pushed closer to the hotel, crushing steel barricades as if they were damp match-boxes. Assistant tour manager Malcolm Cook recalls, 'the front of the Southern Cross was all glass panels and it was terrifying to watch thousands of fists beating against the glass and thousands of bodies throwing their weight into it – it was bigger than a Victorian Football Grand Final. And I remember Tony Charlton from Channel Nine doing a live coverage, staring in horror at the scene before him saying into his mic, "Mothers, if your child is out there you should be ashamed."'

On the other side of the endangered glass the conditions were even more petrifying for any poor soul bearing the responsibility of keeping the peace. The police contingency had grown to 300 but, even bolstered by a military force of 100, order was a lost cause. As the first field hospital was filled to overflowing, another was established in the foyer of the Southern Cross. Dr Ivan Markovics, a hotel guest, played Florence Nightingale, muttering, 'I've never seen anything like this.' Neither had one policeman, who described the situation as 'frightening, chaotic and rather inhuman.' The gentle, festive character of the Adelaide adoration had been somehow superceded by a more brutal, determined clamouring, not at all disimilar to a VFL Grand Final.

In the midst of the sea of bodies, brawls erupted and expired within the space of a few seconds. One youth fell ten feet from a tree branch which gave way; an expensive Italian sports car was crushed from boot to bonnet by hundreds of scrambling feet; one slightly-built young girl commenced hitting a hapless man on the head with her stiletto shoe when he blocked her view; fainted girls were carried along in the crush, held upright like sardines; elderly people attracted by the spectacle were trapped inside the crowd, some crying in fear, and a fleet of ambulances took 40 of the more serious casualties to Royal Melbourne and St. Vincent's Hospital. More than 150 fans received medical treatment. 'The mounted police did a marvellous job,' recalls Kevin Ritchie. 'They could get right into the heart of the crowd, drag fainted kids up and over the front of their saddles and take them off for treatment. Nothing else could have done it.'

They were considered the big capitalist threat during the Cold War. You could bring Rolling Stones albums into the country, later on, but not the Beatles. You know why? I think it's because the Beatles were an event. The Rolling Stones were a rock band, but the Beatles were the cultural event of our century.
— Dr. Yury Pelyushonok, Beatles fan

Within ten minutes of their successful secret entry into the hotel, and midway through a boisterous reunion with Ringo, all five Beatles were rushed out onto the first floor balcony in order to ease the crush on the front doors. All appeared to be cold, with Ringo approaching a shade of blue in the icy winds. The deep resonant roar obliterated any words that the objects of the adulation proferred, so John held one finger to his upper lip and threw a series of Nazi salutes, shouting, 'Sieg Heil.' Below, the surge increased instead of abated. One policeman later explained, 'They pushed forward twenty feet so we mustered all our strength and moved them back fifteen feet – then it started all over again.'

Before the repeated five foot losses of ground could bring the fans to the glass walls, the Beatles retired from the balcony and the satisfied mass quickly dispersed, leaving a loyal core of a few hundred stalwarts. When fainted girls awoke to find that they had missed the appearance, they became hysterical, some rolling about on the floor weeping and screaming, 'I hate the Beatles, I hate the Beatles!'

Back inside the hotel, John admitted that it was all 'a little frightening', naming it 'the greatest reception we have received anywhere in the world', breaking his own code of protocol. At a press conference later in the day, the five Beatles were photographed together for the first and last time. After which, Jimmy was sent to his room to pack.

If Jimmy had felt like an outsider throughout his stint with the group, he might as well not have even existed when Ringo came upon the scene. 'He obviously felt quite uncomfortable with John, Paul and George,' recalls Bruce Stewart, 'and spent most of his time with Sounds Incorporated and the Phantoms.' Dave Lincoln of the Phantoms remembers that some of Jimmy's comments to the press had irritated Brian Epstein, who had already given the instruction that the drummer was most definitely not to return to Sydney to play again with Frances Faye. As Nicol himself would later comment, 'The boys were very kind but I felt like an intruder. They accepted me but you can't just get into a group like that – they have their own atmosphere, their own sense of humour. It's a little clique and outsiders just can't break in.'

During the press conference, John and George spoke with Alan Lappin of 3UZ, who put to John: 'One place you haven't been is the Soviet Union,' to which Lennon replied, 'They think we're some kind of capitalist trick. But it doesn't really matter, I don't think they can afford to buy records there.' Asked if any of the Beatles had ever undergone National Service, John tersely clipped the question with, 'No, we don't like armies or things like that.' Did he ever get a haircut? 'Yes, in fact I need a trim at the moment but I can't find anyone I trust.'

Beatles Down Under: 1964 Australian and New Zealand Tour, Glenn A. Baker, 1986

THE MAN WHO FRAMED
THE BEATLES
By Andrew Yule

This extract from the biography of director Richard Lester, one of the prominent names in 1960s British cinema, recounts how the 1964 filming of the Beatles' first feature film, A Hard Day's Night, *was fraught with difficulty. Nevertheless, Lester captured the essence of the group, and something of the spirit of the times.*

The first day's shooting, on March 2, was on a train hired for six days that would shuttle between Paddington and the west country. 'The plan was to shoot it for real, which was crazy, but we wanted it to look like a real train,' Lester recalls. 'I decided to do the whole thing hand-held, mainly because there wasn't much else to look at, and it needed a documentary flexibility. Unfortunately, in those days you didn't work with a little hidden lapel microphone, you had a boom man using the same instrument originally invented in the 1920s and christened on *The Jazz Singer*. In that sense not much had changed between the era of Al Jolson and the Beatles, so three cars down there was half a wagon full of Westrex recording equipment, massive stuff. Clumsy and awful though it was, everyone watching the movie would know it was a real train.'

With a crowd of onlookers screaming and fighting their way forward at Paddington, even filming the Beatles boarding the train posed problems. Lester grabbed a camera, focused and shot the group attempting to break through the meleé. They did not fully appreciate the immediacy he wanted to capture, and furiously regarded the whole event as a security cock-up, a shaken George even waving his fist at Lester on camera. The shot was captured so quickly that several of the crew blinked and missed it. The continuity girl wrote in her notes that morning: 'First shot, Beatles wearing their own clothes. I was in the toilet. Director was the operator. If this is the way the film is to go on, I'm resigning now.'

At the end of the day's work, the Beatles were dropped off at a prearranged spot out of town, decanted into their own transport and driven off. When the train returned to Paddington the last person to leave was clapper loader Peter Ewens, a small, dark-haired individual sporting a Beatle-style haircut. Carrying the cans of the first day's rushes to get them to the laboratory for night processing, Ewens ran into lingering fans as he stepped off the train. His haircut proved his undoing – the crowd thought he was a Beatle. Since he was loaded down with cans of film, running was out of the question. There was only one thing for it. Throwing the precious reels up in the air, he bolted for his life. Unfortunately, light penetrated the cans, wasting the entire first day's shooting.

Despite the practical problems caused by the fans, the film benefited from their ubiquity.

Lester concedes that the choreographed look of the crowd scenes was largely a matter of luck, as well as judicious editing:

> Their fans tracked them all over the place. Every time we got to a new location there would be these mobs of girls trying to get their hands on them. One day, after we finished shooting, the boys headed for their car to be chauffeured home. I told the cameraman to keep turning, record what ever happened. Just then a drove of screaming fans cut loose and began converging on the car. When I saw the rushes I took one look at the expression on the boys' faces and decided to put the scene in the picture. The rest was pacing and rhythm worked out in the editing. If you look closely at the scene with the Beatles in the train station, you will see that they are wearing one set of clothes on the train and an entirely different set in the car. As far as I know, nobody spotted the discrepancy.

Lester knew that he was freezing in time the catalytic nature of the Beatles' contribution, for better or worse, to the contemporary social revolution in sixties' Britain:

> I think they were the first to give a confidence to the youth of the country, which led to the disappearance of the Angry Young Man with a defensive mien. The Beatles sent the class thing sky-high; they laughed it out of existence and, I think, introduced a tone of equality more successfully than any other single factor that I know. Eventually it became taken for granted that they were singlehandedly breaking Britain's class system without the benefit of an education or family background. They were, of course, much more middle class than most people admitted.

Drawing comparisons with the Marx Brothers (and even Citizen Kane!*) in some quarters,* A Hard Day's Night *met with almost universal critical acclaim on its release in summer 1964.*

The reviews on both sides of the Atlantic were ecstatic, reflecting not only what this author saw as the visual wit and exuberance with which Lester had packed the movie, but the sheer unexpectedness of the venture. (Having seen Lester's earlier *It's Trad, Dad,* I was less surprised. Despite its threadbare budget, the movie had possessed a manic energy that overcame purely fiscal limitations.) 'Fresh and engaging,' *Time* magazine raved. 'Fresh and lively,' *Newsweek* agreed. Bosley Crowther in the *New York Times* found it 'surprisingly good, a whale of a comedy,' while John Coleman in *New Statesman* pronounced it 'Splendidly engaging.' To *Vogue* magazine it was 'fast, energetic and hip,' while Arthur Knight in *Saturday Review* found it 'almost good enough to be taken for a French New Wave work.'

A Hard Day's Night **was one of the truly pleasant surprises of the sixties . . . The splendid reviews that the picture received and the unexpected praise heaped upon the Beatles for their performances made the nation's young people collectively burst with pride. To have their Beatles, their idols who were more than symbolically central to their lives, given 'legitimacy' by establishment critics, whom their elders/parents read and respected, was much more than gratifying – it was liberating.**
– *Danny Peary,* Cult Movies

To Andrew Sarris in the *Village Voice,* the movie was 'the *Citizen Kane* of jukebox musicals, a brilliant crystallisation of such diverse cultural particles as the pop movie, rock'n'roll, *cinema verité,* the *nouvelle vague,* free cinema, the affectedly hand-held camera, frenzied cutting, the cult of the sexless subadolescent, the semidocumentary, and studied spontaneity.' To Arthur Schlesinger, Jr., it was nothing less than 'The astonishment of the month,' although he found it hard to decide who should be granted the lion's share of the credit – Lester, Owen or the Beatles themselves.

The Man Who Framed the Beatles, Andrew Yule, 1994

BEATLE WITH A FUTURE
By Gloria Steinem

Proto-feminist Steinem concentrated on Lennon for her investigation into US Beatlemania. Note how, in the vernacular, she happily mixes with the 'birds' who throng around the group.

In Britain, the Beatles outdraw Queen Elizabeth. In America, they attract bigger crowds than the President and Elizabeth Taylor combined. All over Europe and even in Hong Kong, teenagers turn out in droves whether or not they understand the lyrics. The Beatles have become, quite literally, the single biggest attraction in the world.

Show business experts disagree on the sociology or psychology or simple merchandising behind this success, but they agree on one thing: like every craze from the hula-hoop to the ancient Celts' habit of painting themselves blue, it must come to an end, and probably an abrupt one. At ages 21 to 24, they don't seem to have thought about the problem much, but under pressure of constant questions from reporters, they have come up with a few clues. George Harrison, the youngest Beatle and the only one who shows any interest in the business side of their career, might produce records for other pop music stars. Paul McCartney – at 22, the Beatle with the best looks and on-stage personality – is likely to continue a show business career as a solo. Ringo Starr (born Richard Starkey), the oldest of the four and the prototype of a non-verbal pop musician, hasn't voiced a preference for anything but a future of playing the drums and tossing his eyebrow-length hair. Only John Lennon, 24 and the one married Beatle, has shown signs of a talent outside the hothouse world of musical fadism and teenage worship: he has written a book titled *In His Own Write* – a slender, whimsical collection of anecdotes, poems and Thurber-like drawings – that is in its seventh printing here.

The difficulty of getting to the Beatles at all (one London columnist claimed he had had less trouble interviewing De Gaulle) plus Lennon's extreme reluctance to talk to strangers (he cares, explained Epstein, 'not a fig or a damn or a button for anyone save a tight, close-guarded clique of less than a dozen') have kept him a mystery. Yet he continues to be spoken of as 'the Beatle who will last', 'the intellectual one and 'a popular hero who, like Sinatra, gained fame through teenage adulation, but can keep it through talent.'

Will he last?

There is no sure answer, but an observation of the odd world the Beatles inhabit, a few hours with that 'close-guarded clique' and some words from Mr Lennon himself offer a few clues.

By the end of their recent, 32-day American tour, the Beatles had given concerts in 24 cities, grossed a record $2 million, spent two days relaxing on their first American ranch, flown back to New York via carefully guarded chartered plane ('like,' as one reporter put it, 'a troop movement in wartime or a shipment of gold to Fort Knox'), been spirited by helicopter and car into Manhattan's Paramount Theatre, and were getting ready for their last chore before returning to London: a half-hour performance as the climax of a show benefiting United Cerebral Palsy and Retarded Infants Services, Inc.

Tickets were expensive. . .but the theatre was sold out and screaming, non-ticket-holding fans had forced police to set up barricades near the Paramount at nine o'clock in the morning.

Those fans – the thousands of weeping, screeching girls – surrounded the theatre completely, and wading through them was a process so slow that it was possible to interview a few on the way. Most of them seemed to be lank-haired, single-minded, under sixteen and carrying homemade placards ('I Love You, Ringo', 'If You Can't Marry Me, George Please Just Look at Me'), record jackets to be autographed or photographs of their favourite. (Feather Schwartz, ex-secretary of the Beatles fan club of America, discovered that the average Beatle fan is thirteen to seventeen years old, of middle-class background, white, Christian, a B-minus student, weighs 105 to 140 pounds, owns a transistor radio with an earplug attachment and has Beatle photographs plastered all over her room.) One girl paused in her effort to climb over a five-foot-high police barricade to tell me that she was 'crazy wild about John' because he was 'utterly fab'. Another said she was 'passionately in love with Ringo', and had saved $25 of her allowance to get there from Pennsylvania. Tears were streaming down her face; she had yelled herself hoarse at passing taxis, unaware that her beloved had entered the Paramount secretly, two hours before. Would she go out with Ringo if he asked her? Would she like to marry him? She looked startled. 'I don't think so,' she said. 'I hardly know him.'

When I finally reached a harried policeman, he was turning away a pretty blonde with a letter of accreditation from a high school newspaper in New Jersey. He turned away my press credentials with the same: 'We got orders, lady. No press,' and shoved me back into the crowd. A girl with braces on her teeth and a life-size picture of John pinned to her chest was sympathetic. 'They turned away a guy who said he was from the *New York Times*,' she said soothingly, 'and boy was he mad.'

45 minutes and several pleadings later, a policeman let me in the stage door ('OK lady, I guess you're too persistent to be a nut') and warned me I was on my own. That left only five flights of stairs, six policemen and three private guards between me and Bess Coleman, the representative of the Beatles' New York office who was very apologetic ('I told all the policemen I saw to let you through but there are so many') and assured me that my interview with John Lennon was set.

Miss Coleman ushered me into a room where I was to wait and left me with its assorted occupants: a blonde girl with her hair in purple plastic curlers, four men with black suits and briefcases, a young man in corduroy pants and Beatle-length hair and a pretty matron in a cocktail dress. I walked to the window and looked down. A roar like the distant sound of an Army-Navy football game came up from the crowd five storeys below. 'You better not stand there, honey,' the blonde girl said kindly. 'They go crazy when they see somebody, anybody. The police told us to stay away from the windows.' The pretty matron introduced herself as a writer for a national women's magazine. She had been on most of the month-long tour, she said, but had not yet been able to interview one of the Beatles: if I got to see John, might she sit in and listen? I told her she was welcome to come if it turned out to be a public interview, but that I hoped to talk with him privately. The Beatle-haired young man – identified by the matron as Neil Aspinall, the Beatles' road manager – broke his consultation with the men in black suits and smiled. 'Well, then,' he said with a Liverpudlian lilt, 'we're very optimistic now, aren't we?'

In the hall, while looking for reassurance and Miss Coleman, I discovered two more roomsful of waiting people, glimpsed Ed Sullivan disappearing into a third, answered a ringing pay phone ('Please tell Paul McCartney that he doesn't know me but I'm very pretty and I'll be in the first booth at the Astor drugstore after the show') and was given a paper cup filled with the Beatles' favourite drink, an equal-parts combination of warm Coca-Cola and Scotch. The Beatles, Miss Coleman assured me, were much too exhausted to see anyone before the show; would I mind waiting until afterward? She introduced me to a reed-thin, shirt-sleeved young man named Derek Taylor – head of publicity and public relations for the Beatles – sat us down in the room, now deserted by everyone but the matron, and asked Taylor to turn the other way while she changed her dress.

Eyes to the wall, Taylor explained that they were all exhausted from the long tour of one-night stands and sleeping only on the chartered plane ('In Kansas

City, we stayed in a hotel; the next day the manager was offered $750 for one of the Beatles' sheets'), and that the two-day ranch vacation ('The Beatles rode and fished and stayed up all night playing poker') hadn't helped much. Though the ranch was 13,000 acres in the middle of Missouri and 'surrounded only by the tiniest hamlets', local disc jockeys had learned of the Beatles' presence. By midnight of the first day, all roads to the ranch were jammed and carloads of teenagers had arrived from St Louis. And, though Neil Aspinall had learned by experience how to move the Beatles ('The plane stops at the end of the runway; we use special cars and drivers to back up to hotel and theatre entrances, some-times we use tunnels. There's really no precedent for this sort of thing'), Ringo had had his shirt torn off, and Brian Epstein was once nearly pushed in front of an oncoming train.

There has never been such a crowd. Never. Not even for kings and queens. – *Attendant at John F. Kennedy Airport, 7 February 1964*

It was time for the Beatles' performance. Everyone crowded into the hall, looking expectantly at the room in which the Beatles had been 'incommunicado' and 'resting', the same room into which I had seen Ed Sullivan disappear. Paul McCartney came out first, looking soft-faced and vulnerable as a choirboy. George Harrison and Ringo Starr followed, animated and laughing. John Lennon moved quickly behind them, but his face was stoic and aloof behind his dark glass-es (the face that inspired a London journalist to write, 'It has the fear-neither-God-nor-man quality of a Renaissance painter's aristocrat'). Behind Lennon came three chic young girls, two brunettes and a blonde, in their late teens or early twenties. McCartney jerked his head toward them as he got in the elevator and told some of his staff members to 'look after the birds now, won't ya.'

I turned to Derek Taylor, about to comment that – what with Ed Sullivan and these three – the Beatles hadn't been so incommunicado after all, but Taylor was already looking harassed and apologetic. 'Look,' he said. 'You've got to be patient with them. If you just come to the party they're having afterwards at the hotel, I'm sure John will talk to you.' We were challenged by a policeman but Taylor showed a lapel pass and we got to the elevator. 'You'll be more sure of getting to the Beatles,' he said helpfully, 'if you stick with the birds.'

The Beatles' entourage crowded together in the wings, and I talked to the birds. Were they working for the Beatles or interviewing them? No, they were just friends. 'We met the Beatles at a press conference in Philadelphia,' said the pretty blonde, 'that's where we're from.' Two of them wore wool suits with short culotte skirts. They all looked as if they had stepped from the pages of a teenage fashion magazine, and one carried a comb and hairbrush which she used frequently and passed around to the others. 'Well, two of us had met them,' corrected the friendly blonde, 'and this time we brought along a friend.'

Out in the dark, crowded theatre, we stood by the apron of the stage and watched the show: sobs, shouts and piercing screams ('I'm over here, Ringo. Please!') drowned out all but an occasional drumbeat. Girls were hanging precariously from the two large balconies and standing on the arms of their chairs. Behind me, a woman held her six-year-old on her shoulders and four girls with linked arms were jumping up and down in time to the music and crying.

Taylor stood next to me and tapped my arm just before each chorus of screams reached a crescendo. 'You can always tell,' he explained calmly. 'It happens just after one of them tosses his hair or lifts his guitar.' What about the strange, firecracker bursts of light? Was that part of the lighting effect? 'No,' he smiled. 'It's the flashes from everyone taking pictures.' Three overweight, poorly dressed girls were sobbing and calling out as they pressed against us, and a fourth girl with an exceedingly large nose was waving a banner that said, 'Georgie, You Are My Dream'. 'Sometimes,' said Taylor, 'when we pick a few girls to come in and get autographs, we pick pretty ones like those,' he nodded at the birds who were watching the stage with secret smiles. 'But I usually try to pick the ones with braces on their teeth and acne. Meeting a Beatle helps. And they can impress their friends.'

Ringo tossed his hair, and a fresh wave of screams went up. Paul smiled and looked endearing. John lifted his guitar, setting off more screams, but he sang without smiling ('That's because,' fellow Liverpudlian Neil Aspinall had once explained to a reporter, 'he's giving you his soul when he sings.'). The crush was so great that our arms were pinned to our sides, but a path suddenly cleared as if by magic, and the slim, elegant figure of Brian Epstein – the 30-year-old mastermind behind the Beatles' success – strode to the end of it, leaving a lingering trail of shaving scent. The girl with the banner had been pushed out of the way. 'I don't like Englishmen,' she said, and resumed her screaming. The three birds, who never screamed, looked at her with curiosity. One began idly to brush her hair with her eyes glued to the stage. 'How do you like the Beatles?' the blonde shouted into my ear. 'Fine,' I said. 'Just fine.'

The Beatles were leaving for London early the next morning. That, plus the fact that several Manhattan hotels had turned them down, brought them to the Riviera Motor Inn at Kennedy Airport. The rooms were small, barely big enough for a bureau, twin beds and a television set but they had commandeered a whole floor and there were policemen guarding the halls. Our room was

jammed with carts of Scotch and Coca-Cola, trays of sandwiches and two photographers, the young ladies from Philadelphia, a tall girl who had followed the
Beatles from San Francisco, several journalists who had been on the Beatle tour,
a pretty airline stewardess in a very lowcut dress who was acting as hostess, and,
occasionally, Neil Aspinall and Derek Taylor. Two of the Beatles were in other
rooms, but Ringo Starr and Lennon were in the one adjoining us with the door
locked. It was opened only to admit Aspinall, Taylor, one or two other selected
young men and liquor.

At three o'clock, I had still not seen a Beatle, but I had spent two hours interviewing the entourage, who told me some facts of Lennon's life. . .Everyone
agreed on one thing: Lennon was certainly the most talented in diverse ways, and
therefore the most likely to succeed creatively even after the Beatle craze was
over. As Epstein had written in his autobiography, 'Had there been no Beatles
and no Epstein participation, John would have emerged from the mass of population as a man to reckon with.' 'He's untutored,' said Taylor, 'but he's a natural writer. He loves the sound of words. He's an original.'

The door to the next room opened and Taylor, who seemed to remember
everybody else's problems in spite of his own exhaustion ('I'm worried about
him,' confided the matron, 'he's slept hardly at all for five days'), ushered me in
and introduced me. It was 4 a.m. and the small group – Lennon, Ringo,
American folk singer Bob Dylan, Dylan's manager, the tall girl from San
Francisco, photographer Bob Freeman who designed the titles of the Beatles'
movies and Lennon's book, and an unidentified, bearded journalist – were in the
combined grip of fatigue and a crisis involving Brian Epstein. Taylor, it seemed,
had told the Beatles that Epstein had refused to let the three birds ride in his
limousine, and Epstein was furious at Taylor.

Lennon received me calmly ('Oh, I know about that article') and went on
giving desultory advice to Taylor on the care and handling of Epstein. ('He's all
right, but he doesn't understand people having a few laughs, not even me laughs
with me wife.') The conversation dwindled into silence. Would Lennon come
with me for an interview? 'Oh, well now, I don't have anything to say. My
friends and those other articles will tell you all.' The voice was musical, but the
face behind the sunglasses was impervious.

Wouldn't he like to set the record straight, to check the information I already
had? 'No, I don't think so.' Silence. The tall girl leaned over to Lennon and told
him that his skin was looking mottled again. 'I know,' he said and looked embarrassed. 'It's nerves.'

The phone rang several times and no one answered. I picked it up. A Princess
Mary somebody-or-other was calling from a phone booth. Could she please

speak to a Beatle? I asked Lennon if he would like to speak to the Princess. 'No,' he said. I hung up.

Taylor came back from a conference with Aspinall about whether or not he should leave his post as publicity chief and go back to being a newspaperman ('The Beatles are fine,' said Taylor, 'but their life is unbearable') and asked Lennon if there wasn't something he could do about Paul who had barricaded his door and gone to bed without saying goodbye to his friend from Philly. 'She's rather upset,' Taylor explained. 'After all, Paul did make a big thing of her and now he won't even say goodbye.' 'Look,' Lennon said patiently, 'Paul is Paul and nothing's going to change him.' Ringo, in a purple silk shirt with white polka dots, shifted his weight mournfully. 'Always worrying about people,' he said.

The phone rang again. The Princess, now at her home phone and reduced to saying that she was a friend of the Animals, hoped very much she could speak with the Beatles and invite them to an island hotel. 'No,' said Lennon, 'hang up.' 'Don't answer the phone,' counselled the bearded journalist. 'You can't answer all the calls around here, you'd go crazy.'

Wouldn't Lennon answer any interview questions at all? 'I don't think so,' he said and addressed the journalist. 'You ought to get out of your hotel room, see a little more of our country, beautiful monuments and all that. See the Statue of Liberace.' It was a good imitation of an interview, and we all laughed. 'Statue of Liberace is good,' said Bob Freeman. 'Is that the first time you've used that?'

At that point, Lennon was staring into his drink. Ringo observed meditatively that he didn't see why policemen had to stand right in front of the door, and that in one hotel, the police had stolen souvenirs from their rooms. More silence. It was five a.m.

I told Lennon that I understood how tired he must be of answering questions, and began to say goodbye. He looked surprised. Aspinall came back, explaining comfortingly to Taylor that Brian Epstein had once slapped him, but that was just one of the manager's moods that had to be understood.. . .'Listen,' said Freeman kindly, nodding toward me, 'she's all right. She's a friend of friends.' The effect on Lennon was as magical as an OK from the Mafia. He smiled for the first time, and told me not to leave. 'But she's the press,' Ringo muttered sceptically. 'You see,' said Taylor reasonably, 'they've been exploited so much that it's hard for them to trust anyone.'

Would Lennon like to write another book?

'I would, but you can't plan it. I just put things down and stuff them in my pockets until I have enough.'

Had he been influenced by the authors he was compared to?

'I mean to read Joyce but I never have. I got a laugh from all those intellectuals saying I was like him. I've read some Thurber stories though. And *Alice in
Wonderland*.'

When I was about twelve I used to think I must be a genius but nobody'd noticed. I thought, 'I'm a genius or I'm mad. Which is it? I can't be mad because nobody's put me away therefore I must be a genius.'
– *John Lennon*

We checked a few biographical details and discussed their second movie,
which they plan to begin in February. ('I wouldn't write the script for it. I
wouldn't know how.') He now lives just outside London with his wife and
infant son. He owns a Rolls-Royce. (How does it feel? 'Great!') He likes
America and doesn't like New Zealand. He loves the Crazy Gang kind of comedy, and he adores Peter Sellers. (It's true that he improvised some of the first
film's dialogue, including the interchange between an Old School Britisher and
a Beatle. Britisher: 'I fought the war for your sort.' Beatle: 'And aren't you sorry
now.') He has no plans to retire while the money is coming in, unless the life
should become unbearable. What about reports that, since the Establishment has
accepted them, British teenagers have gone on to other groups? 'That's all the
same. We'll just be us.' He is enthusiastic about rival groups, the Rolling Stones
and the Animals. How much money has he made? 'A lot.' Has success changed
him? 'Yes, it's made me richer.' Does he aspire to change socially? 'No, I'm from
Liverpool.'

Would he like to be a writer?

'I don't know. I guess so. I write what I think of, when I think of it.'

Was he surprised by his good reviews?

'Yes, I love those hellishly intellectual things they say, but I'd keep on writing whether they said them or not.'

What will he do when there are no more Beatles?

'That's the question everybody asks us, but I'll tell you this. I know this thing
can't last. I'm saving the money. And I've got a lot of things I want to do.'

I thanked Taylor who, having made the decision to quit the life of the Beatles
and become a newspaperman again, looked relieved and, for the first time,
cheerful.

I thanked Lennon, who looked worried, and said, 'I hope you're as true as
you seem.'

I said goodbye to the three birds who still sat in the adjoining room. Two were stretched out on the bed and a third was applying eye shadow. ('Women,' Lennon had once told a reporter, 'should be obscene and not heard.') They smiled their Mona Lisa smiles.

A fat policeman, yawning and red-eyed, said goodbye to me.

Outside it was dawn, but four girls were sitting patiently on the curbstone. Had I seen the Beatles, had I touched them? I said yes. A girl in an outgrown raincoat stretched out a Beatle photograph. 'Here,' she said. 'Sign this for me.'

Cosmopolitan, December 1964

NEVILLE CLUB
By John Lennon

When In His Own Write, *Lennon's first collection of prose and poetry, was published in 1964, literary critics compared it to both the 'nonsense' writing of Lewis Carroll and Edward Lear and to James Joyce. American writer Tom Wolfe more cautiously observed in his review, 'Lennon's real test will come when he turns loose his wild inventiveness and bitter slant upon a heavier literary form.' Alas, it was never to be.*

Dressed in my teenold brown sweaty I easily micked with crown at Neville Club a seemy hole. Soon all but soon people accoustic me saying such thing as

'Where the charge man?' All of a southern I notice boils and girks sitting in hubbered lumps smoking Hernia taking Odeon and going very high. Somewhere 4ft high but he had Indian Hump which he grew in his sleep. Puffing and globbering they drugged theyselves rampling or dancing with wild abdomen, stubbing in wild postumes amongst themselves.

They seemed olivier to the world about them. One girk was revealing them all over the place to rounds of bread and applause. Shocked and mazed I pulled on my rubber stamp heady for the door.

'Do you kindly mind stop shoveing,' a brough voice said.

'Who think you are?' I retired smiling wanly.

'I'm in charge,' said the brough but heavy voice.

'How high the moon?' cried another, and the band began to play.

A coloured man danced by eating a banana, or somebody.

I drudged over hopping to be noticed. He iced me warily saying, 'French or Foe.'

'Foe,' I cried taking him into jeapardy.

In His Own Write, John Lennon, 1964

PLAYBOY INTERVIEW WITH THE BEATLES
By Jean Shepherd

This 1965 interview is indicative of the Beatles' massive Stateside profile. Despite its cad-dish image, Playboy's editorial content was taken seriously by Middle America. The mag-azine regularly quizzed cultural figures, politicians and the occasional pop star in its cus-tomarily irreverent and hip style.

PLAYBOY: *OK, we're on. Why don't we begin by. . .*
JOHN: Doing *Hamlet.*
(laughter)
RINGO: Yeah, yeah, let's do that.

PLAYBOY: *When you joined the others Ringo, they weren't quite as big as they are now, were they?*
RINGO: They were the biggest thing in Liverpool. In them days that was big enough.
PAUL: This is a point we've made before. Some people say a man is made of muscle and blood. . .No they don't. . .they say, 'How come you've suddenly been able to adjust to fame,' you know, to nationwide fame and things. It all started quite nicely with us, you see, in our own sphere where we used to play, in Liverpool. We never used to play outside it, except when we went to Hamburg. Just those two circles. And in each of them, I think we were 'round the highest paid, and probably at the time the most popular. So in actual fact we had the same feeling of being famous then as we do now.
GEORGE: We were recognised then, too, only people didn't chase us about.
PAUL: But it just grew. The quantity grew; not the quality of the feeling.
JOHN: In Liverpool, people didn't even know we were from Liverpool. They thought we were from Hamburg. They said, 'Christ, they speak good English!' Which we did, of course, being English. But that's when we first, you know, stood there being cheered for the first time.

PLAYBOY: *There's been some dispute among your fans and critics, about* *whether you're primarily entertainers or musicians. . .or perhaps neither. What's your own opinion?*

JOHN: We're money-makers first; then we're entertainers.

PAUL: . . . we'd be idiots to say that it isn't a constant inspiration to be making a lot of money. It always is, to anyone. I mean, why do big business tycoons stay big business tycoons? It's not because they're inspired at the greatness of big business; they're in it because they're making a lot of money at it. We'd be idiots if we pretended we were in it solely for kicks. In the beginning we were, but at the same time we were hoping to make a bit of cash. It's a switch around now, though, from what it used to be. We used to be doing it mainly for kicks and not making a lot of money, and now we're making a lot of money without too many kicks. . .except that we happen to like the money we're making. But we still enjoy making records, going on-stage, making films, and all that business.

JOHN: We love every minute of it, Beatle people!

It all happened so quickly . . . that I didn't get any chance to turn back – none of us did. It's a good job we all had the right sort of mentality to hold ourselves from going mad, with everything going on round us like it did. But it's been great – what else can you say to this sort of thing when it happens to you? It's like winning the pools!
– *George Harrison, 1964*

PLAYBOY: *You guys seem to be pretty irreverent characters. Are any of you churchgoers?*

JOHN: No.

GEORGE: No.

PAUL: Not particularly. But we're not anti-religious. We probably seem anti-religious because of the fact that none of us believe in God.

JOHN: If you say you don't believe in God, everybody assumes you're anti-religious, and you probably think that's what we mean by that. We're not quite sure *what* we are, but I know that we're more agnostic than atheistic.

PLAYBOY: *Are you speaking for the group, or just for yourself?*

JOHN: For the group.

GEORGE: John's our official religious spokesman.

PAUL: We all feel roughly the same. We're all agnostics.

JOHN: Most people are, anyway.

RINGO: It's better to admit it than to be a hypocrite.

JOHN: The only thing we've got against religion is the hypocritical side of it, which I can't stand. Like the clergy is always moaning about people being poor, while they themselves are all going around with millions of quid worth of robes on. That's the stuff I can't stand.

PAUL: A new bronze door stuck on the Vatican.

RINGO: Must have cost a mighty penny.

PAUL: But believe it or not, we're not anti-Christ.

RINGO: Just anti-Pope and anti-Christian.

PAUL: But you know, in America. . .

GEORGE: They were more shocked by us saying we were agnostics.

PAUL: In America, they're fanatical about God. I know somebody over there who said he was an atheist. The papers nearly refused to print it because it was such shocking news that somebody could actually be an atheist. . .yeah. . .and admit it.

RINGO: He speaks for all of us.

PLAYBOY: . . . *why do you think the rock'n'roll phenomenon is bigger in England than in America?*

JOHN: Is it?

PAUL: Yes. . . If we'd been over there instead of over here, there probably would have been the same upsurge over there. Our road manager made an interesting point the other day about this difference in America. In America the people who are big stars are not our age. There's nobody who's really a big star around our age. Possibly it may seem like a small point, but there's no conscription. . .no draft. . .here. In America, we used to hear about somebody like Elvis, who was a very big star and then suddenly he was off to the Army . . . And the Army seems to do something to singers. It may make them think that what they're playing is stupid and childish. Or it may make them want to change their style, and consequently they may not be as popular when they come out of the Army. It may also make people forget them, and consequently they may have a harder job getting back on top when they get out. But here, of course, we don't have that problem.

JOHN: Except those who go to prison.

PAUL: It's become so easy to form a group nowadays, and to make a record, that hundreds are doing it – and making a good living at it. Whereas when we started, it took us a couple of years before record companies would even listen to us, never mind give us a contract. But now, you just walk in and if they think you're OK, you're on.

PLAYBOY: *Do you think you had anything to do with bringing all this about?*
JOHN: It's a damn fact.
PAUL: Not only us. Us, and people who followed us. But we were the first really to get national coverage because of some big shows that we did, and because of a lot of public interest in us.

PLAYBOY: *How does it make you feel to have millions of effigies of yourselves decorating bedsides all over the world? Don't you feel honored to have been immortalised in plastic? After all, there's no such thing as a Frank Sinatra doll, or an Elvis Presley doll.*
GEORGE: Who'd want an ugly old crap doll like that?

> **I wasn't allowed to go to the [1965] Shea Stadium concert because I was too young. My sister went with her girlfriend Diane, and I had to go to the World's Fair with Dotty, my mother's friend. I was so disappointed. I could hear them screaming. I tried to have a good time; we saw Soupy Sales. But with the Beatles right next door, wouldn't it kill ya?**
> **– Cyndi Lauper**

PLAYBOY: *Would you prefer a George doll, George?*
GEORGE: No, but I've got a Ringo doll at home.

PLAYBOY: *Did you know that you're probably the first public figures to have dolls made of them. . .except maybe Yogi Berra?*
JOHN: In Jellystone Park? Do you mean the cartoon?

PLAYBOY: *No. Didn't you know that the cartoon character is based on a real person. . .Yogi Berra, the baseball player?*
GEORGE: Oh.
PAUL: Well, they're making *us* into a cartoon, too, in the states. It's a series.
JOHN: The highest achievement you could ever get.
PAUL: We feel proud and humble.

PLAYBOY: *Did you know, George, that at the corner of 47th Street and Broadway in New York, there is a giant cutout of you on display?*
GEORGE: Of me?

PLAYBOY: *Life size.*
RINGO: Nude?

PLAYBOY: *No. . .but the reason we mention it is that this is really a signal honour. For years on that corner, there's been a big store with life-size cutouts of Marilyn Monroe, Anita Ekberg, or Jayne Mansfield in the window.*
JOHN: And now it's George.
PAUL: The only difference is that they've got bigger tits.
GEORGE: The party's getting rough. I'm going to bed. You carry on, though. I'll just stop my ears with cotton. . .so as not to hear the insults and smutty language.

Playboy, February 1965
Copyright 1965 Playboy for *Playboy Interview: The Beatles.*

THE MENACE OF BEATLISM
By Paul Johnson

In this New Statesman *piece, Johnson berates 'Beatlism' as the antithesis of highbrow culture. As a left-winger at the time, he saw them as the very epitome of crass commercialism. (Johnson later famously defected to the Right — exchanging his holier-than-thou socialism for holier-than-thou conservatism.)*

Mr William Deedes is an Old Harrovian, a member of the cabinet and the minister in charge of the government's information services. Mr Deedes, it will be remembered, was one of those five ministers who interviewed Mr Profumo on that fateful night and were convinced by him that he had not slept with Miss Keeler. Now any public relations man, even a grand one who sits in the cabinet, can use a touch of credulity; but even so I remember thinking at the time: 'If Deedes can believe that, he'll believe anything.' And indeed he does! Listen to him on the subject of the Beatles:

> They herald a cultural movement among the young which may become
> part of the history of our time. . .For those with eyes to see it, something
> important and heartening is happening here. The young are rejecting
> some of the sloppy standards of their elders, by which far too much of
> our output has been governed in recent years. . .they have discerned
> dimly that in a world of automation, declining craftsmanship and increased
> leisure, something of this kind is essential to restore the human instinct to
> excel at something and the human faculty of discrimination.

Incredible as it may seem, this was not an elaborate attempt at whimsy, but a serious address, delivered to a meeting of the City of London Young Conservatives, and heard in respectful silence. Not a voice was raised to point out that the Emperor wasn't wearing a stitch. The Beatles phenomenon, in fact, illustrates one of my favourite maxims: that if something becomes big enough and popular enough — and especially commercially profitable enough — solemn men will not be lacking to invest it with virtues. So long as the Beatles were just another successful showbiz team the pillars of society could afford to ignore them, beyond bestowing the indulgent accolade of a slot in the Royal Variety Performance. But then came the shock announcement that they were earning £6,250,000 a year-

and, almost simultaneously, they got the stamp of approval from America.

This was quite a different matter: at once they became not only part of the export trade but an electorally valuable property. Sir Alec Home promptly claimed credit for them, and was as promptly accused by Mr Wilson of political clothes-stealing. Conservative candidates have been officially advised to mention them whenever possible in their speeches. The Queen expressed concern about the length of Ringo's hair. Young diplomats at our Washington embassy fought for their autographs. A reporter described them as 'superb ambassadors for Britain'. It is true that the Bishop of Woolwich has not yet asked them to participate in one of his services, but the invitation cannot be long delayed. And, while waiting for the definitive analysis of their cultural significance by Messrs Raymond Williams and Richard Hoggart we have Mr Deedes' contribution on behalf of the cabinet.

Of course, our society has long been brainwashed in preparation for this apotheosis of inanity. For more than two decades now, more and more intellectuals have turned their backs on their trade and begun to worship at the shrine of 'pop culture'. Nowadays, if you confess that you don't know the difference between Dizzy Gillespie and Fats Waller (and, what is more, don't care) you are liable to be accused of being a fascist.

To buttress their intellectual self-esteem, these treasonable clerks have evolved an elaborate cultural mythology about jazz, which purports to distinguish between various periods, tendencies and schools. The subject has been smeared with a respectable veneer of academic scholarship, so that now you can overhear grown men, who have been expensively educated, engage in heated argument on the respective techniques of Charlie Parker and Duke Ellington. You can see writers of distinction, whose grey hairs testify to years spent in the cultural vineyard, squatting on the bare boards of malodorous caverns, while through the haze of smoke, sweat and cheap cosmetics comes the monotonous braying of savage instruments.

One might, I suppose, attribute such intellectual treachery to the fact that, in jazz circles, morals are easy, sex is cheap and there is a permissive attitude to the horrors of narcotics. Men are, alas, sometimes willing to debauch their intellects for such rewards. But I doubt if this is the real reason. The growing public approval of anti-culture is itself, I think, a reflection of the new cult of youth. Bewildered by a rapidly changing society, excessively fearful of becoming out of date, our leaders are increasingly turning to young people as guides and mentors — or, to vary the metaphor, as geiger counters to guard them against the perils of mental obsolescence. If youth likes jazz, then it must be good, and clever men must rationalise this preference in intellectually respectable language. Indeed, whatever youth likes must be good: the supreme crime, in politics and culture alike, is not to be 'with it'. Even the most unlikely mascots of the Establishment are now drifting with the current: Mr Henry Brooke, for instance, finds himself appointing to the latest Home Office committee the indispensable teenager, who has, what is more, the additional merit of being a delinquent.

Before I am denounced as a reactionary fuddy-duddy, let us pause an instant and see exactly what we mean by this 'youth'. Both TV channels now run weekly programmes in which popular records are played to teenagers and judged. While the music is performed, the cameras linger savagely over the faces of the audience. What a bottomless chasm of vacuity they reveal! The huge faces, bloated with cheap confectionery and smeared with chain-store makeup, the open, sagging mouths and glazed eyes, the hands mindlessly drumming in time to the music, the broken stiletto heels, the shoddy, stereotyped, 'with-it' clothes: here, apparently, is a collective portrait of a generation enslaved by a commercial machine. Leaving a TV studio recently, I stumbled into the exodus from one of these sessions. How pathetic and listless they seemed: young girls, hardly any more than sixteen, dressed as adults and already lined up as fodder for exploitation. Their eyes came to life only when one of their grotesque idols – scarcely older than they – made a brief appearance, before a man in a camel-hair coat hustled him into a car. Behind this image of 'youth', there are, evidently, some shrewd older folk at work.

And what of the 'culture' which is served up to these pitiable victims? According to Mr Deedes, 'the aim of the Beatles and their rivals is first class of its kind. Failure to attain it is spotted and criticised ruthlessly by their many highly-discriminating critics.' I wonder if Mr Deedes has ever taken the trouble to listen to any of this music? On the Saturday TV shows, the merits of the new records are discussed by panels of 'experts', many of whom seem barely more literate or articulate than the moronic ranks facing them. They are asked to judge each record a 'hit' or a 'miss', but seem incapable of explaining why they have reached their verdict. Occasionally one of the 'experts' betrays some slight acquaintance with the elementals of music and makes what is awesomely described as a 'technical' point: but when such merit is identified in a record, this is usually found to be a reason for its certain commercial failure.

In any case, merit has nothing to do with it. The teenager comes not to hear but to participate in a ritual, a collective grovelling to gods who are themselves blind and empty. 'Throughout the performance,' wrote one observer, 'it was impossible to hear anything above the squealing except the beat of Ringo's drums.' Here, indeed, is 'a new cultural movement': music which not only cannot be heard but does not need to be heard. As such I have no doubt that it is, in truth, 'first class of its kind'.

If the Beatles and their like were in fact what the youth of Britain wanted, one might well despair. I refuse to believe it – and so I think will any other intelligent person who casts his or her mind back far enough. What were we doing at sixteen? I remember the drudgery of Greek prose and the calculus, but I can also remember reading the whole of Shakespeare and Marlowe, writing poems and plays and stories. It is a marvellous age, an age of intense mental energy and discovery. Almost every week one found a fresh idol – Milton, Wagner, Debussy, Matisse, El Greco, Proust – some, indeed, to be subsequently toppled from the pantheon, but all springing from the mainstream of European culture. At sixteen, I and my friends heard our first performance of Beethoven's Ninth Symphony; I can remember the excitement even today. We would not have wasted 30 seconds of our precious time on the Beatles and their ilk.

> **I like pop as I like coca-cola or wrapped bread or fish fingers. They're instant and they give an illusion of nourishment. But I get very frightened when intellectuals start elevating pop to the level of important art . . . Even the best songs of the Beatles are only simple little lyrics written by young men of no great education and no great knowledge of our literary past; they do a very simple job very adequately. – *Anthony Burgess***

Are teenagers different today? Of course not. Those who flock round the Beatles, who scream themselves into hysteria, whose vacant faces flicker over the TV screen, are the least fortunate of their generation, the dull, the idle, the failures: their existence, in such large numbers, far from being a cause for ministerial congratulation, is a fearful indictment of our education system, which in ten years of schooling can scarcely raise them to literacy. What Mr Deedes fails to perceive is that the core of the teenage group – the boys and girls who will be the real leaders and creators of society tomorrow – never go near a pop concert. They are, to put it simply, too busy. They are educating themselves. They are in the process of inheriting the culture which, despite Beatlism or any other mass-produced mental opiate, will continue to shape our civilisation. To use Mr Deedes' own phrase, though not in the sense he meant it, they are indeed 'rejecting some of the sloppy standards of their elders'. Of course, if many of these elders in responsible positions surrender to the Gadarene Complex and seek to elevate the worst things in our society into the best, their task will be made more difficult. But I believe that, despite the antics of cabinet ministers with election nerves, they will succeed.

New Statesman, 28 February 1964

JOINT HONOURS
By Robert Sandall

The populism of British culture in the mid-Sixties was epitomised when the Beatles were awarded Membership of the British Empire. Ostensibly for their contribution to the export economy, it was a shrewd political gesture by Prime Minister Harold Wilson. It caused predictable outrage in Establishment circles, but reflected the public mood perfectly.

More than 30 years before Tony Blair opened the doors of Number Ten to Noel Gallagher and Alan McGee, while his spin doctors talked up something called 'Cool Britannia', another Labour premier was anxiously trying to associate his party with youthful style and success.

With his white hair, plump figure and permanently smouldering pipe, Harold Wilson looked about as cluelessly 'square' as any other old pop-fearing dad. But wily politician that he was, Wilson had swiftly realised that the Beatles could assist him in sexing up a Labour party which had spent thirteen years out of power. In the spring of 1964, six months before the general election, the Leader of the Opposition had turned up at the Dorchester hotel to present the Beatles with a Variety Club award. Wilson's pretext – that as member for the Huyton constituency near Liverpool, he was a fellow Merseysider – barely disguised his desire to get close to the hottest media property in the land. The fact that none of the group had the slightest idea who he was and that George Harrison mistook him for a 'Mr Dobson' (of Barker and Dobson toffee fame) didn't matter. As the following day's newspapers showed, in massive double page photo spreads, Wilson was the first senior British politician to *get* the Beatles.

A year later, as the leader of a country mired in debt and a government pledged to support 'the white heat of a technological revolution', he was even keener to draw attention to the beat group which had become Britain's most potent export. The Queen's birthday honours list, compiled as always by her Prime Minister, was Wilson's chosen instrument. And so on June 12, 1965, it was duly announced that, along with 182 military men, captains of industry and other elderly worthies, the four Beatles would each receive the MBE – the most junior of the orders of the British Empire.

The group, just back from their second European tour, were taken completely by surprise and they responded individually and in character. Lennon was sarky: 'I thought you had to drive tanks and win wars to get the MBE.' Ringo was self-deprecatingly droll: 'I'll keep it to dust when I'm old.' Harrison drily owned up to his ignorance that such awards could be won 'just for playing rock and roll music'. And McCartney, always the most eager to please and be pleased, said how marvellous it was and asked what his being an MBE made his dad.

For the next four months, the compatibility of Beatles and MBEs sparked a lively national debate with opinion divided across a recently defined 'generation gap'. Several holders of the award returned them in disgust at being joined by what one old sea dog described as 'a gang of nincompoops' – a colonel resigned from the Labour party. But with the group's second feature film *Help!* conquering cinema box offices over the summer and attracting to its premiere the grooviest royal of the day, the Queen's sister Princess Margaret, the Beatles had pretty much won the argument by the time of their autumn investiture at Buckingham Palace.

It's a keen pad and I liked the staff. I thought they'd be dukes and things but they were just fellas. The Queen was lovely. She was just like a mum to us.
– *Paul McCartney*

Never had a ruling monarch been so thoroughly upstaged by a group of her subjects as was Elizabeth II on October 26. The crowds in the Mall were of coronation proportions; the cries of 'God save the Beatles' were not. The arrival of four suited lads from Liverpool, all still only in their early twenties, on the long red carpet in the Palace's white and gold State ballroom was without precedent. It was also the clearest sign yet that the Beatles really had changed the world. At the press conference afterwards they waved their silver crosses and played the cheeky Scousers. McCartney called the Palace 'a keen pad' and said the Queen was 'like a mum'. Ringo said he'd made her laugh by telling her the group had been together for 40 years.

What none of them revealed at the time, perhaps because it didn't happen, was that prior to accepting their awards they'd shared a joint in the royal washroom. The only source of this widely credited but probably apocryphal tale was John Lennon, the Beatle who later sent back his MBE as a protest at Britain's support for the American involvement in Vietnam. Whether the joint was actually present, the story's survival as myth attests to a symbolic truth: The

Beatles didn't just visit the Queen's residence on that October afternoon, they took it over.

The only party in any way injured by Wilson's cunning PR stunt was the person in the Beatles' camp to whom official recognition of this sort mattered most: Brian Epstein. Because Wilson's purpose here was to divert the lustre of the group towards himself and his government, no other intermediaries could be allowed near the event. But it must have niggled this insecure and socially ambitious man to hear Princess Margaret commenting on the newspaper head-lines at the new offices of the *Birmingham Post and Mail* which she happened to be opening on the same day. 'I think MBE must stand for Mr Brian Epstein,' she remarked merrily.

Mojo, February 2002

THE DIARIES
By Noel Coward

Ever the quintessential English gentleman, the dramatist, performer and raconteur, Noel Coward recounts his personal 'shock of the new' on encountering the Beatles in 1965.

Wednesday 23 June 1965

I have finished the rewriting of *A Song at Twilight*, and I really do think I have improved it enormously. The weather has slightly improved. The Swiss social world continues to revolve sluggishly but quite agreeably. I dined with the Chevreau d'Antraigues and visited the Queen of Spain after dinner. The poor old girl is not well and shows signs of breaking up.

There has been another high-flown debate in the House of Lords about suggested (idiotic) amendments to the Homosexual Bill, in the course of which Lord Montgomery announced that homosexuality between men was the most abominable and bestial act that any human being could commit! It, in his mind, apparently compares unfavourably with disembowelling, torturing, gas chambers and brutal murder. It is inconceivable that a man of his eminence and achievements could make such a statement. The poor old sod must be gaga.

The Beatles have all four been awarded MBEs, which has caused a considerable outcry. Furious war heroes are sending back their bravely won medals by the bushel. It is, of course, a tactless and major blunder on the part of the Prime Minister, and also I don't think the Queen should have agreed. Some other decoration should have been selected to reward them for their talentless but considerable contributions to the Exchequer.

Sunday 4 July 1965

Today Audrey [Hepburn] and Mel [Ferrer, her then husband] came to lunch. She enchanting as ever and he really extremely nice. I got back on Thursday after an interlude in Rome in time to dine with Adrianne and Dorothy Hammerstein [Oscar's widow], whom I love. Rome was fascinating and fraught with drama. The temperature all the time hovered between 88° and 98°. Princess Torlonia's wedding was beautiful to look at but too many *paperazzi* flashing cameras all through even the most serious parts of the ceremony. I went with Kay Thompson and Merle Oberon. I then changed into a dinner jacket and went to

133

the *Grand Recepsione* which was *inferno* owing to there being no air-conditioning. It looked beautiful, however, and was crowded with Maria Pias and Maria Gabriellas.

On the Sunday night, I went to see the Beatles. I had never seen them in the flesh before. The noise was deafening throughout and I couldn't hear a word they sang or a note they played, just one long, ear-splitting din. Apparently they were not a success. The notices were bad the next day. I went backstage to see them and was met by Brian Epstein, who told me they had gone back to the hotel and would I go there. So off I went and, after being received by Brian Epstein and Wendy Hanson [the Beatles' publicist] and given a drink, I was told that the Beatles refused to see me because that ass David Lewin [*Daily Mail* columnist] had quoted me saying unflattering things about them months ago. I thought this graceless in the extreme, but decided to play it with firmness and dignity. I asked Wendy to go and fetch one of them and she finally reappeared with Paul McCartney and I explained gently but firmly that one did *not* pay much attention to the statements of newspaper reporters. The poor boy was quite amiable and I sent messages of congratulation to his colleagues, although the message I would have liked to send them was that they were bad-mannered little shits. In any case, it is still impossible to judge from their public performance whether they have talent or not. They were professional, had a certain guileless charm, and stayed on mercifully for not too long.

I was truly horrified and shocked by the audience. It was like a mass masturbation orgy, although apparently mild compared with what it usually is. The whole thing is to me an unpleasant phenomenon. Mob hysteria when commercially promoted, or in whatever way promoted, always sickens me. To realise that the majority of the modern adolescent world goes ritualistically mad over those four innocuous, rather silly-looking young men is a disturbing thought. Perhaps we are whirling more swiftly into extinction than we know. Personally I should have liked to take some of those squealing young maniacs and cracked their heads together. I am all for audiences going mad with enthusiasm after a performance, but *not* incessantly *during* the performance so that there ceases to be a performance.

The Noel Coward Diaries, Noel Coward, edited by Graham Pyn and Sheridan Morley, 1982

YESTERDAY
By Giles Smith

Since appearing on the Help! *soundtrack album in 1965, 'Yesterday' has become the single most covered Beatles song. It's also one of the most covered standards of all time – by artists as varied as Doctor John, Frank Sinatra and Marvin Gaye.*

Everybody knows about the man who turned down the Beatles. Dick Rowe, the rep from Decca, who heard some of the Fab Four's early recordings and decided that he just couldn't see a future in them, has become a legendary figure of fun. But what about the man who turned down the Beatles' biggest song? Doesn't he deserve a pillorying too? Step up, Billy J. Kramer.

It was Kramer who approached Paul McCartney in 1965 and asked him if he had written anything new that he could have for a single. McCartney played him a little ballad he had written on the guitar, with a lyric on a conventional blues theme – the man whose lover has walked out on him, without quite saying why. The first verse went: 'Yesterday/ All my troubles seemed so far away/ Now it looks as though they're here to stay/ Oh, I believe in yesterday.' Kramer thought about it for a minute and decided he didn't rate the song.

Seven years later, what was not good enough for Billy J. had proved acceptable to 1,186 artists around the world, all of whom had seen fit to make recorded versions of 'Yesterday', a song which McCartney had rapidly come to believe was 'the most complete thing I've ever written.'

For 'written', read 'dreamt'. The tune for 'Yesterday' came to McCartney in his sleep. 'I woke up one morning in London in Wimpole Street in an attic flat. Just woke up and I had that tune of "Yesterday" in my head, with no idea where it came from. They gave me an award for it because it's been [broadcast] five million times – and the next song down is three million so it's way out ahead. And I dreamt it, so if that's not magic, what is? Dead jammy.'

The lyrics, though, had to be worked for. At first, McCartney simply attached a couple of prototype lines of daft verse to the tune – a common practice for him while he was weighing up a melody and wondering which way to push the song's mood. But in this case, the lines he hit on could have sunk the song for good. Before 'Yesterday' was 'Yesterday', the words ran 'Scrambled eggs/ Oh my darling, you've got lovely legs.' When a writer reaches the send-up stage this early in a composition, ordinarily he or she is on the verge of throwing the whole thing away and moving on. But something in the tune's solemn roundedness seems to have called McCartney back from the edge and forced him to take the job seriously.

It was still called 'Scrambled Eggs' in January 1964, when he showed it, rather sheepishly, to the Beatles' producer, George Martin. Consider McCartney's predicament: he was 22, at the front of the world's greatest pop group, the writer of mould-breaking snappy teen anthems and heart-melting ballads and yet into his lap had dropped a composition which was stately, formal, oddly classical in the way phrase answered to phrase, and about as hip and youthful as a pot of tea. He told Martin that he was looking for a one-word title for the song, that 'Yesterday' had come to mind, but he was worried that it was too corny. Martin encouraged him to persist.

. . . Noodles sees his face as an old man reflected to the sound of 'Yesterday'; in that first moment the spectator could interpret the look of Robert De Niro as nostalgia for a lost youth, something that the music contributes to . . . – *Roberto Bartual, 'Once Upon a Time in America: An Experimental Epic'*

The song was not recorded until Monday, 14 June 1965. Mark Lewisohn's scholarly guide, *The Complete Beatles Recording Sessions*, informs us that the track was completed in three hours in the evening. McCartney played acoustic guitar and sang, while a classical string quartet accompanied him, filling the track out and plotting its rhythmic direction without need for the heavier certainty of drums. 'Yesterday' marks the Beatles' first use of orchestral instruments, and by no means their last. The strings were Martin's idea. As Andy Partridge, the songwriter from XTC, once said: 'George Martin is often described as the Fifth Beatle; he may well have been the First.'

Whatever, none of the other three contributed to 'Yesterday' (though George Harrison was evidently in the studio during the session). This was widely interpreted at the time as rock-solid evidence that the Beatles were on the verge of splitting – but then, in 1965, very few things weren't interpreted that way. And though 'Yesterday' appeared on the *Help!* soundtrack album (Parlophone 1965) – if not in the movie itself – and was the title track of an EP, it is certainly true that the rest of the band distanced themselves from the song and ribbed McCartney mercilessly for its fuddy-duddiness. McCartney said, 'I remember George saying, "Blimey, he's always talking about 'Yesterday', you'd think he was Beethoven or somebody.'"

In fact, there is nothing fancy or ornate about the song's construction. McCartney's opening guitar part sets the tone – one repeated chord, played with downward strokes of the thumb, which is the most basic kind of strumming. The unique thing, when the song moves into the verse, is its cycle of chords. 'Yesterday' is built on a set of perfectly common cadences but, as you travel through them, you pass across neat little bridging chords so that the movement of the strings beneath the voice appears subtly interleaved.

George Martin has revealed how McCartney was determined that the string players should keep their vibrato to a minimum, so as not to give the song any cumbersome emotionality. The same principle informs his singing, which maintains an understated warmth, even when it climbs high into the middle section. ('Why she had to go/ I don't know/ She wouldn't say/ I said something wrong/ Now I long for yesterday.') The recording is primitive and partly botched: occasionally you hear the voice double up. Not a deliberate effect, this is simply the trace of an earlier take, spilling out of the headphones in the studio. But the key thing about the basic instrumentation is that there is nothing here to betray the song's age, no particular noise pinning it to its era. This has had a double benefit: it made the song sound like a standard, even when it was freshly minted; and it has since rendered it immune to the passing years.

Hence that slew of cover versions. No one has taken the song to No. 1 – but then, neither did the Beatles. (Released as a single retrospectively, in 1976, 'Yesterday' only went as far as No. 8.) Most shots at the piece fall into one of two camps. On one hand, there are those who have realised McCartney's worst fears about the song. Many of these use the presence of strings on the original as an excuse to ladle giant, sticky violin sections all over the arrangement, somehow forgetting that there was only a quartet there to begin with and that it played with rasp and edge. If McCartney had somehow been able to hear Richard Clayderman's dizzyingly sugary instrumental version in advance, can we really believe he would have bothered to complete the song?

On the other hand, there are recordings by Ray Charles and Marvin Gaye whose versions amply support McCartney's hunch that, when he wrote 'Yesterday', he was creating more than just a bauble to hang on Perry Como's *Take It Easy* album (RCA 1990). Charles's 1967 version (*The Collection*, Castle 1990) replaces the guitar with a piano and inserts a moment of silence before each verse. 'Suddenly,' he snaps, 'I'm not half the man I used to be.' It's as if those little gaps are the spaces in which the singer is trying to gather what is left of his strength. On Gaye's version (*That's the Way Love Is*, Motown 1970), a prominent bass drum and cymbal lend the song the slink of a Motown ballad, with Gaye calling out, 'People, now I need a place to hide away.' For all the song's ostensible English poppiness, you barely have to rub at the surface to reveal something of gospel and soul there.

As a rule of thumb, don't trust anyone who slows the song down. It is easy to underestimate the medium pace at which McCartney's version ticks along. 'Yesterday' owes its becoming blitheness, its refusal to wallow, precisely to this. Generally, when people put the brakes on, they are hoping to milk the song for something it cannot give them. This is why the version by the four-woman singing group En Vogue on the *Funky Divas* album (East West 1992) makes a fresh break. They move the tempo up a notch and stuff the track with close-packed harmonies set to a thumping drum machine. In the process they become probably the first act to give the song a defiant swagger.

Better this, certainly, than the decelerated Tom Jones version (*Delilah*, Decca 1968), which is crammed to breaking point with bogus suffering. Jones gives it the big-voice treatment, but, as 'Yesterday' is apt to make clear, size isn't every-thing. Shocking to say, even Elvis Presley, live in Las Vegas (*On Stage*, RCA 1970), exercises more decorum, though a nicely modest vocal delivery is spoilt by the intrusion of backing vocalists, who rather disrupt the song's solitary, con-fessional thrust. ('Yesterday,' sings Elvis: 'Yesterday!' coo the singers, in case you misheard the first time.)

And so it goes on: Dionne Warwick gives the song heart (*Unforgettable*, Castle 1987), Diana Ross empties it of content (*I Hear a Symphony*, Motown 1966); Merle Haggard and Willie Nelson lift it effortlessly (*Help Me Make It Through the Night*, RCA 1984), Ray Conniff sits on it, heavily (*Easy Listening Beatles*, CBS 1985). With 'Yesterday' it can go either way. McCartney seems to have known this even as he wrote the song. But at least he left us, in the shape of his own version, the instruction manual.

Lives of the Great Songs, edited by Tim De Lisle, 1994

JOHN LENNON'S SCHOOL DAYS
By Michael Wood

This analysis of Lennon's lyric writing compares the nonsense verse of A Spaniard in the Works *with songs from the* Sgt. Pepper *era — not yet written when the book was published in 1965.*

A heavy man with glasses sits on a chair looking at a green monster with four legs. Caption? 'An adult looks at a Beatle.' The caption is mine, but the drawing is John Lennon's. It appears in his second book, *A Spaniard in the Works*.

There are four-legged things everywhere in Lennon's drawings: sheep, cats, cows, Sherlock Holmes on his knees. The first book, *In His Own Write*, has a huge Wrestling Dog ('But who would fight this wondrous beast? I wouldn't for a kick off'), and a piece called 'Liddypool' is accompanied by a sketch of chatting quadropuses.

It is a child's world, or a world that Thurber might have drawn for a child. Animals and freaks have comic dignity while adults look silly and too big, bending over and crawling. A double suggestion runs through the writing in both books: adults *are* silly, they give children rubbish to read and expect them to like it; and left to themselves, adults are worse than children – they talk jabberwocky about politics and colour and religion, and they believe what they say.

So we get Enig Blyter's famous five – ten of them taking off for Woenow Abbey – '"Gruddly Pod, Gruddly Pod," the train seemed to say, "Gruddly Pod, we're on our hollidays."' There is a trip to Treasure Ivan with Large John Saliver, Small Jack Hawkins, Cpt Smellit and Squire Trelorgy. But Prevelant ze Gaute also appears, and Docker Adenoid along with Harrassed MacMillion and the late Cassandle of the Mirror on the Wall. The Bible, hymns, newspapers, the telly, bad films: the world shrinks to the nonsense of a book for small children.

The trick is simple, a standard schoolboy game. You retreat to baby talk, to mock-childishness, to the linguistic pranks of Lewis Carroll and Edward Lear. This is your revenge on all the language, life and literature that people are asking you to take seriously. You bend and break what they teach you; you make their world sound like Wonderland. Vile ruperts spread through a village, an old man leaves his last will and testicle, there is dirty weather off Rockall and Fredastaire. A day is a red lettuce day.

139

The jokes are John Lennon's, but they have already seen good service in most grammar schools in this country. The grammar school is the place for this intelligent, informed and infantile humour, I think; and school may have been more important for Lennon and McCartney than either home or Liverpool, whatever sociologists and trendmen say. Grammar school pupils are alert, disciplined and frightened. Their pleasures are psychological – torturing a nervous teacher – and fairly secret.

I remember a joke that ran for months when I was at school. Whenever a teacher left the room, someone would draw a head, side view, on the blackboard. It would be a policeman in a huge helmet or a guardsman in a vast busby. At the side of this would appear a drawing of the policeman or guardsman without his helmet or busby. His head would be exactly the same shape as his hat. Another version showed a grotesque clubfoot – with or without a shoe, it looked the same.

. . . it was far from the image that the world at large has of John Lennon's childhood – far from the image of docks, warehouses, black rats, walking along the Dock Road and dark poverty-struck satanic mills of William Blake's awe inspiring poem 'Jerusalem'.
– David Ashton, 'The Vanished World of a Woolton Childhood with John Lennon'

Thinking back, I can see two things in our enjoyment of those gruesome gags. First, a hope that the world would stay simple, that our fears of mess and complication might prove to be unfounded. Just think. If the mask should fall to reveal a face just like the mask, if the truth about life, which parents and teachers hinted at so darkly, should turn out to be exactly like the facade, then they would be the fools with their conspiracy theories, and we would be right in our scared simplicity. And, secondly, I think we were fascinated by disease and deformity, which represented the future ugliness of life itself. If we could keep that at the level of a joke, if we could tame it in the safeness of school, everything would be all right.

All this is in Lennon. The adult world makes him larf, and his books are a vengeance. He has verbal forms of the clubfoot joke – Mr Borris Morris, in the story of that name, has a happy knack of being in the right place at the right place – and a splendid visual version. Two beggars stand side by side, each complete with stick, trumpet, dog and begging tin. One of them has dark glasses, and his dog has dark glasses too. The man carries a placard on his chest saying: I am blind. The other man also has a placard. It says: I can see quite clearly. Thus does the world shed its secrets for the innocent. Although for the person who can make such a joke, as for the boys who could laugh at our drawings, innocence is already a fantasy, an incipient nostalgia, no longer a state of mind.

But most strikingly, Lennon sets up a gallery of deformed and violent people, a literal menagerie of creatures born on the blackboard during a break. A man clubs his wife to death. A friendly little dog ('Arf, Arf, he goes, a merry sight') is put to sleep. Eric Hearble, who has a growth on his head, loses his job teaching spastics to dance ('"We're not having a cripple teaching our lads," said Headmaster'). Randolph is killed at Christmas by his pals ('At least he didn't *die* alone did he?') and a girl wonders about flowers for her wheelchair at her wedding – luckily her father comes home and cancels the husband. Little Bobby, 39 years old, gets a hook for his missing hand as a birthday present. Only the hook is for the wrong hand, his good left hand, and they have to chop that off to fit the hook.

It is absurd to compare Lennon to Joyce. Lennon's puns are piecemeal, scattered and unequal. Joyce's punning in *Finnegans Wake* is a system, a metaphysic for melding worlds. When Joyce writes of the flushpots of Euston and the hanging garments of Marylebone, the Bible and London really collide. But Lennon has some fine effects. A pun is what Durkheim in another context called a logical scandal, it is an escape from linear meaning. It is language on holiday, and Lennon occasionally gets the authentic glee of this.

'Anything you say may be used in Everton against you.' 'Father Cradock turns round slowly from the book he is eating and explains that it is just a face she is going through.' People dance with wild abdomen, and send stabbed, undressed envelopes.

Why is there so little of all this in the songs Lennon writes with Paul McCartney? McCartney's sobering influence? Hardly. More likely both are being tactful towards their public. They know that people are offended by nonsense, by things they can't understand; they know that people tend to take jokes that baffle them as a personal insult, a calculated exclusion. And their songs after all are a commercial enterprise – Lennon and McCartney have written well over 100 songs since 1962, and their work has been recorded by almost everyone you can think of.

Certainly there are occasional puns – 'It won't be long/Till I belong to you.' 'A Hard Day's Night', the nonsense title of a film and a song, comes from a Lennon story called 'Sad Michael'. There are all the double meanings concerning pot and LSD on the *Sergeant Pepper* album, there is the sound play of by, buy,

141

bye–bye in the song 'She's Leaving Home'. And the songs have developed towards complexity.

Lennon and McCartney's early lyrics were thin and conventional. There was rain in the heart, there were stars in the sky, birds were always threatening not to sing. The tunes were good, some of them as good as those of Rodgers or Leonard Bernstein. But the gap between words and music in pieces like 'If I Fell', 'And I Love Her', 'Ask Me Why', 'Not a Second Time', was embarrassing for anyone who wanted to take the songs seriously. The best lyrics, which went with up-tempo numbers like 'I Feel Fine', 'All My Lovin'', 'Can't Buy Me Love', were the ones which said the least. They said yeh, approximately. I'm not suggesting that Lennon and McCartney didn't know how conventional they were being, or that they couldn't have done better. But they didn't do better, presumably because they weren't interested.

Now they are interested. We get the sharpness of 'Your day breaks/Your mind aches,' where the rhyme really does something. People, characters, begin to take the place of the anonymous lover of the early songs, shouting, sobbing, missing, losing, promising his standardised love. We get Rita the meter maid, and the man who wants to be a paperback writer. We get Eleanor Rigby and all the lonely people, and the sights and sounds of Penny Lane. To say nothing of Billy Shears, Sgt. Pepper and Mr Kite. And we get the complex compassion of songs like 'Wait' ('If your heart breaks/Don't wait') and 'She's Leaving Home', where the girl going off writes a note 'that she hoped would say more', and her parents moan their incomprehension: 'We gave her most of our lives. . .' The whole work develops a sense of waste, of 'tears cried for no one', as one song has it.

But still, the music has developed more than the language, and the language is not a main attraction in these songs. Lennon and McCartney's words are still less important than those of Bob Dylan, or Lorenz Hart, or Cole Porter, or Ira Gershwin. We have to look elsewhere for the link between the songs and Lennon's stories.

The link is not hard to find. It takes us back to school, and Lennon and McCartney's repeated flights into the past. Think of the titles: 'Yesterday', 'The Night Before'. Think of the nostalgia in songs like 'Things We Said Today', or 'In My Life': 'There are places I'll remember all my life.' Think of the echoes of melodrama and music hall in the *Sergeant Pepper* album, the jaunty George Formby tone of 'When I'm 64'. In 'Good Morning, Good Morning' we take a walk past the old school – 'Nothing has changed, it's still the same' - and 'She Said She Said' flings a bewildered boy out of the classroom on to a hard life. The girl tells him that she knows what it's like to be dead, and he can only reply, 'No no you're wrong when I was a boy everything was right. . .' Lennon and McCartney in their songs do indeed 'live the past in the present', as Richard Poirier wrote about them in *Partisan Review* last year. But it is a personal and sentimental past, not a historical one — it is the specific past of good school days, when the world was simpler and adults looked like fools. Lennon and McCartney are not naively nostalgic, but they are nostalgic. Their songs and Lennon's stories express the *good child's* hostility to grown-ups. That is what we mean by the youth of the Beatles, an attitude, not an age — after all, they were in their twenties when they began to make it around 1962. The attitude is not dangerous, at worst it deserves a detention, and this is why adults have been so keen to endorse the Beatles. This is safe play for children, mild naughtiness, and much better than breaking up Margate or digging up Paris.

The Beatles are a middle generation between the old conformers and the new rebels, between those who find it hard to believe that the world will change and those who know it's got to. Lennon and McCartney protest against the world adults have made, of course. They hate its pain and loneliness. But their protests are quiet, and their only answer so far has been escape into dope or India.

But the question remains. The Beatles have by-passed adulthood, and this links them with the revolutionary students who are asking why they should grow up when growing up means napalm, treachery, compromise and Porton Down. For years we have sold maturity as a virtue, we have preached the careful ethic of the status quo. But the Beatles are nearly 30 and wildly successful on anyone's terms. If they haven't grown up yet, why should they now?

New Society, 27 June 1968

HELP!
By Kenneth Tynan

Writer and critic Kenneth Tynan gained instant notoriety by being the first person to utter the word 'fuck' on British TV. His review of the band's big-screen debut draws heavily upon the influences of pop-art literature, and illustrates the affection afforded the Beatles by the 'chattering classes' of the day.

THIS this THIS this THIS is the kind of THING (from outer SPACE?) you can expect from *Help!*, the new (and BAM!! it's new or never) film directed by focus-pulling, prize-winning, gag-spawning, zoom-loving Richard (*The KNACK*) Lester, shot (POWWW!) in Eastmancolour but influenced by *Observer*colour and suggesting whole libraries of colourmags sprung BOING! to instant obsolescent life, complete with COOL gaudy consumer-tailored featurettes (one Lester missed: 'Tread Softly: The Dream-World of Wall-to-Wall Carpeting') and genuine only-connecting ADS (another Lester missed: 'Why not fly to the Aleutians in your custom-built Hammond Organ?'), not to mention FOUR EXPENSIVE TWO-DIMENSIONAL OBJECTS – namely John Lennon, the snickering heavyweight punster; surly, bejewelled Ringo Starr; George Harrison, the twelve-string narcissist; and Paul McCartney, the boy next fibre-glass-electric-eye-operated door (under that wig he's really – GASP! – Anne Rutherford) - who are flung about (URGGHH!), battered (SPLAT!!) and flattened (KER-PLUNK!!!) in a comic-strip chase through tourist-enticing London, the whiter-than-white Austrian Alps and selected sunsoaked Bahamas, pursued by Oriental goodness-gracious villains ('It's a Sellers' market,' quips writer Charles Wood) and guaranteed mad scientists, all plotting to slice (EEK!) a magic ring from surly Ringo's bejewelled finger, while off-beat Lester movie garners harvest of heady hosannas ('LOFTY GROSSES LOOM FOR MOPHEADS' LATEST – Flicker's Total Sexlessness Augurs Wham Family Fare') from notoriously hard-to-please CRITICS (ECCHH!!) in American trade press. . .

In other words, *Help!* is a brilliant, unboring but ferociously ephemeral movie. Richard Lester's direction is a high-speed compendium of many lessons learned from Blake Edwards, Frank Tashlin, Goon comedy, fashion photography and MGM cartoons. The Beatles themselves are not natural actors, nor are they exuberant extroverts; their mode is dry and laconic, as befits the flat and sceptical Liverpool accent. Realising this, Lester leaves it to his cameraman (David Watkin) to create the exuberance, confining the Beatles to deadpan comments and never asking them to react to events with anything approaching emotion. He capitalises on their wary, guarded detachment. 'There's something been in this soup,' says John, having calmly removed from the plate a season ticket and a pair of spectacles.

> **There's one scene in the film where Victor Spinetti is doing that curling, you know, with the big stones and you slide them, and one of them, of course, has a bomb in it. We find this out and we have to run away. And Paul and I ran about seven miles. [laughs] We just ran and ran so we could stop and have a joint and come back. – *Ringo Starr***

The script (by Marc Behm and Charles Wood) is chopped into fragments; hundreds of half-heard gags zip by, of which we are given time to laugh at about two dozen. The best-sustained sequence is the one where Ringo is trapped by an escaped tiger that can be tamed only by a full choral rendering of Beethoven's Ninth. The musical items are superbly shot, and the title song is the most haunting Beatle composition to date.

To sum up *Help!* I must go to Coleridge, who said that whereas a scientist investigates a thing for the sheer pleasure of knowing, the non-scientist only wants to find out whether it will 'furnish him with food, or shelter, or weapons, or tools, or ornaments, or *play-withs*.' *Help!* is a shiny forgettable toy; an ideal play-with.

Tynan Right and Left, Kenneth Tynan, 1967

HIGH-BROWS VS NO-BROWS
By Abram Chasins

While the Beatles had already won over British intellectuals like Kenneth Tynan, their American counterparts were split down the middle after the 'British invasion' hit their shores — hence this spirited defence.

'If you can't fight 'em, join 'em.' Fully ten years ago, I offered this homespun advice to dismayed friends whose children were shrieking and clutching at Elvis Presley. Those who had determined that it was time to assert parental authority had found themselves embroiled in a bitter struggle. The more they objected, the more they encountered hysteria and defiance. Others had passively let the mania run its course — a few in nostalgic remembrance of their own generation's idolatry of Vallee, Crosby and Sinatra; most in tight-lipped resignation that this, too, shall pass.

It did, of course; but only to recur in more frenzied forms, hitting a new high in Beatlemania, today's teen-age trauma. Up to a point, it is a familiar phenomenon, which should remind us that there is nothing completely new under the sun and that, without our lifting a finger, it will fade into oblivion. In its unprecedented duration and degree of intensity, however, Beatlemania is far more than an outburst of common hero worship. Despite its power to provoke bedlam and broken limbs, it is also a phenomenon we could channel constructively to reaffirm the home as a source of standards and behaviour.

Surveys of how parents are coping with their children's 'acting up and dressing down' have revealed that the largest number claims to be waging militant opposition to the craze, yet admits 'no success' or 'some success at the cost of family harmony'. The next largest group claims to be 'relaxing against it', supporting this position behind explanations such as 'It's just adolescence' or 'They're just conforming.'

Anthropologists tell us that the frenzied reaction to rock'n'roll rhythms is a throwback to the aboriginal response to the jungle beat of the tom-tom. Where do we go from there? Barbaric rhythm is also the chief characteristic of most contemporary music, including the greatest classical masterpiece of our century, Stravinsky's *The Rite of Spring*. Evidently, the mature and cultured segments of our society also feel the need for a primitive outlet.

Psychologists and psychiatrists tell us that Beatlemania serves as a revolt against parental authority. Other studies conclude that the outward hysteria of Beatlemania is an antidote for the inner hysteria of 'emancipated' youngsters plagued by the uncertainties of a turbulent world; and that the mass conformism provides status, safety in numbers, and a chance to let off steam in a society that suppresses instinct and emotion. Still another theory is that Beatlemania offers youngsters a chance to 'find themselves' by losing themselves in self-identification with those successful and attractive 'good-bad boys'.

Whether or not these theories are correct, I am not qualified to judge. Music is my beat, and it is the music the Beatles compose and perform that accounts substantially for their immense fame and following.

In this area, music analysts have shown an unwillingness to recognise the extent to which popular music has been a revealing reflection of the emotions of the majority of Americans throughout our history. From the patriotic and political songs of Revolutionary days to the rock'n'roll that has ridiculed traditions and flouted our conventions, popular songs have candidly, though often obviously, mirrored our ever-changing modes of life.

The music of the Beatles is not strictly rock'n'roll, but a synthesis in which it is merely an element. The melodies are mongrels of cowboy and calypso traits, echoes of Anglo-Saxon folklore, all with a northern British accent. The instant appeal of the songs is rooted in the spectacular resurgence of folk singing and dancing. The harmonies are basically orthodox, with unexpected deviations and turns in the modern manner. The rhythm is a lustier and more syncopated Big Beat. Most interesting is the spicy variety of the Beatles' style, from tender ballads to tough twists.

Instrumentally, Ringo handles his drums with all the subtlety of a woodsman felling an oak, while the others slash chords across electric guitars, carefully avoiding anything complicated, as they are obliged to because of their technical limitations. Vocally, they are youthfully hoarse, and their untidy enunciation of corny lyrics is amusingly calculated to satirise our hillbillies.

As they sing and sway, they disclose revealing dualities. They are sophisticated yet disarmingly simple; their material is a composite of cliches, imaginatively woven into a texture of individual sound and style. Especially significant is the sharp intelligence with which the Beatles reverse roles with audiences and, at that point, also act as accompanists to ecstatic fans, whom they shrewdly encourage to jump, shriek and share the show in uninhibited self-expression.

Now, what's behind all this? What can we learn from the Beatles' ability to convert children's pent-up emotions into mutual love and musical enthusiasm? What needs are they fulfilling that we are not? In an effort to answer such questions, I asked teenagers from different localities and different backgrounds how they felt about the Beatles. Their answers made them one. In fact, with the exception of a handful of deviationists, the responses were so startlingly similar that they can be quoted collectively.

'They're adorable, they're young, they're a little kooky like us, and they're in our corner,' the girls murmured dreamily. 'When we wave, they wave back, and they don't tell us to shut up or dress up. Whatever we do is okay with them. They understand.'

'They've got rhythm and a terrific beat,' the boys said. 'Their music is different, but you can get it and it gets you. They make you want to do what they do. They give us the right kind of a "fix" – they fix it so that singing and playing aren't sissy. Believe me, when you can handle a song and a guitar, it sure rates with the girls.'

Both girls and boys said, 'At home, when I play my music, my folks give me a dirty look and walk out. So when they play their music, opera and classical stuff, I walk out.'

'My music.' 'Their music.' Where did they get that? They got it in homes where music, if it existed at all, was never an experience the whole family enjoyed together. They got it from parents who divide music into 'good' and 'bad', who still haven't learned that the more you love music, the more music you love.

The most illuminating single answer came from a youngster of fourteen. 'My parents are driving me nuts,' he said. 'Anything I do that puts me "in" with my gang, puts me "out" with them. My mother made me take piano lessons. After a while, I hated music and I wouldn't practice and I got bawled out. Now I love the guitar, and I formed a combo of kids. I double at the piano, and we're the only ones who have a piano, so I asked the kids up one night to practice, and it was awful. My father put his hands over his ears and ran out of the room. My mother tried to be nice, but you could see she wasn't with it, and when we began to get real hopped up from playing together, she looked scared. When I went to Carnegie Hall to hear the Beatles, she made me feel like I was a delinquent.'

I decided to start my poll of parents with this mother. I pointed out that the Beatles seem to have succeeded precisely where she had failed – in making music a rich and joyful part of her boy's life. Further, that going to Carnegie Hall is the beginning of a good habit. I then asked her whether she wouldn't rather have her son making music with his friends at home, even if it was noisy, than not to know what he was doing.

'I'm amazed at you,' she answered. 'With your standards, how can you think of this in terms of music? It's just childish, cheap stuff. We made every sacrifice to give Billy lessons, so that he would know the difference between this maudlin trash and great music. He resisted it, all of it.'

That's where she was wrong. That's not what Billy resisted. What he did resist, and rightly so, was the whole senseless paraphernalia of making music in a vacuum, the isolated drudgery of practising an instrument not of his own choosing and before he had any desire for music. As for the 'cheap stuff' that had inspired Billy not only to love music, but to read it and practice without pressure in order to participate in it – indeed I call it music, for the ingredients are essentially the same as those that exist in music of more permanent value.

Another parent said, 'The Beatle craze? Rebellious enthusiasm, that's what it is. The madder I get, the more satisfaction my children get from swooning over that junk.'

The harmonic intricacies shared by the Beatles and Debussy might elude the casual listener. But upon closer examination, the tonal qualities and melodic sensibility of the French impressionist composer and Lennon/McCartney are remarkable. Compare 'A Day in the Life' from *Sgt. Pepper* with any of Debussy's melodic piano works. You'll be pleasantly surprised.
– Martin Gorda, 'Rock-to-Classical: A Musical Menu'

'Rebellious enthusiasm.' Take away the adjective, and enthusiasm remains – the most precious of all qualities that bring meaning and joy to our lives. Haven't we all been sick at heart over our children's apathy and blase boredom? The Beatles have given them something to get excited about. We could be more grateful and far more alert to the implications of what they have done.

The parents of the boy who brought his combo home should have realised that, in his enthusiasm, he was trying to include them in this important part of his life. He was paying them the highest compliment possible, trusting them and their reactions in front of his friends. They should have been proud of the good job they had done, up to that point. Then they misbehaved, like children. Equally immature was the attitude of the mother whose untimely emphasis on standards had all but destroyed her boy's innate musicality.

Don't worry about standards; just set them yourself. They're contagious. Children's tastes are always changing, anyway. I remember a battle in our family over my thirteen–year–old cousin, who was an insatiable reader of comic books. Today, he is one of the most literate men I know. Why not? He got the habit of reading.

One parent to whom I told this said, 'It's not the same, if you're implying that the kids are getting the listening habit through the Beatles. How can they listen when they keep shrieking along?' Wait a minute. The kids know all the words and every note, or they couldn't join in. They must have listened, and attentively, to radio or records. As for the excellent habit of collecting records, an enormous number of children told me they started with the Beatles, whose records are now alphabetically stored between Bach and Beethoven.

If we really value the fact that our nation has become the greatest centre of musical interest and activity in the world, every factor that made it so is as healthy as the others. Who cares whether a child is a music lover because Ringo's bongos are the 'status cymbals' of his peers? The only thing wrong with that is our adult snobbery that excludes us and encourages them to oppose us. Won't we stimulate their affection and respect if we show that our broader interest in music has been intensified by their own interest?

Beatlemania was turned to effective account and even to the 'pursuit of excellence' by the mother of the looniest little Beatlebug I know. He had been struggling valiantly but unsuccessfully with a guitar, which he played passionately and poorly. His mother listened, suffered with him, and then bought him a recording by the superb flamenco artist, Montoya. The boy played it from morning till night through an entire weekend. His mother then took him to a concert by Julian Bream and watched her son's eyes grow as big as saucers over that supreme virtuosity and ease.

The next day, the youngster was up at 5:00 a.m. slaving at his guitar. His mother had to drag him away from it to go to school. That night, he blurted out, 'Could I have guitar lessons, please?' He could and did.

And it all started through those boys from Liverpool – from the fun they get and give through music, and because of their warmth, easy humour and astuteness. Their realistic and modest public statements show that they know exactly who they are, where they stand, and that their party may soon be over.

But a humdinger it surely has been and still is. The long list of honours bestowed on these sons of humble parents has now been crowned by Queen Elizabeth with the Order of the British Empire. Their earnings this year and the products named for them are expected to gross over $100 million, and the same figure applies to the number of their records sold.

All this reflects affirmation, not protestation. And we may be certain that none of us could be more pleased than those ingratiating fellows to discover that the vogue which enriched them so handsomely has also enriched their fervent little American fans, in ways that cannot be measured by money.

McCall's, September 1965

ELVIS MEETS THE BEATLES: UNCENSORED

By Chris Hutchins and Peter Thompson

British journalist Chris Hutchins was actually present when the two greatest forces in rock'n'roll met, on 27 August 1965. Although Elvis was considered a spent force by the mid-Sixties, churning out frothy films prior to his celebrated comeback in '68, the Beatles still revered him as their original inspiration. Lennon had declared, 'Before Elvis there was nothing.'

Elvis rose to greet his guests, sun-tanned and outwardly relaxed. Peering round the room like Peter Sellers and putting on an Inspector Clouseau accent to address his reluctant host, John said: 'Oh, zere you are!' The Mersey had finally run into the Mississippi, and already I could see that there were going to be some big waves.

Shooting a quizzical look in Priscilla's direction, Elvis sat down with John and Paul on his right and Ringo and George on his left. There was a sudden silence as the record came to an end. No one spoke. The silence became uncomfortable, and then embarrassing. Everyone looked at Elvis. His nightmare was coming true. Nervously, he picked up the remote control and started changing channels on the big colour TV set.

Throwing the device on to the coffee table, he said: 'If you guys are just gonna sit there and stare at me, I'm goin' to bed. Let's call it a night, right, Cilla? I didn't mean for this to be like the subjects calling on the King. I just thought we'd sit and talk about music and maybe jam a little.'

'That would be great,' enthused Paul, trying to salvage the situation.

'Somebody bring in the guitars,' ordered Elvis.

Electric guitars were produced and plugged into amplifiers scattered around the room, and a white piano was pushed into view. Elvis picked up the bass guitar he had started to learn to play. John and George began tuning up rhythm guitars while Paul sat down at the piano.

'Sorry there's no drum kit for you,' Elvis told Ringo. 'We left that back in Memphis.'

'That's OK,' Ringo replied. 'I'd rather play pool.'

Elvis played a few notes and addressed himself to Paul: 'Still not too good, huh. . .but I'm practising.'

Paul gave him the benefit of some instruction while John played some chords on the guitar he'd picked up.

'Elvis, lad, you're coming along quite well. Keep up the rehearsals and me and Mr Epstein will make you a star,' Paul jibed.

'I hear you guys had a little trouble on the plane ride to Portland,' said Elvis, handling the role of host quite well.

. . . There's two kinds of people in this world, Elvis people and Beatles people. Now Beatles people can like Elvis. And Elvis people can like the Beatles. But nobody likes them both equally. Somewhere you have to make a choice. – *Mia Wallace (Uma Thurman),* Pulp Fiction

'Yeah, like one of the engines caught fire,' replied George. 'Another time, when we were flying out from Liverpool, the window next to me blew open.'

'I took off from Atlanta once,' recalled Elvis. 'The plane only had two engines and one of 'em failed. Boy, I was really scared. I thought my number was up. We had to remove sharp objects from our pockets and rest our heads on pillows between our knees. When we landed, the pilot was wringing wet with sweat even though it was snowin'.'

'Yeah, we've had some crazy experiences,' said Paul. 'One guy ran on stage, pulled the leads out of the amplifiers and said to me, "One move and you're dead!"'

'It was pretty scarin' sometimes,' said Elvis. 'I remember once in Vancouver, we'd only done a number or two when some of the fans rushed the stage. It was lucky the band and I got off in time – they tipped the whole damn rostrum over.'

'When the fans went for you,' John said, 'you were up there all alone. With us, it's four against everybody and we can draw support from each other.'

Priscilla walked into view and I saw John watch her shapely legs glide across the carpet. In a corner of the games room, the Colonel and Joe Esposito had set up a roulette table. 'Ladeez and genel'men,' the Colonel bawled in his best showman's voice, 'the casino is open for business.'

Brian Epstein hurried across the room to join them. [Neil] Aspinall and [Mal] Evans and the members of the Memphis Mafia had moved to the cocktail bar for drinks and tough-guy talk. I was poised near the fireplace between them and the guitar players on the couch. I inspected a model covered wagon, lit from the inside to illuminate the words 'ALL THE WAY WITH LBJ' on top. Priscilla walked over, smiling.

'You've made a big hit,' I told her. 'I can see John likes you.'

'That's his first mistake. Elvis is very jealous.'

'Of you or John?' I asked, only half in jest.

Luckily, she was not required to answer: Sergeant Presley's Lonesome Heartbreak Band was ready to play. In front of a privileged audience of just two dozen people, a billion dollars' worth of talent was lined up to give its one and only performance.

'What's it gonna be?' asked Elvis.

'Let's do one by the other Cilla – Cilla Black,' said Paul, leading into 'You're My World'.

'This beats talking, doesn't it?' said John. He could never resist making some obscure or barbed comment just when things were going well.

The Bel Air All-Stars proved to be pretty good, slipping easily and freely into their individual roles. Elvis's voice rose, richer, deeper and more powerful than the others', his left leg pumping up and down in time to the beat. You could feel the magic and he did it so naturally. Paul, on the piano, joined Elvis in some vocal duets, George worked in some of his neat little riffs and John, even if he were just going through the motions, didn't let the side down. I started to relax a bit and enjoy the piece of music history being enacted before me.

Simultaneously, the roulette game proceeded and Ringo shot pool surrounded by six excited children while the wives and girlfriends watched the jam session with rapt expressions. Each time there was a lull, I slipped off to the bathroom to scribble the notes the Colonel had forbidden but knew perfectly well I would make.

Elvis was getting into the spirit of the evening. 'This is what you guys gave me for my thirtieth birthday,' he said. 'It made me sick.'

He laughed as he led them on bass guitar into 'I Feel Fine'.

'Why have you dropped the old stuff? The rock?' asked John, for once with feeling. 'I loved the old Sun records.'

Elvis squirmed in his seat. This was one line of questioning he had dreaded.

'Listen, just because I'm stuck with some movie soundtracks doesn't mean I can't do rock'n'roll no more,' he said testily. 'I might just get around to cuttin' a few sides and knockin' you off the top.'

John reverted to his Clouseau accent: 'Zis is ze way it should be. . .Ze small homely gathering wiz a few friends and a leetle muzic.'

He walked over to join me near the fireplace, and it was at this moment that he saw the covered wagon. More particularly, he read the slogan 'ALL THE WAY WITH LBJ', emblazoned across it like some piece of gung-ho graffiti scrawled outside a redneck bar. John frowned. To John, LBJ was a warmonger responsible for the slaughter of innocent civilians in what he regarded as a civil war between the Vietnamese people. John's mood could change in an instant, and that is exactly what happened at Elvis Presley's party that night. He reacted a little later when he heard Elvis say: 'I'm making movies at a million bucks a time and one of 'em – I won't say which one – took only fifteen days to complete.'

'Well, we've got an hour to spare now,' said the Beatle with the shark-infested mouth. 'Let's make an epic together.'

Elvis looked stunned, but held his tongue. John had been too clever to mention Vietnam outright, knowing that this would only lead to a political argument in which he would be hopelessly outnumbered. His technique in situations like this was to make people look foolish over something they believed in. By putting Elvis down over his movies, he was, I know, also belittling the King's support for the Vietnam war.

In hindsight, I would classify that crack from John as the final insult, the one that started the feud for real. Before that, the disputed territory between Elvis and the Beatles had been about record sales in the marketplace, public acclaim at the box office and headlines in newspapers. Now it would become a highly personal conflict, which had nothing whatever to do with music but everything to do with politics: a stand-off between Elvis, the staunch American patriot, and John, the anti-war protester.

The former tank corps sergeant got up from the couch and went over to Sonny West and Alan Fortas, a former football player known as Hog Ears. Only Elvis and the Memphis Mafia dared call him that.

'Someone ought to talk to the FBI about that sonovabitch,' Elvis said angrily, almost three years' frustration finally boiling over. 'He's stoned out of his mind.'

Fortas's voice boomed across the room: '*Hey, Beatle!*'

Four mop-topped heads swivelled in unison. Assuming that the command was directed at him, John walked over and told Elvis: 'Talking about money, I've got a Rolls-Royce Phantom Five just like the one you've got parked outside.'

By now, everyone was crowding around in a circle of heaving muscles and tight shirts.

'Great party, Elvis,' I said, joining in. 'They told me not to miss the floor show.'

'Happy now? Got what you came for? Filled that little notebook of yours on all those trips to the bathroom?'

When Brian realised that John had talked his way into trouble, he came over, put a protective arm around his shoulder and led him to a quiet corner. But even as the party broke up around 2.00 am, there was a parting shot from John as we bundled each other out of the front door.

'Sanks for ze music, Elvis,' he said, adding sarcastically: 'Long live ze King!'

Still the peacemaker, the Colonel handed each Beatle a boxful of Elvis

records. Having noted that Brian was partial to liberal quantities of wine and spirits, he promised to order him a cocktail cabinet.

Not one to be outdone in giving thoughtful and extravagant presents, Brian
replied that he would ask Harrods to send the Colonel a Shetland pony to
remind him of his days in the circus. Then, to repair the damage with Elvis, he
invited the King to Beatleville in Benedict Canyon the following evening.

'Well, I'll see,' stalled Elvis. 'I don't know whether I'll be able to make it or not.'

I was in Germany flying a helicopter for the army and just starting to form a band. When I first heard the Beatles, I thought they were great. The first time I saw them perform, I thought they were the absolute pinnacle of performance success. What we admired about the Beatles was that they kept their personal and artistic integrity, and all their success didn't blow them away, like it killed Elvis. – *Kris Kristofferson*

John turned to some of the Guys who had followed us out into the Bel Air night.

'You're welcome to come *with* or *without* him,' he said pointedly.

As we walked to the car, the Colonel said to me: 'Tell the fans it was a great
meeting.'

John laughed and said: 'Tell them the truth – it was a load of rubbish.'

Elvis politely shook hands with chauffeur Alf Bicknell. 'He called me "sir",'
said an astonished Alf, who was more used to Beatle-style informality. 'Elvis
Presley called me "sir"!'

Needless to say. Elvis did not visit the Beatles and he never spoke to John
Lennon again. John, however, was soon talking about Elvis in glowing terms,
which I knew to be totally at odds with his true feelings.

'There's only one person in the United States of America that we ever wanted to meet – not that he wanted to meet us! And we met him last night,' he said.
'We can't tell you how we felt. We just idolised him so much. The only person
we wanted to meet in the USA was Elvis Presley. We can't tell you what a thrill
that was.' Privately, John later gave friends a different opinion. 'It was just like
meeting Engelbert Humperdink,' he said sourly.

Asked to comment, Paul would only say that Elvis was 'odd'. Yet, coming
from the most diplomatic Beatle, that word spoke volumes.

Elvis Meets the Beatles, Chris Hutchins and Peter Thompson, 1994

HIGH TIMES
By Mark Lewisohn

Lewisohn, author of the definitive Beatles Complete Chronicle, *is rightly considered the leading expert on the minutiae of the group's career. Here, he captures the marijuana-influenced atmosphere of the* Rubber Soul *album recording sessions.*

Rubber Soul was the transition. There it sits, between the R&B-tinged pop of *Help!* and the breathtaking kaleidoscope that was *Revolver*. All three albums were released in the space of a year, a feat of work and rate of progress awesome in any context. Mop-tops no longer, at least not in their own eyes, the Beatles had become a studio band before anyone even knew what that meant. While they may have come to despise the commercial pressures put upon them by EMI (and Brian Epstein) they flourished under them, for to flinch in the face of a challenge was simply not in the Beatles' make-up.

For easy definition, *Rubber Soul* is 'the pot album'. Dylan had turned on the Beatles in 1964, and their considerable intake throughout the filming of *Help!* earlier in 1965 is well established. The cover photo – yet another revolutionary image, naturally – shows the guys standing among rhododendron bushes; leaves of a more variegated, illegal kind would have been apposite.

Ringo has since said that the Beatles preferred not to work high, but that they took their high experiences into the studio. This album is the proof. The vision, the articulation, the knowingness – all are rooted in the weed, but the manifestation is clear-headed, economical and purposeful. The Beatles were suddenly painting from an extended palette, applying new shades and textures to new sounds. The album is a particular triumph for John Lennon. Under the influence of Dylan, dope and the first few lumps of acid-imbued Tate & Lyle, his creativity was in full flow, marked by songs of maturity, depth and intelligence – 'Norwegian Wood', 'Girl', 'In My Life', 'Nowhere Man'. Thanks to John himself, this later went down as his 'Fat Elvis' period.

Not merely a collection of fourteen songs but an entity in itself, *Rubber Soul* was a new kind of album; for lyrical wisdom and sheer *savoir-faire* it anticipates *Revolver* and is sometimes its better. Yet, ordained as they were by EMI to fill a million stockings at Christmas 1965, it is all the more remarkable to reflect that the Beatles didn't even begin its recording until the middle of October, by which point only a few of the songs were written. Weekend and late-night sessions – the latter soon became the Beatles' norm – were a necessity. The whole thing was polished off in under a month.

Such autumn almanac particulars aside, it is the songs and musical invention on *Rubber Soul* that still startle, and the album remains as good an indication as any of how the Lennon-McCartney partnership had evolved. Compared to the head-to-head collaborations of, say, 'From Me To You' and 'She Loves You', they were scarcely writing together by this point, yet each was acutely aware of and able to contribute to the other's work. In this period, the Beatles were still tending to record songs in the order they were written, a pattern that had emerged in 1963-64 when the cover versions on several albums prove how many original songs short they were. For the fuller *Rubber Soul* experience, programme the simultaneous single 'Day Tripper'/'We Can Work It Out' into the mix and follow the chronology. Now one can see that John revealed 'In My Life' to his band-mates on a Monday, they took Tuesday off, and on Wednesday Paul brought in 'We Can Work It Out'. John then goes home to Weybridge and comes in the following afternoon with 'Nowhere Man'. When John pulled 'Norwegian Wood' out of his bag, Paul's response was 'Drive My Car', witty and stylish and, in its own fashion, every bit as sardonic. Here were two young men about town, at their absolute coolest and each with a sibling competitive streak a mile wide, battling at the highest level. We were all winners.

Not, of course, that the other two Fabs were mere sidemen. Without frills but with a definite and unique style, and ideal temperament, Ringo was vital to the creative mix, and George's guitar work on *Rubber Soul* was excellent from first cut to last. This was the album when George's songwriting began to emerge. He'd forced only two numbers on to the preceding five albums, here he had two shots in one. It was always George's misfortune that his earliest songwriting efforts were held up to global scrutiny – and compared, too, to the by-now finessed pieces of John and Paul. While neither 'If I Needed Someone' or 'Think for Yourself' rivals 'In My Life' for vision or complexity, they are at home in the setting. They were also the last Harrisongs before George, with LSD in his system and new-found spiritualism in his soul, truly found himself.

Flush with the influences of America and yet still resolutely British, and so very Scouse, *Rubber Soul* drips confidence and delicious arrogance. 'In My Life', such a mature piece of songwriting, ranks as close to perfection as it is possible to achieve. 'Girl' positively aches, and yet it is also witty with its 'tit tit tit' backing vocals and sharp intakes of breath that represented either sexual heavy-breathing or the deep inhalation of a joint, or both. The harmonies throughout *Rubber Soul* are in full flow, too, especially on Ringo's vocal track, 'What Goes

On', one of the Beatles' best Rutles cover versions. As a rock and roll band whose musical influences were so much broader than their genre, the Beatles could also record a song like 'Michelle' with absolute sincerity, recognising and enhancing its beauty.

I was in college at the University of Hawaii when I first started hearing the Beatles. I remember being interested, not overwhelmed. I was overwhelmed, though, when I heard *Rubber Soul*. I was working with a kind of travelling actors' group in the summer of '66, and the stage manager blasted *Rubber Soul* day and night. It just took hold of me, unlocked something in my imagination that I had never experienced in popular music. – *Bette Midler*

In *The Complete Beatles Recording Sessions* I reproduced George Martin's scribbled running order ideas for *Beatles for Sale*. No such document for the other albums seems to have survived, and one gets the firm impression that with *Rubber Soul* the Beatles were, for the first time, much more closely involved in deciding how their music should be presented. It was another shift away from the 'good' old days of Tin Pan Alley, towards major freedom for all bands.

Mojo, February 2002

HOW DOES A BEATLE LIVE?
JOHN LENNON LIVES LIKE THIS
By Maureen Cleave

This otherwise relaxed account of life in the Lennon household gained notoriety for John's declaration that the Beatles were 'more popular than Jesus'.

It was this time three years ago that the Beatles first grew famous. Ever since then, observers have anxiously tried to gauge whether their fame was on the wax or on the wane; they foretold the fall of the old Beatles, they searched diligently for the new Beatles (which was as pointless as looking for the new Big Ben).

At last they have given up; the Beatles' fame is beyond question. It has nothing to do with whether they are rude or polite, married or unmarried, 25 or 45; whether they appear on *Top of the Pops* or do not appear on *Top of the Pops*. They are well above any position even a Rolling Stone might jostle for. They are famous in the way the Queen is famous. When John Lennon's Rolls-Royce, with its black wheels and its black windows, goes past, people say: 'It's the Queen,' or 'It's the Beatles.' With her they share the security of a stable life at the top. They all tick over in the public esteem – she in Buckingham Palace, they in the Weybridge-Esher area. Only Paul remains in London.

The Weybridge community consists of the three married Beatles; they live there among the wooded hills and the stockbrokers. They have not worked since Christmas and their existence is secluded and curiously timeless. 'What day is it?' John Lennon asks with interest when you ring up with news from outside. The fans are still at the gates but the Beatles see only each other. They are better friends than ever before.

Ringo and his wife, Maureen, may drop in on John and Cyn; John may drop in on Ringo; George and Pattie may drop in on John and Cyn and they might all go round to Ringo's, by car of course. Outdoors is for holidays.

They watch films, they play rowdy games of Buccaneer; they watch television till it goes off, often playing records at the same time. They while away the small hours of the morning making mad tapes. Bedtimes and mealtimes have no meaning as such. 'We've never had time before to do anything but just be Beatles,' John Lennon said.

He is much the same as he was before. He still peers down his nose, arrogant as an eagle, although contact lenses have righted the short sight that originally caused the expression. He looks more like Henry VIII than ever now that his face has filled out he is just as imperious, just as unpredictable, indolent, disorganised, childish, vague, charming and quick-witted. He is still easy-going, still tough as hell. 'You never asked after Fred Lennon,' he said, disappointed. (Fred is his father; he emerged after they got famous.) 'He was here a few weeks ago. It was only the second time in my life I'd seen him – I showed him the door.' He went on cheerfully: 'I wasn't having *him* in the house.'

I was passionate about *Alice in Wonderland* and drew all the characters. I did poems in the style of 'Jabberwocky'. I used to love Alice . . . – *John Lennon*

His enthusiasm is undiminished and he insists on its being shared. George has put him on to this Indian music. 'You're not listening, are you?' he shouts after twenty minutes of the record. 'It's amazing this – so cool. Don't the Indians appear cool to you? Are you listening? This music is thousands of years old; it makes me laugh, the British going over there and telling them what to do. Quite amazing.' And he switched on the television set.

Experience has sown few seeds of doubt in him: not that his mind is closed, but it's closed round whatever he believes at the time. 'Christianity will go,' he said. 'It will vanish and shrink. I needn't argue about that; I'm right and I will be proved right. We're more popular than Jesus now; I don't know which will go first – rock'n'roll or Christianity. Jesus was all right but his disciples were thick and ordinary. It's them twisting it that ruins it for me.' He is reading extensively about religion.

He shops in lightning swoops on Asprey's these days and there is some fine wine in his cellar, but he is still quite unselfconscious. He is far too lazy to keep up appearances, even if he had worked out what the appearances should be – which he has not.

He is now 25. He lives in a large, heavily panelled, heavily carpeted, mock Tudor house set on a hill with his wife Cynthia and his son Julian. There is a cat called after his aunt Mimi, and a purple dining room. Julian is three; he may be sent to the Lycee in London. 'Seems the only place for him in his position,' said his father, surveying him dispassionately. 'I feel sorry for him, though. I couldn't stand ugly people even when I was five. Lots of the ugly ones are foreign, aren't they?'

We did a speedy tour of the house, Julian panting along behind, clutching a large porcelain Siamese cat. John swept past the objects in which he had lost interest: 'That's Sidney' (a suit of armour); 'That's a hobby I had for a week' (a room full of model racing cars); 'Cyn won't let me get rid of that' (a fruit machine). In the sitting room are eight little green boxes with winking red lights; he bought them as Christmas presents but never got round to giving them away. They wink for a year; one imagines him sitting there till next Christmas, surrounded by the little winking boxes.

He paused over objects he still fancies; a huge altar crucifix of a Roman Catholic nature with IHS on it; a pair of crutches, a present from George; an enormous Bible he bought in Chester; his gorilla suit.

'I thought I might need a gorilla suit,' he said; he seemed sad about it. 'I've only worn it twice. I thought I might pop it on in the summer and drive round in the Ferrari. We were all going to get them and drive round in them but I was the only one who did. I've been thinking about it and if I didn't wear the head it would make an amazing fur coat – with legs, you see. I would like a fur coat but I've never run into any.'

One feels that his possessions – to which he adds daily – have got the upper hand; all the tape recorders, the five television sets, the cars, the telephones of which he knows not a single number. The moment he approaches a switch it fuses; six of the winking boxes, guaranteed to last till next Christmas, have gone funny already. His cars – the Rolls, the Mini-Cooper (black wheels, black windows), the Ferrari (being painted black) – puzzle him. Then there's the swimming pool, the trees sloping away beneath it. 'Nothing like what I ordered,' he said resignedly. He wanted the bottom to be a mirror. 'It's an amazing household,' he said. 'None of my gadgets really work except the gorilla suit – that's the only suit that fits me.'

He is very keen on books, will always ask what is good to read. He buys quantities of books and these are kept tidily in a special room. He has Swift, Tennyson, Huxley, Orwell, costly leather-bound editions of Tolstoy, Oscar Wilde. Then there's *Little Women*, all the William books from his childhood, and some unexpected volumes such as *41 Years in India*, by Field Marshal Lord Roberts, and *Curiosities of Natural History*, by Francis T. Buckland. This last – with its chapter headings 'Earless Cats', 'Wooden-Legged People', 'The Immortal Harvey's Mother' – is right up his street.

He approaches reading with a lively interest untempered by too much formal education. 'I've read millions of books,' he said, 'that's why I seem to know things.' He is obsessed by Celts. 'I have decided I am a Celt,' he said. 'I am on

Boadicea's side – all those bloody blue-eyed blondes chopping people up. I have an awful feeling wishing I was there – not there with scabs and sores but there through *reading* about it. The books don't give you more than a paragraph about how they *lived*; I have to imagine that.'

He can sleep almost indefinitely, is probably the laziest person in England. '*Physically* lazy,' he said. 'I don't mind writing or reading or watching or speaking, but sex is the only physical thing I can be bothered with any more.' Occasionally he is driven to London in the Rolls by an ex-Welsh guardsman called Anthony; Anthony has a moustache that intrigues him.

The day I visited him he had been invited to lunch in London, about which he was rather excited. 'Do you know how long lunch lasts?' he asked. 'I've never been to lunch before. I went to a Lyons the other day and had egg and chips and a cup of tea. The waiters kept looking and saying: "No, it *isn't* him, it *can't* be him."'

He settled himself into the car and demonstrated the television, the folding bed, the refrigerator, the writing desk, the telephone. He has spent many fruitless hours on that telephone. 'I only once got through to a person,' he said, 'and they were out.'

Anthony had spent the weekend in Wales. John asked if they'd kept a welcome for him in the hillside and Anthony said they had. They discussed the possibility of an extension for the telephone. We had to call at the doctor's because John had a bit of sea urchin in his toe. 'Don't want to be like Dorothy Dandridge,' he said, 'dying of a splinter 50 years later.' He added reassuringly that he had washed the foot in question.

We bowled along in a costly fashion through the countryside. 'Famous and loaded' is how he describes himself now. 'They keep telling me I'm all right for money but then I think I may have spent it all by the time I'm 40 so I keep going. That's why I started selling my cars; then I changed my mind and got them all back and a new one too.

'I want the money just to *be* rich. The only other way of getting it is to be born rich. If you have money, that's power without having to be powerful. I often think that it's all a big conspiracy, that the winners are the Government and people like us who've got the money. That joke about keeping the workers ignorant is still true; that's what they said about the Tories and the landowners and that; then Labour were meant to educate the workers but they don't seem to be doing that any more.'

He has a morbid horror of stupid people: 'Famous and loaded as I am, I still have to meet soft people. It often comes into my mind that I'm not really rich. There are *really* rich people but I don't know where they are.'

He finds being famous quite easy, confirming one's suspicion that the Beatles had been leading up to this all their lives. 'Everybody thinks they *would* have been famous if only they'd had the Latin and that. So when it happens it comes naturally. You remember your old grannie saying soft things like: "You'll make it with that voice."' Not, he added, that he had any old grannies.

He got to the doctor two-and-three-quarter hours early and to lunch on time but in the wrong place. He bought a giant compendium of games from Asprey's but having opened it he could not, of course, shut it again. He wondered what else he should buy. He went to Brian Epstein's office. 'Any presents?' he asked eagerly; he observed that there was nothing like getting things free. He tried on the attractive Miss Hanson's spectacles.

The rumour came through that a Beatle had been sighted walking down Oxford Street! He brightened. 'One of the others must be out,' he said, as though speaking of an escaped bear. 'We only let them out one at a time,' said the attractive Miss Hanson firmly.

He said that to live and have a laugh were the things to do; but was that enough for the restless spirit?

'Weybridge,' he said, 'won't do at all. I'm just stopping at it, like a bus stop. Bankers and stockbrokers live there; they can add figures and Weybridge is what they live in and they think it's the end, they really do. I think of it every day – me in my Hansel and Gretel house. I'll take my time; I'll get my *real* house when I know what I want.

'You see, there's something else I'm going to do, something I must do – only I don't know what it is. That's why I go round painting and taping and drawing and writing and that, because it may be one of them. All I know is, this isn't *it* for me.'

Anthony got him and the compendium into the car and drove him home with the television flickering in the soothing darkness while the Londoners outside rushed home from work.

Evening Standard, 4 March 1966

FIRST STEPS TOWARD RADICAL POLITICS: THE 1966 TOUR

By Jon Wiener

Wiener's posthumous biography of John, Come Together, *was described as 'A sympathetic documentary history of Lennon's political thinking' by Stephen Holden in the* New York Times Book Review. *His review continued, 'During the counterculture's flowering, rock music had real clout in the American political arena. Certainly some government officials thought so, or they wouldn't have initiated deportation proceedings after Lennon aligned himself with the activist Left.'*

When the Beatles arrived in Memphis on their 1966 summer tour, they discovered that a massive Christian rally, organised by a hundred fundamentalist ministers, had been scheduled to protest their appearance. The problem was John. He had recently said the Beatles were 'more popular than Jesus'. The English, in their matter-of-fact way, had concluded he was correct. But in the God-fearing United States, the religious right accused him of 'blasphemy' and took after him like a pack of wolves while the media watched and chuckled. The 'more popular than Jesus' controversy pushed John to take his first steps away from the Beatles and toward the antiwar activism that would become central to his life and work.

The leader of the Memphis ministers had a name that could have come out of a B movie: the Reverend Jimmy Stroad. He issued a grim challenge, declaring that the Christian rally would 'give the youth of the mid-South an opportunity to show Jesus Christ is more popular than the Beatles'. And he offered as competition against the Beatles not only Jesus but also Jay North, the child actor who had played Dennis the Menace on TV.

Until John's 'Jesus' comment the Beatles had been the good boys of rock, in contrast to the nasty and sexually aggressive Rolling Stones. Parents considered the Beatles playful and harmless. Ed Sullivan liked them. But America's fundamentalist ministers saw them in a completely different light. 'What have the Beatles said or done to so ingratiate themselves with those who eat, drink and think revolution?' asked David Noebel, author of a series of anti-Beatle tracts beginning in 1965. 'The major value of the Beatles to the left in general. . .has been their usefulness in destroying youth's faith in God.' He carefully combed through all of John's work and came up with strong evidence that the 'Jesus' remark was part of a larger and more sinister pattern. In John's book *A Spaniard in the Works* he had written about 'Father, Sock and Mickey Most'. (Mickey Most produced records by Herman's Hermits.) That phrase, Noebel felt, did a lot to destroy youth's faith in God and his only begotten sock.

In Memphis the city commission agreed with the fundamentalists. An official statement declared, 'The Beatles are not welcome in Memphis.' Memphis, where Elvis Presley had recorded his first songs, awakening John Lennon from his teenage torpor; Memphis, the subject of a Chuck Berry classic the Beatles had played over and over in their early days; Memphis, where Jerry Lee Lewis had sung about the shaking that was going on; Memphis, a centre of black music, where that very summer of 1966 Carla Thomas recorded the rocking 'Let Me Be Good to You' and Sam and Dave recorded the stirring 'Hold On, I'm Comin'' – how could the Beatles not be welcome in Memphis?

The day after the city fathers issued their statement, Beatles manager Brian Epstein revealed his strategy: apologise for everything. He released a telegram to the press declaring that he 'wished to assure the people of Memphis and the mid-South that the Beatles will not, by word, action or otherwise, in any way offend or ridicule the religious beliefs of anyone throughout their forthcoming concert tour. . .Furthermore, John Lennon deeply and sincerely regrets any offence that he might have caused.'

The week before the concert, the local newspaper was filled with debate, including statements from several ministers attacking the fundamentalist counter-rally. The rector of Holy Trinity Episcopal Church wrote, 'I do not care for the Beatles. I would not go to their concert. I do not even think that the noise which they produce falls in the category of what we call music. Nevertheless, the truth of John Lennon's statement cannot be denied.'

A Methodist pastor quoted part of John's statement and declared that it contained a correct description of the anti-Beatle ministers in Memphis: 'Jesus was all right but his disciples are thick and ordinary. It's them twisting it that ruins it for me.' A Memphis youth attending Louisiana State University wrote that the city fathers should 'for once in their lives overcome the idea that everything that enters Memphis not carrying a cross is evil. . .Is your religion so weak that four rock-and-roll players can shake it?'

The Beatles and their entourage had been frightened as the Memphis date approached. When they left London, fans had screamed, 'John, please don't go; they'll kill you!' John had the same fear. Later he explained, 'I didn't want to tour because I thought they'd kill me – 'cause they take things so seriously there.

They shoot you, and then they realise it wasn't that important. So I didn't want to go. But Brian, and Paul, and the other Beatles persuaded me to come. I was scared stiff.' He wasn't the only one. Paul McCartney had 'a horror of being shot on stage', according to Peter Brown, the Beatles' personal assistant. As the Beatles got off their plane in Memphis, Paul remarked ironically, 'We should be wearing targets here.' Because of the fear of a sniper in the audience, police at the concert were asked to 'keep a lookout for firearms'.

The Beatles opened up a Pandora's box when they hit the United States with their druid/rock beat in the 1960's . . . The flood gates to witchcraft were opened by this pop group from Liverpool in England, and the United States – indeed the WHOLE WORLD – will NEVER RECOVER. – *New Covenant Church of God*

Subsequent accounts of what actually happened at the Beatles concert and the counter-rally were confused. A best-selling history of the Beatles reported that while the Beatles were getting ready to go onstage, 'outside the Ku Klux Klan were holding an 8,000-strong counter demonstration'. In fact, the number of demonstrators outside the concert hall was closer to eight than 8,000, but they were indeed Klansmen, wearing full white-sheet regalia. That never happened to Mick Jagger, despite his efforts to be outrageous. It was an honour of sorts for John to be the only white rock-and-roller to provoke a Klan picket line.

In the middle of their performance a sound like a gunshot rang out. A wave of fear crossed the Beatles' faces. 'Every one of us looked at each other,' John later explained, ''cause each thought it was the other that had been shot. It was that bad. I don't know how I did it.' Each quickly saw the others were okay, and they continued playing without missing a beat. Later they learned that what they had heard was only a cherry bomb.

While 20,000 heard the Beatles, only 8,000 showed up across town for the counter-rally, half of whom were adults. They didn't really count in the battle for the hearts of the mid-South's youth. Reverend Stroad implicitly conceded that Christ did not seem to be as popular as the Beatles, even in Memphis. He issued a new statement: the rally had 'shown the whole world that Christianity will not vanish', so at least John had been disproven on that point.

Poor attendance was not the counter-rally's only problem. Dennis the Menace did not appear. Some of the fundamentalists objected to the program, and a group of 30 walked out of the rally in protest. Their spokesman declared that young people had been 'decoyed' by promises of a 'Christian testimonial service', but instead they had been given music inspired by Satan. They objected in particular to a vocal group that sang Christian songs 'to a modified "twist" while an accompanying combo maintained a throbbing beat,' the newspaper reported. It quoted the protesters: 'We might as well have gone to the Beatles.'

From the beginning of rock and roll, fundamentalist churches and white racists had organised against it. In 1956 the *New York Times* had reported that Southern white church groups were attempting to suppress 'Negro style' rock music because it corrupted white youth. The Alabama White Citizens Council, which had been organised to combat the civil rights movement, also took a stand on rock and roll, calling it 'a means of pulling the white man down to the level of the Negro. It is part of a plot to undermine the morals of the youth of our nation.' Members of the White Citizens Council attacked and beat Nat 'King' Cole during a concert in Birmingham in 1956. Ten years later John's 'Jesus' remark brought the same social forces back into the limelight.

Memphis was not the first American city to witness right-wing protests against Lennon's remark. The first demonstrations had been organized in Birmingham, the city which in 1966 symbolised the violent repression of civil rights. Three years earlier the Birmingham police had attacked civil rights demonstrators with high-pressure fire hoses and arrested 2,543 of them in a single week. Later the same year a black church in Birmingham was bombed, killing four girls. Now, at the end of July 1966, two weeks before the Beatles were to begin their fourth American tour, Birmingham was back in the news, as a local disc jockey named Tommy Charles organised a rally at which 'protesters' tossed their Beatles albums into a giant tree-grinding machine, turning them into dust. Mr Charles told visiting reporters that he was 36 years old 'but I think like a teenager.'

Within a few days, 30 other radio stations announced that they were banning Beatles records. Most were in the South, but stations in Boston and New York joined the ban. They included the one that had first promoted Beatlemania, calling itself 'W-A-Beatle-C'. Newspapers across the country published striking photos of kids in crew cuts grinning at Beatles record-burnings. The TV news showed a girl gleefully ripping the pages out of John's book *In His Own Write* and tossing them into the flames. The Grand Dragon of the South Carolina Ku Klux Klan held a ceremony in which he attached a Beatles record to a large wooden cross and set the cross on fire. The symbolism of the Beatles' music on the cross apparently escaped his notice.

The most striking event took place in Longview, Texas, where a record-burning was held on Friday the thirteenth of August, organised by radio station KLUE. The next day its transmitter was hit by lightning, knocking its news director unconscious and blasting the station off the air. The anti-Beatle organisers failed to draw the obvious conclusion.

The American demonstrations gained international support as the right-wing governments of Franco Spain and South Africa banned all Beatles music. South Africa lifted its ban on the Beatles when the group split in 1970, but continued to prohibit the broadcast of John's records. The Vatican's official newspaper *L'Osservatore Romano* announced that 'some subjects must not be dealt with profanely, not even in the world of beatniks.' Beatniks?

John's 'Jesus' remark had been at the top of the agenda at the first press conference when the Beatles began their tour on August 12 in Chicago. That city had just been the site of organised attacks on black people. The previous month Martin Luther King, Jr., had led a demonstration of 40,000 people in Chicago, seeking to end discrimination in jobs and housing there. The campaign was his first attempt to confront institutional racism in the North. A week before the Beatles arrived in the city, a mob of 4,000 whites, led by members of the American Nazi Party and the Ku Klux Klan, attacked and beat 700 black marchers, including King. He stated afterward, 'I have seen many demonstrations in the South, but I have never seen anything so hostile and so hateful as I've seen here today.'

For the media, however, the big news in Chicago on August 12 was not racist violence, but rather John's apology to Christians: 'If I said television was more popular than Jesus, I might have gotten away with it – I just said what I said and it was wrong, or it was taken wrong, and now there's all this.'

The reporters were unsatisfied. The next question was, 'But are you prepared to apologise?'

John tried again. 'I'm not anti-God, anti-Christ or anti-religion. I am not saying we are greater or better. I believe in God, but not as one thing, not as an old man in the sky. I believe that what people call God is something in all of us. I believe that what Jesus and Mohammed and Buddha and all the rest said was right. It's just that the translations have gone wrong. I wasn't saying that Beatles are better than God or Jesus. I used "Beatles" because it's easy for me to talk about Beatles.'

Reporters continued to press him: 'Are you sorry about your statement concerning Christ?'

'I wasn't saying whatever they're saying I was saying. . .I'm sorry I said it, really. I never meant it to be a lousy anti-religious thing. . .I apologise, if that will make you happy. I still don't know quite what I've done. I've tried to tell you what I did do, but if you want me to apologise, if that will make you happy, then okay, I'm sorry.'

'Would you say you are being crucified?'

I was on the Tuskegee University [Alabama] campus, where I grew up. This is an all-black community and everyone was at home watching the Beatles on *Ed Sullivan.* **There had been such a build-up – 'The Beatles are coming, the Beatles are coming.' Before that, I had only been listening to Motown and Stax. I was thinking, 'This is a phenomenon.' They changed so many things, they really led us. –** *Lionel Richie*

Although the Jesus remark captured the public's attention that summer, the Beatles involved themselves in another political controversy that would become much more important for John: the war in Vietnam. Two months before the 'Jesus' controversy, American disc jockeys had received the new Beatles album, *Yesterday. . .and Today.* Its cover showed the Beatles surrounded by slabs of raw, red meat and decapitated dolls. *Time* announced that the cover was 'a serious lapse in taste', and frightened Capitol Records executives issued an apology for what they called an 'attempt at pop satire'.

John, asked to explain, told reporters the butcher cover was 'as relevant as Vietnam'. He intended to be neither witty nor irreverent. He spoke seriously. The Beatles may not have intended the butcher cover to be a comment on American butchery in Vietnam, but once it was suppressed, John cast it in that light. His statement showed for the first time that John perceived the 'relevance' of Vietnam – that the war was on his mind.

During the Beatles' American tour that summer of 1966, the Johnson administration escalated its war. In June the United States bombed Hanoi for the first time and announced a policy of systematic bombing of North Vietnam. The anti-war movement was growing. The previous year, Students for a Democratic Society had sponsored the first march on Washington protesting the war, and 25,000 people came. Shortly afterward students at Berkeley held a 36 hour teach-in against the war, and 12,000 came to listen. In 1966, anti-war activity was spreading to campuses not usually considered centres of radicalism. When Johnson went to Princeton that spring to defend his Vietnam escalation, he was met with a large demonstration. LBJ questioned the manhood of opponents of the war: he called them 'nervous Nellies'.

John followed the news closely. Maureen Cleave wrote during that summer that he 'recalls all the daily newspapers. . .He watches all TV news coverage.' The air war filled the front pages. As the Beatles left Memphis, the local newspaper reported, 'Reds gun down US' hottest pilot as Communist gunners score their heaviest toll of the war in bringing down US planes. US warplanes struck back, smashing North Vietnam with a record 139 bombing missions. US fliers streaking from Guam bagged their eighteenth MiG and hammered Communist targets in the South.'

When the Beatles held their ritual New York press conference later in the same week, the first questioner asked them to comment on any aspect of the Vietnam conflict. They answered in unison, 'We don't like war, war is wrong,' several times in a row. John later gave his own brief and trenchant answer to the question, what did they think about the war? 'We think of it every day. We don't like it. We don't agree with it. We think it's wrong.'

It was a bold and risky move, which Brian Epstein had urged them to avoid. John was aligning himself with anti-war students. He knew that only ten percent of the public agreed with them at this time, according to opinion polls. And it was unprecedented for a leading rock group to take a political stand of any kind. That was only for Bob Dylan and Phil Ochs. John's 1966 statement deserves scrutiny. British historian Eric Hobsbawm commented, 'Most British people at the time would have said they thought the war in Vietnam was wrong, but very few would have said, "We think about it every day." That's remarkable.'

The contrast with their earlier New York press conferences was striking: no more playful banter, no more smiling faces. The Fab Four looked 'tired and pale', the *New York Times* reported. They were becoming part of the growing political conflict in America. On August 24, the same day the Beatles played their second Shea Stadium concert, newspapers reported that the House Un-American Activities Committee (HUAC) had proposed legislation to set criminal penalties for 'obstruction of the Vietnam war effort'. HUAC had investigated a Berkeley plan, led by Jerry Rubin, among others, to send medical supplies to North Vietnam and block troop trains.

That same day Stokely Carmichael announced a new political strategy for the Student Nonviolent Coordinating Committee, 'Black Power'. 'We must form our own institutions, credit unions, co-ops, political parties, write our own histories,' he declared, calling on white radicals in SNCC to leave the organisation and instead work among whites to fight racism. Newspapers that day also reported that Mao's 'Red Guards for the cultural revolution' held their first major demonstration in Peking.

The anti-war movement, Black Power, Maoism – each of these would become increasingly important in John's life and music over the next few years, first when he denounced radicals 'carrying pictures of Chairman Mao' in his 1968 song 'Revolution' and then when he returned to New York in 1971 wearing a Mao badge, joining Jerry Rubin and sharing the stage with Black Power spokesmen.

John expected the mass media to trumpet the news that the Beatles had joined the anti-war camp. Everything about the Beatles sold newspapers. In fact, Epstein shouldn't have worried. The anti-war statement was published only in local New York newspapers, and even they did not feature it. The *Daily News* devoted six pages to Beatles coverage but only one sentence to the anti-war declaration. *Time* and *Newsweek* ran long stories on the Beatles' tour, focusing on the storm over John's 'Jesus' remark and ignoring the anti-war statement completely. John was portrayed as an arrogant egomaniac who had finally been slapped down by an outraged public. 'Lennon forgiven,' *Newsweek* chuckled, failing to see a crucial event in his life: his first step out of the role of the 'lad from Liverpool' toward radical politics. In the future, John would make sure that his political statements could not be ignored.

Come Together: John Lennon in His Time, Jon Wiener, 1984

REVOLT INTO STYLE
By George Melly

When jazz singer/arts critic Melly's book was published in 1970, it was regarded as a knowing overview of popular culture in the 1960s – from the perspective of a sympathetic member of the older generation.

. . .The Beatles had escaped; they'd broken the pattern.

They had neither gone down with the Liverpool ship nor taken to the show-biz life-boat. They'd become part of 'Swinging London', a catch at trendy parties, defending themselves through irony from such hazards as the Royal Command Performance and the courting of politicians. Their nerve and timing kept them out of trouble.

In 1965 they were awarded MBEs, a reward based partially on the amount they'd earned in dollars, partially on the Labour Party's mistaken belief that to flatter the Beatles was to win over a future electorate. Not that Wilson was alone in this misunderstanding; the Tories too made pro–Beatle noises and aroused the justified if ill-directed scorn of Paul Johnson in the *New Statesman* for doing so; yet it was the Socialists who really made asses of themselves. Wilson himself went so far as to travel up to Liverpool to be present at the opening of a rebuilt and tarted-up Cavern, failing to recognise that, not only was the Cavern scene over but that it was *because* it was scruffy, smelly and disreputable that it had loomed large in young Liverpool's legend.

As for the MBEs, the only result was to infuriate those to whom the right to put letters after their name and shake hands with the Queen meant something.

The Beatles now claim to have accepted their MBEs only to annoy such people but, even if they believe it themselves, I take it with a pinch of salt. Up until 1966 they were still touring, still a group and, whatever the Beatles themselves may have felt about those bits of ribbon, I'm convinced that Epstein, in many ways a very conventional man, thought of them as an honour and a confirmation.

Musically, too, things developed logically. 'Can't Buy Me Love' marked in my view the end of their early period. Issued as a single in March 1964 it was also part of the score of *A Hard Day's Night,* that watershed which marked their defection to London.

Inevitably they lost their naïvety. Throughout 1965 I found their single

172

releases less and less interesting while at the same time more contrived, more knowing. Influenced perhaps by the success of their new rivals, the Rolling Stones, they sacrificed audibility in favour of volume and a rather synthetic excitement. For me, 'Paperback Writer' was a poor thing, a falling off.

The Beatles were kind of silly. We were very unimpressed with the Beatles. I mean, we were more impressed with the Rolling Stones because they came out of the tradition of jazz. And that was the kind of music I liked. The Beatles, certainly when they first came along, were very square. They looked silly with their little haircuts and little double-breasted suits . . . they were like the Monkees. I mean, the Monkees were as ridiculous as the Beatles. – *David Bailey*

At the same time, and somewhat confusingly, their LPs were becoming more rather than less convincing. Up until then, the British pop LP had been of little interest, a string of single hits with a few 'standards' added for good measure. The Beatles set about altering that. They not only composed and performed more experimental pieces on their long-playing records but also, whether consciously or not, they gave the impression of working towards the creation of an internal unity or at any rate a musical and emotional balance. They had gradually dropped their early habit of performing other people's songs. *Rubber Soul*, issued at the end of 1965, was entirely Beatle music, mostly Lennon and McCartney with two tracks by Harrison. While 'the happy little rockers' were perhaps losing their grip on their single releases, the Beatles, as mature and conscious artists, were maturing on LP.

This split between what was considered commercial and experimental material was in fact unnecessary. McCartney's over-sweet 'Michelle', for instance, was put out as singles by several other artists and went zooming up the charts. Yet admirable as most of the material on *Rubber Soul* was, it was no breakthrough. The impression I got from this LP was that Lennon and McCartney were gradually moving into that exclusive class: the aristocracy of popular song, and that they would have to be rated, as both composers and lyricists, alongside Cole Porter or Gershwin. In confirmation of this their music was everywhere. It tempted the quality jazz singers and not, you felt, simply on commercial grounds. And it wasn't only jazz singers; they changed the guard to oompa'd versions of 'A Hard Day's Night'; others arranged Beatle compositions in imitation of Bach.

173

Yet it was also a fact that, despite a limited technique and no particular vocal brilliance, Beatle songs sounded better performed by Beatles.

My personal feeling that they were tending to underestimate the singles market was confirmed in August 1966 when two tracks from their new and brilliantly original LP, *Revolver,* were issued as a 45 release. Not only did it make Number One, but one side at least broke right through the conventions of the very best traditions of popular song, let alone pop. It was with a sense of delighted awe that that summer in Wales I heard, for the first time, 'Eleanor Rigby'. It seemed to me that pop had come of age.

Revolt into Style, George Melly, 1970

ELEANOR RIGBY
By Steve Turner

Author and poet Turner has written one of the best 'stories behind the songs' books about the Beatles' music, A Hard Day's Write.

As in many of his songs, the melody and the first line of 'Eleanor Rigby' came to Paul as he sat playing his piano. Initially though, the fictional church cleaner featured in the song was to be called Miss Daisy Hawkins not Eleanor Rigby.

Paul started by imagining Daisy as a young girl, but soon realised that anyone who cleaned churches after weddings was likely to be older. If she was older, he considered that she might not only have missed the wedding she was having to clear up after, she might also have missed her own. Maybe she was an ageing spinster whose loneliness was made worse by her job and having to clear away the debris left behind by family celebrations. 'I couldn't think of any more so I put it away,' he remarked.

Paul toyed with the song for a while but wasn't comfortable with the name of Miss Daisy Hawkins. He thought it didn't sound 'real' enough. Sixties folksinger Donovan remembered Paul playing him a version of the song where the protagonist was called Ola Na Tungee. 'The words hadn't yet come out right for him,' says Donovan.

Paul has always thought that he came up with the name Eleanor because of having worked with Eleanor Bron in Help!. Songwriter Lionel Bart, however, is convinced he took it from a gravestone in a cemetery close to Wimbledon Common, where they were both walking one day. 'The name on the gravestone was Eleanor Bygraves,' says Bart, 'and Paul thought that would fit his song. He came back to my office and began playing it on my clavichord.'

Paul came across the name Rigby in January 1966, while in Bristol visiting Jane Asher, who was playing the role of Barbara Cahoun in John Dighton's *The Happest Days of Your Life*. The Theatre Royal, home of the Bristol Old Vic, is at 35 King Street and, as Paul was waiting for Jane to finish, he strolled past Rigby & Evens Ltd, Wine & Spirit Shippers, which was then on the opposite side of the road at number 22. This gave him the surname he was looking for.

The song was finally completed at Kenwood when John, George, Ringo and Pete Shotton crowded into the music room where Paul played it through. They all contributed ideas to move the story along. Someone suggested introducing an old man rifling through garbage cans whom Eleanor Rigby could have a romance with, but it was decided that would complicate the story. Paul had already introduced a character called Father McCartney. Ringo suggested that he could be darning his socks, an idea which Paul liked. George came up with a line about 'lonely people'. Pete Shotton suggested that it be changed from Father McCartney because people would think it was a reference to Paul's dad. A flick through the phone directory produced McKenzie as an alternative.

. . . I began reading all the lyrics of Beatles' songs and finding, or imagining, all kinds of hidden meanings. One phrase in particular staggered me: 'keeping her face in a jar by the door,' from 'Eleanor Rigby'. This seemed to me pure surrealism. – *Alan Aldridge,* **The Beatles Illustrated Lyrics**

Paul was then stuck for an ending and it was Shotton who suggested that he bring the two lonely people together in a final verse as Father McKenzie takes Eleanor Rigby's funeral and stands by her graveside. At the time, the idea was dismissed by John who thought that Shotton had missed the point but Paul, who didn't say anything at the time, used the scene to finish off the song, and later acknowledged the help he'd received.

Extraordinarily, sometime in the Eighties the grave of an Eleanor Rigby was discovered in the graveyard of St Peter's Parish Church in Woolton, Liverpool, within yards of the spot where John and Paul had met in 1957. It's clear that Paul didn't get his idea directly from this grave but is it possible that he saw it as a teenager and that the pleasing sound of the name lay buried in his subconscious until called up by the song? At the time he said: 'I was looking for a name that was natural. Eleanor Rigby sounded natural.'

In a further coincidence, the firm of Rigby and Evens Ltd, whose sign had inspired Paul in Bristol in 1966, was owned by a Liverpudlian, Frank Rigby, who established his company in Dale Street, Liverpool in the nineteenth century.

A Hard Day's Write, Steve Turner, 1994

BOMB CULTURE
By Jeff Nuttall

Bomb Culture is a similar overview of the 1960s to Melly's Revolt into Style, *but from a countercultural perspective. Nuttall's point of comparison for the Beatles is the work of Brian Patten — regarded as the most mature of the 'Liverpool Poets', who emerged during that decade.*

The Beatles were and are the biggest single catalyst in this whole acceleration in the development of the sub-culture. They robbed the pop world of its violence, its ignorant self-consciousness, its inferiority complex. They robbed the protest world of its terrible self-righteous drabness, they robbed the art world of its cod-seriousness. They reflected the scene from which they came, where all this fusion of art, protest and pop had happened previously, in microcosm, for the world to follow; so that Allen Ginsberg, visiting Liverpool a year after the Beatles left, was moved to pronounce it 'the centre of consciousness of the human universe', a statement more perceptive than extravagant. In Liverpool, however, the peaked caps, mini-skirts, long haircuts, drugs, happenings, collages, poetry readings and pop clubs generated a significantly different atmosphere from that of the London Scene. Liverpool is a roaring, seedy, working-class port. It has something of the old red-nose Lancashire comedian about it. It has the crumbling grandeur of the nonconformist north. It has the whimsicality and drunken recklessness of an Irish docker. It lacks completely the 'Swinging London' feeling, the Kings Road, debby, two-seater, sports model element. There's nothing toffee-nosed about Liverpool. Marcel Duchamp once said that his life had been devoted to removing the preciosity of art. Liverpool was the place where his idea paid off. Already it had produced Billy Fury and Clinton Ford. It went on to produce Cilla Black and Gerry and the Pacemakers besides the Beatles. Freddy and the Dreamers, a scatty surrealist group, came from nearby Manchester. The so-called Mersey beat was a Lancashire version of the heavily negroid Tamla Motown sound. The Liverpool Poets, Adrian Henri, Roger McGough, Brian Patten, Mike Evans, Tonk, and their many local followers, formed a style for public reading with pop groups which, like the work of Milligan and the Alberts, constituted a sort of gentle music-hall surrealism. The music/satire group, the Scaffold, thrived on a local audience. John Lennon of the Beatles wrote in a far more savage mood with pungent sick overtones and illustrated his work with sophisticated little drawings. As the Beatles went their own way more and more, their lyrics more and more reflected the Liverpool spirit – 'Yellow Submarine' is a perfect example. On the same album, *Revolver*, the Beatles introduced influences of Indian music, electronic music, chamber music and brass band music, a collage technique which is borrowed completely from Liverpool pop art and happenings. 'She's Leaving Home' and 'Eleanor Rigby' both have a strong Patten influence. Brian Patten, the outstanding poet of the whole group, has moved on to a far more individual style. Nevertheless the religious nature of his recent work, derived from meditation and LSD, follows a curiously similar pattern to that of the Beatles' public image.

Bomb Culture, Jeff Nuttall, 1968

PORTRAIT OF THE ARTIST AS A ROCK & ROLL STAR

By Robert Christgau and John Piccarella

Despite the consensus that 1967's Sgt. Pepper *represents the high point of the Beatles' creativity,* Revolver, *which preceded it in 1966, is the more radical progression. The vivid imagery of 'Eleanor Rigby', George's embracing of Indian music, innovations in electronic sound, and the ultimate 1960s children's song ('Yellow Submarine'), all served as catalysts in the Beatles' transition from a 'live' to a 'studio' band.*

And then, nine months after *Rubber Soul*, came *Revolver*, and psychedelia was in flower. Even in the US, where its impact was dulled somewhat by the inclusion of three of John's *Revolver* songs on *The Beatles – 'Yesterday' and Today* two months before, it seemed, well, revolutionary at the time. With its string octet and French-horn solo and soul brass, its electronics and tabla-and-sitar, its kiddie sound effects and savage guitar breaks, its backward tapes and backward rhythms, its air of untrammeled eclecticism, mystic wandering and arty civility, this was really where the Beatles stopped being a bar band. More than any specific song, what's most remarkable about John's presence is his vocals, because he's just about stopped shouting – his campy, kissy-lipped back-up harmonies have turned into the sometimes almost prissy lead voice of a yea-and-nay-saying oracle, lyrical one moment and bummed out the next. On the nowhere man's victory cry 'I'm Only Sleeping' he achieves this effect solely with mouth and larynx, but on 'And Your Bird Can Sing', a two-minute 'Queen Jane Approximately' and 'Dr. Robert', which caricatures a pill-scripting jet-setter, he's added his own double-tracking to Paul's. And on 'She Said She Said' and 'Tomorrow Never Knows', the climactic side-closers that are John's only showcases on the US release, a filter makes him sound, as one of us wrote at the time, 'like God singing through a foghorn.'

This is not the voice of a lover because John is leaving what few love songs the Beatles are singing to his mates. From a man who'd snuck the word 'trivialities' into 'When I Get Home' two years before, 'She Said She Said' is even more strikingly basic English than 'She Loves You', but with a big difference: This time the simple diction is about impoverishment rather than

179

outgoing charity, satirising mind-damaged bad-tripping pretension and posit-
ing a tranquil if illusory childhood certainty against it. And 'Tomorrow Never
Knows' dispenses with pop song altogether. Incorporating violin snatches,
mock war whoops, barrelhouse piano and lots of run-it-backward-George
into a rhythmic layout rooted in Ringo's off-centre pattering and a static bass-
and-tamboura drone, the song ignores ordinary verse-chorus-break structure.
There's only the continuous downstream unfolding of the same melody going
nowhere, like time, or consciousness, until it circles around to a conclusion
that is also a rebirth: 'Or play the game existence to the end/ Of the begin-
ning/ Of the beginning.'

Barrett said that the reason the kids dig the Beatles . . . is not so much because of their music, but because they always do what they want to do and to hell with everyone else. 'That's why the kids dig them – because they do what they want. The kids know this.' – *'Interview with Syd Barrett'*, Melody Maker, *9 December 1967*

The Ballad of John and Yoko *by the Editors of* Rolling Stone, *1982*

INTERVIEW WITH JOHN LENNON
By Leonard Gross

This interview defines a period when the Beatles had ceased live performances and Lennon began to seek an individual path – beginning with his non-Beatle role in a film.

Whoever would have dreamed that beneath that mop lurked a Renaissance man? Yet there, shorn, sits John Lennon, champion minstrel, literary Beatle, coarse truthsayer, who turned Christendom on with one wildly misunderstood gibe at cant. Now, face white, tunic red, playing wounded in a field of weeds, this pop-rock De Vinci is proposing to act for real. Relaxed to all appearances, he is all knots inside.

'I was just a bundle of nerves the first day. I couldn't hardly speak I was so nervous. My first speech was in a forest, on patrol. I was suppose to say, "My heart's not in it any more" and it wasn't. I went home and said to myself, "Either you're not going to be like that, or you're going to give up."'

As he casts his weak brown eyes at the camera, the entire movie company jockeys for a glimpse. 'I don't mind talking to the camera – it's people that throw me.' Sure enough, he blows his lines. He waggles his head in shame. 'Sorry about that.' But under the low-key coaxing of director Dick Lester, Beatle John becomes Private Gripweed, a complex British orderly, in an unorthodox new film, *How I Won the War*.

Lennon on his own – rich for life at 26, yet poor still in what men of all seasons crave – full knowledge of himself. Beatling by itself, he has found, is not enough. 'I feel I want to be them all – painter, writer, actor, singer, player, musician. I want to try them all, and I'm lucky enough to be able to. I want to see which one turns me on. This is for me, this film, because apart from wanting to do it because of what it stands for, I want to see what I'll be like when I've done it.'

They stood silently in the deserted German square that Sunday morning, three young British actors costumed like the soldiers who had taken the town 22 years before. Then the one whose notorious locks had recently been chopped short observed, 'I haven't seen so much fresh air together for about four years.'

For John Lennon, the Beatles' leader, it had been one swift crazy ride to the

181

top. But now, there were distortions, and he had recoiled. Grownups were twisting a Beatles' kids' song into an LSD trip – an ingenious lament that he and Beatle Paul McCartney had polished off one wild night was, current rumor had it, actually the synopsis of an opera so bitter it could not be sung. A passing remark about religious hypocrisy had made Lennon a devil or a saint, depending on your tastes. Others might enjoy them, but to Lennon, who is nothing if not honest, the distortions had become a threat.

'I don't want people taking things from me that aren't really me. They make you something that they want to make you, that isn't really you. They come and talk to find answers, but they're their answers, not us. We're not Beatles to each other, you know. It's a joke to us. If we're going out the door of the hotel, we say, "Right! Beatle John! Beatle George now! Come on, let's go!" We don't put on a false front or anything. But we just know that leaving the door, we turn into Beatles because everybody looking at us sees the Beatles. We're not the Beatles at all. We're just us.

'But we made it, and we asked for it to an extent, and that's how it's going to be. That's why George is in India [studying the sitar] and I'm here. Because we're a bit tired of going out the door, and the only way to soften the blow is just to spread it a bit.'

In that kind of mood, a Dick Lester set was just the therapy for Lennon. Each man is the kind who makes the New Theologians jump. To them, the individual is more thrill than threat – a unique being who should be taken for what he is. Lester, who directed both Beatle films, gratefully recalls his first meeting with the group, when the movies were just an idea. 'They allowed me to be what I damn well pleased. I didn't have to put on an act for them, and they didn't put one on for me.'

This is what a Lester set is like: Once more, they are in a deserted German square, now, with all the paraphernalia of movie-making, with British 'soldiers', Lennon among them, ready to comb the streets, with German 'soldiers' lying in wait. 'Quiet please!' an assistant shouts – just as a little boy walks into the scene. Apoplectic, the assistant rushes forward and shoves the child aside. Lester, whose normal weapon is humour, flushes. 'Don't push!' he commands.

Once again, they are ready to shoot – and once again, the child intrudes. For fifteen seconds, Lester eyes the man silently. Then, 'Boo,' he calls, and 'Boo,' the cast joins in.

For Lester, a director makes no statement against violence by having thousands die. To him, each death must matter – and in his new film, each does. Such were the ideas that captured Lennon, despite his doubts about himself.

He did not doubt alone. *How I Won the War* is staffed with seasoned British actors, all trained in repertory, all well-known at home and all suspicious. But none is today.

Samples: 'We expected someone a bit kinky, bitchy, arrogant. He is none of those things. He's completely natural.'

I didn't realise that the alienation process would also alienate the audience. I also failed to understand that when you hire John Lennon, even when you tell the press 30 times that he is playing a straight role because he wants to, that people would still say, five minutes into the performance, 'Why hasn't he played the guitar yet?' He didn't, and they felt cheated, that he had been brought in under false pretences. – *Richard Lester, on* **How I Won the War**

'You're not working with another actor, you're working with an OBE, a multimillionaire – in sterling, not dollars – whose every word will be reported in the world press. The miracle is that he's so normal. I could wrap him up dialectically in two minutes, intellectually, in three. But he's got a certain inborn, prenatal talent. I have my talent, which I think is considerable, but it doesn't compare in his field.'

'I don't think he does anything with a conscious thought of trying to impress. He's remarkably free. He does not act the part.'

'We talk about him all the time. All of us feel the same thing. We find it difficult to be as normal with him as he is with us.'

Lennon's lack of pretense astonished the actors. 'He's someone who just tries anything,' one of them marveled. 'No stand-in, no special treatment, no chair for him.'

During a break for tea one raw morning, Lennon queued with the rest. When his turn arrived, his heart's desire was gone. 'You don't have to be a star to get a cheese sandwich,' he mused. 'You just have to be first.'

They like his humour too. That same morning, a German mother pushed her three-year-old son up to the Beatle, clutching his autograph book in his hand. 'Sign it!' she demanded. Lennon did as bidden, telling the boy, 'Yes, sir, you put us where we are today.' On location in Spain one afternoon, the script required Lennon to drive a troop carrier along the beach. Accelerating too fast, he spun the wheels; the rear of the carrier sank. As his crestfallen director approached the cab, Lennon peered sheepishly over his glasses and gave him a limp salute.

Lennon is not on; he is simply original. 'America used to be the big youth place in everybody's imagination. America had teenagers and everywhere else just had people.' He recognises his own impact on the changes since then, but he refuses to concede that youth today is all that different – particularly youth in England.

The last generation might have been just like today's young adults, he maintains, had it not had to fight the war.

'If they said, "Fight the war now," my age group would fight the war. Not that they'd want to. There might be a bit more trouble getting them in line – because I'd be up there shouting, "Don't do it!"

'It just so happens that some groups playing in England are making people talk about England, but nothing else is going on. Pop music gets through to all people all over the world, that's the main thing. In that respect, youth might be together a bit. The Commie youth might be the same as us, and we all know that, basically, they probably are. This kind of music and all the scene is helping. But there's more talk about it than is actually happening. You know, swinging this, and all that. Everybody can go around in England with long hair a bit, and boys can wear flowered trousers and flowered shirts and things like that, but there's still the same old nonsense going on. It's just that we're all dressed up a bit different.

'The class thing is just as snobby as it ever was. People like us can break through a little – but only a little. Once, we went into this restaurant and nearly got thrown out for looking like we looked until they saw who it was. "What do you want? What do you want?" the headwaiter said, "We've come to bloody eat, that's what we want," we said. The owner spotted us and said, "Ah, a table sir, over here, sir." It just took me back to when I was nineteen, and I couldn't get anywhere without being stared at or remarked about. It's only since I've been a Beatle that people have said, "Oh, wonderful, come in, come in," and I've forgotten a bit about what they're really thinking. They see the shining star, but when there's no glow about you, they only see the clothes and the haircut again.

'We weren't as open and as truthful when we didn't have the power to be. We had to take it easy. We had to shorten our hair to leave Liverpool and get jobs in London. We had to wear suits to get on TV. We had to compromise. We had to get hooked, as well, to get in and then sort of get a bit of power and say, "This is what we're like." We had to falsify a bit, even if we didn't realise it at the time.'

If Lennon is compulsive about anything today, it's about truth as he sees it. But he protests when he's labeled a cynic.

'I'm not a cynic. They're getting my character out of some of the things I write or say. They can't do that. I hate tags. I'm slightly cynical, but I'm not a cynic. One can be wry one day and cynical the next and ironic the next. I'm a cynic about most things that are taken for granted. I'm cynical about society, politics, newspapers, government. But I'm not cynical about life, love, goodness, death. That's why I really don't want to be labeled a cynic.'

It is in the context of the young man who recoils at distortion that his now-famous remark should be viewed. 'I said it. I said we were more popular than Jesus, which is a fact.' What he could not explain then was why.

He does not feel that one need accept the divinity of Jesus – he, personally, does not – in order to profit from his words. A frequent reader of ancient history as well as philosophy (his current lists includes a book on Indian thought and Nikos Kazantzakis's *Report Greco*), he contends that man has mishandled Christ's words throughout the centuries.

'I believe Jesus was right, Buddha was right, and all of those people like that are right. They're all saying the same thing – and I believe it. I believe what Jesus actually said – the basic things he laid down about love and goodness – and not what people say he said.'

Christianity has suffered, he believes, not only because Christians have distorted Christ's words but because they concern themselves with structures and numbers and fail to listen to their vows. They 'mutter' and 'hum' their prayers, but pay no attention to the words. 'They don't seem to be able to be concerned without having all the scene about, with statues and buildings and things.

'If Jesus being more popular means. . .more control, I don't want that. I'd sooner they'd all follow us even if it's just to dance and sing for the rest of their lives. If they took more interest in what Jesus – or any of them – said, if they did that, we'd all be there with them.'

Would he call himself a religious person? 'I wouldn't really. I am in the respect that I believe in goodness and all those things.' And if being religious meant being 'concerned', as Paul Tillich the late Protestant theologian, once put it? 'Well, I am then. I'm concerned alright. I'm concerned with people.'

At the age when most men are just beginning to adjust to the world, John Lennon has already nudged it a bit. The hysteria that surrounds him can no longer disguise the presence of a mind. His ideas are still rough, but his instincts are good and his talent extraordinary. You may love him, you may loathe him, but this you should know: As performer, composer, writer or talker, he'll be around for a long, long time.

Look Magazine, 13 December 1966

PRIVATE ON PARADE
By Jon Savage

Lennon's role in How I Won the War *is sometimes identified as the point at which his anti-war stance became overt, as in this article. However, the influence of director Richard Lester (then a very fashionable figure) in casting Lennon for the part shouldn't be overlooked.*

Five days after returning home from the Beatles' final paying concert at Candlestick Park, John Lennon flew out to Germany for his next role – as Private Gripweed in Dick Lester's *How I Won the War*. The next day, his coiffed hair was brutally cut to just over army regulation length: a drastic new look that, together with the granny glasses that he assumed for the role and would retain thereafter, marked the psychic and emotional changes occurring within.

If 1966 was the crux year for the Beatles, then Lennon's assumption of a comparatively minor role in a satirical war movie was an act both out of character and born of desperation. As he revealed in 1980, 'I was always waiting for a reason to get out of the Beatles from the day I made *How I Won the War* in 1966. I just didn't have the guts to do it, you see. Because I didn't know where to go. I did it because the Beatles had stopped touring and I didn't know what to do.'

Indeed, *How I Won the War* remains better-known for its part in the Beatles' story than as a piece of cinema. Lester's film, written by the *Help!* screenwriter, Charles Wood, attempts to harness fast-cutting surrealism to hard-hitting war protest with unhappy results. The point about the absurd illogic of war is quickly made, while the episodic script, the endless speeches to camera and the military-decibel voices remove any sense of involvement or enjoyment.

Lennon is a pleasure, as alvays, but the script does not give him much to do. Gripweed is a slimy, servile little character – a working-class ex-Fascist, no less – which must have been satisfyingly iconoclastic for the man who played him. He gets off a few good lines and hisses 'bastard' at all the right points, but when he gets blown up by a mortar shell at the film's climax, you don't really care. After all, the script takes care of that: 'I knew this would happen,' Gripweed moans, holding his stomach. 'You knew it would happen, didn't you?'

Place it within the context of its times, however, and you can give all concerned a medal for bravery. In 1966, Britain was still awash with films celebrating the war; criticism only became acceptable at the box office with Richard Attenborough's 1969 *Oh! What A Lovely War* – which took several pointers from Lester's effort. As much to the point is the fact that it occurred at the point where the Beatles, and John Lennon in particular, were at their most explicit about their opposition to war – especially the rapidly escalating American involvement in Vietnam. Interviewers had asked the Beatles about military matters during their early tours of the US, but they usually parried the topic. There would he occasional asides – like John's 1964 comment, 'all our songs are anti-war' – but, under advice from Brian Epstein, they avoided direct confrontation.

Sometime in late 1965, according to Barry Miles, Paul McCartney went to see the philospher, veteran pacifist and CND avatar Betrand Russell who alerted him to the fact that 'Vietnam was a very bad war, it was an imperialist war.' The first overt statement comes with John Lennon 's retort to the banning of the 'Butcher' sleeve in spring 1966: it was 'as relevant as Vietnam'. There were also some sharp exchanges in the June 30 Tokyo press conference. When asked, 'How much interest do you take in the war that is going in Vietnam now?', Lennon replied: "Well, we think about it every day, and we don't agree with it and we think it's wrong. That's how much interest we take. That's all we can do about it. . .and say that we don't like it.'

Describing the situation in Iraq as 'terrible', [Yoko] Ono said Lennon would have 'told off' President Bush and Prime Minister Tony Blair about 'how stupid it is to go through this.' – BBC World News, *28 March 2003*

Interviewed by *Look Magazine* on the set of *How I Won the War*, Lennon said he wanted to do the film 'because of what it stands for'. The report catches a nervous young man out of his usual environment: the other actors find it difficult to relate to him and he is not sure about his own abilities. He is also under no illusions about the new youth community: 'If they said, Fight the war now, my age group would fight the war. Not that they'd want to. There might be a bit more trouble getting them in line because I'd be up there shouting, Don't do it.'

How I Won the War took eight weeks to film, during which Lennon visited Hamburg and Paris, smoked marijuana, got very bored and wrote 'Strawberry Fields Forever'. Save some post-production dubbing, that was the limit of his involvement until the film's premiere on October 18, 1967. The experience gave him an enforced detox from Beatle life which offered him a chance to refill the creative well and acquire some perspective: his comments about British society in the *Look* interview prefigure his infamous 'Lennon Remembers' rant.

How I Won the War stands with the 'Butcher' cover and the Jesus controversy as marking the moment – and the year, 1966 – when the Beatles stepped out from behind the boy band image and started to talk about what was really on their minds and in their hearts. As beneficiaries of the decision to stop National Service in the UK, the Beatles, at first intuitively and later ideologically, rejected militarism past (all those war films) and present (Vietnam). In doing so, they helped to influence successive generations against, as Derek Taylor later wrote, 'war and violence as a means of dealing with the problems that politicians had allowed to get out of hand'.

Mojo, February 2002

GOING UNDERGROUND
By Barry Miles

Miles was the proprietor of the Indica Bookshop (which Paul helped to fund) in the mid-Sixties, and later the Indica Gallery (where John met Yoko). He was a central figure in the 'Swinging Sixties' avant-garde, and, contrary to conventional wisdom, claims the same was true of McCartney.

In 1965, the cutting edge of experimental music was represented by AMM, a free-improvisation music group headed by composer Cornelius Cardew, former assistant to Karlheinz Stockhausen. Cardew had worked with John Cage in Europe and was the leading advocate of Cage's ideas in Britain. He held weekly sessions with AMM in the basement of the Royal College of Music on Prince Consort Road, where he was a professor of composition.

Early in 1966, I attended one of the events with Paul McCartney. We arrived late and the 'music' had begun. Cardew was a multi-instrumentalist but on this occasion he sat by the piano. About twenty people sat around on the floor, facing AMM who were making noises on instruments ranging from tenor saxophone and violin to various percussion instruments and wind instruments. A number of transistor radios stood among the instruments but were only rarely turned on, usually to provide a more dense layer of sound if several players were performing at once – channels of static or distorted music from far-away stations were preferred.

Cardew sometimes tapped the piano leg with a small piece of wood. Once or twice he leaned inside the piano to pluck a string, tap the frame or lid, but at no point did be actually play a note. There was no melody, no rhythm, just noises or 'notes' in relation to one another, the performers listening intently, responding to the texture and pace of the progression of sounds. The audience was encouraged to contribute: Paul ran a penny along the side of an old-fashioned steam radiator and, after the break, used his beer mug as an instrument to tap. Though Paul did not find the evening satisfying musically – 'It went on too long' – he said that you did not have to like something in order to be influenced by it

It was Paul's involvement in this type of of event that John Lennon envied but did not participate in until he got together with Yoko, years later. In the meantime, Paul would report the latest fantastical hash-induced ideas to him and John would encourage him excitedly : 'Do it! Do it!' But Paul was cautious, he was very conscious of bringing Beatles fans along with them slowly, rather than alienating them with too much weirdness. Paul did contemplate a solo album and even had a title for it, *Paul McCartney Goes Too Far*, but nothing came of it.

In the mid-Sixties, Paul patrolled London with his antennae out, omnivorous, wide open for experience. Through Jane Asher he met playwrights, actors and film directors: Bernard Miles, Harold Pinter, Arnold Wesker; through art dealer Robert Fraser he met David Hockney, Andy Warhol, Jim Dine, as well as Michelangelo Antonioni, whom Paul screened his experimental home movies for at half speed. He commissioned pop artists Peter Blake and Richard Hamilton to design Beatles album sleeves and as he was the only Beatle living in London, it also fell to him to supervise their production.

I was approached to do a film script for the Beatles. I said it would have to be an absolutely original script. Paul McCartney said do whatever you like . . . . we finally get this little note from Brian Epstein, that it wasn't suitable for the Beatles . . . . by page 25 they had committed adultery, murder, dressed in drag, been in prison, seduced the niece of a priest, blown up a war memorial and all sorts of things like that. I can't really blame them but it would have been marvellous. – *Joe Orton*

His taste was eclectic and each week was crammed with events: a lecture by Luciano Berio; Cliff Richard in concert; *Ubu Roi* by Alfred Jarry. He would sit on the floor at the UFO Club, listening to the Soft Machine and the Pink Floyd (the only Beatle to go there) and the next night watch a cabaret at the Blue Angel. He hung out at the Indica gallery, helped to lay out *International Times*, Britain's first underground paper, and got very involved in the underground scene. At John Mayall's house he enlarged his knowledge of blues and R&B, and at my flat he listened to Albert Ayler, William Burroughs cut-ups and John Cage, particularly *Indeterminacy*, where electronic sounds and piano sometimes drown out the Zen-like stories Cage recounts. Paul was intrigued by Cage's ideas: that you can play anything – a screwed up ball of paper can be flattened and used as a score; all sound is potentially musical

All this was dissected and processed, to finally emerge, unrecognisable, in Beatles music. The best example is 'A Day in the Life', beginning with the lyrics which were were partly found by John and Paul pulling phrases from a copy of

the *Daily Mail* to which they added a fragment that McCartney had already written. The music was constructed like a building; Paul had roadie and friend Mal
Evans count off 24 bars out loud and then ring an alarm clock. Paul: 'It was just
a period of time, an arbitrary length of bars, which was very Cage thinking'

The 24 bars were recorded with an ever-increasing reverb so there was a
tremendous echo on it towards the end. The tape was left for a week while Paul
decided what to do next. His idea shocked George Martin but was loved by
Lennon: 41 players were hired from the New Philharmonia and instructed to
play as one instrument. Paul: 'I told the orchestra, there are 24 empty bars. On
the ninth bar the orchestra will take off, and it will go from its lowest to its highest note. You start with the lowest note in the range of your instrumnent and
eventually go through all the notes of your instrument to the highest. But the
speed at which you do it is your own choice. So that was the brief, the little
avant-garde brief.'

Mojo, February 2002

ALL YOU NEED IS EARS
By George Martin

Producer George Martin was central to the Beatles' creative dynamic from the moment they first stepped into EMI's Abbey Road studios. His workmanlike book, All You Need Is Ears, *gives an entertaining blow-by-blow account of the production process behind their classic recordings.*

Then came Christmas, and we agreed to get together again after they had written some more material. But in the meantime EMI and Brian Epstein had told me that they needed another single, since they hadn't had one for a while. I said: 'OK. It means we'll have to find extra material for the album, but let's couple the best two we have so far – 'Strawberry Fields' and 'Penny Lane' – and issue them as a double-A-sided record.' To this day I cannot imagine why that single was beaten to the number one spot, because for my money it was the best we ever issued. But there it was, and now we were left with 'When I'm 64' on its own for the new album.

We started work again in February 1967, and the boys began bringing in the various songs they had written. But 'Sergeant Pepper' itself didn't appear until halfway through making the album. It was Paul's song, just an ordinary rock number and not particularly brilliant as songs go. Nor was there anything difficult or special about the recording of it. But when we had finished it, Paul said, 'Why don't we make the album as though the Pepper band really existed, as though Sergeant Pepper was making the record? We'll dub in effects and things.' I loved the idea, and from that moment it was as though *Pepper* had a life of its own, developing of its own accord rather than through a conscious effort by the Beatles or myself to integrate it and make it a 'concept' album.

'A Little Help from My Friends', for example, was originally conceived as a separate entity, specially written for Ringo – we always felt there had to be some corner of each album that was forever Ringo! The boys backed him with vocal choruses and so on, since he never did have a very brilliant voice, but the song suited him admirably.

Again, George's contribution, 'Within You Without You', was, with all deference to George, a rather dreary song, heavily influenced by his obsession with Indian music at that time. I worked very closely with him on the scoring of it, using a string orchestra, and he brought in some friends from the Indian Music Association to play special instruments. I was introduced to the dilruba, an Indian violin, in playing which a lot of sliding techniques are used. This meant that in scoring for that track I had to make the string players play very much like Indian musicians, bending the notes, and with slurs between one note and the next.

But even such widely differing songs as these two seemed to merge into the whole once they had become the 'work' of Sergeant Pepper himself, from that first moment on the record when you hear the tuning-up noises of the band and the atmosphere of an audience. The way in which the record seemed to generate its own 'togetherness' became particularly apparent during the editing. A perfect example of that was 'Good Morning', an up-tempo, fairly raucous song with a curious, irregular metre to it. We normally faded out the music at the end of a song, but this time we decided to cover the fade with a host of sound-effects, particularly animals. We shoved everything in, from a pack of hounds in full cry to more basic farmyard noises. The order we had worked out for the album meant that that track was to be followed by a reprise of the 'Sergeant Pepper' song, and of course I was trying to make the whole thing flow. So imagine my delight when I discovered that the sound of a chicken clucking at the end of 'Good Morning' was remarkably like the guitar sound at the beginning of 'Sergeant Pepper'. I was able to cut and mix the two tracks in such a way that the one actually turned into the other.

That was one of the luckiest edits one could ever get. At other times, we could only fall back on our own mad ideas in order to achieve the effects we wanted: no more so than with 'Being for the Benefit of Mr Kite'. Like most of John's songs, it was based on something he had seen; he would often pick up a newspaper and see some item which was the spur to a song. In this case it was an old placard for a circus and fair, which he had hanging in his house. It announced, 'Being for the benefit of Mr Kite, a Grand Circus, the Hendersons, Pablo Fanques' Fair. . .' and included all the acts which would appear, including Henry the Horse. When we came to the middle section of the song, where 'Henry the Horse dances the waltz', we obviously had to go into waltz-time, and John said he wanted the music to 'swirl up and around', to give it a circus atmosphere. As usual, having written a great song, he said to me, 'Do what you can with it,' and walked away, leaving me to it.

In order to get a hurdy-gurdy effect, I got Mal Evans, the roadie, to play his enormous bass harmonica, while John and I did our thing on two electric organs, a Wurlitzer and a Hammond. John was to play the basic tune, and around it I was to play the swirly noises – chromatic runs based on it. Unfortunately, my digital capacities on an organ fall short of spectacular, and I found that I couldn't achieve the speed I wanted for these runs. So I told John: 'What we'll do is to slow the whole thing down by a half. You play the tune twice as slow and an octave down, and I'll do my runs as fast as I can, but an octave down as well. Then, when we double the tape speed, it'll come out all nice and smooth and very swirly.'

Of course, we could always have got a professional organist in to do it, but our attitude was 'Why the hell! Why should we let someone else in on our fun?' Besides, we were doing it all off the top of our heads: to bring someone else in would have meant delay and a lot of tedious explanation.

I think there's a lot of facts about *Pepper* that people get wrong, they say, 'Yeah, the greatest thing made on four-track.' But, how many four-tracks was it made on? Fill up one, bounce to another. So, eventually they probably had as many as 40 tracks of stuff piled up . . . I think getting all those musicians though, not to play in the traditional sense, that ascending line they play [on 'A Day in the Life'] to get to the chord was an incredible feat on George Martin's part. – *Andy Partridge, XTC*

But even when we had done it this new way, it still didn't sound quite right, and I told John that I would think about it. Then I found the answer. I got together a lot of recordings of old Victorian steam organs – the type you hear playing on carousels at county fairs – playing all the traditional tunes, Sousa marches and so on. But I clearly couldn't use even a snatch of any of them that would be identifiable; so I dubbed a few of the records on to tape, gave it to the engineer and told him, 'I'll take half a minute of that one, a minute and a half of that one, a minute of that one,'and so on.

'Then what do I do with them?' he asked.

'You cut that tape up into sections about a foot long.'

'What?!!'

'Cut it up into little parcels about a foot long, and don't be too careful about the cuts.'

Clearly thinking I had lost my senses, he did it, leaving me with a bunch of pieces of tape some one foot long – about 60 in all. '*Now* what?'

'Fling them up in the air.'

Believing by now, I suppose, that the world had gone completely insane, he did as asked.

'Now,' I said, 'pick them up in whatever order they come and stick them all back together again.'

The poor chap couldn't contain himself. 'What did you do *that* for?!!'

'You'll see,' I said.

After he had laboriously stuck them all together again, we played the tape and I said: 'That piece there's a bit too much like the original. Turn it round the other way, backwards.' We went on like that until the tape was a whole amalgam of carousel noises, but meaningless in musical terms because it was composed of fragments of tunes connected in a series of fractions of a second. It was an unreal hotch-potch of sound, arrived at without rhyme or reason; but when it was added as a background 'wash' to the organ and harmonica track we had already made, it did give an overall impression of being in a circus.

Compared with Paul's songs, all of which seemed to keep in some sort of touch with reality, John's had a psychedelic, almost mystical quality. 'Lucy in the Sky with Diamonds' was a typical John song in that respect, and a lot of analysts and psychiatrists were later to describe it as the drug song of all time. They were talking rubbish, but the tag stuck. I was very offended recently when I saw a television programme about the drug raid, Operation Julie, in which some major world suppliers of LSD were rounded up. The programme was prefaced with 'Lucy', as though it were *the* drug song – a 'fact' which people have taken as finally proven simply because 'Lucy', 'Sky' and 'Diamonds' happen to start with the letters LSD.

The gospel truth of the matter is that Julian, John's young son, came home from school one day carrying a picture of a little girl in a black sky with stars all round her. John asked if he had done the picture, and when Julian said he had, John asked him, 'What is it, then?'

Julian's best friend at school was a little girl called Lucy, and he replied, 'It's Lucy, in the sky, with diamonds.'

John's imagery is one of the great things about his work – 'tangerine trees', 'marmalade skies', 'cellophane flowers'. I hope it doesn't sound pretentious, but I always saw him as an aural Salvador Dali, rather than some drug-ridden record artist.

On the other hand, I would be stupid to pretend that drugs didn't figure quite heavily in the Beatles' lives at that time. At the same time they knew that I, in my schoolmasterly role, didn't approve, and like naughty boys they would slope off into the canteen, lock the door and have their joints. Not only was I not into it myself, I couldn't see the need for it; and there's no doubt that, if I too had been on dope, *Pepper* would never have been the album it was. Perhaps it was the combination of dope and no dope that worked, who knows?

All You Need Is Ears, George Martin, 1979

BEATLES NOT ALL THAT TURNED ON
By Alan Aldridge

British illustrator Aldridge – responsible for the two acclaimed books of Beatles Illustrated Lyrics *– interviewed Paul about their psychedelic-era songs. According to McCartney, some of the drug inferences detected by listeners just weren't there.*

'There's a fog upon L.A. and my friends have lost their way,' sings Beatle George Harrison in 'Blue Jay Way', named for a road in the Hollywood hills. And there is a fog, one that has led to sundry articles, calls to talk radio stations, asides from disc jockeys and myriad conversations and arguments over the significance of Beatles' lyrics in such songs as 'A Day in the Life', 'Dr. Robert' and 'Strawberry Fields Forever'.

All this crypto-analysis has produced more murk than light and, since Beatles records are the most-played, most-sold, most-memorised, most-discussed pop product of the decade, their meanings and intents – whether subliminal or super-liminal – have heavy social impact. Realising the magnitude of confusion, British writer-artist Alan Aldridge interviewed Beatle Paul McCartney to get a foun-tainhead perspective of their words. His article may answer some questions. Then again, it may not.

It seems to me your songs appeal to two entirely separate audiences, the mass teeny-boppers who accept your work at a humming and dancing level, and the new semi-intellectual audience which analyses and seeks hidden meanings behind the lyrics.
We write songs; we know what we mean by them. But in a week someone else says something about it, says that it means that as well, and you can't deny it. Things take on millions of meanings. I don't understand it.

A fantastic example is the inner track on the back of *Sergeant Pepper* that plays for hours if your automatic doesn't cut off. It's like a mantra in yoga and the meaning changes and it all becomes dissociated from what it is saying [the chang-ing meaning of an endlessly repeated phrase is the subject of experiments by Dr Chris Evans at the National Physical Laboratory]. You get a pure buzz after a while because it's so boring it ceases to mean anything.

To be honest it wasn't until I heard 'Eleanor Rigby' ('she keeps her face in a jar by the door') that I became aware that your songs had a lot more to offer than 'yea yea yea'. Perhaps we could talk about this for a start?

Well, that started off with sitting down at the piano and getting the first line of the melody, and playing around with words. I think it was 'Miss Daisy Hawkins' originally; then it was her picking up the rice in a church after a wedding. That's how nearly all our songs start, with the first line just suggesting itself from books or newspapers.

At first I thought it was a young Miss Daisy Hawkins, a bit like 'Annabel Lee', but not so sexy; but then I saw I'd said she was picking up the rice in church, so she had to be a cleaner; she had missed the wedding, and she was suddenly lonely. In fact she had missed it all – she was the spinster type.

Jane [Asher] was in a play in Bristol then, and I was walking round the streets waiting for her to finish. I didn't really like Daisy Hawkins – I wanted a name that was more real. The thought just came: 'Eleanor Rigby picks up the rice and lives in a dream' – so there she was, The next thing was Father MacKenzie. It was going to be Father McCartney, but then I thought that was a bit of a hang up for my dad, being in this lonely song. So we looked through the phone book. That's the beauty of working at random – it does come up perfectly, much better than if you try to think it with your intellect.

Anyway, there was Father MacKenzie and he was just as I had imagined him, lonely, darning his socks. We weren't sure if the song was going to go on. In the next verse we thought of a bin man, an old feller going through dustbins; but it got too involved – embarrassing. John and I wondered whether to have Eleanor Rigby and him have a thing going, but we couldn't really see how. When I played it to John, we decided to finish it.

That was the point anyway. She didn't make it, she never made it with anyone, she didn't even look as if she was going to.

Like 'Dr. Robert' – he seems to be a psychiatrist?

Well, he's like a joke. There's some fellow in New York, and in the States we'd hear people say: 'You can get everything off him; any pills you want.' It was a big racket, but a joke too about this fellow who cured everyone of everything with all these pills and tranquilisers, injections for this and that; he just kept New York high. That's what 'Dr. Robert' is all about, just a pill doctor who sees you all right. It was a joke between ourselves, but they go in in-jokes and come out out-jokes because everyone listens and puts their own thing on it, which is great. I mean, when I was young I never knew what 'Gilly Gilly Elsa Feffer Cats. . .' was all about, but I still enjoyed singing it. You put your own meaning at your own level to our songs and that's what's great about them.

Is that how you wrote Sergeant Pepper?

I was just thinking of nice words like Sergeant Pepper, and Lonely Hearts Club, and they came together for no reason. But after you have written that down you start to think, 'There's this Sergeant Pepper who has taught the band to play, and got them going so that at least they found one number.' They're a bit of a brass band in a way, but also a rock band because they've got the San Francisco thing. We went into it just like that: just us doing a good show.

> It was my idea to say to the guys, 'Hey, how about disguising ourselves and getting an alter ego, because we're the Beatles and we're fed up? Every time you approach a song, John, you gotta sing it like John would. Every time I approach a ballad, it's gotta be like Paul would.' And it freed us. It was a very liberating thing to do. – *Paul McCartney*

Why did you put all those people on the cover, like a school photograph gone wrong?

These were all just cult heroes. George chose a few of his schoolmates he liked, and the rest of us said names we liked the sound of: Like Aldous Huxley, H. G. Wells, Johnny Weissmuller.

Those Indian people have amazing stories. There's one called Panmahansa Yogananda, who died in 1953 and left his body in an incredibly perfect state. Medical reports in Los Angeles three or four months after he died were saying, This is incredible; this man hasn't decomposed yet. He was sitting there glowing because he did this sort of transcendental bit, transcended his body by planes of consciousness. He was taught by another person on the cover and he was taught by another, and it all goes back to the one called Babujee, who's just a little drawing looking upwards.

You can't photograph him – he's an agent. He puts a curse on the film. He's the all-time governor, he's been at it a long time and he's still around doing the transcending bit.

These are all George's heroes?

Yes. George says the great thing about people like Babujee and Christ and all the governors who have transcended is that they've got out of the reincarnation cycle; they've reached the bit where they are just there; they don't have to zoom back.

So they're there planning the spiritual thing for us. So, if they are planning it, what a groove that he's got himself on our cover, right in the middle of the Beatles' LP cover! Normal ideas of God wouldn't have him interested in Beatles music or any pop – it's a bit infra dig – but obviously, if we're all here doing it, and someone's interested in us, then it's all to do with it. There's not one bit worse than another bit. So that's great, that's beautiful that he's right on the cover with all his mates.

Whatever it is, it's what is doing all those trees and doing us and keeping you going; which someone must be doing.

The yogi goes through millions of things to realise the simplest of all truths, because while you are going through this part, there's always the opposite truth. You say, 'Ah, well, that's all there is to it then. It's all great, and God's looking after you.' Then someone says, 'What about a hunchback then? Is that great?' And you say, 'Okay then, it's all lousy.' And this is just as true if you want to see it. But the truth is that it's neither good nor lousy; just down the middle; a state of being that doesn't have black or white, good or bad.

Is that what George's number is about?
I think George's awareness has helped us because he got into this through Indian music – or as he calls it, 'all-India radio'. There's such a sense of vision in Indian music that it's just like meditation. You can play it forever; there's just no end to what you can play on a sitar and how good you can get.

It struck me that Sergeant Pepper is one of the first LPs that has looked at the idiom either like a symphony or a paperback: trying to present a complete show that lasts an hour.
That's it. We realised for the first time that someday someone would actually be holding a thing that they'd call 'The Beatles' new LP' and that normally it would just be a collection of songs or a nice picture on the cover, nothing more. So the idea was to do a complete thing that you could make what you liked of; just a little magic presentation. We were going to have a little envelope in the centre with the nutty things you can buy at Woolworth's: a surprise packet.

'Late of Pablo Fanques Fair' – Where did you get that?
John has this old poster that says right at the top, 'Pablo Fanques Fair presents the Hendersons for the benefit of Mr Kite,' and it has all the bits of things that sound strange: 'Over men and horses, hoops and garters, lastly through a hogshead of

real fire.' 'The Hendersons' – you couldn't make that up.

There's one part that must be one of John's puns: 'Somersets' instead of 'somer-saults'.
No, that's from the poster as well.

The pop scene before you came along went to great lengths to create names. I suppose we ought to realise that you can't do better than real fact – your own actual experience of life.
There's no need to make things up. We started on interviewers who would say, 'What do you believe?' and we'd say, 'We do not believe in gold-lame suits: That's trying to glory it up and doesn't even do it well.' That detaches you from the real thing. That's why Daisy Hawkins wasn't any good – it sounds like Daisy Made-up. Billy Shears is another that sounds like a schoolmate but isn't. Possibly one day we'll meet all these people.

One of the most obviously ambiguous of your songs, the one that everybody can see something in, is 'Lucy in the Sky with Diamonds'.
This one is amazing. As I was saying before, when you write a song and you mean it one way, and then someone comes up and says something about it that you didn't think of – you can't deny it. Like 'Lucy in the Sky with Diamonds', people came up and said, cunningly, 'Right, I get it. L-S-D,' and it was when papers were talking about LSD, but we never thought about it.

If you take LSD as a sort of pun, the whole song is a trip.
What happened was that John's son, Julian, did a drawing at school and brought it home, and he has a schoolmate called Lucy, and John said, 'What's that?' and he said, 'Lucy in the Sky with Diamonds' – so we had a nice title. We did the whole thing like an *Alice in Wonderland* idea, being in a boat on the river, slowly drifting downstream and those great cellophane towers towering over your head. Every so often it broke off and you saw Lucy in the sky with diamonds all over the sky. This Lucy was God, the big figure, the White Rabbit. You can just write a song with imagination on words and that's what we did.

It's like modern poetry, but neither John nor I have read much. The last time I approached it I was thinking, 'This is strange and far out,' and I did not dig it all that much, except Dylan Thomas, who I suddenly started getting, and I was quite pleased with myself because I got it, but I hadn't realised he was going to be saying exactly the same things.

It's just that we've at last stopped trying to be clever, and we just write what we like to write. If it comes out clever, okay. You get to the bit where you think, if we're going to write great philosophy it isn't worth it. 'Love Me Do' was our greatest philosophical song: 'Love me do/You know I love you/I'll always be true/So love me do/Please' simple and true, means that it's incredibly simple.

People have told me that 'Fixing a Hole' is all about junk, you know, this guy, sitting there fixing a hole in his arm.
This song is just about the hole in the road where the rain gets in; a good old analogy – the hole in your make-up which lets the rain in and stops your mind from going where it will. It's you interfering with things as when someone walks up to you and says, 'I am the Son of God.' And you say, 'No you're not; I'll crucify you,' and you crucify him. Well that's life, but it is not fixing a hole.

It's about fans too: 'See the people standing there/Who disagree and never win/And wonder why they don't get in/Silly people run around/They worry me/And never ask why they don't get in my door.' If they only knew that the best way to get in is not to do that, because obviously anyone who is going to be straight and like a real friend and a real person to us is going to get in; but they simply stand there and give off, 'We are fans, don't let us in.'

Sometimes I invite them in, but it starts to be not really the point in a way, because I invited one in, and the next day she was in the *Daily Mirror* with her mother saying we were going to get married. So we tell the fans, 'Forget it.'

If you're a junky sitting in a room fixing a hole then that's what it will mean to you, but when I wrote it I meant if there's a crack or the room is uncolorful, then I'll paint it.

'She's Leaving Home' is a great song, very simple, similar to 'Eleanor Rigby'.
It's a much younger girl, but the same sort of loneliness. That was a *Daily Mirror* story again: This girl left home and her father said, 'We gave her everything, I don't know why she left home.' But he didn't give her that much, not what she wanted when she left home.

Fine. What's 'Lovely Rita' all about?
I was bopping about on the piano in Liverpool when someone told me that in America they call parking-meter women meter maids. I thought that was great, and it got to Rita Meter Maid and then Lovely Rita Meter Maid and I was thinking vaguely that it should be a hate song: 'You took my car away and I'm so blue today.' And you wouldn't be liking her; but then I thought it would be better to love her and if she was very freaky too, like a military man, with a bag

on her shoulder. A foot stomper, but nice.

The song was imagining if somebody was there taking down my number and I suddenly fell for her, and the kind of person I'd be, to fall for a meter maid, would be a shy office clerk and I'd say, 'May I enquire discreetly when you are free to take some tea with me.' Tea, not pot. It's like saying, 'Come and cut the grass' and then realising that could be pot, or the old teapot could be something about pot. But I don't mind pot and I leave the words in. They're not consciously introduced just to say pot and be clever.

After the line 'a little like a military man' there's a fantastic 'whoop whoop'. How did you do that?
It's done with a comb and paper. We had it in the bit after and it sounded too corny; it wasn't quite good enough to have twice, but in a way that's nice because you listen for it to come around again.

There's a lot of random in our songs – Strawberry Fields is the name of a Salvation Army School – by the time we've taken it through the writing stage, thinking of it, playing it to the others, writing it, and letting them think of bits, recording it once and deciding it's not quite right and do it again and then find, 'Oh, that's it, the solo comes here and that goes there,' then bang, you have the jigsaw puzzle.

That happens with all our- songs, except the ones we want to keep really simple, like 'When I'm 64' and 'Fixing a Hole'.

What kind of scene are you thinking of when you say, 'Took her home and nearly made it, sitting on the sofa with a sister or two'?
That's it: There are a couple of sisters around so that is why I never made it.

I could see a whole scene of naked bodies writhing on the sofa. . .
If it had been really made. . .

Then the tricky one that the BBC banned – 'A Day in the Life'. It's been said that this is a sort of requiem to Tara Brown [the heir to the Guinness Trust, killed in 1966 in a car crash in London].
I've heard that. I don't think John had that in mind at all. The real words to that are 'read the news today'. There'd been a story about a man who'd made the grade, and there'd been a photograph of him sitting in his car. John said, 'I had to laugh.' He'd sort of blown his mind out in the car.

Literally, with a gun?

No, he was just high on whatever he uses, say he was in this big Bentley, sitting at the traffic lights. He's driving today; the chauffeur isn't there, and maybe he got high because of that. The lights have changed and he hasn't noticed that there's a crowd of housewives and they're all looking at him saying,' Who's that? I've seen him in the papers,' and they're not sure if he's from the House of Lords. He looks a bit like that with his Homburg and white scarf and he's out of his screws.

That's a bit of black comedy. The next bit was another song altogether but it just happened to fit. It was just me remembering what it was like to run up the road to catch a bus to school, having a smoke and going into class. We decided, 'The hell with this, we're going to write a turn-on song.' It was a reflection of my school days – I would have a Woodbine then, and somebody would speak and I would go into a dream.

This was the only one in the album written as a deliberate provocation. A stick-that-in-your-pipe. But what we want is to turn you on to the truth rather than pot.

The law against marijuana is immoral in principle and unworkable in practise – *SOMA ad, the* London Times, *24 July 1967, paid for by Paul McCartney and signed by all four Beatles*

'Yellow Submarine' has connotations – I read that in Greenwich Village they call yellow phenobarbital capsules – Nembutals – 'yellow submarines'.
I knew it would get connotations, but it really was a children's song. I just loved the idea of kids singing it. With 'Yellow Submarine' the whole idea was, 'If someday I came across some kids singing it, that will be it,' so it's got to be very easy – there isn't a single big word. Kids will understand it easier than adults. 'In the town where I was born/ There lived a man who sailed to sea/ And he told of his life in the land of submarines.' That's really the beginning of a kids' story. There's some stuff in Greece like icing sugar – you eat it. It's like a sweet and you drop it into water. It's called submarine; we had it on holiday.

But some of your songs are real places and real facts. Can you remember the little influences that made 'Penny Lane', for example?
Penny Lane is a bus roundabout in Liverpool; and there is a barber's shop show-ing photographs of every head he's had the pleasure to know – no that's not true, they're just photos of hairstyles, but all the people who come and go, stop and say hello. There's a bank on the corner, so we made up the bit about the banker

in his motor car. It's part fact, part nostalgia for a place which is a great place, blue suburban skies as we remember it, and it's still there.

I've heard it said that George Martin writes most of your music.
He always has something to do with it, but sometimes more than others. For instance, he wrote the end of 'All You Need Is Love' and got into trouble because the 'In the Mood' bit was copyrighted. We thought of all the great cliches because they're a great bit of random. It was a hurried session and we didn't mind giving him that to do – saying, 'There's the end, we want it to go on and on.' Actually what he wrote was much more disjointed, so when we put all the bits together we said, 'Could we have "Greensleeves" right on top of that little Bach thing?' And on top of that we had the 'In the Mood' bit.

George is quite a sage. Sometimes he works with us, sometimes against us; he's always looked after us. I don't think he does as much as some people think. He sometimes does all the arrangements and we just change them.

Finally, many people in the trade tell me Ringo can't drum.
That's extraordinary. He wasn't on our first record; with 'Love Me Do' Ringo was on the LP and Andy White on the single, and you really notice the difference. What a long time ago that was.

Washington Post, 1969

AWOPBOPALOOBOP ALOPBAMBOOM
By Nik Cohn

Journalist Cohn's entertaining, highly opinionated account of rock music as it stood at the end of the Sixties took its title from Little Richard's intro to 'Tutti-Frutti'. Its summation of the Beatles' four individual personalities dates from their psychedelic era.

Between them, the four of them being so complementary, they managed to appeal to almost everyone.

Lennon, for instance, trapped the intellectuals. He started writing books and he knocked out two regulation slim volumes, *In His Own Write* and *Spaniard in the Works*, stories, poems, doodled drawings and assorted oddments. Mostly, they were exercises in sick, sadistic little sagas of deformity and death, written in a style halfway between Lewis Carroll and Spike Milligan.

Predictably, the critics took it all with great solemnity and, straightaway, Lennon was set up as cultural cocktail food, he got tagged as an instinctive poet of the proletariat, twisted voice of the underdog. He himself said that he only wrote for fun, to pass time, but no matter, he was turned into a heavy Hampstead cult.

Meanwhile, he sat around in discotheques and tore everyone to pieces. He was married and had a son. He lived in a big suburban mansion in Weybridge and he was sharp as a scythe. He wrote songs as if he was suffocating. Still, he was powerful and he generated a real sense of claustrophobia, he had great command of irony and he owned one of the best pop voices ever, rasped and smashed and brooding, always fierce. Painful and obsessive, his best songs have been no fun whatever but they've been strong: 'I Am the Walrus', 'A Day in the Life', 'Happiness Is a Warm Gun' and, most racked of all, 'Strawberry Fields Forever'.

On stage, he played monster and made small girls wet their knickers. He hunched up over the mike, very tight because he couldn't see an inch without his glasses on, and he'd make faces, stick his tongue out, be offensive in every way possible. On 'Twist and Shout', he'd rant his way into total incoherence, half rupture himself. He'd grind like a cement mixer and micro-bops loved every last dirty word of him. No doubt, the boy had talent.

Paul McCartney played Dick Diver. He was stylish, charming, always elegant and, whenever he looked at you, he had this strange way of making you feel as if you were genuinely the only person in the world that mattered. Of course, he'd then turn away and do exactly the same thing with the next in line but, just that flash while it lasted, you were warmed and seduced and won over for always.

He was a bit hooked on culture: he went to all the right plays, read the right books, covered the right exhibitions and he even had a stage when he started diluting his accent. No chance – Lennon brought him down off that very fast indeed. Still, he educated himself in trends of all kinds and, when he was done, he emerged as a full-blown romantic, vastly sentimental, and he wrote many sad songs about many sad things, songs that were so soft and melodic that grannies everywhere bought them in millions.

In their different styles, then, both Lennon and McCartney had gotten arty and their music changed. In the first place, their work had been brash, raucous, and the lyrics very basic – 'She Loves You', 'Thank You Girl', 'I Saw Her Standing There'. Good stuff, strong and aggressive, but limited. From about 1964 on though, they got hooked on the words of Bob Dylan and their lyrics, which had always been strictly literal, now became odder, quirkier, more surreal. Message and meaning: suddenly it was creative artist time.

My own feeling is that Lennon has heavy talent and that McCartney really hasn't. He's melodic, pleasant, inventive but he's too much syrup.

Still, they do make a partnership: Lennon's toughness plays off well against McCartney's romanticism, Lennon's verbal flair is complemented by McCartney's knack of knocking out instantly attractive melody lines. They add up.

Of course, when McCartney runs loose with string quartets, some horribly mawkish things happen – 'Yesterday', 'She's Leaving Home' – but he has a certain saving humour and he's usually just about walked the line.

At any rate, he looks sweet and more than anyone, he made the Beatles respectable at the start and he's kept them that way, no matter what routines they've got involved in. Even when he confesses to taking acid or bangs on about meditation, he invariably looks so innocent, acts so cutely that he gets indulged, he's always forgiven. Regardless, he is still a nice boy. Also, not to be overlooked, he is pretty and girls scream at him.

More than any of the others, though, it was Ringo Starr who came to sum the Beatles up.

America made him. In England, he was always a bit peripheral, he always sat at the back and kept his mouth shut but, when the Beatles hit New York, they were treated very much like some new line in cuddly toys, long-haired and hilarious, and Ringo stole it.

Big-nosed and dogeyed, he had a look of perpetual bewilderment and said hardly anything: 'I haven't got a smiling mouth or a talking face.' He only bumbled, came on like some pop Harry Langdon and women in millions ached to mother him. In fairness, it has to be said that this was not his fault – he looked that way by nature and couldn't change.

Every now and then, out of deep silence, he'd emerge with some really classic line. No verbal gymnastics like Lennon, not even a joke – just one flat line, so mumbled and understated as to be almost non-existent.

My own favourite was his summing-up of life as a Beatle: 'I go down to John's place to play with his toys, and sometimes he comes down here to play with mine.'

. . . it has to do with who they were at that time. They had successfully shed their clean-cut Moptop image, added psychedelia to their sound and depth to their lyrics, grew their hair out and experimented with drugs. – Hollywood Bitchslap *review of* Magical Mystery Tour

He's solid. When he got married, he chose no model, no starlet, but a girl from Liverpool, a hairdresser's assistant. He'd known and gone steady with her for years. And when all the Beatles went meditating in India with the Maharishi, he said that it reminded him of Butlins and came home early.

Really, he summarises everything that's best in the English character – stability, tolerance, lack of pretension, humour, a certain built-in cool. He knows he's not a great drummer and it doesn't upset him. Not very much upsets him in fact: he only sits at home and plays records, watches television, shoots pool. Simply, he passes time.

He is hooked on Westerns and he loves new gadgets and he spends a lot of his time just playing. He sits with his wife and his children. Well, he may be slightly bored at times because he has nothing much to do any more but he isn't too bothered and, quite genuinely, he would make out all right if the Beatles went broke on him and he had to get a nothing job again. No matter what, he ticks over.

George Harrison is more problematic.

To begin with, he wasn't much more than a catcher, a trampoline for the others to bounce off. On stage, he'd set himself a little way back from the mike and play along without smiling. He hardly moved and he'd look cut off, vaguely bored.

His big moment used to be when he and Paul McCartney would suddenly bear down hard on the mike together and, cheeks almost touching, they'd shake their heads like mad. This gesture used to provoke more screams than almost anything else. But when it was over, Harrison never followed it up, he only dropped back and looked bored again.

In interviews, too, he was less than impressive. He was slower than the rest, less imaginative, and he tended to plod a bit. In every way, he was overshadowed by Lennon/McCartney.

At this stage, his most publicised interest was money and he got very tight with Epstein, who used to explain the complexities of Beatle finance to him. Epstein, who worshipped the Beatles and was greatly afraid of losing touch with them, loved this and used to speak of Harrison as his most favourite son.

Still, as Lennon/McCartney got increasingly arty, Harrison was stung and he began chasing. He went on a heavy intellectual streak himself.

First up, he got interested in Indian music and took lessons on sitar from Ravi Shankar. Second, he was to be seen flitting in and out of London Airport wearing beads and baggy white trousers. Third, he started writing Indian-style songs, all curry powder and souvenirs from the Taj Mahal, very solemn. And finally, he went up a mountain with the Maharishi Mahesh Yogi, guru to the stars, and came down again a convinced mystic. From here on, he was a philosopher, a sage, and his interviews were stuffed full of dicta, parables and eternal paradoxes. Sitting crosslegged in Virginia Water, he hid his face behind a beard, a moustache, two Rasputin eyes and he was almost unrecognisable as George Harrison, guitar-picker.

Awopbopaloobop Alopbamboom, Nik Cohn, 1970

YESTERDAY: THE BEATLES REMEMBERED
By Alistair Taylor

Having been the most money-conscious of the four Beatles during the hectic years of Beatlemania, George Harrison's anti-materialistic volte-face was even more surprising when he subsequently embraced yoga, meditation and the Hare Krishna sect.

Wow, it's hot! In London today the temperature must have broken all records, but I've been lucky enough to spend the afternoon with George at Kinfauns.

I enjoy being with George; it's always been peaceful at Kinfauns and there's none of the pressure to do things that I sometimes feel when I'm with John or Paul. Just sitting indoors listening to George learning to play his sitar is very relaxing and the hours seem to fly by without me noticing.

Take it away. That's bullshit, man. Karma Yoga, remember? It isn't the answer. The answer's in your own head. Isn't it? I don't want that. Get it away and thanks anyway. – *George Harrison, refusing psychedelic drugs in Haight-Ashbury, 1967*

Today we were outside, sitting on the grass next to George's little pool. This isn't a swimming pool; it's more like a pond, about six feet wide and a couple of feet deep. George and I talked about all manner of things and in an idle moment he looked at the pool.

'You see that water?' he said.

There were all sorts of tiny little creatures wriggling and swimming around in the greenish water.

'A few weeks ago, I filled that pool up with water, clear tap water with nothing in it, and now there are living things in it. Where have they come from?'

We were already talking about life and the great mysteries, so we veered off the subject of the pool on to religion and the Indian theology that George is studying. But that's George. With most people, infested tap water would have led to a discussion about water works and their efficiency, or lack of it; with George, everything leads to the cosmic meaning of life.

Yesterday: The Beatles Remembered, Alistair Taylor, 1988

SGT. PEPPER AND FLOWER POWER
By Jon Wiener

Journalist Wiener describes how the Beatles' soul-searching and self-indulgence was at odds with the political action taking place elsewhere at the time. John Lennon would later declare, 'The dream is over,' and become radicalised – to the extent where the authorities tried to have him deported from the USA. Wiener worked for years to gain access to the FBI's files on Lennon, eventually publishing them under the title Gimme Some Truth: The John Lennon FBI Files.

Songs about childhood: that was the first project John and Paul undertook in 1966. Each did one, and the Beatles put more effort into recording them than they had given to most of their albums. The songs came out as opposite sides of the same single, with Paul's 'Penny Lane' on the A side. He sang sweetly and affectionately about the 'blue suburban skies' of his childhood shopping centre.

John's feelings about his childhood were not sweet. His childhood experiences hurt him. How badly he would not be able to say until the *Plastic Ono Band* album in 1970. But the song he recorded at the end of 1966 represented a step in that direction: 'Strawberry Fields Forever'.

The song was part of his first attempt to move beyond the Beatles. He wrote it in Spain, during the shooting of *How I Won the War*. He worked on the song for six full weeks – 'time to think', he called it.

When he sang, 'I'm going to Strawberry Fields,' he was singing about a real place in Liverpool: a grim orphanage. It was not far from his Aunt Mimi's, with whom he lived from the age of five, after his father abandoned him and his mother decided to have his aunt raise him. His sense of loss over these childhood traumas was expressed for the first time in the song. He was taking his first steps toward the awful screams, 'Mama, don't go/ Daddy, come home' on the opening track of the *Plastic Ono Band* album.

When he sang, 'Nothing is real,' he was doing something he had never done before: naming the childhood feeling that had intensified during his life as a Beatle. The line anticipated the project of 'becoming real', which he declared in 1970. But in 1966 he couldn't imagine overcoming that sense of unreality. He could barely express his feelings of isolation – 'No one I think is in my tree' – and hopelessness – 'it doesn't matter much to me.'

Few understood what John was doing. He wanted it that way. He had carefully concealed his ideas in a dizzy, dreamy *tour de force* of sound that saturated the listener with music. But the Beatles had ceased to exist as a band on that song; John was alone, his music coming from electronic devices in the recording studio, not from the Fab Four. The promotional video for the song helped conceal John's real purpose, opening with the Beatles romping in a big field on a beautiful sunny day. He knew what people wanted from the Beatles: their playful optimism, not the terrifying truth about his feelings of abandonment, isolation, and hopelessness.

After the Beatles released 'Strawberry Fields Forever', Paul got an idea for a new album: bring the songs together around a single concept. The Beatles would assume the identities of another band, old-time music-hall entertainers, and the music on the album would take rock on a tour of popular styles of the century: marching bands, circus music, folk songs, jazz hits, the new psychedelic sounds. They would create dazzling effects in the studio, effects that had never been put on a pop album before.

Sgt. Pepper's Lonely Hearts Club Band, with its rich variety of sounds and feelings, seemed to show that rock had become broad enough and free enough to express anything. Greil Marcus, writing on rock for the San Francisco underground *Express Times*, recalled listening to an advance copy with friends: 'You mean this thing is going to be in the stores, we can buy it, listen to it ourselves?' The album made history in a dozen ways: it brought art to pop; it mixed good-time rock and roll with thoughtful ballads; its cover – a collage of the Beatles surrounded by heroes and celebrities – was amazing; its budget – $75,000 – and sales – 1.7 million in the United States – were unprecedented. But John's work on the album pulled him off the road leading from *How I Won the War* to the radical art of the *Plastic Ono Band* album. For him *Sgt. Pepper* was a step backward.

The album was mostly Paul's. He was the principal composer of seven of the twelve songs. 'She's Leaving Home' was a gem of realism, and his whimsy was never more delightful than on 'Lovely Rita' and 'When I'm 64.'

After the reprise of the 'Sgt. Pepper' theme, after the end of the music hall performance, John sings about real life, right now, with its loneliness and horrors. 'A Day in the Life' presents a vivid contrast to the playful optimism of the rest of the album.

The opening line took on a terrible new meaning after John was killed: 'I read the news today oh boy.' The 'oh boy' seems too real: sad, vulnerable, and puzzled. The lyrics represent a kind of dream journalism in which the facts of an ordinary day do not connect. John tells how terrible events are presented by the media as a form of entertainment, leaving the viewer feeling confused, isolated, anxious, and filled with dread. The images are concise and chilling: a suicide in a car, crowds that stand and stare and then turn away. John sings with a controlled intensity. His voice is at first subdued; soon it almost cracks with despair. The insistent beat disintegrates. The music reaches a crescendo of dissonance.

Paul's bridge interrupts: the narrator awakens, and with a routinised, nervous energy, gets ready to go to work, where he falls back into his 'dream'. John returns with more of the day's news: '4,000 holes in Blackburn, Lancashire'. Later he explained this image as coming from a newspaper article on potholes in the street, near the article describing the man who committed suicide. The newspaper regards the terrible suicide and the insignificant potholes equally as 'news'. Sgt. Pepper's band ended its concert complimenting its 'lovely audience'. John then describes the audience in the Albert Hall as 'holes', lifeless and empty.

His response to these terrifying images is to propose to turn us on. But this trip will not be fun, it will not be getting high with a little help from our friends. This is turning on in pain and defeat, to escape the misery of 'a day in the life'. At the end John's terror and despair have turned into an irrevocable hopelessness. The music culminates in a dissonant, formless, nightmarish orchestral crescendo, ending with a 43-second chord of utter finality.

John's other songs included 'Good Morning, Good Morning', which hinted at his dark feelings, and then denied them: 'I've got nothing to say but it's okay.' He contributed the weakest song on the album, 'Being for the Benefit of Mr. Kite'. Its elaborate circus sound effects only emphasised that it lacked something. The song of John's that caused the most excitement was 'Lucy in the Sky with Diamonds'. It was psychedelic.

John had fun telling straight reporters the song's title came not from the initials LSD, but from something his four-year-old son Julian had written. The reporters didn't really need to ask. If they had read the words on the jacket sleeve, they would have seen that the song described an acid trip. If they had actually listened, they would have heard John's effort to simulate a trip with sounds. The music captured some of the swooning euphoria of the acid experience, but the lyrics were cloying, even in 1967: 'rocking horse people eat marshmallow pies.'

The line about 'flowers that grow so in-cred-ibly high' did provide a nice image for a central chapter in the history of youth culture: flower power and psychedelia. LSD, its advocates promised, brought a new kind of experience and knowledge. It broke down the barriers that separated people from the rich, hidden utopia within themselves. It gave people an immediate, sensuous experience of colours and sounds, and promised a direct, authentic knowledge of the self and others. It revealed the extent to which bourgeois culture locked people into drab routines, cutting them off from their true feelings and perceptions. It exposed the isolation and repression of daily life in straight society. It brought emotional experiences so intense you would never be the same afterward.

There was also the possibility that this experience would be too intense, this self-knowledge too frightening, unbearable: the 'bad trip'. People had killed themselves on bad trips, people had gone into mental hospitals when they came down. For John, with his feelings of isolation and hopelessness, taking LSD required either recklessness or courage.

When John took it, and thereby joined the counterculture elite, he wanted to make music out of his experiences. Bob Dylan had shown it could be done in 'Mr. Tambourine Man', which conveyed the dreamy quality of one kind of marijuana high. John set out to do the same for LSD. His song 'Tomorrow Never Knows' on *Revolver* described the psychedelic quest for knowledge with strange, distorted sounds that had nothing to do with rock music: violin snatches, barrelhouse piano, tapes running backward. The lyrics were paradoxical and stirring: 'Play the game existence to the end/ Of the beginning.' 'Lucy in the Sky' emphasised simply the visual weirdness induced by LSD – the marmalade skies. This was the acid trip at its most trivial.

The way to self-knowledge through LSD was to dissolve the ego, to let go of desire and ambition, John explained in 'Tomorrow Never Knows'. You found yourself by losing yourself. This approach combined a life-affirming optimism with a profound passivity. For some, LSD provided an intense form of recreation; for John it was the basis of a completely serious search for himself. As critics Robert Christgau and John Piccarella put it recently, he 'went with the flow down into the flood'.

Although this search for self-knowledge through LSD was an honourable one, it didn't work for John. Three years later in *Lennon Remembers* he explained, 'I got the wrong. . .message on acid – that you should destroy your ego. And I did, you know.' It nearly brought him to disaster. But at the end of his LSD experience, isolated from the Beatles, with his defences broken down, he would be compelled to return to basics, to start over.

During the summer of 1967, however, none of this was clear. The Beatles as a group stood not only for the quest for self-knowledge through LSD but for 'flower power'. Flower power seemed hopelessly apolitical to New Left activists, but it represented a profound cultural revolution. The hippies rejected virtually all of bourgeois society: its sexual repression, private property, individualism and competition, authoritarian family, definitions of masculinity and femininity, linear logic, and compulsive cleanliness. Flower power asserted a utopian politics. Its communes brought to life an alternative community and culture on the fringes of the straight world. This community valued play over work, spontaneity over order, shared poverty over individual acquisitiveness.

I mean, can you imagine if they had the Beatles goin' zing zing zing zing zing zing zing, all that jump and shout, you know, and all of a sudden they put on an ad where the guy comes on very straight: 'You ought to buy Brillo because it's rationally the correct decision and it's part of the American political process and it's the right way to do things.' You know, fuck, they'll buy the Beatles, they won't buy the Brillo. – *Abbie Hoffman*

Flower power opposed the politics not only of the mainstream but also of the left. Hippies saw the confrontation tactics and mass demonstrations of the anti-war movement as a mirror of the status quo: they addressed the same issues, sought the same kind of power, reproduced the straight world's forms of domination and repressive work routines.

Despite this explicit rejection of political activism, the hippies contributed to the development of the New Left – perhaps in spite of themselves, and typically without any conscious intention. They expanded the arena of the political. The government's foreign and domestic policies were not the only, or even the most important, forms of oppression that had to be challenged. Domination in the family, the oppressive organisation of work and play, sexual repression – the hippies insisted that a radical movement had to address these issues of personal life, had to pursue a politics of liberation.

They insisted also that the challenge to bourgeois society had to go beyond criticism and protest. The values of the counterculture had to be put into practice every day. The radical project was not just for some distant future; the work of creating a new society had to begin immediately, in the interstices of the old one.

The forms of protest with which the hippies confronted straight society were playful, imaginative, and improvised. When buses brought tourists to stare at Haight–Ashbury in 1967, hippies ran alongside holding up mirrors. Hippie street life emphasised the put-on; hippies were happy to shock straight people. This style made its mark on the movement's tactics. It demonstrated how new forms

of protest and resistance could be created. It expanded the definition of the political act.

Hippies understood that revolutions require a transformation not only of
social and political organisation but also of consciousness. They understood better than the early New Left that society exercised domination not just over the
organisation of daily life but also over forms of thought. Thus they sought to create new kinds of subjectivity, to liberate the imagination. Over the next several
years John would embrace each of these central themes of the counterculture and
work to bring them into New Left politics.

During the summer of *Sgt. Pepper*, however, these links between the counterculture and the New Left remained murky for John and for everyone else.
The underground press began to express the values and concerns of both movements, but was not yet making any sustained effort to examine the area of antag-
onism and alliance. The first underground papers – the Los Angeles *Free Press*,
the Berkeley *Barb*, New York's *East Village Other* – were satisfied to mix articles
about the drug culture, sexual freedom, police brutality, macrobiotics, and
protest demonstrations with record reviews. A serious debate about Sixties music
and politics would not begin for another year, and it would be provoked by John
and his song 'Revolution'. In the meantime, virtually everyone loved *Sgt. Pepper*.

Robert Christgau, who would lead in developing the self-consciousness of the
New Left and the counterculture about music and politics, was writing in a music
magazine called *Cheetah* at the time. He called *Sgt. Pepper* 'the best rock album
ever made' because of its 'exploration of the formal possibilities' of 'aboriginal
rock and roll', and because it served as a 'catalyst for the entire youth movement'.
The youth movement, he wrote, 'sadly, perhaps, is not about overthrowing society. It is about living with it, coping. . .One part of me feels ashamed every day
for my own society, another part of me is very much of that society.'

The Beatles' right-wing critics argued that *Sgt. Pepper* was communistic. The
proof, they said, was on the album cover, where among the figures standing
behind the Liverpool lads they found Karl Marx. The critics failed to note that
Marx stood next to Oliver Hardy and behind an Indian guru who has never been
identified. And Marx was the only political figure. The other radical heroes of
the decade – Fidel, Che, Mao, Ho Chi Minh – were absent. But the immediate
predecessors of the counterculture were there, those antagonists of bourgeois
respectability, Lenny Bruce and William Burroughs.

Sgt. Pepper found listeners in the most unlikely places. A writer for *Christian
Century* recalled that 'With a Little Help from My Friends' was played at 'an
underground Eucharist service' held by a group planning a Lutheran conference
on war and racism. The worship leader explained that 'while many people

thought "friends" were drugs, Beatles lyrics usually had more than one meaning, and people who were sticking their necks out on the Vietnam issue would indeed need "a little help from their friends."

Time magazine devoted a cover story to *Sgt. Pepper*. The Beatles' early music had 'blended monotonously into the parched badlands of rock', the magazine declared with breathtaking ignorance. But *Sgt. Pepper* had changed all that. It turned pop music into 'an art form'. 'A guaranteed package of psychic shivers,' the record made 'parents, professors, even business executives' into Beatle fans. This was supposed to be a compliment.

The *Time* story made Richard Goldstein's penetrating review seem particularly impressive. 'For the first time, the Beatles have given us a package of special effects, dazzling but ultimately fraudulent,' he wrote in the *New York Times*. The Beatles had turned away from their achievements on *Revolver* and *Rubber Soul*, 'the forging of rock into what is real. It made them artists, it made us fans. . .We still need the Beatles, not as cloistered composers, but as companions. And they still need us, to teach them how to be real again.'

Sgt. Pepper contained no hint of the social and political conflicts that intensified through 1967. That spring, while the Beatles worked on the album, the anti-war movement in America took some big steps. Martin Luther King, Jr., finally declared, 'We must combine the fervour of the civil rights movement with the peace movement.' Women Strike for Peace demonstrated at the Pentagon; 5,000 scientists petitioned for a bombing halt; and University of Wisconsin students forced Dow Chemical recruiters off campus. Dow manufactured napalm, the jelly dropped from American planes which clung to the skin of the Vietnamese as it burned.

Ramparts magazine revealed in March that the National Student Association had received more than $3 million from the CIA through dummy foundations. The magazine subsequently revealed that 30 other organisations and publications which claimed to be independent had been secretly funded by the CIA. On April 15 the largest anti-war demonstration to date was held in New York City, as 250,000 people marched down Fifth Avenue in a 'peace parade', while 50,000 more marched in San Francisco. Heavyweight boxing champion Muhammad Ali was arrested after refusing induction into the Army. He had been denied conscientious-objector status. Boxing authorities immediately stripped him of his title as sports became politicised around the issues of war and race.

The summer of *Sgt. Pepper* was also the summer of ghetto rebellions in the United States. In mid-July Newark exploded: blacks battled police over a ten-square-mile area. After five nights, 24 blacks had been killed, more than 1,500 were injured, and 1,397 were arrested. A commission set up by the governor criticised the 'excessive and unjustified force' used by National Guardsmen and police, who shot at black people indiscriminately and vandalised black business-es. A week later the Detroit ghetto exploded. Snipers held off National Guardsmen, and for the first time in 25 years officials summoned federal troops to quell a civil disturbance. The toll in Detroit was 36 blacks killed along with seven whites, over 2,000 injured, 5,000 arrested, and 5,000 left homeless from 1,442 fires. Smaller riots broke out in Harlem, Milwaukee, Cambridge, Maryland, Minneapolis, and Chicago.

The ghetto uprisings revealed to white America the rage of the black under-class. They demonstrated the indiscriminately brutal response of white authority and suggested the tremendous gulf that separated white youth in the summer of *Sgt. Pepper,* flower power, and the peace movement from ghetto youth shout-ing, 'Burn, baby, burn.' Census statistics released later in the year showed the material basis for black rage: 41 percent of non-white families earned less than $3,000 a year, compared to twelve percent of white families; the unemployment rate for blacks was double that for whites; most black young people attended seg-regated schools.

John Lennon said a lot of great things in his day . . . it's more than apparent that he had a remarkable degree of insight into the human condition. John Lennon also said a lot of very absurd things in his day – anyone consuming as much LSD as he was can only be allowed at least a few non sequiturs – but far and away the most ridiculous thing he ever said was 'All you need is love.' – *'All You Need Is Hate'*, University of Oregon Magazine

The Six-Day War in the Mid-East took place that same summer. Israel launched a surprise attack on Egypt in June, responding to Egypt's military build-up, expulsion of the UN emergency force from the Sinai, and alliance with Syria, Jordan, and Iraq. Peter Brown described how the war touched the Beatles: 'There was enormous pressure from the Jewish establishment in London during the war to get the Beatles to appear in a benefit concert for Israel. Brian said, "Absolutely not." He would never do benefits. He argued that you can't select these things wisely, so it's better not to do them at all: Our aim is to sell records, he said, so we should keep out of anything controversial. The pressures Jewish leaders applied were really pretty nasty ones. People like Lew Grade and Co. really put the old screws on Brian. It wasn't that he didn't sympathise with the cause. It was that he'd made this rule and he wasn't going to bend it, even if it affected something so close to him.'

In the middle of that summer of conflict, the Beatles played a new song, written and sung by John: 'All You Need Is Love'. 700 million people heard it in a worldwide TV satellite broadcast. It became the anthem of flower power that summer. Radicals continued to denounce John for it for the rest of his life.

The song expressed the highest value of the counterculture. In retrospect, 'love' seems an absurdly naïve slogan. For the hippies, however, it represented a call for liberation from Protestant culture, with its repressive sexual taboos and its insistence on emotional restraint. John's song seemed to say that to find happiness, you didn't 'need' the traditional bourgeois virtues of individualism, aggressiveness, competition, acquisitiveness. All you needed was love.

Neither the song's fans nor its critics had listened to it closely. John did not say that love would solve the world's problems. He suggested that the world's problems would take care of themselves; thus life could be devoted to love instead of to solving problems and achieving distant goals. The song presented the flower-power critique of movement politics: there was nothing you could do that couldn't be done by others; thus you didn't need to do anything about the killing in Vietnam or the oppression of America's blacks. Everyone should relax and enjoy this place – and this moment. John was arguing not only against bourgeois self-denial and future-mindedness but also against the activists' sense of urgency and their strong personal commitments to fighting injustice and oppression.

As usual, New Left writers were not unanimous about 'All You Need Is Love'. Most objected to John's message of acquiescence in the status quo, but some found things to like in the song. The SDS paper at Cornell University argued that it conveyed a 'gentleness combined with strength' that distinguished it from most of rock, which was 'an assault'. The movement needed more of this non-violence, and John was pointing the way.

On the flip side was a sweet self-satire, 'Baby You're a Rich Man', in which Paul asks John questions in a soprano voice: What music is he going to play in the new key he's found? They were thinking about psychedelia at the time, but that question – what to do with his new ideas – was one John would start asking himself more and more seriously.

John followed that with 'I Am the Walrus', released at the end of November 1967, the wildest music the Beatles ever recorded. Later he said he understood the Walrus in the Lewis Carroll poem to be a symbol of socialism, resisting the capitalist Carpenter. He was wrong about that. The Walrus and the Carpenter were both villains, eating the poor oysters they lured to take a walk with them. That isn't what made the Walrus important to John. He remembered the lines, "'The time has come," the Walrus said, "to talk of many things: of shoes and ships and sealing-wax, of cabbages and kings."' When John sang 'I Am the Walrus', he was identifying with this articulate symbol of the imagination.

The first line referred to the LSD-inspired project of destroying his ego – 'I am he as you are he" – and asserted the Sixties communal ideal: 'we are all together.' In each verse, John poured out a torrent of disjointed images, ending with 'I'm crying.' He sang that line without expression, with a blankness that was frightening. He was hinting that LSD wasn't working for him, but he was also disguising his bad feelings in a dizzying spectacle of sounds and words, as he had done with 'Strawberry Fields Forever'. He was not yet able to tell the truth simply and directly.

The triumph of *Sgt. Pepper* served as a challenge to the Rolling Stones, Bob Dylan, and the rest of pop music in the summer of 1967. The Stones had started recording new material when *Sgt. Pepper* came out; they stayed in the studio another three months, working on the album that would be measured against the Beatles' masterpiece. Their work was interrupted by Mick Jagger's and Keith Richards' trials on drug charges. Two days before *Sgt. Pepper*'s release, Jagger was found guilty of possessing four amphetamine pills and sentenced to six months in prison; Richards, found guilty of permitting his house to be used for the smoking of hashish, was sentenced to one year. Even the ruling-class *Times* of London had to object, publishing an editorial titled 'Who Breaks a Butterfly on a Wheel?'. The Beatles jointly made a political statement, signing a full-page ad in the the *Times* three weeks after the release of *Sgt. Pepper* calling for the legalisation of marijuana.

Jagger's drug bust and draconian sentence drove him to the left. 'The way things are run in Britain and the States is rotten and it is up to the young to change everything,' he declared after his trial. 'The time is right now, revolution is valid. The kids are ready to burn down the high-rise blocks and those stinking factories where they are forced to sweat their lives away. I'm going to do anything, anything that has to be done, to be a part of what is about to go down.'

Their Satanic Majesties Request; recorded between June and September and released in November 1967, had none of this anger. It was the Stones' attempt to be more psychedelic than *Sgt. Pepper*, and it was a failure. Jagger had pushed to do it, and Brian Jones had opposed it, arguing the Stones should stay true to their roots in rhythm and blues. Americans missed the pun in the title: British passports read, 'Her Britannic Majesty. . .requests and requires.' The Stones were referring to their recent drug busts, which made it impossible for them to travel freely. They tried to hide the weakness of the music by putting a 3-D cover on the album. At least the Beatles couldn't top that.

Sgt. Pepper was loved by the counterculture and imitated by the Stones, but it was challenged by Bob Dylan. In January 1968, six months after the Beatles' album appeared, he released his first album since his motorcycle accident a year and a half earlier: *John Wesley Harding*. The Beatles' music sounded extravagant; Dylan simply strummed his acoustic guitar. The Beatles were playful; Dylan was serious. The Beatles' sources ranged from the British music hall to the Indian raga; Dylan drew strictly on American music. Even the cover of *John Wesley Harding*, a plain black and white photo of Dylan surrounded by two Native American musicians and one woodsman, was a reply to the cover of *Sgt. Pepper*. Dylan's response to the Beatles, Robert Christgau wrote in May 1968, was 'salutary' and 'mature'.

John Wesley Harding offered not only an artistic alternative to *Sgt Pepper* but also a political one. While none of the songs spoke directly about the war, the entire album expressed a subtle awareness of it and showed how it was affecting Dylan. The Beatles' playfulness and fantasy ignored the war's existence, while Dylan's new songs acknowledged it by trying to be real, and by playing fewer games than ever before. The best song on Dylan's album, 'All Along the Watchtower', expressed a new commitment to truthfulness and seriousness. The song opened with the old Dylan, 'the joker', looking for a way out. But he had learned that life is too short for joking. New Left critics were less happy with 'Dear Landlord', which seemed like his coming to terms with authority in society. But it was hard not to like the tender 'I'll Be Your Baby Tonight'.

Dylan himself was talking about John. 'The last time I went to London I stayed at John Lennon's house,' he told an interviewer. 'You should see all the stuff that Lennon bought: big cars and a stuffed gorilla and thousands of things in every room in his house, cost a fortune. When I got back home I wondered what it would be like to have all those material things. I figured I had the money and I could do it, and I wondered if it would feel like anything real. So I bought all this stuff and filled my house with it and sat around in the middle of it all. And I felt nothing.' He wasn't a working-class lad from Liverpool.

Meanwhile, in a different realm of popular music which for a while seemed untouched by artistic or political ambitions, the Beach Boys had been perfecting their sound, a celebration of complacent white middle-class suburban youth. Jim Miller has written sensitively about the contradictions faced by their brilliant leader Brian Wilson: 'His business was the revitalisation of myths he wished were true and knew were false.' 'California Girls' peaked at Number Two that sum-mer. A masterpiece of white pop harmony, it later became a shampoo commer-cial. The Beach Boys' most ambitious album, *Pet Sounds*, somehow became obsolete when the new Beatles album appeared. After *Sgt. Pepper* the Beach Boys never got one of their songs into the Top Ten. Suddenly their records had become oldies.

During the summer of *Sgt. Pepper* the alternatives posed by soul music and soft rock became clearer than ever before. When *Sgt. Pepper* was released in June, the Number One song was Aretha Franklin's 'Respect'. Her album *I Never Loved a Man (The Way I Love You)* followed. More than anyone else, she brought the apocalypse of gospel to the white rock audience, singing with desperation and urgency. 'Respect' was a powerfully rocking statement of feminist, black pride.

'Respect' was replaced in the Number One spot by the Fifth Dimension's 'Up Up and Away', which realised its potential later when it became a TWA commercial. Smokey Robinson's greatest song, 'The Tracks of My Tears', did-n't get any higher than Number Nine. This was also the season of the shlock flower-power anthem that told people going to San Francisco to be sure to wear a flower in their ear.

At the end of the summer of *Sgt. Pepper* the Beatles seemed to have every-thing: they were a critical and popular triumph, they had the power to do any-thing they wanted. Then manager Brian Epstein died of an accidental overdose of sleeping pills. He was 32 years old and a millionaire. 'I knew we were in trouble then,' John said later in *Lennon Remembers*. 'I thought, "We've fucking had it."'

Come Together: John Lennon in His Time, Jon Wiener, 1984

LENNON REMEMBERS
By Jann S. Wenner

When Rolling Stone *editor-in-chief and founder Wenner conducted a lengthy inteview with John in 1970, it was the frankest ever with an ex-Beatle. This extract lifts the veil on the Maharishi experience, with some barbed comments concerning his old songwriting partner's drive to keep the group going after Epstein's death.*

Where were you when you heard Brian died?
We were in Wales with Maharishi. We'd just gone down after seeing his lecture the first night. And we went down to Wales and we heard it then. And then we went right off into the Maharishi thing.

Where were you?
A place called Bangor in Wales.

In a hotel?
No, we were just outside a lecture hall with Maharishi. It just sort of came over. Somebody came up to us – the press were there 'cause we'd gone down with this strange Indian. And they said, 'Brian's dead.' I was stunned. We all were. And the Maharishi – we went into him, 'He's dead,' and all that. And he was sort of saying, 'Oh, forget it, be happy.' Fucking *idiot*. Like parents: 'Smile.' That's what Maharishi said. So we did. And we went along with the Maharishi trip.

What was your feeling when Brian died? Do you remember?
The feeling that anybody has when somebody close to them dies. There's a sort of little hysterical sort of 'hee-hee, I'm glad it's not me,' or *something* in it, that funny feeling when somebody dies. I don't know whether you've had it. I've had *a lot* of people die on me. And the other feeling is, 'What the fuck? What can I do?' I knew that we were in trouble then. I didn't really have any mis-conceptions about our ability to do anything other than play music. And I was scared. I thought, 'We've fuckin' had it.'

What were the events that immediately happened after Brian died?

Well, we went with Maharishi. I remember being in Wales and then I can't remember. I'll probably have to have a bloody [primal] session to remember it. I can't remember. It just all happened.

Then you went to India.
Yeah, I think so.

I remember very little about the Maharishi because the weekend was so traumatic – it was there that the news came that Brian Epstein had died. It was simply terrible how lost, how heartbroken, the Beatles were. They kind of went into close family mode from the sorrow and pain. – *Marianne Faithfull*

What about the funeral?
Oh, that was bullshit. I was offended enough that I've forgotten. Funerals are. . .

And how did Paul. . .
I don't know how the others took it. I can never tell how, it's no good asking me. It's like me asking how you took it – I don't know. I'm in my own head, I can't be in anybody else's. I don't know what George, Paul and Ringo think any more than I do about. . .I know them pretty well, but I don't know anybody *that* well. Yoko I know about the best. I don't know how they felt. I was in my own thing. We were all just like dazed.

So Brian died and then what happened is Paul started to take over?
I don't know how much of this I want to put out, I'll tell you. I think Paul had an impression – he has it now, like a parent, that we should be thankful for what he did, for keeping the Beatles going. But when you look upon it objectively, he kept it going for his *own* sake. Not for my sake did Paul struggle. But Paul made an attempt to carry on as if Brian hadn't died. By saying, 'Now, now, boys, we're going to make a record.' And being the kind of person I am, I thought, 'Well, you know, we're going to make a record, alright.' So I went along, we went and made a record. And I suppose we made *Pepper*, I'm not sure.

That was before.
That was before Brian. Oh, I see. Well, we made the double album then. But it was like that, you know. Was *Magical Mystery Tour* after Brian? Paul had a

tendency to just come along and say, 'Well, [I've] written ten songs, let's record now.' And I said, 'Give us a few days and I'll knock a few off.' Or something like that. He came and showed me what his idea was for *Magical Mystery Tour* and this is how it went, it went round like this, the story and production, and he said, 'Here's the segment, you write a little piece for that.' And I thought, 'Fuckin' hell, I've never made a film, what's he mean?' He said, 'Write a script.' So I ran off and wrote the dream sequence for the fat woman and all the things – the spaghetti and all that. So it was like that. George and I were sort of grumbling, 'Fuckin' movie, well we better do it.' A feeling that we owed the public to do these things. So we made it.

When did your songwriting partnership with Paul end?
That ended, I don't know, around 1962 or something. If you give me the albums, I can tell you exactly who wrote what, and which line. We sometimes wrote together and sometimes didn't. But all our best work – apart from the early days, like 'I Want to Hold Your Hand', we wrote together, and things like that – we wrote apart always. Even 'One After 909' on the whatsit LP, it's one I wrote when I was seventeen or eighteen in Liverpool separately from Paul. 'The Sun Is Fading Away' and things like that Paul wrote. We always wrote separately. But we wrote together because we enjoyed it a lot sometimes and also because they'd say, 'You're going to make an album.' We'd get together and knock off a few songs. Just like a job.

Whose idea was it to go to India?
I don't know. Probably George's, I have no idea. We [John and Yoko] met around then. I was going to take [Yoko], but I lost me nerve because I was going to take me wife *and* Yoko and I didn't know how to work it [*laugh*]. So, I didn't do it. I didn't quite do it.

You wrote 'Sexy Sadie' about the Maharishi.
That's about Maharishi, yeah. I copped out and wouldn't write, 'Maharishi, what have you done, you made a fool of everyone.' [*leaning into mike of tape recorder*] But now it can be told, fab listeners.

When did you realise that he was making a fool of you?
I don't know, I just sort of saw.

While in India, or when you got back?
Yeah, there was a big hullabaloo about him trying to rape Mia Farrow or trying

to get off with Mia Farrow and a few other women, things like that. And we went down to him and we'd stayed up all night discussing, was it true or not true? And when George started thinking it might be true, I thought, 'Well it must be true, 'cause if George is doubting it, there must be something in it.' So we went to see Maharishi, the whole gang of us the next day charged down to his hut, his very rich-looking bungalow in the mountains. And I was the spokesman – as usual, when the dirty work came, I actually had to be leader, whatever the scene was, when it came to the nitty gritty I had to do the speaking. And I said, 'We're leaving.'

'Why?' Hee-hee, all that shit. And I said, 'Well if you're so cosmic, you'll know why.' He was always intimating, and there were all his right hand men intimating that he did miracles. He said, 'I don't know why, you must tell me.' And I just kept saying 'You know why' – and he gave me a look like, 'I'll kill you, bastard.' He gave me such a look, and I knew then when he looked at me, because I'd called his bluff. And I was a bit rough to him.

YOKO: You were expecting too much from him.

JOHN: I always do. I always expect too much. I'm always expecting my mother and don't get her, that's what it is. Or some parents. I know that much.

Lennon Remembers, Jann S. Wenner, 2000

THE BEATLES AND THE GURU
By William F. Buckley

Right-wing American journalist Buckley was the scourge of liberals everywhere. His scathing, pro-Christian put-down of the Beatles' adoption of Eastern mysticism says as much about his own narrow world-view as his subjects' naïvety.

London, Feb. 28 – The doings of the Beatles are minutely recorded here in England and, as a matter of fact, elsewhere, inasmuch as it is true what one of the Beatle-gentlemen said a year or so ago, that they are more popular than Jesus Christ. It is a matter of considerable public interest that all four of the Beatles have gone off to a place called Rishikesh, in India, to commune with one Maharishi Mahesh Yogi.

The gentleman comes from India, and the reigning chic stipulates that Mysterious India is where one goes to Have a Spiritual Experience. Accordingly, the Beatles are there, as also Mia Farrow, who, having left Frank Sinatra, is understandably in need of spiritual therapy; and assorted other types. It isn't altogether clear what is the drill at Rishikesh, except that – and this visibly disturbed a couple of business managers of the Beatles – a postulant at the shrine of Mr Yogi is expected to contribute a week's salary as an initiation fee. A week's salary may not be very much for thee and me, but it is a whole lot of sterling for a Beatle, and one gathers from the press that the business managers thought this a bit much, and rather wish that the Beatles could find their spiritual experience a little less dearly.

The wisdom of Maharishi Mahesh Yogi is not rendered in easily communicable tender. It is recorded by one disciple that he aroused himself from a trance sufficiently to divulge the sunburst, 'Ours is an age of science, not faith,' a seizure of spiritual exertion which apparently left him speechless with exhaustion, I mean, wouldn't you be exhausted if you came up with that? It is reported that the Beatles were especially transfigured when the Maharishi divulged, solemnly, that 'speech is just the progression of thought'. One can assume that the apogee of their experience was reached upon learning, from the guru's own mouth, that 'anything that comes from direct experience can be called science'.

I am not broke, but I think that if I were, I would repair to India, haul up a guru's flag and – I guarantee it – I would be the most successful guru of modern times. I would take the Beatles' weekly salary, and Mia Farrow's, and the lot of them, and I would come up with things like: 'Put on therefore, as the elect of God, holy and beloved, bowels of mercies, kindness, humbleness of mind, meekness, longsuffering; forbearing one another, and forgiving one another, if any man have a quarrel against any; even as *** forgave you, so also do ye. And above all these things put on charity, which is the bond of perfectness. And let the peace of God rule in your hearts, to the which also ye are called in one body; and be thankful.'

I don't believe in Buddha / I don't believe in mantra / I don't believe in gita / I don't believe in yoga.
– *John Lennon, 'God'*

Can it be imagined that I would be less successful, quoting these lines, from a single letter of St Paul, than Maharishi Mahesh Yogi has been? The truly extraordinary feature of our time isn't the faithlessness of the Western people, it is their utter, total ignorance of the Christian religion. They travel to Rishikesh to listen to pallid seventh-hand imitations of thoughts and words they never knew existed. They will go anywhere to experience spirituality – except next door. An Englishman need go no further than to hear Evensong at King's College at Oxford, or to hear high Mass at Chartres Cathedral; or to read St Paul, or John, or the psalmists. Read a volume by Chesterton – *The Everlasting Man*; *Orthodoxy*; *The Dumb Ox*; and the spiritual juices begin to run, but no, Christianity is, well, well what? Well, unknown. The Beatles know more about carburettors than they know about Christianity, which is why they, like so many others, make such asses of themselves in pursuit of Mr Gaga Yogi. Their impulse is correct, and they reaffirm, as man always has, and always will, the truism that man is a religious animal. If only they knew what is waiting there, available to them, right there in Jollie Olde Englande, no costlier than 2/6d at the local bookstore. It is too easy nowadays to found new religions, though the vogue is constant. Voltaire was once abashed at the inordinate iconoclasm of one of his young disciples who asked the Master how might he go about founding a new religion. 'Well,' Voltaire said, 'begin by getting yourself killed. Then rise again on the third day.'

National Review, 12 March 1968

THE BEATLES IN
PERSPECTIVE
By John Gabree

This opinion piece provides a balance to the near universal adulation heaped on Sgt. Pepper, *and sets the Beatles in context against those contemporaries the author has greater admiration for – not least the Stones.*

It is important to get this straight: the Beatles never have been in the vanguard of pop music. They are not now and are unlikely ever to be.

The group's impact has been staggering, but it has been mostly sociological and only negligibly musical. Beatlephiles admit that the early work of the masters was largely imitative ('revitalising', 'opened our eyes to what was right in our own back yards', etc.). But, they argue, the Beatles then went on to become the *avant garde*, the pacesetters of pop music. This is quite simply not true.

There is a good and obvious reason why and how this confusion developed: most critics don't know their rock. Most people who write about rock today probably weren't listening a year ago, certainly not two, and aren't really listening now. They come in late, already thinking the Beatles are it. They pick up *Revolver* or *Sgt. Pepper* and have a revelation. But very few are willing to take the foursome's work for what it is: an introduction to a world of creative adventure, of which the Beatles are merely the popularisers, not the creators.

My first reaction to the recent *Time* cover story on the Beatles was to go blank (which is quite often my reaction to *Time* cover stories). *Time's* reporter, Luce-ly flinging about half (in)formed judgments about pop music, turned in an essay full of deft cracks about 'the rhythmic caterwauling of Elvis Presley' and the 'doldrum of derivative mewing by white singers,' etc., none of it much to the point.

Later I realised that though the *Time* article *is* wrong-headed, it is, sadly, no more so than most writing on rock. The only critic with any perspective on the Beatles, for example, is Richard Goldstein of the *Village Voice*. The *New York Times*, not surprisingly, has introduced a chap named Tom Phillips, whose entire *raison d'etre* seems to be to defend the Beatles from Goldstein. To the popular press, the Beatles are the darlings of the day, the Andy Warhols of rock.

The real story is this:

In the late Fifties, white rock, like the rest of pop culture, was at a low. Things weren't quite as bad as Beatle-lovers like to pretend, but they weren't good. There was a doldrum, all right, produced by the *ennui* excreted in such massive doses during the Eisenhower years. With Kennedy came change. After 1960, the civil rights movement caught fire, and black culture became a focus of attention. Simultaneously, activist youth turned to folk music, looking for an outlet with more meaning than could be derived from Bobby Rydell and his friends from Philadelphia.

Presley and the Everly Brothers, meanwhile, had been away in the Army (and anyway, Presley had sold his soul to Hal Wallis), Jerry Lee Lewis and Chuck Berry had been driven off for performing unmentionable nasties, Buddy Holly was dead, and Fats Domino and Little Richard in retirement, leaving poor Chubby Checker, a sort of musical Uncle Tom, alone on the stage. Everybody else was black, which the communications media viewed like death and still do.

Perhaps it was inevitable that the revitalisation of pop music would occur through a medium, the Beatles, that filtered out the elements that mass cultists found offensive – you can only get to C from A by going to B, but, if B was a necessary intermediate step, it should not have been allowed to become a hang-up. In physics experiments, a balloon that would be small under normal circumstances inflates out of proportion when introduced into a pressureless glass bell. That is what happened to the Beatle balloon when it was inserted into the vacuum of pop music in the early Sixties.

I first heard the Beatles while standing in front of the record store on the corner of Thayer and Angell streets in Providence, R.I. A raucous imitation of the Isley Brothers' 'Twist and Shout' was blaring from a speaker inside. Like much of their work since then, the cut was a mediocre copy, but unlike most of their duplications it reached a smaller audience than the original.

Their brashness made it immediately evident that the Beatles *had* to catch on. They were fresh, while American pop music hadn't produced a new face of lasting significance in a half-dozen years. They had a good ear for harmony and a nearly perfect sense of taste when choosing whom to imitate. They sounded raw and vital when compared with their vapid contemporaries on the Top 40 stations. But they were also safe, being white and having none of that aggressive sexuality that had been so upsetting in the likes of Elvis – all they wanted to do, remember, was hold your hand.

Their playing and singing during this early period was thoroughly unimaginative, not to say monotonous, and what we seek today, if we listen at all to songs like 'I Want to Hold You Hand' or 'She Loves You' (the latter unaccountably called 'Yeah, Yeah, Yeah' by the percipient Phillips), is nostalgia rather than musical pleasure.

With that sure sense of self-preservation that always had characterised the Establishment, America embraced the Beatles. At a time when the civil rights movement was at an all-time high of enthusiasm and seeming success, when we were becoming involved in an unpopular war in Southeast Asia, when much of the cream of our youth was opting for non-Establishment solutions to anti-Establishment goals, when rhythm-and-blues and country-and-western abounded with authentic talent, when the folk music revolution had already produced Bob Dylan and a revived interest in the blues – in the midst of all this we settled for very thin soup in rock-and-roll.

There was a jukebox in Sex. Somebody put on a Beatles record, 'I'm Down', and someone yelled, 'Awwww! My God! The Beatles,' and then grabbed it. They started kicking this Beatles record around the shop. 'We hate the fucking Beatles!' I thought: How brilliant! They hate the Beatles . . . You just didn't say it! – *Marco Pirroni, quoted in* Rotten: No Irish, No Blacks, No Dogs *by John Lydon*

Jazz, which has not been widely accepted in pop circles since the end of the big war, offers no parallel situation (except, perhaps, the West Coast jazz phenomenon), but folk music provides an interesting example of a group that performed the same function as the Beatles now do for rock. The Weavers were a highly eclectic (the word is used more than any other in connection with the Beatles) folk quartet that was central in attracting the pop cultists and intellectuals to folk music in the Fifties. Without the Weavers, there could have been no folk revolution at the beginning of this decade. In the same way, it is hoped, the pop critics and, more important, the audiences who have recently discovered the Beatles, will be tempted to look beyond them to see what is really happening.

Probably the change will come, but so far it hasn't. For now the press, the pop-cultists, the Establishment, are using the Beatles to make it possible to ignore more significant happenings, happenings that are genuine responses to the fact that this society is in trouble, and happenings they cannot tolerate. There is, for example, an increasing alienation (which even poor *Time* is aware of) that is making itself felt in a variety of ways: the non-violent peace movement has failed, and the black community seems increasingly taken with the angry rhetoric of black power; the horrible, pointless, corrosive war in Vietnam has finally undermined our blind faith in the government, seriously impaired whatever value there was in the President's domestic program, inspired rejection of U.S. involvement in the affairs of other nations, and drowned the spirits and hopes of many. Cities are in flames, while Congress fiddles; the black and the poor are demonstrating a new-found militancy; materialism, greed, and lack of concern for others seem to characterise the national posture; and the young are forever reminded of their essential powerlessness.

The reaction of youth to all this has been threefold: activist alienation of the black power, ghetto-organising, rent-strike, draft-resistance variety on the left, and sour yearnings for the eighteenth century on the right; hippie alienation of the turn-on, tune-in, drop-out type; or simple alienation of the good old silent Fifties style. Not a very happy collection of alternatives.

It is not unfair to the Beatles to say that they are relevant to none of this. Their job – and they have done it well – has been to travel a few miles behind the *avant garde*, consolidating gains and popularising new ideas.

The criticism for their undeserved domination of the scene must be directed at the press and the media who have deified the Beatles at the cost of neglecting more adventuresome creators in rock. (On a recent morning, a Chicago disc jockey, who gets a lot of mileage out of some supposed connection with the Beatles – and who somewhat tastelessly played 'A Day in the Life' in honour of Brian Epstein before it finally was decided he had not killed himself – spun, at a listener's request, 'I'm So Glad' by Cream, one of the best of the experimental groups, and then spent several moments savagely and unnecessarily putting the group down.) Kept in perspective, the Beatles are obviously a vitally important group, as for that matter are the Monkees and Herman's Hermits, but it's useless to contend that musically they are movers and makers.

None of this is a comment on the Beatles as individuals, or as pop leaders in non-musical ways. When John Lennon responded to an interviewer's stock question about the origin of the group's name with the story of a figure that one day rose out of the sea, pointed at them, and said, 'You're Beatles – with an a,' he provided an example of healthy looseness and irreverence that has had a strong influence on the new left-style of the young. And certainly their support of marijuana reform legislation and their admission to having used LSD are courageous acts. And if everything that has been said in advance about *How I Won the War* is true, Lennon has taken a significant stand against war.

On the other hand, they have been at the escapist end of the range of artistic responses possible to the phenomena of the Sixties: not apolitical in the manner of the Lovin' Spoonful or Herman's Hermits, they are political in that clouded way usually associated with liberal U.S. politics. Their movies, *Help!* and *A Hard Day's Night*, can be viewed as dramatisations of the whole male-adventure-fantasy syndrome, and they succumbed quite completely to manager Epstein's attempt to make them camp heroes, as wholesome as bread pudding.

What they have accomplished, besides demonstrating excellent taste in their selection of influences, is to write several first-rate compositions, especially the compassionate 'Eleanor Rigby', and produce two or three pop masterpieces ('Eleanor Rigby' and 'A Day in the Life') and one brilliant album, *Revolver*. The album was important because, with the Rolling Stones' *Aftermath* (released about the same time), it constituted a summation of previous developments in rock.

Here were the blues, hard-rock, ballads, Near Eastern and jazz harmonics, c&w, baroque, etc. In addition, *Revolver*, like *Aftermath*, was restrained and dignified, eschewing the sensationalism that must have been a tremendous temptation for both groups, and which the Beatles have finally given in to in *Sgt. Pepper's Lonely Hearts Club Band*. With rare exceptions, none of the compositions in the latter album have the melodic quality so often present previously in their work. Gone, too, is the restraint, the tastefulness that used to signal them when to stop. The affectation of 'unity' is a sham – and a seeming afterthought – that has been seized on by the reviewers. The press got so silly that even the *Christian Science Monitor* hailed the album's release with a gushy editorial (as still more trail blazing by the fantastic Beatles), managing at the same time never to mention that the Who are performing rock mini-operas or that there is a rock oratorio on each side of the Mothers of Invention's *Absolutely Free*.

There are only two reasons why *Sgt. Pepper* deserves to be more modestly acclaimed. 'A Day in the Life' is a harshly ironic performance juxtaposing Lennon's introverted ramblings ('I read the news today, oh boy/ About a lucky man who made the grade') against McCartney's flat recounting of the day's events ('Found my coat and grabbed my hat/ Made the bus in seconds flat'). And the album as a whole reinforces the importance of electronics in future pop and rock.

But these are not techniques that originated with the Beatles, and they are not even used by them in terribly original ways. There already had been excellent studio work on albums and singles by the Byrds, Donovan, the Beach Boys, and others, including Judy Collins' brilliantly eclectic *In My Life*. The question here also becomes whether we are to credit the group, the producer, or the engineer. I have heard – and whether it is apocryphal or true, it is true enough – that 'A Day in the Life' was born when the Beatles' producer, engineer, and musical midwife, George Martin, soldered together the strands of two separate compositions. Shouldn't we laud Martin instead of the quartet?

More important, however, is the fact that *Sgt. Pepper*, only a slight technical improvement on *Revolver*, has already been left behind by the work of other groups: The 'operettas' of the Mothers of Invention; the Who's dynamic performances and advanced compositions; the Yardbirds' newfound assurance; Cream's brilliant experimentation; the advanced blues stylings of Canned Heat and Big Brother and the Holding Co.; the unique and adventuresome psychedelic experiments of Jefferson Airplane, the Grateful Dead, and Country Joe and the Fish; jazz-rock explorations by the Gary Burton-Larry Coryell team and by Jeremy Steig and the Satyrs; and the continuing excellence of the Rolling Stones.

The Stones present the most telling case. They started in about the same place as the Beatles, with perhaps a shade more expertise, a brilliant vocalist in Mick Jagger, and an orientation that leaned closer to a purely blues-based style. Jagger and Keith Richard developed quickly into songwriters comparable to Lennon and McCartney, and anyone else you might choose to name. But they have been ignored by the press – except for an occasional finger of admonishment – mostly because they provide a musical parallel to the civil rights movement, the anti-Vietnam war protests, and the sexual and drug revolutions. They are almost the very embodiments of the alienation the pop cultists would like to ignore.

John Goodman, writing in the *New Leader*, points out that 'as to themes, the Stones like to satirise sex, the everyday, drugs, and the cool attitude. In the album *Flowers*, the red-eyed chick on drugs is put down hard: "You may look pretty, but I can't say the same for your mind" ("Ride on, Baby"). "Mother's Little Helper", the yellow pill "helps her on her way, gets through her busy day," with ironic consequences. In *Between the Buttons* yesterday's girls are like "Yesterday's Papers" – who wants them? But the Stones' finest scorn is reserved for those women of affectation who are "Complicated" or "Cool, Calm, and Collected". The humour here is winning, for it is both bitter and warm, reflective and spontaneous. The Stones have learned how to make their protest mature, viable, and musical.'

The only point left to emphasise is that they are authentic originals who have been content to go their own way, sometimes in the face of considerable opposition. For example, few groups would have had the chutzpah to release 'Let's Spend the Night Together'; in Beatledom, this would never happen.

In reaction to the emphasis in the hippie community on love in its various manifestations, the Beatles felt compelled to honor the subject in song. Not sure which way the wind was blowing and not wanting to be left either pro- or anti-love, they compromised with a mindless composition called 'All You Need Is Love'. The result of their confusion is a mishmash that delights writer Phillips as much as it confuses him. The Stones, meanwhile, produced 'We Love You', a much more assured and inventive song, which managed to be warmly ironic about love and to satirise the Beatles at the same time. The argument is not that art must serve politics, or even that an artist must deal with political issues, but it is necessary to point out that the songs and performances of the Beatles have all been executed with clearly prescribed limitations imposed by the desires and needs of the disseminators of pop, the radio and television outlets, the press, and lately the intellectual and 'concerned' magazines.

And my brother's back at home with his Beatles and his Stones/We never got off on that revolution stuff/ What a drag, too many snags.
– David Bowie, 'All the Young Dudes'

It has been suggested to me by one correspondent that the Beatles are really a contemporary equivalent of Hector Berlioz, a composer whose unengaged romanticism expressed itself in brilliantly orchestrated productions of quite ordinary musical ideas. In the same way, the Beatles never achieve the tension that underlies all great art. Nor have they, except on rare occasions, written memorable compositions. Lovely often but memorable seldom. Art must simply be true to itself, and this, I believe, is the Beatles' failure. The foursome has been compared to Johnny Appleseed, sowing musical seeds, but they have really spent the last four years picking apples in other people's orchards to make their own (sometimes delicious) pies.

As *Time* approvingly points out, throughout their career the Beatles have maintained 'their exemplary behaviour'. Who can help but embrace four such charming lads who can have the good sense to proclaim – as they do stolidly on *Sgt. Pepper* – in the disintegrating fall of 1967, 'I have to admit it's getting better – it's getting better all the time'?

Down Beat, 1967

THE BEATLES' HOME MOVIE
By Charles Marowitz

A quietly damning review of the self-indulgent Magical Mystery Tour *film, by critic and theatrical director Marowitz.*

Cutting through the soft white pastry of Christmas 1967 like a dose of laudanum came *The Magical Mystery Tour*, a 50-minute television film conceived, written, directed, composed, edited, and shot (off-the-cuff) by the Beatles. In a medium that makes a great point of sucking back its hair and cleaning under its fingernails, the Beatles' jump-cutting, hand-held home movie came over as a calculated affront to professionalism.

The day after, the po-faced critics complained of anarchy and confusion, of fashionable *avant-garde* techniques mindlessly applied, of self-indulgence and even effrontery. Others who recognised they were dealing here with *the* trendsetters of our time, patted the film cautiously, deciding (ultimately) it had better be approved of for qualities it *probably* possessed although not apparently to the uninitiated, meaning themselves. (Unbeknownst to them, that included most everyone.) No one was particularly rude. No one was particularly enthusiastic. Everywhere there was a sense of occasion. The first film made by the Beatles themselves (one paper compared it with Welles's debut on *Citizen Kane*) and everywhere one was conscious that the occasion had not quite ushered in an event.

The next day, answering their TV critics, the put-upon lads from Liverpool explained: 'We tried to present something different. . .We thought we would not underestimate people and would do something new. It is better being controversial than purely boring.' But controversial usually means passionate pros and equally passionate cons, whereas the general consensus was negative to indifferent. Even the *Guardian* critic, who alone of all the dailies was not disappointed, praised the film for being an alternative to the glossy packages jutting out of all the other network stockings – rather than an achievement in its own right. The next day, however, finding himself drafted to carry the banner, he damned all the downputters for missing the point which, 24 hours and two television discussions later, he was able to expound.

The film is a kind of *collage-cauchemar* which starts with Ringo buying a ticket for a Mystery Tour and then proceeds to document the discontinuous odyssey of a bus-load of merry-makers who encounter what four magicians (the Beatles) devise from their metaphysical control tower above. (The necessity to provide enchantment for the customers being a subtle indictment of the public's expectations of its idols.) There are set pieces in which numbers from their latest album (a poor relation of *Sgt Pepper's Lonely Hearts Club Band*) are illustrated with trick photography, out-of-focus panning, jump-cuts, and endless footage of what actually happened to the people on the bus. There is an unexceptional strip-number, and a fascinating sequence in which George Harrison, quadruply projected, sits in the lotus position and sings a mildly Westernised Indian ballad. Victor Spinetti does a rough-and-ready imitation of the square-bashing act he did in *Oh! What a Lovely War* and Ivor Cutler, a lachrymose composer-cum-comedian, looks mournfully at one and all. There are a few refreshing subliminal flashes during the musical numbers, but more often than not the pictures mickey-mouse the lyrics. Despite a poverty of visual imagination, the picture captures the frolicsome atmosphere its makers induced in their cast, and that is probably its most vital asset.

MAIN POINTS
Coach Tour – 3 days with people onboard./Week Sept 4 – Cameraman, Sound, Cast, Driver./Hotels arranged for 2 nights./Magical Mystery Tour emblem to be designed./ Yellow coach to be hired – Sept 4 to Sept 9 Microphone system in coach . . . good all around vision./Tour staff – Driver, Courier, Hostess./3 staff uniforms required./Coach destination – Cornwall??/ After coach – Shepperton Studios – 1 week./Write outline script./Decide cast. Engaged cast./Decide when shooting starts./ Sets for studios./Fix completion date.
– *Paul McCartney's itinerary for* Magical Mystery Tour, *written on a napkin*

The Magical Mystery Tour is based on the now-fashionable principles of indeterminacy, chance-selection, and improvisation, without the guiding intelligence that men like Cage or Cunningham bring to the same principles. Being divided among four sensibilities (each of the Beatles was allowed to shoot whatever appealed to him), no uniform vision links the disconnected imagery, and the disparity of temperaments among the four makes the film divide rather than coalesce. Many of the images, like four English bobbies holding hands in a dance formation which is the exact duplicate of the anti-riot squad position, are slyly chosen and memorable. The bus trip, which may be a metaphor for a drug trip (although giving the Beatles the benefit of the doubt, I wouldn't expect them to be that obvious), shuttles from anarchy to fantasy without creating rich confusion or refreshing otherworldliness. In spite of a maniacally fleet rhythm, the result of brutal chop-cutting, the film is slow in many places because it lingers on shots – not for effect but from uncertainty as to where to go next.

What I liked about the film was its relentless privacy; its naive assumption that what it found interesting would interest others, and if it didn't, *tant pis*. It is not an artistic success, but why should a home-movie expect to be? The unconscious 'magical' concept in the picture was the Beatles' magical belief that anything they did was bound to come off, because they were the Beatles and, in some magical way, all the usual criteria for artistic achievement would be temporarily in abeyance. If one complains of the film (and one does) it is not because one expected plot, characters, and situation (the Beatles' lame defence the other night) but because it didn't realise its own surreal potentialities.

Brainwashed by the Maharishi and committed blindly to the Cage-Cunningham principle that what *is* is art and the less the organising-mind interferes the better, the Beatles have had a bash. What they failed to realise is that some underlying instinct – call it taste or talent, it remains an invisible thermostat regulating the artist's unconscious – is an indispensable part of the creative process, and without it no principles, no matter how fashionable, can possibly work.

However, it is ridiculous to discuss the film in these terms. It is another foray in the battle for anti-art, and I am not at all sure we have developed the criteria by which such works can be judged.

Village Voice, 4 January 1968

METAMORPHOSIS OF THE BEATLES
By Pauline Kael

US film critic Kael's review of Yellow Submarine *emphasises its appeal as an animat-ed feature film. The film further defined the Beatles' changing image: from leatherclad rock-ers, via cuddly mop-tops, to dandyish hippies. As they withdrew from live performance, and, in many ways, 'real life', what could be more apt than their metamorphosis into car-toon characters?*

From the nursery to the boutique is now a very short path; *Yellow Submarine* trav-els it with charm and ease. The Beatles, represented by cartoons, go to the rescue of the people of Pepperland and save them from the Blue Meanies, their weapons being (who'd have guessed it?) music and love – but what is so pleasant about *Yellow Submarine* is its lighthearted, throwaway quality, and the story seems as dis-posable as the banter and the images. If the movie tried to be significant, if it had 'something to say', it might be a disaster. One of the best characters is a gluttonous consumer with a vacuum snout, who devours the universe, yet the movie itself sucks up an incredible quantity of twentieth-century graphics. If *Yellow Submarine* were not so good-natured and – despite all the 'artistic' effects – unpretentious, one would be embarrassed; its chic style can't support much more than the mes-sage of 'love'. You could almost make a game of how many sources you can spot, but, because of the giddy flower-childishness of it all, this not only seems all right but rather adds to one's pleasure. The eclecticism is so open that it is in itself entertaining – we have the fun of a series of recognitions. A little Nolde here, a bit of Klimt there, the hotel corridor from *The Blood of a Poet*, with *The Mysteries of China* now become Indian, and good old Birnam Wood moving once again – it's like spotting the faces in Tchelitchew's *Cache-Cache*.

The movie is extravagantly full of visual puns and transformations, but not too full (though there are places where one might wish for an extra instant to savour what is going by). The Beatles' non-singing voices are not their own, but they're good. The verbal jokes invite comparison with Edward Lear but can't sustain it. The movie seems to get its spirit back each time one of the Beatles' songs (sung by the Beatles) comes on (there are ten, three of them new), and this is not just because of the richer verbal texture but because the animation, ingenious as it is, is not much more than a shifting series of illustrations. The movie works best when the images (even though they don't quite connect with the meaning of the lyrics) are choreographed to the music.

In animation, anything can turn into anything else, and children love it for the illogic that is a visual equivalent of their nursery rhymes and jingles and word games. Recent American commercial cartoons have been so undistinguished visually and limited so much of the time to the reversibility of destruction that *Yellow Submarine*, with its bright pop flourish and inventiveness, restores the pleasure of constant surprise, which has always been the fun of good animation. Yet what will probably make *Yellow Submarine* a great success is its superlogical development: the Beatles walk by, and flowers grow out of them. They're no longer the rebellious, anarchistic pop idols that parents were at first so outraged by; they're no longer threatening. They're hippies as folk heroes, enshrined in our mythology. The name 'Beatles' no longer suits them; they have become quaint – such gentle, harmless Edwardian boys, with one foot in the nursery and the other in the boutique, nothing to frighten parents. The movie is a nostalgic fantasy – already nostalgic for the happy anarchism of 'love'. It finally goes a bit flat because love is no longer in bloom.

No doubt we can all do with less threat and less stress in the environment, and yet there's something depressing about seeing yesterday's outlaw idols of the teenagers become a quartet of Pollyannas for the wholesome family trade. And if one looks at a list of the merchandise being promoted in conjunction with the movie, one may long for the simpler days of Mickey Mouse watches. That omnivorous consumer better get ready to suck up seven different *Yellow Submarine* books and a die-cast submarine and clocks and masquerade costumes and sweatshirts and stuffed dolls and inflatable swim toys and posters and lunchboxes and pillows and aprons and lamps and about 50 other products. Wasn't all this supposed to be what the Beatles were *against*? The way attacks on the consumer society become products to be consumed is, to put it delicately, discouraging. The Beatles had already become part of a comic-strip world in *Help!*. By now, they have replaced Mickey Mouse as symbols of the union of art and popular success. Their loss of corporeality seems perfectly natural and right.

Movies are treacherous. I don't fully respect what the director, George Dunning, has done in *Yellow Submarine*; I don't truly admire much of what the chief designer, Heinz Edelmann, has done. And yet the movie is charming. They have done what hasn't been done before in animation – at least, not on anything like this scale. And if it's derivative, so was the Disney style – though not so obviously, since it was more unified. Despite all the enthusiasm registered in the press for animated features, this. is one of the handful of palatable ones.

Without human characters, an animated feature is likely to be a bore, but animated human figures have never quite worked. Erwin Panofsky provided a reasonable explanation: 'The very virtue of the animated cartoon is to animate; that is to say, endow lifeless things with life, or living things with a different kind of life. It effects a metamorphosis, and such a metamorphosis is wonderfully present in Disney's animals, plants, thunderclouds, and railroad trains. Whereas his

I was laying in bed in the Ashers' garret, and there's a nice twilight zone just as you're drifting into sleep and as you wake from it – I always find it quite a comfortable zone. I remember thinking that a children's song would be quite a good idea . . . I just made up a little tune in my head, then started making a story – sort of an ancient mariner, telling the young kids where he'd lived. – *Paul McCartney*

dwarfs, glamorised princesses, hillbillies, baseball players, rouged centaurs, and *amigos* from South America are not transformations but caricatures at best, and fakes or vulgarities at worst.' Still, this may be a little too pat. In the arts, one can never be altogether sure that the next artist who comes along won't disprove one's formulations. *Yellow Submarine* does not exactly disprove Panofsky, but one sequence, the dancing couple for 'Lucy in the Sky with Diamonds', is a stunning use of stylised human figures – an apotheosis of Rogers and Astaire. Rather surprisingly, Edelmann follows the Disney and U.P.A. artists very closely in most of the human characters, making the Beatles as limply boneless and sweet as Snow White, and the Meanies grisly caricatures constantly displaying their cruel teeth. Even so, they shake Panofsky's formulations a bit, because in *Yellow Submarine* this weakness is not as crucial as in the Disney films. Where there is so much to choose from and the style is a collection of rejectable items, something bad may not matter very much. Aesthetic theories don't always allow for the variety of what we enjoy; we may like a certain amount of caricature and grisliness, and I preferred Popeye and Mr Magoo to most animal characters in cartoons, because they were wittier. The Beatles provide a frame of reference that holds this movie together, though as cartoons they are weak facsimiles, with less character than the movie's fish, who are like wind-up toys, and its strange made-up monsters, or even its professorial little Boob. The single worst sequence in the movie – even worse than the addendum of filmed live Beatles – is the montage of photographed cities as the cartoon Beatles leave Liverpool; it disrupts the fantasy. But raiding the arts – shooting the works in animation – succeeds. It becomes an equivalent of the way kids dress now – cutting through the anxieties about what is appropriate and the class structure of good taste, wearing what they feel like wearing, and making life a fancy-dress ball. The movie has something of this freshness; throwing in a multiplicity of styles – even a couple of startling Op sequences – is a fluke solution to a problem that more rigorous-minded men have failed to solve.

The Disney artists' animation was pre-Pop pop of a simple, consistent, and often stupid kind, and this was true, oddly, of *Animal Farm*, the last animated feature to come from England. But pop has now become a style; *Yellow Submarine* uses pop heroes and Pop Art deliberately, and with sophistication. And it works. But it is merely a further development of what ads and commercials have already been doing. People who want to make animated features may now have an easier time getting backing, but the aesthetic problems haven't been solved. Animators can't just keep on ravaging the art of the twentieth century; after the orgy of *Yellow Submarine* it's going to look worn out.

The New Yorker, 30 November 1968

BEATLES
By Adrian Mitchell

Poet Mitchell was a firm fixture in the 1960s British counterculture. More recently, he edited McCartney's anthology Blackbird Singing: Poems and Lyrics 1965-1999, *and performed with him at a poetry rendition at Liverpool's Everyman Theatre. He wrote this utopian view of the Beatles as potential social saviours in response to the authorised Hunter Davies biography.*

William Huskisson, President of the Board of Trade, was standing between the lines in Liverpool welcoming the first train. 'I declare this railway well and truly – AARAGH!' SPLAT! It was the best death scene since an eagle dropped a tortoise on the head of Aeschylus (THUNK!) but it only rates 21 words in Hunter Davies's *The Beatles*, although however already this official biography is a long trudge compared with Michael Braun's sprinting Penguin (*Love Me Do*), yet notwithstanding perhaps there's some fair scenery along the way, especially when Mr Davies shows how various songs were fitted together. So much for criticism.

> The average Englishman wakes up one morn-
> ing to find himself born,
> and starting to explore
> what his body is for
> finds there's rhythm and blues
> in his shoes
> and that's news
> because a few years ago
> the average British toe
> could only go
> slow slow quick slow slow.
> Now the offbeat of the heartbeat
> is the children's choice
> and the human voice
> can shake while it sings and twist and shout
> because some of the fear's flown out.
> Most of us are mostly afraid –
> Murder Incorporated has to be paid

and there's terror in the bone
because of Al Capone
from Canterbury, Baby-Face Calvin
and the spiritual Chicago of Rome.
And though you chain up the door
of your rentokilled home –
Matthew, Mark, Luke and John
surround the bed that you lie on with dread,
each of them armed with a nuclear warhead.

But the Beatles roared along
at the wheel of an independently suspended song
and they saw the rows of English feet
and they knew that feet without a beat are just meat,
so they rolled down the windows to let the word be heard
and every time they passed a naked human has-been
they all shouted out – it's a clean machine.
Jehovah, Jesus, Holy Ghost and Ringo Starr,
Four-faced jubilee weeping in the public bar,
Suddenly flowering home-made submarine –
Shift all the slag heaps from Aberfan to Esher Green.
I'm not trying to paint you a quartet of saints
or musical Guevaras.
But the standard of loving has
plopped through the bottom of the graph.
So the few who do any kind of thing
that shakes out the horrors
are quadruply welcome
especially if they make us laugh.

The fashion-go-round of the underground
may forsake them,
the Army or the CIA may take them,
but we'll meet again. . .

So to the point as fast as possible. When Allen Ginsberg was last over here, he gave a reading of Blake and Ginsberg at the Roundhouse, Chalk Farm, at a time when all honest chalk farmers were in bed dreaming of the sprouting pink, blue and white lengths of chalk which decorate the dusty fields around the blackboard forest. Between poems Ginsberg talked about fear. He said that ten or fifteen years ago he had been full of fear, but that he'd worked at cutting down his terror ration and had changed until he was hardly afraid of anything. I sat in the audience and felt the lump of fear which I always carry diminish.

I asked Bobby Dylan/I asked the Beatles/I asked Timothy Leary/But he couldn't help me either. – *Pete Townshend, 'The Seeker'*

The Beatles appear to be moving, zigzag, in the Ginsberg direction. They've already shown some courage in a traditionally cowardly trade – for in pop music the aim is to be loved by everyone, villains included. Maybe it was foolhardiness when they filmed their own *Magical Mystery Tour*. It contained some images – policemen holding hands on top of a concrete bunker or shelter while the Beatles played below in Disney masks – which were way beyond the heads of most of the critics. The progress of their songs from 'Please Please Me' (instantly likeable and who, at that time, could ask for anything more?) to 'Penny Lane' (poetry) and 'A Day in the Life' and 'I Am the Walrus' (adventurous poetry) has been an exciting voyage to follow. After all, everyone knew Francis Chichester wasn't going to fall off the edge of the world, but the Beatles might.

Snipers from the press will keep trying to shoot them down and keep missing, because the Beatles have more to offer than the press. Most people, without envy, wish them good luck on their journey. More than that, many people hope that their courage increases, and not just for the sake of their art. There are obviously more important issues.

Take one of these. For many years England has been unofficially, sometimes shamefacedly and often silently racialist. Then along came Enoch Powell, strumming on the nerves of the nation, speaking the language of cold sweat. Suddenly he became the first popular politician since the war – has anyone else so rallied the Right? Enoch Powell has changed and will continue to change English politics from blatantly selfish to patently lunatic. The weakness of both Heath's and Wilson's responses proves how scared they are.

I'm not suggesting that Powellism could be stopped if the Beatles applied their considerable wits to a record called *Enoch*. But they would be heard. They would also lose votes. They would be subject to a great deal of hatred. They have taken risks in the past, but this would be a higher risk, one that might mean imprisonment (in a bad future) or might, by amplifying the small chorus of brave voices, mean that the future might be less bad.

The Listener, 3 October 1968

THE BEATLES
By Hunter Davies

Davies' biography was the 'official authorised' account. As the Beatles were still functional as a unit, it was clearly in their interests to control how the image of the group was presented.

John lives in a large mock Tudor house on a private estate full of mock Tudor houses in Weybridge, Surrey. Ringo lives on the same estate. John's house cost him in all £60,000, although it was only £20,000 to buy. He spent the other £40,000 doing it up, knocking rooms around, decorating and furnishing, landscaping the garden and building a swimming pool. He has spent too much on it, which he knows. 'I suppose I'd only get half the money back if I sold it, about £30,000. I'll need to find a pop singer to sell it to, someone soft anyway.'

In the garden he has a psychedelically painted caravan, which was done to match the patterns of his painted Rolls Royce. The house is on a slight hill, with the grounds rolling beneath. There is a fulltime gardener, a housekeeper called Dot and a chauffeur called Anthony. None of them lives in.

Inside, the front hail is dark and book-ridden but the rooms beyond are bright and large and lushly decorated. There are long plush sofas and huge pile carpets and elegant drapes, all of which look brand new and unused, like a Hollywood set. But amongst them are scattered irrelevant ornaments, old posters and bits of antiques. They look highly used and personal, obviously chosen by John, rather than an interior decorator, but just dumped and forgotten about once the initial whim wore off.

These reception rooms might as well be corridors. Nobody ever seems to use them, although they are kept beautifully dusted. They just walk through them to get out. All the living is done in one little rectangular room at the back of the house. It has one wall completely made of glass and looks over the garden and trees beyond.

John, his wife Cynthia and their son Julian (born 8 April 1963) spend most of their time in this living-room and kitchen. The surrounding opulence seems to have nothing to do with them. Dot looks after that.

Inside their quarters, Cyn looks after her family on her own, doing all the cooking for the three of them - though John sometimes makes tea. She looks after Julian by herself. She has never had a nanny, although Dot does a lot of baby sitting. It was she who looked after Julian while John and Cyn were in India in early 1968.

Cyn gets worried now and again by the expense of having and not using such a big house. John, when he thinks about it, finds it a laugh.

'Everything seems to cost a fortune,' she says. 'John spends impetuously and it's catching. I'm always feeling guilty. I have to pull myself together now and again, when I realise how much something would mean to some people. Our food and drink bill is amazing. It's mostly bread, tea, sugar, milk, cat food and soft drinks, as we don't drink. Yet it somehow comes to £120 a month. I don't know how.'

They have five cats. Their names chart the stages in John's life. There's Mimi, after his aunt, and Neil and Mal, after their road managers. One kitten, born in the summer of 1967, at the height of their Yogi summer, is called Babidji.

A lot of the regular bills, like gas and electricity, are paid direct by their accountant. Cyn pays the rest.

'I sometimes open them when they arrive,' says John. 'If I don't like the look of them I put them away and forget about them till they start complaining. Now and again I do query them, but they just go on about "Well, sir, it's like this sir." You never get anywhere.'

All the Beatles receive a weekly sum of £50 in fivers to cover any personal expenses, like staff. They rarely carry any money personally.

'I don't know how much money I've got,' says John. 'I'm not conscious of having a treasure chest full of it at the bottom of the garden. It's all hypothetical, but I know it's not as much as some people think.

'It's all tied up in things, in various forms. I did ask the accountant once how much it came to. I wrote it down on a bit of paper. But I've lost the bit of paper.'

Their little rectangular living-room is crammed high with posters, ornaments and photographs. A large notice pinned on one wall says 'Milk is Harmless'.

They eat in this room, watch telly in this room and when it's cold or rainy John spends most of his time, when he's not recording or writing a song, curled up on a small sofa in this room, doing nothing. The sofa is far too small for him. He would obviously be more comfortable on one of the lush ones from the other room. But he curls his legs round and can lie for hours.

When it's fine, he opens the sliding glass door and goes out and sits on a step in the garden, looking down at his swimming pool and his English country garden.

Anthony or Dot usually answer the front door, though if he's in the mood, John does. He rarely answers the telephone. It is almost impossible to get him on the telephone anyway as he has an answer phone system which takes messages. This in itself puts off most people trying to get through to him. There is a recorded voice which says 'This is Weybridge Four, Five, Wubbleyoo, Dubbleyoo, please leave your message now.'

His ex-directory number is always being changed which is supposed to be one way of keeping it secret. It's a secret from John anyway. He can never remember it.

An ordinary evening at the Lennons is ordinary. This particular ordinary evening, two door-to-door salesmen had come to the door, saying they were Australian students selling magazines. John happened to open the door and had let them in. They said they were in a competition to see who could get most subscriptions. The prize would help their studies. That was their story anyway. John said yeh, very good, come on then, what do you want me to do? They got out the list of the magazines and asked John to tick the ones he would like to read. He ticked a lot and the two salesmen-students said it would come to £74. John said OK, hold on till I find some money. He could only find the packet with the £50 housekeeping cash. He gave them that. They said that would do fine. They thanked him very much and left.

John and I both came from comfortable homes but he never knew the love and support that there was in my family. So when the whole Beatles thing happened I kept my feet on the ground while he went off on some kind of lunar trajectory. – *Cynthia Lennon*

Cyn made the evening meal for her family. They started with a slice of melon followed by a plate of cold meat with vegetables. John didn't have the meat, as he'd become a vegetarian. They all drank cold milk with it.

John had a filling coming out of his tooth which he constantly played with, making a sluicing noise as he ate his food. He went to the fridge in the kitchen to get some more milk. He drank it ice cold from the bottle. Cyn said that wouldn't do his tooth any good.

Throughout the meal, the television was on. They all turned their seats to watch it. Now and again Cyn or John would change the station. They never seemed to watch any programme for more than ten minutes. John stared silently at it, lost and abstracted through his specs. Cyn was reading the *Daily Mirror* at the same time. Julian watched it and chattered. Then he got down from the table and lay on the carpet and started to do a drawing. Cyn got him some coloured biros. They both watched him, asking him what his drawing was. He said it was a bird cage, like the one in the garden. He explained all the things happening in his drawing. John and Cyn smiled at him as he did so.

John then opened the large sliding window, and sat on a step to get some fresh air, looking down upon the pool. On the surface of the pool the automatic filter buzzed round and round, like a space ship which had just landed. Julian came out and went down to the pool. He threw some oars in, then got them out again and came back to the house. Cynthia cleared up.

Terry Doran arrived and was greeted warmly by all, including Julian who sat on his knee.

'Do you want your Dad to put you to bed?' said Cyn, smiling at John, who grinned back. 'Or do you want Terry?' Julian said he wanted Terry. But she picked up Julian herself and put him to bed.

'Are you going to roll us a few then?' said John to Terry. Terry said yes. John got up and brought out a tin tool box which he opened for Terry. Inside was some tobacco wrapped in silver tin foil plus some cigarette papers. Terry rolled a couple of cigarettes which they smoked, sharing them between them. This was during the pot-taking period, which is now over.

Cyn came back. The television was still on. They all sat and watched it, still

I haven't broken it off, but it is broken off, finished . . . I know it sounds corny, but we still see each other, and love each other, but it hasn't worked out. Perhaps we'll be childhood sweethearts and meet again, and get married when we're about 70.
— public statement by Jane Asher, 20 July 1968

changing programmes all the time, until about midnight when Cyn made some cocoa. Terry left and John and Cyn went to bed. John said he was going to read a paperback book someone had given them. Cyn said oh, she wanted to read that first.

While the other three moved out into stock-broker Surrey, Paul remained the only London Beatle. He took a large detached three-storey house in St John's Wood, near Lord's cricket ground and just round the corner from EM I's recording studios. He bought it at the end of 1966 for £40,000. He didn't do much knocking about, compared with John and Ringo. The garden became a jungle, completely overgrown, inhabited only by the prowling Martha. When he'd moved in it had been very pretty. Everybody kept on at him, especially his Dad, to do something about it. He seemed to delight in its wildness and the way it annoyed some people. But at the end of 1967 he decided to start having it tarted up. He got the idea of building a magical house in it, a sort of pagoda on a raised platform with an open glass roof onto the skies. When he got that finished, he and Jane started thinking about moving to a smaller house in the country.

The house is guarded by a high brick wall and large double black gates which are controlled from the house. You speak into a microphone, someone inside answers and, if you say the right thing, the doors swing open and then clank shut again to keep out the fans.

All the Beatle homes have fans hanging around, but Paul has most, being Paul and also being in London. They keep up a permanent watch outside, usually sitting in rows on the wall of the house opposite. From there they can just see over the wall and make out any movements around the front door. Coming into the street you can tell Paul's house by the rows of girls hanging precariously from his wall, a couple of feet off the ground, craning to look over.

The basement of the house contains a staff flat. He had a couple for a long time, Mr and Mrs Kelly, who both lived there. She did the housekeeping and he was the sort of butler, but both really mucked in and were just there. After them, he's had a succession of people. They just seem to arrive at random and he keeps them on sometimes, however unsuitable. He could really do with a secretary, to organise his house and his visitors, but he says he would never do that. Very often he has nobody living in the house and when he's been abroad his dad Jim sometimes has come down to look after the house and Martha.

Not that Paul worries about it. It doesn't bother him that people arrive whom he's promised to see and instead he's gone off to Africa or America. All he likes around is a nice motherly lady who serves up a fried breakfast at about one o'clock and at other hours of the day as required. When Jane is not working, she does a lot of the cooking and is very good.

The ground floor contains the kitchen, which is very large and well appointed, a large haughty dining-room which looks completely unused, and his living-room at the back, which is the most used of any Beatle room. This is very large and comfy with French windows opening on to the back garden. It has a large soft green Edwardian suite, nicely faded. There is a large wooden table in this living-room where most meals are served, rather than in the dining-room. It is usually covered with an elderly white lace tablecloth, very working-class posh. The room is usually in chaos, with stuff piled everywhere, ornaments, flashing lights, packages, newspapers and bits of equipment. This is where the Beatles and Mal and Neil and others congregate before recording sessions and in fact most times they are in London. It has an unpretentious lived-in feeling. 'Everywhere I've lived always ends up like this. At Forthlin it was the same. Things might look a bit different now, like a big colour TV, but the atmosphere's always the same.'

On the first floor is his bedroom, a large L-shaped room with an extravagant bed with a large carved headboard. Jane helped him to furnish this room. There are two other bedrooms. On the top floor is his work room, where he and John do most of their hard slog together when they need some more songs to fill up an album. This is where he has the Paolozzi sculpture. Very interesting, that piece. Paolozzi was Stu Sutciffe's hero and teacher.

The famous Martha (if you don't think she's famous you should read *Beatles Monthly*) is a very large, shaggy good-natured old English sheep dog. She's good-natured even when she has a few fleas. She has her own trap door into the garden for her regular prowls, but Paul tries to take her for a proper walk as often as he can. He usually goes to Primrose Hill or Regent's Park. He did go to Hampstead Heath once but Martha had a fit and he hasn't taken her back. There are also several cats, and kittens, which seem to vary in number from day to day. All the Beatles have cats, and all their births are faithfully reported in *Beatles Monthly*.

Paul manages his walks with Martha with surprising lack of recognition. The fans never realise where he's going, when he rushes out. And in the park, he usually has his jacket collar up and walks round the remotest parts with Martha, meeting only elderly dog lovers who are more interested in the enormous Martha than Paul.

He exchanges the time of day with other people and makes polite dog chat. He even shouts out at people he vaguely recognises, something the other Beatles wouldn't do, not being as sociable as Paul. He was on the top of Primrose Hill one day when he saw an actor he slightly knew. He shouted at him, but the actor walked past, as if to say I don't know you so please don't shout, there's a good chap. He was a terribly upper-class young English type actor. He gave a great backwards Hello, when he at last recognised Paul. Paul had met him once through Jane. He'd been acting in the same play and had invited Jane and Paul to his house for dinner.

Paul asked him how he was doing, then. The actor said, very coyly, that he had a chance of a play in New York. 'Oh aye,' said Paul. 'What?'

'Can't tell,' said the actor, going even coyer. 'Sorry. Never do. When there's something in the offing one might spoil it by talking about it, mightn't one? Don't you find that, hmm?' Paul smiled and said yeh, he supposed so. 'Well, bye then,' said the actor. He breezed off, swinging his arms, looking up and breathing heavily at the lovely day. You could almost see him reading the stage directions.

'Strange, isn't it?' said Paul, walking back to the car. 'How somebody like that just can't relax. It's impossible for him to be natural. Yet he's OK, he's a nice enough bloke, once he relaxes and has a few drinks. By the end of that dinner we had with him he was almost normal. I feel sorry for people like that, really. It's the way they've been conditioned.

'When I was a kid of sixteen, all adolescent and awkward and shy, I was dying to be an actor like that, all smooth and in command, always coming on dead confident. But it was worth going through that awkward stage, just to be natural now. Jane has a little bit of the same trouble, with her background. She can't help it. It's how they've been brought up.'

The Beatles, Hunter Davies, 1968

A TWIST OF LENNON (2)
By Cynthia Lennon

This second extract from the memoirs of Lennon's first wife describes how he deserted her for Yoko Ono – and demonstrates more sympathy for her ex than might be expected.

John had taken acid once more, but this time he said it was wonderful. His friend had told him that all was marvellous and that he was a great guy. This for John was such a revelation since he was always the one to boost others' egos. His own had been neglected until that moment.

'Cyn, it was great,' he enthused. 'Christ, Cyn, we've got to have lots more children. We've got to have a big family around us.'

At this point I burst into tears, much to John's amazement.

'What the hell's the matter with you, Cyn, what are you crying for?'

All I could blurt out was that in no way could I see us as he did. One trip did not guarantee a secure future and it was no use using the promise of a large family to solve our problems. I was so disturbed by John's outburst that I even suggested that Yoko Ono was the woman for him. John protested at my crazy suggestion and said that I was being ridiculous. But nothing he said could dissuade me from my premonitions.

Although life went on as usual, my fears grew. I felt nervous, depressed, as though I was sitting on the edge of a volcano. John was aware of my depression and suggested that as he had to work for long hours in the recording studios for a few weeks, I should accompany Jenny, Donovan, Gypsy and Alexis on a holiday to Greece. The very thought of sun and sea really brightened my outlook. I felt that the complete change would help me to get things into perspective. I would be able to return refreshed and renewed. I felt that when I returned I would be able to cope with a situation that was fast getting out of hand.

The two weeks in Greece were wonderful, a total change. My mind began to unwind, the cobwebs of doubt and fear eventually began to disperse. I was happy and hopeful for the future. I had decided to banish my fears and premonitions. I wanted to be back with John again and to start afresh. All I could think of on the journey home was John and Julian and our future. We spent a night in Rome and following lunch the next day, we caught a flight back to London. I kept saying, 'Won't it be great! Lunch in Rome and we'll drag John out for dinner in London. We'll make a day of it, do the jet-set bit.'

Our arrival home, it seemed, was unexpected. It was four o'clock in the afternoon. The porch light was on and the curtains were still drawn. There were no signs of life, no Julian to welcome me with his usual shouts of delight, no John, no Dot, just an ominous silence. My heart was in my mouth. The front door was not locked so we all trooped into the house shouting, 'Hello, where are you? Is anyone home?' No response, until we walked into the morning-room where we heard quiet murmurings of conversation. When I opened the door I was confronted by a scene that took my breath and voice away. Dirty breakfast dishes were cluttering the table, the curtains were closed and the room was dimly lit. Facing me was John sitting relaxed in his dressing-gown. With her back to me, and equally as relaxed and at home, was Yoko.

The only response I received was 'Oh, hi,' from both parties. Although I knew that Yoko would in some way loom large in John's life, the reality and the shock of the situation stunned me more than I could have imagined. They looked so right together, so naturally self-composed under the unusual circumstances. I felt totally superfluous. The ground was taken from beneath my feet and I was incapable of dealing with such an occasion. I was a stranger in my own home. Desperately trying to cover up my shock, all I could think of saying was, 'We were all thinking of going out to dinner tonight. We had lunch in Rome and we thought it would be lovely to have dinner in London. Are you coming?' It sounded so stupid in the light of the changed circumstances. The only reply I received was 'No thanks.' And that was it. I wanted to disappear and in fact that is just what I did. I rushed out of the room upstairs, gathered random personal belongings together with the speed of lightning. All I knew was that I had to get out, get away from a scene that created so much pain. I was in a terrible state of shock. As I ran along the landing, I noticed a pair of Japanese slippers neatly placed outside the guest bedroom door. Instead of feeling incensed, I just wanted to run.

A Twist of Lennon, Cynthia Lennon, 1978

BORN UNDER A BAD SIGN
By Tony Palmer

*TV producer/director Palmer wrote his useful analysis of rock culture and the countercul-
ture at the end of the Sixties, including this account of the Beatles and their floundering
Apple empire.*

'I declare,' wrote Timothy Leary, 'that the Beatles are mutants. Prototypes of
evolutionary agents sent by God, endowed with a mysterious power to create a
new human species – a young race of laughing freemen.'

The Beatles tore the hackneyed pants off pop music like frenzied lovers.
They completely squashed the Coke-soaked, chocolate sundae bunch of singers
which had dominated the scene since Elvis and the Everly Brothers had gone off
into the army. In the late Fifties, Jerry Lee Lewis and Chuck Berry had been
almost driven off stage for performing 'distasteful nasties'. Buddy Holly had been
killed in an air crash and Fats Domino and Little Richard were in retirement.
Everyone else who was anyone was black – which for the communications
media such as television meant instant depth. In response to this vacuum, the
Beatles grew large. The hysteria with which they were greeted was nothing new.
Heine's description of the effect that the composer-pianist Liszt had had upon
women sounds as if it might have been written of the Beatles. 'Women shrieked,
fainted and fought,' wrote Heine, 'when the great pianist arrived because of
magnetism, galvanism and the electricity of histrionic epilepsy, tickling musical
cantharides and other unmentionable matters.' The Beatles were used by those
who would make the Beatles part of their own romantic fantasies. They looked
like being heroes who would promise never to rock the boat. They 'did their
thing' and it just happened to coincide with one of society's needs. So their
record *Sergeant Pepper* was the great success it was, partly because we wanted it
to be. It tidied up the drug scene and made psychedelia as mind-blowing as *Late
Night Line-Up*. That has always been one of the Beatles' functions – to make pop
and the pop scene socially acceptable.

The Beatles are the great democratic principle at work in pop, reducing
everything to the ordinary. They wanted to outwit the media who didn't want
to know about the things that hurt. As Nat Hentoff said, the Beatles 'turned on
millions of American adolescents to what had been hurting all the time. . .but

the young never did want it raw; consequently they absorbed it through the Beatle filter.' So the Beatles performed an essentially middle-class function – they filtered out the 'hurting'. They served as the introduction to and the popularisers of a whole new world of creative adventure. They travelled only a few miles beyond the *avant-garde*, consolidating gains and making acceptable new ideas. In this way they cleaned-up the lyrics of rock'n'roll, and used the most obvious aspects of black music – the big beat amplification (picked up from Chuck Berry), ensemble singing and a vague hint of blueness – as the foundation of their wrongly labelled 'new' music. 'Yeah' thus became the bridge word from black to white music. The *Times Educational Supplement* noted that 'Lennon and McCartney's lyrics represent an important barometer to our society – sentiments which are shared by pupils in every classroom in Britain. . .If [*Sergeant Pepper's*] understanding were to be reflected in Britain's teachers, our schools might be more sympathetic institutions than some are now.' Richard Goldstein in the *New York Times* noted that 'their jester's approach to "serious" music and "deep" thought clamours for interpretation, and their intentional embrace of ambiguity sets a tempting critical trap; how hard it is to resist when Ideas are the part.'

The Beatles are Divine Messiahs. The wisest, holiest, most effective avatars that the human race has yet produced. – *Timothy Leary*

Wilfred Mellers, Professor of Music at York University, declared that the essential quality of the Beatles – which they had in common with Boulez, John Cage and Bob Dylan – was 'an attempt to return to magic, possibly as a substitute for belief.' McCartney himself admitted – in an interview with Miles in the *International Times*: 'With any kind of thing, my aim seems to be to distort it, distort it from what we know it as, even with music and visual things and change it from what it *is* to see what it *could* be. To see the potential in it all. To take a note and wreck it and see in that note what else there is in it, that a simple act like distorting it has caused. It's all trying to create magic; it's all trying to make things happen so that you don't know why they've happened.'

'Their story,' says Derek Taylor, their close friend and publicist, 'is the biggest running story in history. Longer than the Second World War. But nobody died.' 'They've got enormous momentum,' said one of their legal advisers. '*Whatever* they do has a measure of popular support. If they were to start an undertaker firm tomorrow, teenagers would be making provisions in their wills that they should be buried by the Beatles.' 'The Beatles,' says Derek Taylor, 'have the capacity of very attractive children for really getting away with it. They've said, "we are more

popular than Jesus," tried LSD and admitted it, signed the Legalise Marijuana petition and two of them have been heavily fined for smoking it, and followed the
Maharishi. They've survived all that and still people smile when they see them.
They no longer feel they have to be anything but themselves, but they're still a
continuously big event and *you* don't want to miss it.'

En route, almost by accident it seems – these four likely lads from Liverpool,
who were only one of 350 groups to suddenly emerge from that city, removed
what felt like the sterile martyrdom from Art, and revived its sensual qualities. In
a very short time, they composed over 200 songs, some worthy of any comparison, and amassed a fortune. In a sense, therefore, Liverpool's poor were to make
England rich, in song, in fashion, in youthful energy and in foreign currency.

Since 1963, the Beatles' records have grossed at least £100 million – much
of it in dollars. Sales of their 230 songs topped the 200 million mark some while
back – and that's not including the 10,000 or so cover versions. 'Yesterday' alone
has 119 different recordings. Each Beatle has earned enough £1 notes to make
a pile one-and-a-half miles high; it would take you five months of solid count-
ing at the rate of two £1 notes per second to get through their total earnings.
John and Paul, for example, used to be paid four-and-three-quarter pennies per
single and 1/8d. per LP, by way of publishing royalties. This revenue was
assigned to a small private company called Northern Songs Ltd., over which they
only recently lost control. The two Beatles originally owned twenty per cent
each of its shares. In its first eighteen months, the company earned £289,292.
The company then went public, offering its shares at an initial 7/9d., thus making it worth £1,937,500. Within a week, both John and Paul sold a quarter of
their holdings, netting £96,875 each, tax free – the capital gains tax was not yet
in force. For a group whose first record sold all of five copies, whose early fee
for a gig could be as much as £4, whose first public appearance was as a rather
indifferent supporting act for 'Wump and the Werbles', and whose career is even
now only eight years old, that's a considerable achievement.

Although their personal fortunes (after tax) are probably far less than is popularly imagined, there's little doubt that if they continue at anything like the
same rate – and in 1968 alone they wrote 40 new pieces, one of them called,
ironically, 'Northern Song' – they will *earn* in their lifetime more than the total
present national debt of the country whose mood and temperament they so
accurately embody. Their financial problem used to be quite simply what to do
with such resources; and the answer seemed to be an apple, for they sank their
fortunes into a multi-million pound entertainment, electronics and merchandising enterprise called Apple Corps Ltd. 'It's a pun,' said Paul – helpfully.

'The aim of the company,' said John, 'wasn't a stack of gold teeth in the

bank. We'd done that bit. It's more of a trick to see if we could get artistic freedom within a business structure, and to see if we could create things and sell
them without charging three times our cost.' Apple Corps was conceived primarily by Harry Pinsker, then one of the Beatles' chief financial advisers, though
he declines responsibility for the name. It was effectively a reincarnation of the
old Beatles Ltd., the company into which the Beatles' vast income from the years
of Beatlemania had been poured. 'I suggested to the boys,' said Pinsker, 'that
they bought freehold property and went into retail trading.' The Beatles
responded with that infectious enthusiasm which they had – until then – reserved
for Indian mysticism and jam butties. 'We want to be like Marks and Spencer's,'
they told Pinsker.

The organisation needed to achieve this extraordinary ambition set itself up
in eight countries. Its permanent administrative staff of 36 were housed in a
£500,000 office block at 3, Savile Row – premises previously occupied by the
impresario Jack Hylton.

The Apple offices were designed conventionally. The atmosphere, according
to one report, was one of 'casual efficiency enlivened by surrealistic incident'.
Occasionally, a Beatle drifted by clothed in yellow satin frills and white bell-bot-
tomed trousers. Almost everyone looked aggressively young and extravagantly
hirsute in the current manner. A thin girl behind a reception desk would say,
'I'm sorry, we're not equipped to handle poetry at present.' It all liked to give
off the impression of a respectable firm which had been seized during a hippy sit-
in and was now being run in the cause of revolution.

In the basement was to be a recording studio described by Paul as the most
technically sophisticated in the world; but plans for four feature films, a couple
of mod clothing stores and for the development of some eighteen patented
inventions by a tame Greek colleague nicknamed 'Magic Alex', seem to have
gone slightly astray. These inventions included, apparently, a two-inch square,
eighth-of-an-inch thick metal plate which – when attached to an ordinary bat-
tery, became red-hot within twenty seconds. If the positive and negative attachments were reversed, it became ice-cold – also within twenty seconds. With this
invention, it was hoped to revolutionise refrigerators and all manner of heating
appliances. Another tit-bit was an audio-visual memory-bank for a telephone.
You tell the telephone the name of the person you wish to call, and the telephone automatically connects you to the person wherever he may be. The
nationwide AT and T Telephone Corporation of America was reported to have
offered the Beatles $1 million for the invention.

John and Paul became worried about the falling sales of discs in the United
States. With the development of the mini tape recorder, or cassette, record buyers

found it cheaper to tape the songs off the radio than to buy the disc. Under the Beatles' sponsorship, an electronic device was developed to prevent this happening, and the grateful record companies were reported to be desperate to buy this world-patented invention. It seemed quite possible that within a few years, every single record sold anywhere in the world would carry this device, and thus pay to the Beatles a royalty. With the number of records being manufactured annually throughout the world exceeding 100 million, it seemed like a good scheme.

As their various contracts with recording companies, distribution agents, publishing houses and film producers expired (the last runs out in 1976), the Beatles intended their affairs to be solely administered and accounted by Apple and its subsidiaries. They offered £20,000 as a starting salary for anyone who thought they could cope with the financial management of their affairs, but for a long time no one whom they interviewed impressed them as being serious enough in their commitment to the cause. Paul intended to start a staff insurance scheme and would have liked to have had a works brass band. He had no intention, however, of becoming a white-collar businessman. 'This *is* a business,' he says. 'But we want to have fun doing it.'

Elvis went downhill because he seemed to have no friends, just a load of sycophants. Whereas with us, individually we all went mad, but the other three always brought us back. – *Ringo Starr*

To that end, they held their first US board meeting aboard a hired Chinese junk, which sailed – appropriately – up and around the Statue of Liberty in New York harbour. For Liberty was precisely what they aimed to have within their new organisation. Liberty – not only to run their own affairs – but to offer to others the kinds of opportunity they themselves felt had been closed to them. 'We *wanted* to help other people,' said Paul. 'But without doing it like charity and without seeming like patrons of the arts.' Even Stravinsky had noted that the two biggest patrons of the arts in America – the Ford and Rockefeller Foundations, were buying up surplus symphonies as the government bought up surplus corn. 'If you came to see me and said, "I've had such-and-such a dream",' continued Paul, 'I would say, "Here's so much money. Go away and do it." We'd already bought all *our* dreams. We wanted to share that possibility with others. When we were touring, and when the adoration and hysteria were at a peak, if we'd been the shrewd operators we were often made out to be, we might have thought – *that's* nice! Aha. Click. Let's use this for our own evil ends. But there's no desire in any of our heads to take over the world. That was Hitler.

That's what he wanted to do. There is, however, a desire to get power in order to use it for good.'

Could the Rev. David Noebel have imagined such a statement when, shocked by initial American reaction to the Beatles, he told his Baptist audience in Claremont, California: 'You listen to this, Christians. These Beatles are completely anti-Christ. They are preparing our teenagers for riot and ultimate revolution against our Christian Republic.' It's all part of a 'Communist Master Music Plan'. The Communists are recording songs with a beat 'synchronised' to the 82 per minute beat of an infant's heart, thus inducing a hypnotic state. 'Those sneaky Beatles step up the beat and add Marxist lyrics which could mass hypnotise the American youth.' The first Beatles LP released in the United States was aptly titled *This is the Savage Young Beatles*.

'You meet a lot of people,' continues Paul, 'who think we planned a lot of this. This power thing. But we haven't, you know. We've never planned anything. I *still* don't know what *Sergeant Pepper* is all about. We only think of ourselves as just happy little songwriters, just playing in a rock group. But – alas – it gets more important than that after you've been over to America, and got knighted.'

Certainly, if it *was* planned, it all got off to a terrible start. John's last school report noted that 'he is on the road to failure'. Ringo's knowledge of music theory was poor. John's father left home when he was eighteen months old and his mother died when he was young. George was nearly thrown out by his parents for being an 'out-and-out teddy boy'. Paul failed in all his academic ambitions. Ringo, an only child ('they gave up after me'), was just 'educated at Butlins'. A career, if such you could describe it, in the tatty world of rock'n'roll was for them the equivalent of becoming a boxer at the turn of the century. It was the only quick way to escape poverty and to acquire an OK ticket to wealth and fame. But even in their chosen career, they were a disaster. The story of how they trouped around Liverpool and Hamburg, first as the Quarrymen, then as the Rainbows, then as John and the Moondogs, then as the Silver Beatles and finally as the Beatles, is well documented in all their fan books and assorted hagiography. For nearly five years, they had neither luck nor recognition. A founder member, Stu Sutcliffe, died of a brain haemorrhage; the original drummer, Pete Best, was sacrificed for a recording contract, although John now says that they never really liked him anyway. Recording manager George Martin had suggested he wasn't up to scratch. Brian Epstein just seemed like a good bet for a manager. To four working class layabouts, Brian – with his big car, his proper accent, his education, his apparent knowledge of the business – seemed okay.

What is less well documented, and in a way more to the point, is their persistent rudeness and aggressiveness to all whom they encountered. Nowadays we like to call this quality a 'sophisticated detachment' or 'an endearing honesty'. Whatever euphemism we give it, however, it is undoubtedly the quality that has caused them to survive, both as people and as artists. For it is not their musical ability nor their minor talent for poetry nor the accidental expression in their songs of the deep feelings of a whole new generation, that has carried them to their present authority. It is this abrasiveness, this mockery, this gentle rudeness, inherent in them and their work, that has brought them to success. More than anything else, it prevented them from being swept away in the deluge of adulation that was to come hurtling their way, and it enabled a quick and readily acceptable identification between us, who wanted to cock a snoop, and them, who were so obviously willing and able to do so. Their triumph against musical snobbery and social prejudice was our triumph also. And their success against authority and demagogy and pedantry was our success also.

What is peculiarly twentieth century, moreover, is that success has always been as necessary to the Beatles as failure was to Mozart. For theirs is the story of how a whole society – not otherwise noted for its generosity to poets – managed to subsidise its revolutionary subconscious to the tune of around £25 million per year. If that society once became aware that its revolutionary subconscious was no longer being satisfied, then hey presto, the bubble would explode. Thus, as the Beatles committed themselves more and more exclusively to Apple, and not just to its financial advantages and rewards, but more importantly to its philosophies and idealism, so the success or failure of that particular enterprise embodied the success or failure of their ability to keep pace with the insistent demands of this revolutionary subconscious. It seemed as if *we* were asking the Beatles to do for us in business organisation and in artistic sponsorship and patronage, what they had already done for us in song, namely to revitalise the language in which we choose to express the way we are, and the way we live.

'It's all right if people don't like us,' says George. 'As long as they don't deny us.' From the start, partly because of this persistent rudeness, denying the Beatles has been hard to do. After their first recording audition, the Beatles were asked by George Martin to tell him what they didn't like. 'As a starter,' said George Harrison, 'I don't like your necktie.' During their first visit to America, they were invited to a reception by the British Ambassador in Washington, Sir David Ormsby-Gore, now Lord Harlech. Confused about their names, the Ambassador asked John if *he* was John. 'No,' said John. He was Fred. Then, pointing to George he said, '*He's* John.' Sir David started to address George as John. 'No,' said George. 'I'm Charlie,' and pointing to Ringo, 'He's John.' As the Beatles left, Ringo turned to the unsettled said Ambassador and inquired: 'And what do *you* do?' 'People in the cheaper seats, please clap,' said John to a West End audience that included, according to the famous story, the Queen Mother. 'The rest of you, just rattle your jewellery.' At earlier performances, John used to appear in bathing trunks, wearing a toilet seat around his neck. 'We're unassuming,' said Ringo, 'unaffected and British to the core. Someone asked me once why I wore four rings on my fingers, and when I told him it was because I couldn't get them on my nose, he didn't believe me.' 'We're rather crummy musicians,' says George now; 'we can't really sing.' 'We can't really do anything,' adds Paul, 'but we're having a great laugh.' 'Don't you think the joker laughs at you?' sang John in his song 'I Am the Walrus'.

This extraordinary lack of self-consciousness and innate aggressiveness also protected them from the massive dose of intellectualisation that was to follow their sensational debut as public property. No-one could quite understand how four rough rug-headed kerns whose apparent intelligence was nil and whose apparent musical inclination was crude and worthless, could seize the imagination of so many in so short a time. Even Billy Graham broke one of his strictest rules never to watch TV on the Sabbath to observe the lads. Richard Buckle called them the greatest composers since Beethoven. William Mann, music critic of the London *Times*, spoke in awed tones of 'pandiatonic clusters' and 'flat-submediant key-switches'. Ned Rorem, an American musicologist and noted commentator, said that 'She's Leaving Home' is equal to any song of Schubert, and Leonard Bernstein cited Schumann. Glenn Gould explained away the success of Lennon and McCartney by pointing to 'our need of the common chord as purgative'. This analytical game reached absurd heights, or depths, in 1968. Derryck Cooke, writing in *The Listener*, said of 'Strawberry Fields': 'it has a first nine-bar section divided into one-and-a-half, two, two, one-and-a-half and two, the penultimate bar being in 6/8 instead of 4/4, quaver equalling quaver. After a delaying six-beat major phrase harmonised by the tonic chord ("Let me take you down, 'cos I'm going"), the tune plunges fiercely on to the flat seventh, harmonised by the minor seventh on the dominant, for a solidly rhythmic beat phrase (*to* "Strawberry Fields").' Musicologically, Mr Cooke was absolutely correct – whether the Beatles liked it or not. But it's as well to remember that he was actually referring to four happy little rockers who can neither read nor write a note of music. Similarly, Jack Kroll of *Newsweek* described 'Day in the Life' as the Beatles' 'Waste Land'. Cyril Connolly thought John's books much influenced by Joyce.

John had never read Joyce. He did buy *Finnegans Wake* subsequently but couldn't manage more than the first page. He framed William Mann's 'pandiatonic clusters' review, but thinks the rest just laughable. To the psychiatric pedantry which reckoned that the Beatles 'are speaking in an existential way about the meaningless actuality', and to the hip-religious fervour which suddenly descended upon them when, for example, a Rev. Ronald Gibbons wanted the Beatles to make a tape-recording of 'O Come All Ye Faithful, Yeah, Yeah, Yeah' because, he said 'the Beatles cult can be the very shot in the arm that the Church needs today,' and to the semi-political band-wagonning which gave them the MBE and caused a Mr. K. Amirvdham, an Indian Communist MP, to refer to their sojourn with the Maharishi as evidence that they were 'not only Western Imperialist war-mongering lackeys, but spies' – to all this, John replied, for example, by drawing anti-religious cartoons depicting among other things Christ hanging on the Cross with a pair of bedroom slippers at the foot. His MBE used to dangle idly from a dummy inside his front door. It then sat on his Aunt Mimi's television. In the days when he lived in Weybridge, his private telephone at one time had an answering device which said, 'This is an answering machine that will not answer you.' And then laughed.

This is not to say that they are ignorant of what it is they are up to, both socially and musically. Indeed, it is because their awareness was often too acute to be comfortable, that their careers took their two most far-reaching twists; firstly, to give up public performance altogether, and secondly to live artistically almost entirely in their electronic playroom, the recording studio. Both decisions were accelerated by the intolerable pressures of Beatlemania touring, but Derek Taylor recounts what seems to him to have enforced the first decision. 'We were in Australia. In a hotel. Suddenly, the manager came to me and said: "The cripples are ready." I said, "What are they ready for? For the Beatles?" He said "yes". "What do they want?" I said. He said, "Well, they can't move that much, so maybe if the Beatles patted them that would be enough." I said, "You mean, lay their hand on them. Faith-heal them!" He said "yes". So I went into the boys' rooms and said, "There's a dozen paraplegics waiting for you in wheelchairs." So good enough, they trooped out, touched them, grinned and said, "See you again." But it left its mark. And when it happened over and over and over again, they treated it like a joke. But they never forgot.'

The second decision came with a growing realisation – shared by others – that pop as it existed then, could no longer contain what they themselves wanted to express through the medium called pop music. To effect this second decision, it became clear that the full resources of the recording studio would have to be utilised. Thus, although pop was already more varied in its sources than jazz had been 40 years earlier, and although the young white pop musician was less shackled by the diatonic-harmonic tradition which had dominated and finally suffocated the jazz and swing eras, the *deus ex machina* of recording techniques gave pop its ultimate advantage and its ultimate newness. Phil Spector had been the first to understand this, but in George Martin, the Beatles found an equally sympathetic record-producer. 'Recording,' he said, 'gave us the advantage of being able to make up music as we went along.'

What had started as the Sound of Soul in America's Deep South and had since absorbed everything from Memphis Rock to British Music Hall, suddenly took on the full paraphernalia of sophisticated music-making. Their first LP was recorded in a day. *Sergeant Pepper* – described by a lecturer at New York's Free University as 'the great contemporary Bible' – took three months and 700 hours of studio time to create. Their next LP, called *The Beatles*, took longer. The orchestration for *Sergeant Pepper* included combs and paper over a string octet and harp for 'Lovely Rita'; multiple-tracked percussion and strings, into which tambouras and swormandels are embedded for 'Within You, Without You' whose rhythm alternates continually between 4/4 and 5/4; three tambouras, a dilruba, a tabla, an Indian table-harp, a sitar, three cellos and eight violins for 'She's Leaving Home', John on Hammond organ, recorded at different speeds and then overlaid with electronic echo and four harmonicas for 'Mr. Kite', and a 41 piece orchestra for 'A Day In The Life' which provided the song-cycle with a final crescendo reminiscent for some of a giant, crippled turbine, struggling to spin new power into a floundering civilisation. By chance perhaps, this desire to spin new power into a floundering civilisation also became the artistic ambition of Apple.

In tonality it ['Sgt. Pepper's Lonely Hearts Club Band'] is curiously ambiguous: for while it gravitates towards a smiling G major, the introduction wobbles between dominant sevenths of D and F, and when we reach the tune itself and the Band, having been introduced, plays and sings, the rhythms of the tootling arpeggiated tune are tipsily displaced by cross accents (three against two) and the open tonality is clouded by blue false relations. – *Wilfred Mellers*

Apple has existed for two years – since the death of Brian Epstein. Its list of products to date reads like the handout for some none too prosperous cottage industry rather than the export list of the dynamic liberator of artistic and business freedom it had been cracked up to be. Less than eighteen months after it had been set up, John Lennon publicly announced that if things carried on the way they were going, the Beatles would be broke within the year. 'I'm down to my last £50,000,' said John. 'My bank balance is really scratching the desk. It would do it good to get back to work.'

Apple's first adventure into retailing – the 'Apple Shop', in London's Baker Street, was in trouble from the start. Its gaudily painted exterior survived for only six months before local residents objected and it was painted out. The shop changed management twice, its staff designers went, it made a loss, and then closed. The Beatles gave away the remaining £20,000 worth of stock. Apple Shop had been run by Terry Doran, 'the man in the motor trade' from 'She's Leaving Home'. He also managed a group called Grapefruit, another Apple off-shoot which so far has failed to make any hit records. A second shop in which, Paul said, 'We shall sell clothes, radios, records and books. If somebody wants to sell something, they can just bring the things in.' 'Apple will be like a bazaar,' he said. It actually turned out to be a smart King's Road boutique called Apple Tailoring (Civil and Theatrical), with an exclusive gents' hairdressing salon in the basement. Apple Films did do a bit better, for a while, with a world-wide financial disappointment – *Magical Mystery Tour*, a cartoon it bought – *Yellow Submarine*, which couldn't get any general release in the United Kingdom, three tiny promotional films and a rag-bag of plans to its credit. Headed by 42-year-old Denis O'Dell, an associate of Richard Lester, these plans included such startling epics as *The Jam*, officially described as 'the story of a traffic jam and the love-hate selfishness and greed it can cause'. Apple Merchandising was run by John Lyndon, a one-time Portobello Road store-keeper. He planned to start up a mail-order catalogue, but so far, nothing. Peter Asher, brother of Jane, ran the new artistes who included Mary Hopkin and James Taylor, and then left. In management, there was 26-year-old Peter Shotton, John's schoolboy chum and a former member of the former Beatle's group, the Quarrymen. Eventually, he was made John's personal assistant, at £30 per week. He had previously been a skilled washboard player. Managing director is Neil Aspinall, one-time road manager, bouncer, and all-purpose hefty. Actually, he's quite small and has eight GCE's. He is, therefore, an intelligent member of the group.

The electronics division – whose devices, it was claimed, would cause a revolution or two in the refrigeration and recording business especially when headed by Alexis Mardas, has so far produced almost nothing. Mardas is said to have arrived in Britain knowing only two people here: the Duke of Edinburgh and Lord Snowdon. It seemed natural enough that he should have soon met the Beatles, who had asked him what he did with that direct curiosity they share with Alice. 'I invent things,' quipped Mardas. Within the turning of an eye, they promptly set him up on a workshop in Marylebone with four research assistants.

Another key figure used to be John's private astrologer. He made his calculations daily before John arrived at the office. On these, John planned his day. So if an important business trip to America had been planned and the astrologer predicted that long journeys over water were unwise, the trip would be cancelled and that was that, so the rumour went.

It's ironic that the word 'béatilles' used to be defined in sixteenth century cook-books as 'all kinds of ingredients that may be fancied put together into a pie, viz.: Cock's combs and bottoms of Hartichokes,' for that's about the mixture that goes into Apple. There is no regularity of purpose or of planning. In their former office accommodation in Wigmore Street, no-one was ever quite sure who lived in what office because from time to time (often twice a day) people would change round – just for fun. 'It wasn't being run like a business,' said John. 'It was more like a fun-fair.' An American businessman, called Allen Klein, previously associated with the Rolling Stones, was brought in to try and sort things out. For these services he was awarded twenty per cent of the Beatles' income.

When the Beatles had first moved to their new offices in London's Savile Row, the four leaders would come in daily to oversee the operation. Klein or no Klein, they drank tea and listened to records. Ringo thought it would be fun to go into the building industry, but that didn't come to much because, as he said, 'No-one wanted to buy the houses we put up.' John would say that he suddenly needed a £1,500 cine-camera with all available attachments to film a tit-bit he had decided was memorable. A minion would be dispatched to bring back the goodies. No-one thought twice or even once about the expense involved.

'At EMI,' (their parent recording company), says Paul, 'we said we wanted to spend £5,000 on a cover and we think it'll be worth it and they reel back and take Disprin and say, *we only spend £75.*' EMI, of course, had recently taken over ATV, and ATV suddenly tried to take over Northern Songs Ltd. – the company which handled many of the Beatles' songs. ATV is part of the Grade Organisation, the joint managing director of which is none other than Bernard Delfont. 'Once again,' said Paul, 'we found ourselves fighting the men in white overalls and big machines and corporate bodies. We're adults now, we're not kiddies any more. Leave us alone, and we'll give in the product and come home with our tails wagging behind us.'

One of the most bizarre aspects of this new adulthood occurred when George and John became co-directors of Hayling Supermarkets Ltd. Someone suggested accordingly – perhaps a little unkindly – that it was the *supermarket* that would prove to be the forum in which the power that the Beatles had won so ferociously, would be displayed. What dreams will they buy there and whom will they sponsor? They'll have endless fun no doubt, but to what end? and for whose good? Can Savile Row really be the apotheosis of all that they have dared? Elgar has his chemical industry, Sir William Walton his villas. Beethoven had his nephew, Mozart his wife. The Beatles have Apple. It's like a congenital,

occupational hazard – this need of artists to dote upon the worthless and irrelevant. It is also the ultimate self-indulgence, and for the Beatles it must surely
diminish their ability to capture that revolutionary subconscious which is the
source of their power. Being businessmen must also transform their relations
with those whom they need. To sell, and continue selling successfully, you
require good PR – quiet, efficient and regular. Out must go the rudeness and
aggressiveness, once essential to their survival. And in its place? The myth of the
omni-powerful Beatles will carry them along for a time. And then? The tragedy
would be if their new vocation stifled their priceless gift of song.

The tension that this playing at businessmen has provoked has not been without its toll. George Harrison had a terrible row and threatened to leave the
Beatles forever. Again, John and Paul seemed to be aware of what was happening to them. Hence their escape to India, not so much to pursue the Maharishi
– by then a failing interest, but just to get enough peace and quiet to write some
more songs. Even that seemed at first sight impossible. According to one of those
apocryphal Ringo stories, a day with the Maharishi began with piped music
throughout the camp, and a broadcast request to 'wakey, wakey'. Nonetheless,
John, Paul and George managed 32 new songs. But after their return, the creative pace slackened. Their LP called *The Beatles* got further and further behind
schedule and recording sessions were sandwiched in between, or even interrupted by business meetings.

Most pop-stars record intensively, and at night. A session can start around six
p.m. and not finish till five or six the following morning. Such was the schedule
of the Rolling Stones, for example. Of late, the Beatles have preferred more normal working hours, two until ten p.m., but this very normality, lacking as it does
the solitude of the night, has also conspired against their freedom. In their desire
to free themselves from what they correctly perceived to be outmoded, restric-
tive business and sponsorship practices – like Brian Epstein's old organisation,
NEMS Enterprises, they gradually enchained themselves more securely than ever
before to an ideology whose very liberality looked as if it might bring about its
own destruction.

One reaction to this sense of impending doom and also to the increasing
boredom of being constantly required to play the Beatles, was that each of them
began to pursue their own separate interests. 'This was the big thing of last year,'
says Paul. 'This great self-realisation thing. We started talking about ourselves as
a third person.' (John looks round and asks, 'Would the Beatles like to do that?'
Then he turns to George Martin – their record producer – and says, 'Yes, I think
they might want to.') Ringo went off to co-star in Peter Sellers' film of *The Magic
Christian*. George Harrison, having already anointed the nineteen sitar strings

with the oil of newness, became completely absorbed in things Indian and then wrote the soundtrack for the film *Wonderwall*. Paul got lost in running Apple and John married the Japanese artist, Yoko Ono.

To John and Yoko's credit, they seem to have survived all kinds of private and public bitchery and appear to be living happily ever after. Together, they have taken to film making. Her art exhibition – 'To Yoko from John', John had filmed by candid camera. At one time, Yoko had had a camera crew follow her about with her previous husband so that every time they had a fight, it could be filmed for posterity. John and Yoko made a film called *Rape* which won critical acclaim and was concerned with ridiculing the documentary technique of *ciné-verité*. The film told of how this technique could only be honestly truthful at terrible cost to the subject matter. The subject matter was, in effect, raped. An earlier film had just shown John smiling. In a sense it was the apotheosis of the Beatles who for a long time had drawn us into a fantasy world of their own creation, and thus produced entertainment without involvement. Now we were faced with the prospect of John, the vanishing Lancashire cat, with nothing left but the smile.

'John and I are very shy people, very vulnerable,' said Yoko. 'Really quite naïve. People have sent us *such* strange letters. "If you (John) have anything to do with that Jap (me), don't forget that we were fighting the Japs only twenty years ago, and if you're not careful she'll slit your throat." My film *No. 5* is in Technicolor and stars John and is directed by me. It consists of John smiling. Just that. At one time I wanted every government in the world to send me their smile shots and so build up a big library of smiles. But eventually I just took John's face as sort of representative. It's a very polite film. And we hoped that the smile would send vibrations all around the world. But not just for now. The vibrations should keep on going for people to get a thousand years from now. After all, the love vibrations that were sent by some people *two* thousand years ago, I can still feel, can't you? John and I are fighters. We don't compromise. There wasn't any point in just making love, secretly, and everything. We had to make a film which had the same vibrations as making love. By being together, John and I are making good vibrations which we hope other people will catch.'

Just in case they didn't, John and Yoko sent Acorns for Peace to the heads of every government throughout the world, and made a record called *Two Virgins* on the sleeve of which they appeared holding hands and stark naked, front and rear view. When asked whether he was just laughing at our desperate and pathetic attempts to interpret his meaning and get his message, Lennon replied: 'No more nor less than *you* are laughing at us.' As Richard Goldstein noted, 'the Beatles became the clown-gurus of the Sixties,' mocking us as we had mocked them.

Has John Lennon gone mad? It's a question that everyone seemed to want to ask. He spent his honeymoon in bed and then invited all peace-lovers through-out the world to join him and his wife in their bed-in for peace. 'If everyone stayed in bed for a week,' said John, 'there would be no killings.' Everyone thought that was such a groovy joke that no-one did anything about it. John and Yoko then went to Montreal where they checked in at the Hotel Reine Elisabeth for another seven-day stint. They sent a telegram to Prime Minister Trudeau inviting him to join them or to plant his acorn for peace. Trudeau was too busy for peacetalk and sent an apology telegram 'with regrets'. It was in room 1742 of the hotel that John and Yoko and 40 friends calling themselves the Plastic Ono Band, recorded the Hawaiian lovechant later called 'Give Peace a Chance'. It was like a football crowd shout-a-long, instantly memorable and endlessly repetitive.

. . . It was the British press who labelled me the Dragon Lady. A dragon is a very powerful creature, and I've decided not to be a victim, but to change my fate. – *Yoko Ono*

John had begun to promote peace as if it were washing powder. 'Think Peace today, and keep Nixon away,' ran the slogan. In a consumer society, believed Lennon, Peace had to be sold like any other commodity. As a result, all his massive talent and all his declining resources were being sunk into that one aim. 'We will keep going until peace comes, until we've got them all indoctri-nated with peace. Including the students. I'd like the militant students to show me one militant revolution that worked. We all have Hitler in us,' concluded John, 'but we also have love and peace. So why not give *peace* a chance for once?' John had once said he was more popular than Jesus. By a tragic twist, he had become, for many young people, Jesus himself and so we treated him in the same way. We declared that he was mad.

John held a press reception for his new record at Chelsea Town Hall. Somehow it had to be Chelsea Town Hall. How many electioneering speeches must that hall have heard? How many tin-pot self-important Aldermen have cuckooed banalities on its stage? Across the balcony hung an enormous banner proclaiming, 'Give Peace a Chance', and across the stage another saying, 'Think Peace'. If it hadn't been a private gathering, those slogans would have been ripped down as anarchist trash by some local church-going do-gooder who would probably then have got the OBE for services to the community.

In peace-loving Australia, meanwhile, another new Beatles disc 'The Ballad of John and Yoko' had been banned because of the chorus which said: 'Christ, you know it ain't easy.'

It remains a miracle that in spite of having become the most famous people in the entire world, probably in the entire history of the world, and in spite of the gradual enchainment entailed in their pursuit of business freedoms, they still manage to go on making music and writing songs with an effortless ease and apparent simpleness that can only be described as miraculous. In a sense, the whole tradition of song-writing, which is at the centre of all musical expression descended upon the Beatles. Big time vocalists like Maria Callas are, for economic reasons, no longer primarily concerned with miniature forms. 'Serious' composers like Stockhausen are, for scientific reasons, no longer primarily concerned with human utterances – of which singing is the most primitive and hence the most expensive. And since a master like Stravinsky has never been famous for his solo vocal writing, all our expectations of good song-writing tended to shift towards the Beatles. Two LP's at least seemed to fulfil these expectations – *Sergeant Pepper's Lonely Hearts Club Band*, and *The Beatles*. A single copy of one of their sleeves came to be almost as valuable as any holy relic ever was.

The idea of making *Sergeant Pepper* into a coherent and continuous song-cycle – thought by some to be the result of a brilliant master plan, in fact occurred only halfway through the project, which would account for the apparent 'irrelevance' of the mystical 'Lucy in the Sky with Diamonds', the ludicrously banal 'Within You, Without You', and the early Seventies sound of 'A Day in the Life' – this last appropriately banned by the BBC. The record contains thirteen songs altogether – all of them, with one exception, by Lennon and McCartney. It took about three months to record (Mozart wrote *Don Giovanni* in less) and was plugged more assiduously than any recent Beatle record in recent Beatle history.

Its pop-art cover 'staged' by Peter Blake and the very lovely Jann Haworth set the uniformed, pop-art Beatles *and* their wax doubles (?), firmly amongst photo cut-outs of the all time greats – Diana Dors, Peter O'Toole, Tony Curtis, Dylan Thomas and other worthies. The 62 faces and figures – and especially those wax doubles – clearly indicated that the Beatles felt themselves to be living not only in the shadows of those whom they admire, but also of themselves. As the song says:

And the time will come
When you will see we're all one

It was all like some victory photograph gleaned from the archives of a gratefully absurd Spanish American revolution. Like the music recorded therein, it had a ritual cynicism that passed for intelligence, an irrepressible lust for fun that passed for a desire to please, and a sarcasm that masqueraded as hip.

Serious criticisms of the Beatles and their music has become an almost forgotten privilege. The *New Statesman* – a left organ, plastered itself so richly with cliches, that its all purpose do-it-yourself review made one gasp for Cliff Richard – sing us one of the old songs, Cliff. 'The Beatles,' groaned the organ, 'despite their priceless simplicity, aren't as simple as all that.' The record, 'though it starts from the conventions of pop, it becomes "art" – and art of an increasingly subtle kind.' 'The triumph [of the Beatles] is equivocal, though not double-faced.' According to the *New Statesman*, the Beatles had cunningly devised a song-cycle which depicted the transformation of old-style camaraderie into new-style aloneness, the aloneness of God's little children who are left only 'with the things that make us simple, social creatures' (greed, violence, bitterness, anger, dreams?).

The august Mr William Mann of *The Times* (the first serious-minded Beatle advocate) preferred to think in terms of the mixolydian and pentatonic. Shapely bass-lines and hurricane glissandi appealed to him greatly. A pity he did not mention the mumbo-jumbo recorded on the inside track of side two which owners of automatic disc-players luckily escaped, or the high-pitched dog-whistle singing away simultaneously with the last chord of the last song just so that the doggies weren't forgotten.

It was ironic that most of the songs were now so electronically complicated, so manifestly the product of a recording studio, that very few could ever be performed in public sounding as they do when they had been devised in private. As if wishing to be *nothing* but moustachioed and clapped-out dandies, the Beatles discovered the *need* for this monster playroom to keep themselves collectively amused. In this way, they have been able to go on gaining energy from one another, to go on regenerating themselves and equipping themselves for survival.

All this is not to deny that when the record first appeared, the Beatles actually resurrected the hope that 'light-music' just might be as interesting and worthy of attention as is what is nervously referred to as 'serious music'. Undoubtedly, they are a standard which other groups are forced to emulate in order to stay fashionable: an aloof and insistent reminder of the woeful ordinariness of much of popular culture; an affront to the sentimental and mealy-mouthed: for some, the Beatles are an uncomfortable even forbidding gesture towards the hordes of the respectable and the coach parties from Luton. Surprisingly, they have never protested nor marched. They are not Left Wing, nor Empire Loyalist. Yet they are political in a way that Mr Wilson is not, for they and not he are the mentors of an age, the spokesmen – artistically – for all colours.

The most eloquent, and also the most frightening of these spokesmen, is John

Lennon, whose fine gift for pun and understatement has disarmed many a high-minded critic. But on the Beatles' own testimony, Lennon has withdrawn more and more, even from them. His white Rolls-Royce – once painted all over in yellowy flower-patterns, used to have darkened one-way windows through which he viewed the world but through which the world could not view him. His house in Weybridge had a room full of halfs – half a chair, half a radio, half an ironing-board, half a bookcase, half a kettle and half a shoe – all of them painted white. Four white hammers hung on a piece of string above the fireplace and he used a chess set, the members of which were *all* white. His conversation is elliptical and visionary. He is scornful of critics – favourable or hostile. His music is harsh and brittle and his poetry a bleak and terrifying outburst. The Walrus, the voice of corporate society, wears 'corporation tea-shirts', weeps crocodile tears and is a raving maniac. Society itself is depicted as a sordid madhouse. Another song – 'Day in the Life', used at the funeral service of the murdered British playwright, Joe Orton, begins:

I read the news today oh boy
He blew his mind out in a car.

Whether this is a dirge for a friend of John's killed in a car crash, and whether it is a lament for the assassination of President Kennedy, it doesn't matter. Like Joyce, it works on all levels. But there remains a dazzling simplicity about the image, and a pitiful grimness about its use. There is a cynicism about the occasion described, and a hopeless despair about its implication. 'Within You' ends the cruellest of laughs, giving all the songs a strange double-edge. For Lennon, the society into which – through no choice of his own – he had been born, had for him deliberately enervated the souls of men and thus noiselessly unwound the springs of action. Such choice as he had, must surely be the freedom to choose how he would exercise his mind, and how he would stimulate his imagination – provided he did not thereby restrict the freedom of others.

And so we live, a life of ease –
Everyone of us, that's all we need

That simple verse from a song dismissed as trite, says much about the aspirations of a man like John Lennon. They are the aspirations of Locke, of Hume, of Mill, of Plato, of Aristotle. They neither worship false gods, nor praise famous men. They are not concerned with power or pomp, with sex or sin, with violence or with victory. They are not words of wisdom or even of authority. These are merely a personal statement of a dream more real than the fabric of any dogma that society would wish to impose upon it.

> Always, no sometimes, think it's me
> But you know I know when it's a dream

A work of art is, after all, nothing more than a reflection of man's image as he imagines it in a mirror. But the mirror has no reality of its own, only the reality of what it reflects. So even 'Yellow Submarine' has its bitter laugh before the final chorus. Our freedom is a freedom to give the Beatles theirs.

Perhaps we cannot forget the image of unruly little rockers that it once suited the Beatles to promote; perhaps we find it hard to overcome the suspicion that wealth and popularity can mean anything but vulgar success and cunning promotion. Perhaps the cheapness of their public sycophants and the arbitrariness of their imitators who must number millions, destroy the uniqueness which alone would give them their freedom. But Lennon does seem to have escaped into a kaleidoscope world all his own. Whilst he mocks the semi-detached conventions that crowd our public behaviour –

> She. . . is leaving (sacrificed most of our lives)
> home (we gave her everything money could buy)

he offers also the hope of a better life than was our father's:

> Picture yourself in a boat on a river
> with tangerine trees and marmalade skies. . .

It is a hopeless vision, unworldly and unreal; but whether it is expressed in Love-Ins or Be-Ins, or whether it is sought through drugs or stimulants, it is not deserving of prison or even handcuffs. And it is infinitely preferable to talk of war and hatred, of racial discrimination and snobbery of all kinds. However muddled its message, it is at least worth our sympathetic attention. Just as its urban poetry is worth our reading, and its hunted music worth our hearing.

In spite of the *New Statesman*, and all of them.

A year later came an even more extraordinary record called, simply, *The Beatles*. It was wrapped in a plain white cover adorned by the song titles and those four faces alone, faces which for some still represent the menace and illogicality of long-haired youth, for others the beginnings of a profound cultural Renaissance and for others the desperate, apparently endless struggle against cynical, defunct so-called betters. In their eyes, as in their songs, we see again the fragile fragmentary mirror of the society which sponsored them, which interprets

271

and makes demands of them and which punishes them when they do what others reckon to be evil; Paul, ever hopeful, wistful; Ringo, every mother's son; George, local lad made good; John, withdrawn, sad, but with a fierce intelligence clearly undimmed by all that organised morality can throw at him. They were all our best hope – heroes for all of us, and better than we deserved.

Do you think you're a genius?
Yes, if there is such a thing as one, I am one . . . I used to say to me auntie, 'You throw my fuckin' poetry out, and you'll regret it when I'm famous,' and she threw the bastard stuff out. I never forgave her for not treating me like a fuckin' genius or whatever I was, when I was a child. It was obvious to me. – *from* **Lennon Remembers**

It's not as if the Beatles ever seek such adulation. The extraordinary quality of the 30 songs on the double-album was one of simple happiness. The lyrics now overflowed with a sparkling radiance and sense of fun that it was impossible to resist. Almost every track was a send-up of a send-up of a send-up, rollicking, reckless, gentle, magical. Like their subsequent LP *Get Back* [finally released as *Let It Be*], they seemed to have become obsessed by parody and self-parody. This obsession had always been clear in their public statements, thus making many of their utterances (including the ones quoted in this chapter) untrue, misquoted, irrelevant or all three. But it never seems to matter. Nor did it when the subject matter of the songs ranged from piggies ('have you seen the bigger piggies/ In their starched white shirts') to Bungalow Bill of Saturday morning film-show fame ('He went out tiger hunting with his elephant gun/ In case of accidents he always took his mom'), from 'Why Don't We Do It in the Road?' to 'Savoy Truffle'. The skill at orchestration had matured with finite precision. Full orchestra, brass, solo violin, glockenspiel, saxophone, organ, piano, harpsichord, all manner of percussion, flute, sound effects, were used sparingly and thus with deftness. Electronic gimmickry had been suppressed or ignored in favour of musicianship. References to or quotations from Elvis Presley, Donovan, Little Richard, the Beach Boys, Blind Lemon Jefferson were woven into an aural fabric that had become the Bayeux Tapestry of popular music. It was all there if you listened. Aristophanes had lengthily misquoted Sophocles and Euripides. Shakespeare had re-written Holinshed. The Beatles had copied and absorbed everybody – including themselves. Even a line from *King Lear* Act IV, Scene Six, had got into 'I Am the Walrus'. Possibly, this willingness to accept anything and everything that they absorb, has – like Janis Joplin – caused a lack of critical distance between them and their art which might lead to self-indulgence. But with the Beatles, the questioning always remains. Lennon sings, 'I told you about Strawberry Fields' and 'I told you about the fool on the hill.' And now?

The Beatles are competent rather than virtuoso instrumentalists – but their ensemble playing is intuitive and astonishing. They bend and twist rhythms and phrases with a unanimous freedom that gives their harmonic adventures the frenzy of anticipation and unpredictability. The voice – particularly that of Lennon – had become just another instrument, wailing, screeching, mocking, weeping. Like the greatest composers, their music thrives on the unexpected. They always manage to make the words go against the music. Beneath the words is a harmonic shiftiness which gives them a continuous uneasiness. The introduction to 'Michelle' actually changes key in the second bar. This element of suspense has enabled the Beatles to be the generous masters but never the creatures of their audience.

There was also in *The Beatles* a quiet determination to be finally rid of the bogus categorisation that often had surrounded them and their music. The words were almost deliberately simpleminded – one song was just called 'Birthday' and included lines like 'Happy birthday to you'; another just went on repeating, 'Goodnight'; another said, 'I'm so tired, I haven't slept a wink.' The music was likewise stripped of all but the simplest of harmonies and beat – so what was left was a prolific outpouring of melody, music-making of unmistakable clarity and foot-tapping beauty. The sarcasm and hostility that had always given their music its edginess still bubbled out – 'Lady Madonna trying to make ends meet – yeah/ Looking through a glass onion.' The harshness of the imagery was, if anything, ever harsher; 'The eagle picks my eye/ The worm he licks my bone,' black birds, black clouds, broken wings, lizards, destruction. And, most grotesque of all, was a terrifying track just called 'Revolution Nine', which comprised sound effects, overheard gossip, backwards-tapes, janglings from the subconscious memories of that floundering civilisation, cruel, paranoiac, burning, agonised, hopeless – given shape by an anonymous bingo voice which just went on repeating, 'Number nine, number nine, number nine' – until you wanted to scream. McCartney's drifting melancholy overhung the entire proceedings like a veil of shadowy optimism – glistening, inaccessible, loving.

At the end, all one could do was stand and applaud. Whatever your taste in popular music, you could find it satisfied here. If you thought that pop music was Engelbert Humperdinck, then the Beatles had done it better – without sentimentality but with passion; if you thought that pop was just rock'n'roll, then the Beatles had done it better – but infinitely more vengefully; if you thought that pop was just mind-blowing noise, then the Beatles had done it better – on distant shores of the imagination that others had not even sighted. It is, perhaps, a curious quirk of our psychological vulnerability that everybody still seems to demand the existence of heroes, whether they be lone yachtsmen, generals, God, TV personalities, cultural leaders, or pop stars. Being semi-myth, moreover, these heroes seem increasingly neither to feel nor care in a way that we are able to understand. But the best of pop heroes, and in particular the Beatles, do care and care with increasing desperation about the way we organise our lives and the way we express what we believe in. They express with indefinable accuracy the sense of outrage felt by most civilised people against all human indignity, whether in Vietnam, in Alabama, or in London.

If nothing else, pop music – with the Beatles undeniably to the fore, is now describing this sense of outrage with a great tenderness. And if the Beatles can overcome their present preoccupations, we may yet look to them again for the fulfilment of that revolutionary subconscious. But if Apple goes broke, then so might they – both as businessmen and as artists. Are the Beatles only in it for money? The interesting thing about *that* question is that *we* keep on asking it and never get a satisfactory reply.

John gave a hint as to his real intentions. He gave back his MBE in protest against Britain's involvement in the Biafran war. He indicated also that the Beatles were dead and that he wished to begin the Seventies not as John Lennon, MBE, not as Beatle John Lennon, but as plain Mr Lennon. One newspaper described the MBE event as the irrelevancy of the decade. Bertrand Russell wrote to congratulate John.

But perhaps the best hope lies in John's first unpublished book, which was called *Sport, Speed and Illustrated, Edited and Illustrated by J. W. Lennon.* It had a serial story which ended: 'If you like this, come again next week. It'll be even better.' John was seven at the time.

Born Under a Bad Sign, Tony Palmer, 1970

THE LONGEST COCKTAIL PARTY
By Richard Dilello

The 'House Hippie' during the anarchic days of Apple, Dilello chronicled the day-to-day madness that permeated their Savile Row offices. It's an often hilarious, sometimes sad memoir of the group during the last year or so before they imploded as a unit.

If you did a quick walk-through and caught it all from the corner of your eye, the reception lounge at 95 Wigmore Street in that summer of 1968 looked like the waiting room at a VD clinic in Haight-Ashbury at the height of the Acid Madness of '67. Ground traffic control had a hard time scheduling the flow.

It seemed that every singer, songwriter, fast-buck artist, apache and second-story man in town was hitting the fan and winding up at Apple. Well over half the Apple staff had been recruited from NEMS and the Liverpool days when Brian Epstein had actively discouraged his employees from talking to the Beatles beyond a brisk 'Hello.' Thank God the world had changed a little since then. Everyone from that old scene had to make rapid, major readjustments in their psyches to survive.

It was a matter of self-preservation. A fairly effective system of filtration had been worked out by July to protect the Beatles and their senior staff from abrasive situations that could prove embarrassing and potentially volatile. The underground had come up blinking into fluorescent lights and proved surprisingly aggressive.

And Poetry and Prose just kept rolling through the doors, wave upon wave. If it didn't come in tucked under a clutching arm, dogeared and coffee-stained, then it found its way through the mail. The pile of manuscripts was inflating itself to grosser proportions day by day.

The majority of the letters that accompanied these offerings shared the same mood, no matter what corner of the globe they came from. The running order was very much the same.

The first paragraph was always an apology for having written in the first place. It was intimated by the writer of the letter and the creator of the verse that obviously the reader (especially if it were a Beatle) had better things to do than read stuff like this, having by now forgotten that it was Apple that had invited the submission in the first place.

It was to have been a beautiful place where you could buy beautiful things, but it was in danger of becoming just an ordinary chain of stores. It may all look very surrealistic and gimmicky, but it's not really. We're just cutting back on a few of our interests. We can't try to run 50 businesses at once. And anyway, you know we always make our mistakes in public. – *Paul McCartney, on the 1968 closing-down giveaway sale at the Apple Boutique*

The second paragraph apologised for the actual contents of the package, making it quite plain from the start that what was inside was not as gifted an offering as any of the Beatles might have produced had he made the same effort.

The third paragraph apologised for the presentation and was usually crammed with footnotes. The more desperate ones then sank to demand that the unclean be cleansed. It was that old hangover from the barnstorming days of Beatlemania; only this time the supplications took on the guise of artistic faith healing.

But Poetry and Prose was only a fraction of the hustle.

For the most part it was the young who were attracted. The hopelessly straight and middle-aged shied away. But the gutter publicity had spread lavalike over London. Apple was a soft touch if you could crack the security cordon. It was actually a soft touch only because everyone was determined that the experiment should succeed.

One afternoon, as the House Hippie moved through the reception lounge heading for the Press Officer's room, he felt a sharp tap-tapping on his shoulder. Turning in that direction he heard a voice asking for a few minutes of his time. 'Sure man, a few minutes is my middle name.'

And then the House Hippie took a good look at the man who had asked the question. It was the Deranged Filthy Faun Raincoat. The only colour the poor fellow seemed to radiate was the green, carpetlike moss on his teeth. Flecks of saliva were gathered at the corners of his mouth. His eyes were dissolute pools of the most intense grayish madness and the accumulation of old sleep seeds made him look like the victim of terminal conjunctivitis. His neatly water-combed, slicked-back hair was as greasy as the ventilation shaft of a third-string hamburger emporium. The dandruff on top looked like a heavy snowfall in

January. The House Hippie took one step back.

'You see the reason I'm here, young man, is because I've evolved a system and I must speak to John Lennon about it.'

'What kind of a system?'

'Ahh! It's an amazing system really. I've cracked the barrier that separates humans from the creatures of the animal kingdom and the only person who will be able to understand me is John Lennon.'

'Uhh – '

The Faun Raincoat pulled from his pocket a sheet of crumpled paper covered in some private, incomprehensible shorthand.

'And this poem here,' he pointed to some inky gibberish, 'I wrote this afternoon at the zoo while I was having my lunch. The first verse is by *me* and the next verse is by *them*. It goes on like that to the end of the poem.'

And then he pulled out the uneaten half of his lunch, a rancid-looking, dried-out tomato and cheese affair and offered it to the House Hippie.

'No thanks, I've just eaten.'

'Well, in that case I'll finish it myself.'

He did it in three chews with a huge grin, never taking his eyes from the House Hippie.

'Delicious! Well, you know all the animals in the Regent's Park Zoo are my friends, all of them, and I'm going to write a book about them but, uhh, I'm a little short on funds. However with a little financial support; well, perhaps it would be more appropriate if I discussed this matter with John Lennon.'

'Uhh – '

At that moment the Press Officer's secretary's lovely face came into focus.

'Richard, Derek wants to see you right now.'

'Excuse me, sir – ' and the House Hippie was gone, leaving the Faun Raincoat breathless with darting eyes sweeping the reception lounge for someone else who might get him to John Lennon.

'Derek doesn't want to see you but I just had to rescue you from that fucking maniac out there. He latched on to me a few weeks back and wouldn't stop.'

The House Hippie shook his head up and down in silent appreciation, wilting from relief. He had just been 'Beatled' for the very first time.

All systems were go. Mid-July 1968 was a very crucial month for Apple. In addition to the projects on the board in films, electronics and merchandising there was the one that assumed precedence above all others: the launching of Apple Records. The music was, after all, the rock that the dream was built on.

The response to the ads placed in the trade papers and the poster campaign had in fact proved too successful. The number of tapes coming in was out of all proportion to the Publishing and Records Departments' ability to give each one a fair share of a listen. Most of the musical discoveries were coming by word of mouth.

Ron Kass was winging his way back and forth between America, London, Europe and South America with a singular, determined regularity, tying up all the last-minute strings with Capitol and EMI for the August world debut of Apple Records.

By now two songs had been recorded and regarded as Apple's royal flush: 'Hey Jude' by the Beatles and 'Those Were the Days' by Mary Hopkin. Everyone said they couldn't help but become number-one worldwide smash hits.

The Longest Cocktail Party, Richard Dilello, 1970

INTERVIEW WITH JOHN LENNON
By Jonathan Cott

A slightly fragmented, but telling interview from late 1968 – touching on Lennon's relationship with Yoko Ono, with whom he had now been living for several months, and his retrospective feelings about the Maharishi experience.

I've listed a group of songs that I associate with you, in terms of what you are or what you were, songs that struck me as embodying you a little bit: 'You've Got To Hide Your Love Away', 'Strawberry Fields', 'It's Only Love', 'She Said She Said', 'Lucy in the Sky', 'I'm Only Sleeping', 'Run for Your Life', 'I Am the Walrus', 'All You Need Is Love', 'Rain', 'Girl'.

The ones that really meant something to me. . .Look, I don't know about 'Hide Your Love Away', that's so long ago. Probably 'Strawberry Fields', 'She Said', 'Walrus', 'Rain', 'Girl', there are just one or two others, 'Day Tripper', 'Paperback Writer', even. 'Ticket To Ride' was one more, I remember that. It was a definite sort of change. 'Norwegian Wood'. . .that was the sitar bit. Definitely, I consider them moods or moments.

There have been a lot of philosophical analyses written about your songs, 'Strawberry Fields', in particular. . .

Well, they can take them apart. They can take anything apart. I mean, I hit it on all levels, you know. We write lyrics, and I write lyrics that you don't realise what they mean 'til after. Especially some of the better songs or some of the more flowing ones, like 'Walrus'. The whole first verse was written without any knowledge. And 'Tomorrow Never Knows'. . .I didn't know what I was saying, and you just find out later. I know that when there are some lyrics I dig, I know that somewhere people will be looking at them. And I dig the people that notice that I have a sort of strange rhythm scene, because I've never been able to keep rhythm on the stage. I always used to get lost. It's me double off-beats.

What is Strawberry Fields?

It's a name, it's a nice name. When I was writing 'In My Life' – I was trying 'Penny Lane' at that time – we were trying to write about Liverpool, and I just listed all the nice-sounding names, just arbitrarily. Strawberry Fields was a place near us that happened to be a Salvation Army home. But Strawberry Fields – I mean, I have visions of Strawberry Fields. And there was Penny Lane, and the Cast Iron Shore, which I've just got in some song now, and they were just good names – just groovy names. Just good sounding. Because Strawberry Fields is anywhere you want to go.

There are places I'll remember
All my life, though some have changed
– *John Lennon, 'In My Life'*

Pop analysts are often trying to read something into songs that isn't there.
It is there. It's like abstract art really. It's just the same really. It's just that when you have to think about it to write it, it just means that you labored at it. But when you just *say* it, man, you know you're saying it, it's a continuous flow. The same as when you're recording or just playing. You come out of a thing and you *know*, 'I've been there,' and it was nothing, it was just pure, and that's what we're looking for all the time, really.

How much do you think the songs go toward building up a myth of a state of mind?
I don't know. I mean, we got a bit pretentious. Like everybody, we had our phase and now it's a little change-over to trying to be more natural, less 'newspaper taxis', say. I mean, we're just changing. I don't know what we're doing at all, I just write them. Really, I just like rock and roll. I mean, these. . .[*pointing to a pile of Fifties records*]. . .are the records I dug then, I dig them now and I'm still trying to reproduce 'Some Other Guy' sometimes, or 'Be-Bop-A-Lula'. Whatever it is, it's the same bit for me. It's really just the sound.

The Beatles seem to be one of the only groups who ever made a distinction between friends and lovers. For instance, there's 'baby' who can drive your car. But when it comes to 'We Can Work It Out', you talk about 'my friend'. In most other groups' songs, calling someone 'baby' is a bit demeaning compared to your distinction.
Yeah, I don't know why. It's Paul's bit that. . .'Buy you a diamond ring, my friend'. . .it's an alternative to *baby*. You can take it logically, the way you took it. See, I don't know really. Yours is as true a way of looking at it as any other way. In 'Baby, You're a Rich Man' the point was, stop moaning. You're a rich

man and we're all rich men, heh, heh, baby!

I've felt your other mood recently: 'Here I stand, head in hand' in 'You've Got To Hide Your Love Away', and 'When I was a boy, everything was right' in 'She Said She Said'.
Yeah, right. That was pure. That was what I meant all right. You see, when I wrote that I had the 'She said she said', but it was just meaning nothing. It was just vaguely to do with someone who had said something like he knew what it was like to be dead, and then it was just a sound. And then I wanted a middle-eight. The beginning had been around for days and days and so I wrote the first thing that came into my head and it was, 'When I was a boy,' in a different beat, but it was real because it just happened. It's funny, because while we're record-ing we're all aware and listening to our old records and we say, we'll do one like 'The Word'. . .make it like that. It never does turn out like that, but we're always comparing and talking about the old albums – just checking up. What is it?. . .like swatting up for the exam – just listening to everything.

Yet people think you're trying to get away from the old records.
But I'd like to make a record like 'Some Other Guy'. I haven't done one that satisfies me as much as that satisfied me. Or 'Be-Bop-A-Lula' or 'Heartbreak Hotel' or 'Good Golly, Miss Molly' or 'Whole Lot of Shakin''. I'm not being modest. I mean, we're still trying it. We sit there in the studio and we say, 'How did it go, how did it go? Come on, let's do *that*.' Like what Fats Domino has done with 'Lady Madonna' – 'See how they ruhhnnn.'

Wasn't it about the time of **Rubber Soul** *that you moved away from the old records to something quite different?*
Yes, yes, we got involved completely in ourselves then. I think it was *Rubber Soul* when we did all our own numbers. Something just happened. We controlled it a bit. Whatever it was we were putting over, we just tried to control it a bit.

Are there any other versions of your songs you like?
Well, Ray Charles' version of 'Yesterday'. . .that's beautiful. And 'Eleanor Rigby' is a groove. I just dig the strings on that. Like Thirties strings. Jose Feliciano does great things to 'Help!' and 'Day Tripper'.

   'Got To Get You Into My Life' – sure, we were doing our Tamla Motown bit. You see, we're influenced by whatever's going. Even if we're not influenced, we're all going that way at a certain time. If we played a Stones record now, and a Beatles record – and we've been apart – you'd find a lot of similarities. We're all heavy. Just heavy. How did we ever do anything light? What we're trying to do is rock'n'roll, with less of your philosorock, is what we're saying to ourselves. And get on with rocking because rockers is what we really are. You can give me a guitar, stand me up in front of a few people. Even in the studio, if I'm getting into it, I'm just doing my old bit – not quite doing Elvis Legs but doing my equivalent. It's just natural. Everybody says we must do this and that but our thing is just rocking, you know, the usual gig. That's what this new record ('The White Album') is about. Definitely rocking. What we were doing on *Pepper* was rocking – and not rocking.

'A Day in the Life' – that was something. I dug it. It was a good piece of work between Paul and me. I had the 'I read the news today' bit, and it turned Paul on. Now and then we really turn each other on with a bit of song, and he just said 'yeah' – bang bang, like that. It just sort of happened beautifully, and we arranged it and rehearsed it, which we don't often do, the afternoon before. So we all knew what we were playing, we all got into it. It was a real groove, the whole scene on that one. Paul sang half of it and I sang half. I needed a middle-eight for it, but that would have been forcing it. All the rest had come out smooth, flowing, no trouble, and to write a middle-eight would have been to write a middle-eight, but instead Paul already had one there. It's a bit of a *2001*, you know.

Songs like 'Good Morning, Good Morning' and 'Penny Lane' convey a child's feeling of the world.
We write about our past. 'Good Morning, Good Morning', I was never proud of it. I just knocked it off to do a song. But it was writing about my past so it does get the kids because it was me at school, my whole bit. The same with 'Penny Lane'. We really got into the groove of imagining Penny Lane – the bank was there, and that was where the tram sheds were and people waiting and the inspector stood there, the fire engines were down there. It was just reliving childhood.

You really had a place where you grew up!
Oh, yeah. Didn't you?

Well, Manhattan isn't Liverpool.
Well, you could write about your local bus station.

In Manhattan?
Sure, why not? Everywhere is somewhere.

In 'Hey Jude', as in one of your first songs, 'She Loves You', you're singing to someone else and yet you might as well be singing to yourself. Do you find that as well?

Oh, yeah. Well, when Paul first sang 'Hey Jude' to me. . .or played me the little tape he'd made of it. . .I took it very personally. 'Ah, it's me,' I said, 'It's *me*.' He says, 'No, it's *me*.' I said, 'Check. We're going through the same bit.' So we all are. Whoever is going through a bit with us is going through it, that's the groove.

In the Magical Mystery Tour theme song you say, 'The Magical Mystery Tour is waiting to take you away.' In 'Sgt. Pepper' you sing, 'We'd like to take you home with us.' How do you relate this embracing, 'come sit down on my lawn' feeling in the songs with your need for everyday privacy?

I take a narrower concept of it, like whoever was around at the time wanting to talk to them talked to me, but of course it does have that wider aspect to it. The concept is very good and I went through it and said, 'Well, okay. Let them sit on my lawn.' But of course it doesn't work. People climbed in the house and smashed things up, and then you think, 'That's no good, that doesn't work.' So actually you're saying, 'Don't talk to me,' really. We're all trying to say nice things like that but most of the time we can't make it – 90 percent of the time – and the odd time we do make it, when we do it, together as people. You can say it in a song: 'Well, whatever I did say to you that day about getting out of the garden, part of me said that but, really, in my heart of hearts, I'd like to have it right and talk to you and communicate.' Unfortunately we're human, you know – it doesn't seem to work.

Do you feel free to put anything in a song?

Yes. In the early days I'd. . .well, we all did. . .we'd take things out for being banal cliches, even chords we wouldn't use because we thought they were cliches. And even just this year there's been a great release for all of us, going right back to the basics. On 'Revolution' I'm playing the guitar and I haven't improved since I was last playing, but I dug it. It sounds the way I wanted it to sound. It's a pity I can't do it better. . .the fingering, you know. . .but I couldn't have done that last year. I'd have been too paranoiac. I couldn't play: ['Revolution' guitar intro] *dddddddddddddd*. George must play, or somebody better. My playing has probably improved a little bit on this session because I've been playing a little. I was always the rhythm guitar anyway, but I always just fiddled about in the background. I didn't actually want to play rhythm. We all sort of wanted to be lead – as in most groups – but it's a groove now, and so are the cliches. We've gone past those days when we wouldn't have used words because they didn't make sense, or what we thought was sense. But of course Dylan taught us a lot in this respect.

Another thing is, I used to write a book or stories on one hand and write songs on the other. And I'd be writing completely free form in a book or just on a bit of paper, but when I'd start to write a song I'd be thinking: *dee duh dee duh do doo do de do de doo*. And it took Dylan and all that was going on then to say, 'Oh, come on now, that's the same bit, I'm just singing the words.' With 'I Am the Walrus', I had, 'I am he as you are he as we are all together.' I had just these two lines on the typewriter, and then about two weeks later I ran through and wrote another two lines and then, when I saw something, after about four lines, I just knocked the rest of it off. Then I had the whole verse or verse and a half and then sang it. I had this idea of doing a song that was a police siren, but it didn't work in the end [*sings like a siren*] 'I-am-he-as-you-are-he-as. . .' You couldn't really sing the police siren.

Do you write your music with instruments or in your head?
On piano or guitar. Most of this session has been written on guitar 'cuz we were in India and only had our guitars there. They have a different feel about them. I missed the piano a bit because you just write differently. My piano playing is even worse than me guitar. I hardly know what the chords are, so it's good to have a slightly limited palette, heh heh.

What did you think of Dylan's version of 'Norwegian Wood'?
I was very paranoid about that. I remember he played it to me when he was in London. He said, 'What do you think?' I said, 'I don't like it.' I didn't like it. I was very paranoid. I just didn't like what I felt I was feeling – I thought it was an out-and-out skit, you know, but it wasn't. It was great. I mean, he wasn't playing any tricks on me. I was just going through the bit.

Is there anybody besides Dylan you've gotten something from musically?
Oh, millions. All those I mentioned before. . .Little Richard, Presley.

Anyone contemporary?
Are they dead? Well, nobody sustains it. I've been buzzed by the Stones and other groups, but none of them can sustain the buzz for me continually through a whole album or through three singles even.

You and Dylan are often thought of together in the same way.

Yeah? Yeah, well we were for a bit, but I couldn't make it. Too paranoiac. I always saw him when he was in London. He first turned us on in New York actually. He thought 'I Want To Hold Your Hand' – when it goes, 'I can't hide' – he thought we were singing, 'I get high.' So he turns up with Al Aronowitz and turns us on, and we had the biggest laugh all night – forever. Fantastic. We've got a lot to thank him for.

Do you ever see him anymore?
No, 'cuz he's living his cosy little life, doing that bit. If I was in New York, he'd be the person I'd most like to see. I've grown up enough to communicate with him. Both of us were always uptight, you know, and of course I wouldn't know whether he was uptight, because I was so uptight. And then, when he wasn't uptight, I was. . .all that bit. But we just sat it out because we just liked being together.

> **Bob [Dylan] handed the joint to John, who immediately handed it to Ringo. 'You try it!' John commanded . . . . 'Inhale with a lot of oxygen,' I instructed. 'Take a deep breath of air together with smoke and hold it in your lungs for as long as you can.' –** *Al Aronowitz*

What about the new desire to return to a more natural environment? Dylan's return to country music?
Dylan broke his neck and we went to India. Everybody did their bit. And now we're all just coming out, coming out of a shell, in a new way, kind of saying, remember what it was like to play.

Do you feel better now?
Yes. . . and worse.

What do you feel about India now?
I've got no regrets at all, 'cuz it was a groove and I had some great experiences meditating eight hours a day – some amazing things, some amazing trips – it was great. And I still meditate off and on. George is doing it regularly. And I believe implicitly in the whole bit. It's just that it's difficult to continue it. I lost the rosy glasses. And I'm like that. I'm very idealistic. So I can't really manage my exercises when I've lost that. I mean, I don't want to be a boxer so much. It's just

that a few things happened, or didn't happen. I don't know, but *something* happened. It was sort of like [*snaps fingers*] and we just left and I don't know what went on. It's too near – I don't really know what happened.

You just showed me what might be the front and back album photos for the record you're putting out of the music you and Yoko composed for your film **Two Virgins**. *The photos have the simplicity of a daguerreotype. . .*
Well, that's because I took it. I'm a ham photographer, you know. It's me Nikon what I was given by a commercially-minded Japanese when we were in Japan, along with me Pentax, me Canon, me boom-boom and all the others. So I just set it up and did it.

For the cover, there's a photo of you and Yoko standing naked facing the camera. And on the backside are your backsides. What do you think people are going to think of the cover?
Well, we've got that to come. The thing is, I started it with a pure. . .it was the truth, and it was only after I'd got into it and done it and looked at it that I'd realised what kind of scene I was going to create. And then suddenly, there it was, and then suddenly you show it to people and then you know what the world's going to do to you, or try to do. But you have no knowledge of it when you conceive it or make it. Originally, I was going to record Yoko, and I thought the best picture of her for an album would be her naked. I was just going to record her as an artist. We were only on those kind of terms then. So after that, we got together, it just seemed natural for us, if we made an album together, for both of us to be naked. Of course, I've never seen me prick on an album or on a photo before: 'What-on-earth, there's a fellow with his prick out.' And that was the first time I realised me prick was out, you know. I mean, you can see it on the photo itself – we're naked in front of a camera – that comes over in the eyes, just for a minute you go!! I mean, you're not used to it, being naked, but it's got to come out.

How do you face the fact that people are going to mutilate you?
Well, I can take that as long as we can get the cover out. And I really don't know what the chances are of that.

You don't worry about the nuts across the street?
No, no. I know it won't be very comfortable walking around with all the lorry drivers whistling and that, but it'll all die. Next year it'll be nothing, like miniskirts or bare tits. It isn't anything. We're all naked really. When people attack Yoko and me, we know they're paranoiac. We don't worry too much. It's the

ones that don't know, and you know they don't know – they're just going round in a blue fuzz. The thing is, the album also says: 'Look, lay off will you? It's two people – what have we done?'

Lenny Bruce once compared himself to a doctor, saying that if people weren't sick, there wouldn't be any need for him.
That's the bit, isn't it? Since we started being more natural in public, the four of us, we've really had a lot of knocking. I mean, we're always natural. I mean, you can't help it. We couldn't have been where we are if we hadn't done that. We wouldn't have been us either. And it took four of us to enable us to do it; we couldn't have done it alone and kept that up. I don't know why I get knocked more often. I seem to open me mouth more often, something happens, I forget what I am till it all happens again. I mean, we just get knocked, from the underground. . .the pop world. . .me personally. They're all doing it. They've got to stop soon.

Couldn't you go off to your own community and not be bothered with all of this?
Well, it's just the same there, you see. India was a bit of that, it was a taste of it. It's the same. So there's a small community, it's the same gig, it's relative. There's no escape.

Your show at the Fraser Gallery gave critics a chance to take a swipe at you.
Oh, right, but putting it on was taking a swipe at them in a way. I mean, that's what it was about. What they couldn't understand was that – a lot of them were saying, 'Well, if it hadn't been for John Lennon nobody would have gone to it,' but as it was, it was *me* doing it. And if it had been Sam Bloggs it would have been nice. But the point of it was – it was me. And they're using that as a reason to say why it didn't work. Work as what?

Do you think Yoko's film of you smiling would work if it were just anyone smiling?
Yes, it works with somebody else smiling, but she went through all this. It originally started out that she wanted a million people all over the world to send in a snapshot of themselves smiling, and then it got down to lots of people smiling, and then maybe one or two and then me smiling as a symbol of today smiling – and that's what I am, whatever that means. And so it's me smiling, and that's the hang-up, of course, because it's me again. But they've got to see it someday. . . it's only me. I don't mind if people go to the film to see me smiling because it doesn't matter, it's not harmful. The idea of the film won't really be dug for another 50 or a hundred years probably. That's what it's all about. I just happen to be that face.

It's too bad people can't come down here individually to see how you're living.
Well, that's it. I didn't see Ringo and his wife for about a month when I first got together with Yoko, and there were rumors going around about the film and all that. Maureen was saying she really had some strange ideas about where we were at and what we were up to. And there were some strange reactions from all me friends and at Apple about Yoko and me and what we were doing – 'Have they gone mad?' But of course it was just us, you know, and if they are puzzled or reacting strangely to us two being together and doing what we're doing, it's not hard to visualise the rest of the world really having some amazing image.

International Times *recently published an interview with Jean-Luc Godard. . .*
Oh yeah, right, he said we should do something. Now that's sour grapes from a man who couldn't get us to be in his film. . .[*One Plus One*, in which the Stones appear]. . .and I don't expect it from people like that. Dear Mr Godard, just because we didn't want to be in the film with you, it doesn't mean to say that we aren't doing any more than you. We should do whatever we're all doing.

But Godard put it in activist political terms. He said that people with influence and money should be trying to blow up the establishment and that you weren't.
What's he think we're doing? He wants to stop looking at his own films and look around. *Time* magazine came out and said, look, the Beatles say 'no' to destruction. There's no point in dropping out because it's the same there and it's got to change. But I think it all comes down to changing your head and, sure, I know that's a cliche.

What would you tell a black-power guy who's changed his head and then finds a wall there all the time?
Well, I can't tell him anything 'cuz he's got to do it himself. If destruction's the only way he can do it, there's nothing I can say that could influence him 'cuz that's where he's at, really. We've all got that in us, too, and that's why I did the 'Out, and In' bit on a few takes and in the TV version of 'Revolution' – 'Destruction, well, you know, you can count me out, and in,' like yin and yang. I prefer 'out'. But we've got the other bit in us. I don't know what I'd be doing if I was in his position. I don't think I'd be so meek and mild. I just don't know.

Rolling Stone, 23 November 1968

ROCK AND FINE ART
By Carl Belz

The double 'White Album' (aka The Beatles*) represented an attempt by the group to get back to basics, after the more elaborate production of 'Strawberry Fields'/'Penny Lane',* Sgt. Pepper *and* Magical Mystery Tour. *Despite its more down-to-earth attitude, however, the pretentiousness of the critics never abated.*

Since its release, the Beatles' 1968 album has provoked extensive controversy. It has been called a 'put-down' and a 'put-on' and it has been said to represent the Beatles' way of 'dropping out' of the rock picture. These judgments are related to a superficially disturbing aspect of the album itself: the fact that it contains references to the overall history of rock music. That is, many of its songs are openly derived from earlier rock, from the Beach Boys, Chuck Berry, Bob Dylan, and even the Beatles' own records; and from trends such as country and western, rhythm and blues, popular folk, folk-rock, acid rock, electronic rock, psychedelic rock and others that have appeared during the 1960's. But the references are used loosely; few songs on the ablum are based exclusively on one past rock style. 'Back in the USSR' contains musical allusions to both Chuck Berry and the Beach Boys; 'Birthday' is lyrically reminiscent of a long tradition of songs dealing with the same subject, while its instrumentation frantically obscures the lyrics in the manner of such classics as the Kingsmen's 'Louie, Louie'; 'Rocky Raccoon' refers at once to Bob Dylan's early style and to the tradition of country music narratives generally. Other links to the past are numerous: 'Me and My Monkey' and 'Helter Skelter' both have a heavy, acid-rock orientation; 'Yer Blues' and 'Why Don't We Do It in the Road?' are clear examples of the Negro blues tradition; 'Martha My Dear' and 'Honey Pie' express the camp sensibility which has brought about a revival of the 1930's; and 'I Will', 'Blackbird' and 'Julia' are like the tender ballads of the early Beatles, for instance 'If I Fell' and 'Do You Want To Know a Secret?'.

To many listeners, these references to the past are disturbing because they envision the Beatles as rock music's *avant garde*, as the signal for each new direction; for these listeners, the Beatles have suddenly 'dropped out' of the rock evolution. Moreover, the Beatles have invariably been viewed as the most sophisticated of rock groups. Their return to the music of earlier periods therefore seems inconsistent with their previous development away from it. Because of this seeming inconsistency, listeners have concluded that the Beatles must either be 'putting down' earlier rock or 'putting on' their own audience, joking with them about the musical fads of the past.

Myth means putting on the audience, putting on one's environment. The Beatles do this. They are a group of people who suddenly were able to put on their audience and the English language with musical effects – putting on a whole vesture, a whole time, a Zeit. – Marshall McLuhan, The Medium is the Massage

Actually, the Beatles are not entirely alone in their enterprise. During 1968, there were several events which indicated a comparable direction in the overall rock movement. *John Wesley Harding*, by Bob Dylan, shows a return to Dylan's earlier lyric and instrumental style. As in *The Beatles*, such a return implies a critical disengagement from the concept of rock 'progress', a concept which has been applied to Dylan almost as frequently as it has to the Beatles. Still, the self-awareness of Dylan's music is not as blatant as that of *The Beatles*, nor does it compel recognition with the same authority. It is not insisted upon.

The 1968 album, *Cruising with Ruben and the Jets*, by Frank Zappa and the Mothers of Invention, also involves a conscious return to earlier rock music, particularly to the ballad style of the 1950's and the early 1960's, to Little Caesar and the Romans, for instance, the Flamingos, Don Julian and the Meadowlarks and the Jaguars. And the songs on the album were all written by Zappa and his group. They are not merely revival versions of Oldies But Goodies, although in style they could easily be mistaken for their historical counterparts whereas the Beatles' 1968 songs could not. A fascinating aspect of *Cruising with Ruben and the Jets* concerns the album notes. They include 'The Story of Ruben and the Jets', an amusing, tongue-in-cheek description of a (fictitious?) rock group of the 1950's; but they also contain a direct statement of intention on the part of the Mothers of Invention, namely that the record was created out of respect for the style of music it emulates. Against the experience of the album itself, however, this statement seems odd. The music does not elicit respect for rock history in the way that the written statement insists it should, or in the way that *The Beatles* elicits respect for its own sources. It appears to have a mixed response toward the past, finding quality in it on the one hand, but feeling embarrassment about it on the other. And the album notes which claim to 'really like' old rock ballads also call them 'greasy love songs' characterised by 'cretin simplicity'. The ambivalence of this statement parallels the ambivalence of Frank Zappa's music. By comparison, the Beatles' songs are in no way ambivalent in their treatment of rock history.

I want to argue that the Beatles' return to the past is neither a 'put-down' nor a 'put-on', but an expression of consciousness which is unprecedented in the history of rock and which defines the 1968 album as fine art. Specifically, it is a consciousness of the fact that the record is, after all, a record. That is, the album is non-metaphoric: Its primary purpose is not to talk about the world, create pictures of it, or refer to specific experiences within it. The primary purpose of *The Beatles* is to present a conscious experience of music as music.

The record's consciousness of itself is shown in many ways. In the first place, the variety of its songs presents a singular, unified subject: rock music as it has existed and changed during a decade and a half. More precisely, the subject of the record is rock history as experienced by the Beatles. What is their attitude to rock on this record? The evidence suggests that the Beatles have a profound respect for the music which provides their subject matter. The Beatles do not use album notes to 'explain' their intentions. The question about their attitude toward rock can only be answered by what a listener feels is the aesthetic quality of the songs in the album. Each song, it seems to me, implies respect for its subject because it is a fine interpretation of that subject – that is, of each example in the spectrum of rock sub-styles. Songs derived from the Beach Boys have an elegant harmony; the Chuck Berry inspirations are rocking, explosive and humorous; the rhythm and blues examples have a direct and heavy beat; and the Beatle-style ballads are tender and restrained. The songs isolate and emphasise the best musical aspects of their subjects. They do not imply that their musical subject matter is inane, insignificant, or in any way embarrassing. Only the listener who personally feels embarrassment about the songs he formerly liked can interpret the Beatles' album as sharing that response. But such an interpretation results from arbitrarily reading into the album instead of accepting musical evidence from it.

In this album, the Beatles are going back over musical territory which they have already covered, which they already know, and which they have left. The consiousness with which they look back is significant for the history of rock because it has been transformed into artistic content. In part, the transformation is achieved by the overtness with which the past is used. That is, it is most immediate and most real at those moments when the listener clearly recognises that the record does in fact involve a return to the past. Listeners who are not aware of either rock history or the Beatles' own past, are not likely to grasp this. In other words, the sophistication manifested by so many aspects of Sixties rock becomes, in the case of the Beatles' 1968 album, a literal prerequisite for understanding the record's full content and historical significance – although not necessarily for feeling some of its aesthetic impact; it is a great record, even for listeners who do not know what it means in terms of rock history. In comparison to *The Beatles*, an awareness of Chuck Berry, the Beach Boys, and other rock artists was never the *content* of the Beatles' early songs. Those artists were simply influences on them. In the 1968 album, they are recognised *as* influences, and this recognition or consciousness openly pervades the entire record and becomes its content. Moreover, because *The Beatles* is aware of itself, it cannot be regarded as a revival of the past or an imitation of it. As a musical statement, the album clearly belongs to the Beatles; its overall style is consistent with the group's previous development, although it extends that development into a new area.

Consistency between the Beatles' 1968 album and their earlier records is evident in several ways. Like *Rubber Soul*, *Revolver* and particularly *Sgt. Pepper*, *The Beatles* has an extraordinary range and extraordinary inventiveness. Lyrically, the songs shift from the straightforward 'Julia', 'I Will' or 'Dear Prudence', to the elusive and quasi-surrealistic 'Glass Onion' and 'Happiness Is a Warm Gun'; the lyrics also range from simple narrative in 'Rocky Raccoon' to virtual anti-narrative in 'Why Don't We Do It in the Road?', which consists merely of three lines, two of which are identical; in addition, they include numerous expressions of humour as in 'Back in the USSR', 'Ob-La-Di, Ob-La-Da', and 'The Continuing Story of Bungalow Bill'; and, in George Harrison's 'Piggies', social commentary. The range of writing in *The Beatles* is unprecedented in either past or present rock history. Moreover, such virtuoso writing underscores the album's consciousness: It summarises the richness and variety of rock lyrics as they have existed in the idiom up to, and including, the present.

The same virtuosity is apparent in the music of *The Beatles*. As I said, it covers the history of rock sub-styles and influences. Yet, each of these is clearly personalised by the English group as they at once acknowledge the past and place upon it their unique stylistic stamp. Whether rock ('Back in the USSR') or blues ('Yer Blues'), country ('Rocky Raccoon') or ballad ('I Will'), each song combines ease with restraint, resulting in the cool refinement which has become characteristic of the Beatles' music during the past five years. Moreover, there are no 'repeats' in the album. Each of the softer ballads makes a distinct impact, and the same is true of the rock numbers, the psychedelic numbers, and the Thirties reminiscences. No other group has been able to move so authoritatively through such a varied texture of rock expressions.

Still, the lyric and musical virtuosity of *The Beatles* is not simply an end in itself. The album is not a narcissistic 'demonstration piece' which intends to show the rock world that the Beatles are more accomplished than any other group.

Certainly, it can be accepted this way, but to do so would undermine the impact of the album as an aesthetic experience in itself, and it would imply that the Beatles had turned their backs on the meaning of creativity expressed by their earlier work – as if their purpose was now to minimise other groups when it had never been their purpose before. It seems to me that neither effect is substantiated by the album itself. Rather, I think that the virtuosity in *The Beatles* serves the purpose of making a statement about rock music: It validates the extraordinary range and power of rock expressions. Such a statement could not be made unless the Beatles had the musical ability to produce songs which were as varied and good as their subjects. So the album does mark a new phase in the Beatles' enterprise. In their records before 1968, they were learning what rock consisted of and they were learning to make their own brand of rock music. But *The Beatles* involves a breakthrough: a conscious looking back at their own musical experiences.

While paying the Beatles the supreme tribute of parody, the Mothers are also putting the gods of Liverpool in a slightly less exalted light than we've been used to seeing them in. Suddenly the Beatles look much too pretty, and not a little bit plastic in all those satin uniforms. – Rolling Stone *review of* We're Only In It for the Money, *Frank Zappa and the Mothers of Invention's* Sgt. Pepper *parody*

The Beatles' album *can* be regarded as a 'drop out', but not in the sense that most listeners suppose. They have questioned the idea of progress in rock music. During the late Sixties, rock has been looked upon as becoming more advanced, more sophisticated, more electronic, and more like fine art than it was in the past. The Beatles' record asks, 'Is it necessarily becoming *better*?' They have questioned whether progress and artistic quality are the same. The Beatles have experienced an undeniable artistic quality in earlier rock *in spite* of the fact that the previous music was *not* advanced, sophisticated, electronic or like fine art. But *The Beatles* has this meaning only to the extent that it possesses high quality itself. In other words, the album relies on quality alone to substantiate its vision.

The equation of progress and quality is characteristic of the folk mentality. In many cases, progress is tangible and immediate; it can be pinpointed, isolated and demonstrated. Unconscious folk artists and audiences do not realise how these features may imply quality in technology, say, without implying quality in art. A marked tendency in the Sixties is to say that rock has become art because it is complex, because it is technically accomplished, or because it contains references to fine art – that is, to Stockhausen, Cage, Mozart, Bach and other composers who are acknowledged to represent fine art. In addition, it is suggested that freedom of interpretation and far-ranging instrumental improvisation constitute fine art. Examples of these tendencies are Cream, Vanilla Fudge, and the Jimi Hendrix Experience. But these are folk claims: They equate sophistication with quality, just as they equate progress with quality.

The Beatles' consciousness of itself as music is not just suggested, it is compelled. In the song 'Ob-La-Di, Ob-La-Da', for instance, the lyrics concern a married couple named Desmond and Molly, but, in describing the lives of Desmond and Molly, they arbitrarily interchange the names so that neither person can be established as the husband or wife. The effect is amusing and disturbing, but only if one regards the song as being directly about *people* in the world. It is non-metaphoric: it is primarily a good *song*. 'Revolution One' sings about revolution and changing the world. The lyrics are identical to the lyrics of 'Revolution', a single released by the Beatles before their 1968 album. The difference between the two versions lies in the way they are sung: 'Revolution' is a fast, rocking record, but 'Revolution One' is performed slowly, as though the first song had been decelerated to half-speed. And the album also contains 'Revolution Nine', which is almost entirely an electronic, tape-music composition. So, are they about revolution? I want to argue that, as much as Claude Monet's paintings of haystacks or Frank Stella's stripe paintings are about painting, 'Revolution One', 'Revolution', and 'Revolution Nine' are about music. They constitute a series for which the subject of revolution is a common denominator, a constant, or a 'control', so to speak, which merely functions as a point of reference for the primary concern, the music.

There are other ways in which The Beatles stresses the experience of itself as music. The lyrics for all the songs are printed on a separate sheet that is included with the album. The Beatles first did this with Sgt. Pepper, where the lyrics are printed on the album itself. In both cases, the gesture obviates the task of 'figuring out' what the lyrics actually are – the task that rock listeners were traditionally confronted with prior to the Beatles. Admittedly, it can be argued that printing the lyrics in this fashion actually adds to their importance as 'poetry' which exists independently of music. Certainly, this is the case with Bob Dylan's albums, several of which contain 'poems' which are distinct from the ones on the recording, but whose similarity to them lends the songs a 'poetic' significance. With the Beatles, however, knowing the lyrics seems to facilitate listening to the music; it enables the music to exist by itself, unencumbered by efforts to grasp the words and intellectualise their 'meaning'. Those activities can take place when the record is not being played.

In addition to 'Ob-La-Di, Ob-La-Da', 'Revolution One', and 'Revolution Nine', several other songs serve to emphasise the self-contained musical experience of *The Beatles*. For instance, 'Back in the USSR' presents a subject that, for most listeners, is nonsensical, although certainly humorous, if it is related to extra-musical realities. 'Glass Onion' also restricts the listener from making direct associations between musical experience and non-musical experience. Its lyrics openly refer to other Beatles songs – 'Strawberry Fields', 'I Am the Walrus' and 'Lady Madonna' – but they suggest that the effort to interpret those songs via the context of ordinary, day-to-day experiences is absurd, like 'fixing a hole in the ocean'. For the Beatles, in other words, music elicits its own kind of experience, one that is valid by itself and requires no justification through references to the non-musical world. Thus, at a moment when rock writers are increasingly anxious to make meaningful and intelligent statements about the world, the Beatles have chosen to investigate their own musical experiences. Such a decision is daring, but it is consistent with the unique position the Beatles have occupied ever since they entered the rock picture.

The Beatles' transformation of consciousness into content has a clear parallel in the history of fine art, particularly in the history of modernist painting. In painting, a comparable breakthrough was achieved by Edouard Manet. Manet made the distancing experience of consciousness the content of his work; he blatantly used the art of the past as his subject matter rather than allowing it merely to influence him; he acknowledged the quality of earlier art, and he recognized that his personal contribution as a painter could only be substantiated if it was good; finally, he was accused of 'putting down' the history of his medium and of 'putting on' the audience of French art. Modernist painting has directly and indirectly explored the implications of Manet's art for more than a century. This fact should lend caution to predictions that rock music will suddenly follow the Beatles' direction.

I have tried to emphasise the Beatles' 1968 album in terms of its consciousness and, correspondingly, its fine art identity. In doing so, I am aware of alternative interpretations of the record's meaning, particularly those interpretations which might stress the album's links with its folk past. Admittedly, not all of the songs insist upon non-metaphoric listening with the same authority. Moreover, the album's internal richness and complexity thwart attempts to straitjacket all of its parts into a single, rigid viewpoint. From the point of view of this book, however, the album's art-consciousness constitutes its major historical achievement. And that achievement matters for one all-important reason: It is couched in supremely good music.

The Story of Rock, Carl Belz, 1969

THE PENDULUM YEARS –
BRITAIN AND THE SIXTIES
By Bernard Levin

The acerbic British journalist and broadcaster Bernard Levin was gentler than usual, if a little cynical, in this recollection of John and Yoko's celebrated 'bed-in for peace'. It took place at the Amsterdam Hilton Hotel in March 1969, after their wedding in Gibraltar.

Most celebrated of all the experimenters in other-worldly ways of life were some of those very Beatles, one of whom, towards the end of the decade, caused great offence to many by going to bed in public with his new bride, a Japanese lady who was variously described as a sculptress and a film-maker, though none could remember seeing any sculpture by her, and the only film she was known to have made consisted entirely of shots of naked buttocks moving, with more or less grace, away from the camera. Mr and Mrs John Lennon, then, having been married, elected to spend their honeymoon entirely in bed, a custom which was, after all, not entirely original. What made their honeymoon different from most is that it was spent in conditions of extreme public exposure, in a suite at the Hilton Hotel, Amsterdam, to which reporters, interviewers, newspaper and television photographers and other interested parties were free to come, and in suitable cases invited to join them in the bed, and there celebrate with the loving couple what was supposed to be the point of the entire proceedings, to wit a demonstration on behalf of personal and international peace. To this end, the walls of the bedroom were decorated with signs reading 'Bed Peace', 'Hair Peace', 'Stay in Bed', and 'Grow Your Hair', and the peaceful two argued, reasonably enough, that if everyone stayed in bed, occupying themselves in growing their hair, there would be no wars. To the question, what would happen if most stayed in bed and grew their hair but a few of the more ruthless declined to do so, they had clearly not addressed themselves, for the philosophy behind the performance was summed up by Mr Lennon, who said that all would be well if the Vietnamese, both North and South, would only take their trousers off, followed by the Arabs, the Israelis, the Russians and the Americans, while Mrs Lennon unwittingly touched upon the fallacy in the argument by proclaiming that their mood could be summed up in the words: 'Remove your pants before resorting to violence.' It might, of course, be objected that this is the spirit which in practice presumably guides every rapist, but granting that Mrs Lennon meant to say that he who removes his pants will be unable to resort to violence, it still left unresolved the problem of what to do about those whose pants stayed resolutely on, and still more the problem of how to deal with those who had learnt to do violence while naked from the waist down, or up, or even both.

I remember once, when I was about thirteen, I borrowed 'The White Album' from [my sister] Patti, and my mother got upset when she heard me listening to 'Happiness is a Warm Gun'. It really bothered her a lot. I don't think you can separate the Beatles from what was going on in the Sixties. That whole period changed a lot of people and brought on some new attitudes – and I'm not saying it was all good. There certainly were excesses. – *Ronald Reagan, Jr.*

It cannot be denied that much of the nonsense talked by the young idols, in particular Mr and Mrs Lennon, invited much of the criticism, though as against that one might reflect that the intimate conversation of the newly married is not usually expected to be either coherent or profound, though as against that one might reflect that the intimate conversation of the newly married is not usually expected to be filmed, recorded and made public. Nor can it be denied that much of the nonsense, even when it was not so extreme or so obtrusive as to invite the more extreme or obtrusive criticism, was still nonsense. Nevertheless it differed from most of the nonsense talked, under the guise of philosophy, by those who were in the business of making money out of popular entertainment in two crucial particulars. First, there was nothing either proselytising or pernicious about it; second, it was gentle, introspective, and pacific. A deep sense of unease afflicted many of those who studied this phenomenon, so much so that their unease took the form of extreme hostility to it; it seemed as though they feared for their ordered, aggressive and interfering world, though in truth there was little danger to it from the young people who sat cross-legged on the floor in kaftans. . .

The Pendulum Years - Britain and the Sixties, Bernard Levin, 1971

1969: HELTER SKELTER
By Ed Sanders

Ed Sanders was a pivotal figure in New York bohemia during the Sixties, leading the anarchic folk jug band the Fugs. His classic account of Charles Manson's infamous 'family' makes the claim that the murders of actress Sharon Tate and four others in August 1969, followed by that of businessman Leno LaBianca and his wife, were fuelled by imaginary messages from 'The White Album'.

By the middle of January 1969, the new Beatles' white double album had already grossed $22 million in the United States alone. The white double album was the first cultural instruction from the Beatles since the album *Magical Mystery Tour* a year previous. Even its all white cover was symbolic to the family – all white, dig it?

Something freaked Manson out in early 1969 enough for him to prepare for the end of Western civilisation. He had already talked about an impending Armageddon of some sort, but he had always preached 'submission is a gift, give it to your brother.' This is, walk humble beneath the violence.

Along oozed Helter Skelter.

Manson had a hypnotic rap about how the modern blacks were arming themselves, how he, Manson, had talked to blacks in prison and he had learned of heavy arms caches here and there.

He had a way of stirring up paranoia that was legendary. Goose bumps shivered the back of the arms during his whispered superstitious lectures on karma and imminent doom. With language as flawed as a president's announcing an invasion of a South Asian country, he announced that the blacks would rise up, kill a few million whites, take over the reins of government.

Then, the story continues, after 40 or 50 years the blacks would turn the government over to Manson when they supposedly found themselves unfit to run the world. Oo-ee-oo.

It was the pig Christian wealthy Americans that were going to get cut. He, Christ, he, Devil, was going to pull off the Second Coming. 'Now it's the pigs' turn to go up on the cross,' he would say.

On a metaphysical plane, Manson linked the impending Helter Skelter with the concept of the Hole. For inside this mystic Hole in Death Valley, Manson and his family would live and dwell while the blacks and the whites in the cities would fight to a bloody end and then the blacks would take over.

From the City in the Hole, Manson would make forays to sack cities with his hairy locusts of the Abyss. And the blacks, through their 'super awareness' – in the words of the family – would know that Charlie was where it was at, and nod him into the power.

On a higher level, if *higher* is any word to be used, Manson taught that the family bringing the seven holes on the seven planes into alignment would be the ones to squirt through to the other side of the universe. And the Hole was to be the magic paradise – magic, because where else can you find subterranean chocolate fountains?

He even over-dubbed a weirdo exegesis atop the chapters and verses of the Book of Revelation, to back up his claims.

The dune buggies were the horses of Helter Skelter with those 'breast plates of fire', described in the Book of Revelation of St John the Divine, Chapter Nine. And the Beatles, unknown to them, were the 'four angels' who would wreak death upon a third part of mankind. And Manson found a scriptural basis for announcing that the Beatles were destined to have a fifth member or 'angel' – the angel of the bottomless pit, otherwise known as guess who.

One of Manson's favourite passages from Revelation Nine was: 'Neither repented they of their murders, nor of their sorceries, nor of their fornication, nor of their thefts' – words he would quote over and over again, preparing his worshippers to kill. And did not the family have 'hair as the hair of women, and their teeth were as the teeth of lions'?

And was not Manson the king of the pit?

'And they had a king over them, which is the angel of the bottomless pit, whose name in the Hebrew tongue is Abaddon, but in the Greek tongue hath his name Apollyon.' When they translated the Bible from Latin to English, the translators left out another name in the text besides Abaddon and Apollyon, for the angel of the bottomless pit. The name in Latin is Exterminans.

Exterminans – what a word to sum up Charles Manson.

The correlations that Manson found between the Book of Revelation and the Beatles and his own crazies could be continued in moonfire profusion but the reader will be spared.

Manson began to listen to the song 'Helter Skelter' off the new Beatles' album with earphones and somehow, as of a miracle, he began to hear the Beatles whispering to him urging him to call them in London. It is unfortunate that Manson evidently did not know that a helter skelter is a slide in an English amusement park.

The girls say that at one point Manson placed a long-distance phone call to London to try to talk to the Beatles. There is no doubt that the song 'Helter Skelter' on the white Beatles double album is a masterful, insistent, rock and roll number – and it is very weird-sounding, especially the long final section which

If you listen to 'Helter Skelter' and listen to the MC5 and the Stooges, it's that sound. They sound exactly like that record. And that song, the way it's played, is the birth of punk rock as we know it. – *Noel Gallagher*

fades out twice at the end, sounding like a universal march of wrecked maniacs.

'Charlie, Charlie, send us a telegram' was what he thought lay beneath the noise plexus of the composition 'Revolution Nine'. It was felt that if one were to listen closely on headphones, one could hear the Beatles softly whispering just that. As it is, so be it.

'Rise! Rise! Rise!' Charlie would scream during the playing of 'Revolution Nine' (which Manson associated with Revelation, Chapter Nine). Later they wrote *Rise* in blood on the LaBiancas' wall.

It is necessary to listen to the Beatles white double album to understand what Manson was hearing and seeking to hear. The album, as a whole, is of confusing quality. It has flashes of the usual Beatle brilliance but it was produced at a time that the Beatles were locked in bitter quarrels and it is reflected in the album.

The album has the song 'Piggies', of course, and, more creepily, a song called 'Happiness Is a Warm Gun'. Other songs like 'Blackbird', 'Rocky Racoon', etc., were interpreted strictly as racist doom-songs.

The song 'Sexie Sadie' must have sent Susan Atkins, aka Sadie Mae Glutz, into spasms of happiness. 'Sexy Sadie, you came along to turn everybody on,' the song croons, and 'Sexy Sadie, you broke the rules, you laid it down for all to see.'

The Family, Ed Sanders, 1971

ALL YOU NEEDED WAS LOVE
By John Blake

Blake's account elaborates on the 'White Album' hypothesis relating to the Manson murders. Despite Manson's denials, it appears that he used the album – and 'Helter Skelter' in particular, an uncharacteristically hard McCartney song oft misattributed to Lennon – to trigger the participation of his young followers.

Charles Manson had got caught up in the whole San Francisco hippy scene after a young boy walked up to him in the street and handed him a flower. 'It just blew my mind,' he later recalled.

He grew his hair long and started playing music. He experimented with LSD and delved into the fashionable areas of religion and philosophy. The Beatles were fairly central to his existence, which was true of most people at this time. But when they released *Sgt. Pepper's Lonely Hearts Club Band* in June 1967, Manson saw in them a significance far beyond their music. He linked them directly with the Book of Revelations in the Bible.

'Look, it's all so obvious, it's all in Chapter Nine,' he told his girlfriend excitedly. 'There it is in verse fifteen – "The four angels were loosed" – those "four angels" are the Beatles. They are telling everyone what to do. God has sent them here to prepare us.

'Then in verse three it says: "And there came out of the smoke locusts upon the earth: and unto them was given power as the scorpions of the earth have power." Locusts or Beatles, both are the same – there is no difference in the Hebrew.

'I am meant to interpret these words, I am destined to be part of the plan,' he shouted triumphantly.

'Their faces were as the faces of men. And they had hair as the hair of women' – an obvious observation about the men who had brought long hair for men back into fashion. The 'breastplates of fire' and 'out of their mouths issued fire and smoke and brimstone' were references to their electric guitars and the voices that had scorched their way into the consciousness of the world.

Manson was particularly struck by a verse which said that man should not worship idols of gold, silver, brass, stone and wood. This was, he said, why the hippies were so right. The straight world worshipped all their cars, their jewellery, their material possessions and placed such things higher in their lives than their

301

fellow human beings. Armageddon was beginning now: the Beatles had foretold it.

Some time later Charles Manson started his notorious 'family'. At first he had just moved girls in to share his flat, where he taught them about mysticism and they all dropped acid and smoked dope.

Then they moved on from San Francisco and their peculiar brand of eccentricity grew stronger in the arid isolation of Death Valley. Several of the girls had babies, possibly Manson's – nobody seems too sure. He had sex with them at random, as did the other crazy-eyed men he allowed to follow him. A number of the girls were so in awe of him that they believed he was a reincarnation of Christ.

Then just after Christmas 1968 he returned to the house in Death Valley almost feverish with excitement, holding a double LP record in his hands. The record looked curious because it was in a plain white sleeve with just the words 'The; BEATLES' embossed on it.

Manson studied the record interminably, listening to every chord, every lyric, sometimes scribbling notes on scraps of paper, sometimes exclaiming aloud when a particular interpretation struck him. His eyes, always wild, took on a: glittering, demonic quality. He looked, said one of the girls: reverently, like a man receiving a communication from God. Which, as it happens, is exactly what Charles Manson, aged 33, believed himself to be.

Later, in January, Manson feared the cold of Death Valley might kill them so they all moved to a very ordinary suburban house in Gresham Street, in the San Fernando Valley district of Los Angeles.

By this time he believed implicitly that he had been chosen to lead the way out of the chaos that was to come and eventually to restore sanity and a new order to the world. He was preposterous and insane, of course. But he was also possessed of a quite extraordinary charisma, an incandescent power, which made it possible for him to bend people, like willow wands, to his will. He knew that the Beatles were not simply pop musicians: they were prophets, possessed of: supernormal powers. They had already influenced and changed tens of millions of people around the globe and now they were preparing for the final scene in their potent drama. But the new white album was the last record they would make; it was a prelude to global warfare.

But Manson's interpretations of the songs on the record were themselves to have bloody consequences.

'Blackbird' was an invitation for the black people of the world to destroy the white man. And as the next track was 'Piggies', and angry blacks had dubbed their white foes 'pigs', this merely reinforced the idea that the time had come for them to give the whites their just deserts – 'a damn good whacking'. 'Happiness Is a Warm Gun' told them explicitly how to take their revenge – 'bang bang, shoot shoot.'

'Helter Skelter', too, was another key song. Manson believed that 'Helter Skelter' was the code name for the war – he'd never heard of the spiralling slides found at British fun-fairs. Battle would commence in a small way, he said. To begin with, a couple of angry black people would come up from the ghetto into Beverley Hills, to the houses where the piggies lived. The blacks would commit atrocious murder. There would consequently be terror among other rich whites which would turn into a blind fury against the blacks of America. This would lead some whites to drive into the ghettoes where they would simply mow down the first black people they saw.

In their eyes there's something lacking. What they need's a damn good whacking. - *George Harrison, 'Piggies'*

These victims, however, would be the Uncle Toms, the blacks who had been playing ball with the whites all along, happy to remain subjugated and exploited without ever dreaming of striking back. The militant blacks, the Panthers and the Muslims, would be far away, laying low, biding their time. When thousands of blacks had been slaughtered a few militants would emerge to appeal to the whites in authority, and this appeal would split the ranks of the whites, causing furious argument between the reactionary, murderous hawks and the liberal, trendy doves. The two factions would grow so angry with one another that civil war would begin. Modern weaponry would mean that millions upon millions of people would die around the world. But then the Black Panther forces would come out of hiding to massacre the few weak, remaining whites.

Manson and his family would survive, however. As predicted in the Book of Revelations, they would spend the war thriving and proliferating in a bottomless pit. This bottomless pit, Manson told his followers, was located in Death Valley. By the time it was all over the family would have grown to 144,000 people, again as predicted in the Bible.

Finally the family would become the master race at the request of the black people, who themselves would be relegated to servants. And Charles Manson would become ruler of all the earth.

For the moment, though, Manson listened to the white album, a five-foot-two, silently ticking, human time-bomb. 'Sexy Sadie' referred to one of Manson's most passionate female followers whom he had re-christened Sadie Mae Glutz.

'Rocky Raccoon' again stressed the role that the 'coons' – black people – were being called upon to play. Not surprisingly 'Revolution One' and 'Revolution Nine' directly predicted the coming holocaust.

And, as he listened to the album, something else became apparent: the Beatles knew Charlie was somewhere on earth and they warned to make contact with him.

If you've got a real solution, they sang on 'Revolution One', let us know your plan.

This meant to Manson that the Beatles wanted him to make an album to reply to the white album: the white album foretold Armageddon, his would start it.

Charlie also told his followers that the Beatles knew he was living in Los Angeles. He based this assertion on 'Honey Pie', in which they referred to Hollywood and asked that Honey Pie cross the Atlantic Ocean.

Charlie feared that the Beatles didn't realise that it was they – not he – who had to sail across the Atlantic. They didn't yet know that the bottomless pit was in Death Valley, that they had to come to him to be saved. Desperately Manson and his followers sent the Beatles letters and telegrams in London and made attempts to telephone them. But the whole world seemed to be trying to reach the four young men from Liverpool that year, and the family were unable to make contact.

At the house in Los Angeles Manson worked feverishly on songs for the album he was to make in reply to the Beatles. He wanted each number to be as subtle and yet as lucid as the Beatles themselves had been.

Manson had numerous contacts in the music business. He had lived with Dennis Wilson, the Beach Boys' drummer and singer, in his mansion on Sunset Boulevard and, through him, he had got to know many powerful and influential people. At one point Dennis had rented a recording studio for Manson – but the resulting tapes had not been particularly successful. Eventually, however, Wilson and Manson had quarrelled and the Beach Boy asked his manager to arrange for Charlie and his followers to be evicted from the house.

When he had finished writing his songs, therefore, Manson turned not to Dennis Wilson but to another acquaintance – Terry Melcher, who was the son of Doris Day and boss of a thriving record company – to produce the record. But the project again came to nothing.

Manson was convinced that helter-skelter would have to be triggered off that summer of 1969, but he worried that the blacks had not understood the Beatles' message. In his strange, convoluted mind he gradually decided that it was incumbent upon him – as the future leader of the world – to show the Panthers what had to be done.

Manson had his tribe completely in his power by this time. He invented a new game called creepy-crawly which entailed breaking into people's houses while they slept, moving things around and then leaving – all without the victims realising that an intruder had visited their home. The games and the fears welded the family ever-closer, made them into a tight fraternity of outlaws. Then, at last, Charlie was ready for them to play the biggest game of all.

All You Needed Was Love, John Blake, 1981

LET IT BE
By Peter Doggett

This account of the almost painful recording of the Let It Be *album captures the tensions that had begun to engulf the group.*

Although it was the chasm between Harrison and McCartney that was high-lighted in the *Let It Be* movie, relations between George and John Lennon were scarcely any easier. Harrison seems to have had more trouble than McCartney in relating to Yoko Ono; there was still the legacy of Lennon's disinterest in Harrison's material during the laborious sessions for 'The White Album'. John made belated gestures of solidarity after the group had split up: 'I can't speak for George, but I know pretty well that we got fed up being sidemen for Paul.' But as the early days at Twickenham became bogged down in boredom, Harrison was as enraged by Lennon's refusal to communicate as he was by McCartney's condescending attitude.

When the cameras began to roll on 2 January 1969, the Beatles had precise-ly sixteen days to prepare an album's worth of new material for their live con-cert and TV special. Shortly after 10:00 that morning, John Lennon, Yoko Ono, and George Harrison arrived at Twickenham Studios. While the Beatles' road manager, Mal Evans, set up their equipment, Michael Lindsay-Hogg's crew was already in position. Besides the film cameras scattered around the room, two Nagra tape recorders maintained almost unbroken audio monitoring of the ses-sions – capturing the Beatles' music and also, crucially, their conversations. Over the next four weeks, these Nagra tapes documented the everyday trivia of the group's working life. More important, they bore witness to an unfolding series of dramas, conflicts, and power plays. . .

At that first session, there was no hint of the crises to come. The tapes began to roll as Lennon and Harrison swapped fragments of their new songs. Lennon offered 'Don't Let Me Down' and 'Dig a Pony'; Harrison responded with 'All Things Must Pass' and 'Let It Down'. Amicably, they settled on 'Don't Let Me Down' for their initial rehearsal.

By the time Starr and McCartney reached the studio, Lennon and Harrison had already worked up some rough harmonies for the song. Running it through for the others, John regularly segued into a showy piece of guitar picking, obviously much practiced, over which he sang vaguely, 'Here is the sun king.' Over the next four weeks, such improvisations would be extracted and molded into songs – or, just as often, toyed with, then forgotten forever.

Almost immediately, the Beatles were unsettled by the size of the film studio and its spartan facilities. 'Where's the console and all that?' Harrison asked plaintively as the session began. 'Where are the mixer and the eight-tracks?' 'We'd do better to rehearse in a small room,' Lennon added.

Another concern was the lack of up-tempo material the four Beatles had

For me, that was the great thing about splitting up: to be able to go off and make my own record and record all those songs that I'd been stockpiling. And also to be able to record with all these new people, which was like a breath of fresh air, really. – *George Harrison*

brought to the sessions. 'We'll probably write some fast ones here, all of us,' Lennon muttered hopefully, as he vamped at a riff from his 1968 composition 'Revolution'. In answer, Harrison sang a line or two from Bob Dylan's 'I Shall Be Released' – an escape route that he continued to use throughout the sessions.

It wasn't just the apposite nature of Dylan's lyrics, or memories of his recent stay with the songwriter in Woodstock, that prompted George to drift into Dylan's songs whenever the tension at Twickenham mounted. Like virtually everyone who'd heard them, Harrison had been struck by the intimacy and enigmatic humour of the home demos – the so-called *Basement Tapes* – that Dylan and the Band had taped in the summer of 1967. Not intended for public release, the recordings had nonetheless circulated among the rock aristocracy, and Harrison had brought back copies from the United States for the Beatles. He must have hoped that his group might be able to conjure up a little *Basement Tapes* spirit during these Twickenham sessions.

Classic Rock Albums: Let It Be/Abbey Road, Peter Doggett, 1998

THOSE INVENTIVE BEATLES
By William Mann

Here, music critic Mann waxes enthusiastic about Abbey Road. *It was the group's penultimate album release, preceding the much-delayed* Let It Be *(for which the basic tracks were already recorded earlier that year), but contained the last studio recordings the Beatles would ever make as a unit.*

If adverse reviews elsewhere have dissuaded you from buying *Abbey Road,* the Beatles' new LP, do not hesitate any longer. It teems with musical invention – mostly by Lennon and McCartney, though all four contribute songs – and the second side, as a piece of musical construction, is altogether remarkable and very exciting indeed. The stereo recording will be called gimmicky by people who want a record to sound exactly like a live performance: how can that guitarist (presumably George Harrison) in 'Here Comes the Sun' hop three or four yards sideways so quickly? He can't, but the effect is agreeable and adds a non-visual drama to the music. Like the back-tracked horns in 'Maxwell's Silver Hammer', and the electronic distortion of voice in 'Oh! Darling', the stereo manipulation is used for a musical purpose, not just to sound ravey.

The first two songs on side one, 'Come Together' and Harrison's 'Something', have been put out as a single. Nice as they are – especially the lazy ostinato bass in the former – they are minor pleasures in the context of the whole disc. For mass appeal I would have pinned greater hopes on 'Maxwell', a neo-vaudeville comic song about a jocular murderer, and Ringo Starr's 'Octopus's Garden' which might be called 'Son of Yellow Submarine' and, like 'Maxwell', delights the teenybopper in all of us. Side one ends with a long piece, 'I Want You', which is really two alternating tunes: the second of these (actually heard first as an instrumental prelude), 'She's So Heavy', is built on a haunting ground-bass that eventually monopolises a grand build-up, in the manner of 'Hey Jude', growing and proliferating and getting louder until the only solution was to cut the tape dead when the side is full. Most exciting.

But not as marvellous as side two. This begins with George Harrison's slow, torrid 'Here Comes the Sun', much the most powerful song he's written so far, only hinted at for the moment. It melds into 'Because', not Guy d'Hardelot but Lennon-McCartney, mind-blowing close harmony (it reminds me of 'This Boy' all those years ago, though the harmonies are more subtle nowadays) over an asymmetrical three plus five rhythmic pulse. Then a wistful romantic tune, 'You Never Give Me Your Money', with a down-to-earth second half in honky-tonk style that fades into a further instalment of 'Sun King' with words in a mixture of Spanish and Italian. This blends into a whole series of rock'n'roll songs that seem to find their tunes in developments of the same initial mood and musical invention.

Some have called this a medley but the effect is more dramatic, more structural; to tie the music further together there is even a back-reference to the ground-bass of 'She's So Heavy'. The last portion of the side begins softly with a new tune to the old words 'Golden slumbers kiss your eyes': towards the end of the Beatles' double LP there was a send-up ballad called 'Goodnight' and 'Golden Slumbers' is a companion to it, but straight rock ballad, not send-up cyclamate.

It merges into a new refrain with a heavy rock beat, 'Boy you're gonna carry that weight', and this includes a reprise, with full symphony orchestra, of the 'You Never Give Me Your Money' tune that got lost a long way earlier: its return is as satisfying as the discovery of a ten-bob note you've been missing for a week. The tempo steps up for a one-line tune that never gets as far as line two because guitar and drums go off on their own in an inspired duet until quick piano chords introduce the last song-epigram: 'And in the end the love you take is equal to the love you make.' The record seems to be over but the long pause is followed by a mini-tribute to 'Her Majesty' in which voice and guitar walk slowly across the room.

A pity the words of the songs aren't supplied with the record. John Lennon has said that *Abbey Road is* an attempt to get away from experiment and back to genuine rock'n'roll, so I suppose they don't want us to study the words: a pity because learning by ear isn't as accurate. In any case, when anyone is as naturally inventive as the Beatles to try non-experimentation is a forlorn hope.

The Times, 5 December 1969

SOMETHING
By Nicholas Barber

George Harrison's 'Something' ranks as one of the most covered of all the Beatles' songs after 'Yesterday' — a rarity for a non-Lennon/McCartney composition.

It hit me while I was listening to Isaac Hayes's interpretation of 'Something' (*The Isaac Hayes Movement*, Stax 1970). Eight or nine minutes in, between the first and second fiddle solo, after he shouts, 'You can't make me! I don't wanna!', but before the drum rolls and the wah-wah guitar outburst, it occurred to me that the history of 'Something' was a history of liberties taken.

George Harrison was taking a liberty when he wrote it in his spare time during the 'White Album' sessions in October 1968. The first line is the title of a song by James Taylor. Taylor had come over to London from Boston as a teenager, while attempting to kick heroin, and had signed to that drug-free establishment, Apple Records. On his eponymous album of 1968 (Paul McCartney's bass makes an appearance) he sings: 'There's something in the way she moves/ Or looks my way or calls my name! That seems to leave this troubled world behind.' But the title does not occur elsewhere in the song, and Harrison can hardly be accused of plagiarising the Dylanish acoustic picking and ruminative vocal. Taylor was unruffled: 'I often notice traces of other people's work in my own songs. If George either consciously or unconsciously took a line from one of my songs then I find it very flattering.'

Ironically, the track which precedes 'Something' on *Abbey Road* (Parlophone 1969) is 'Come Together', which begins with the opening line of Chuck Berry's 'You Can't Catch Me'. Berry's lawyers weren't as charitable as Taylor. Nor, a few years later, were those of Bright Tunes Music Corporation, who accused Harrison of pinching 'My Sweet Lord' from the Chiffons' 1963 hit, 'He's So Fine'.

The liberties taken with 'Something' after it left Harrison's hands are plenty. Smokey Robinson and the Miracles sew it into a smooth and stylish medley with 'Something You Got' (EMI 1970). On Booker T and the MGs' *McLemore Avenue* (Stax 1970, featuring covers of every song on *Abbey Road*) it receives a whole new section centred on some mean guitar chops. Shirley Bassey's *Something* (EMI 1970; her next album was *Something Else*) is one of the many versions that throw a symphony orchestra at the middle eight. On Elvis Presley's

Aloha from Hawaii (RCA 1973), the female backing vocal sounds like the theme of *Star Trek*. There are glossy disco strings and gospel voices calling, 'You know it must be something' on Martha Reeves and the Vandellas' rendition (*Motown Sings the Beatles*, 1984), and an enormous choir backs Brian Keith's rough-hewn vocal on the Congregation's *Softly Whispering I Love You* (EMI 1972).

And so it goes. 'Yesterday' is the only Beatles song which has been recorded more often. 'This I suppose is my most successful song with over ten cover versions,' says Harrison in *I, Me, Mine*, his 1979 'autobiography', a gold-embossed leather-bound scrapbook that was initially going to be called *The Big Leather Job*. 'My favourite version is the one by James Brown – that was excellent. When I wrote it, in my mind I heard Ray Charles singing it, and he did do it some years later. I like Smokey Robinson's version too.'

'Something' attracts covers like almost no other song not just because it is an irresistible, whistlable pop ballad, but also because both lyrically and musically there is room to manoeuvre. John Lennon once criticised 'Yesterday' because it didn't 'resolve': you didn't learn enough about the protagonists' situation. It resolves a lot more than 'Something'.

While recording for the *Let It Be* film, Harrison couldn't even resolve the first couplet. 'What could it be, Paul?' he says. 'Something in the way she moves! Attracts me like. . .I can't think what it was attracted me at all.' Lennon suggests: 'Just say whatever it is that comes into your head each time – 'attracts me like a. . .cauliflower' – until you get the word.' The lyric was briefly, 'Attracts me like a pomegranate,' which beats even the 'scrambled eggs' incarnation of 'Yesterday'. You have to wonder if the Beatles were getting enough to eat at the time. It then became, 'Attracts me like no other woman,' and finally 'no other lover', a negative simile which tells you nothing at all about the attracter. 'Something in the way she woos me' is equally unenlightening. (The woozy vocal sway on the word 'woos' is evoked in the lyric sheet's spelling: 'wooo's me'.) 'I don't want to leave her now,' we probably could have taken as read and, 'You know I believe and how. . .' – well, it serves its purpose in that it rhymes with the line before. The middle eight is even more nebulous. 'You're asking me will my love grow/ I don't know, I don't know/ You stick around now it may show/ I don't know, I don't know.' He doesn't know. No room for debate there.

The song was inspired by Harrison's wife, Patti, a supermodel and the face of Smiths' crisps. But 'Something' is hardly a narrative along the lines of 'The Ballad of John and Yoko'. Instead, the paradox is that it portrays love eloquently because it is so happily tongue-tied, as it giddily fails to sum up the enigmatic 'her' in words. Why do I love her? It's, well, it's her. . .I suppose, it's, you know. . .something. Apart from the intriguing twist of 'Somewhere in her smile she knows!

That I don't need no other lover,' the song is as vague as the title would suggest.

Taking this universal haziness a step too far is the extra verse, a facsimile of which appears in *I, Me, Mine*: 'You know I love that woman of mine and I need her all of the time/ and you know what I'm telling you, that woman that woman/ dont make me blue.' [GH's punctuation]

Luckily, it was excised from the finished article, although there is something about 'Something' which would probably have allowed us to put up with the additional doggerel, anyway. It's the potency of cheap music, the guileless charm of the lyric and the blissfully soothing, unhurried melody. 'It's probably the nicest melody line I've ever written,' said Harrison in 1969.

I'd like to perform this song as a tribute to Mr. Lennon – and to Mr. McCartney. – *Frank Sinatra, introducing his version of 'Something' by George Harrison*

Hence its appeal for romantic crooners, none of whom quite matches Harrison's own conviction: slurring, pained Joe Cocker (*Joe Cocker!*, EMI 1970; Harrison offered Cocker the song before the Beatles used it); big-hearted Finbar Furey (*Love Letters*, Ariola); bluesy Johnny Mathis (*Raindrops Keep Falling on My Head*, Columbia 1970); sultry, sulky Shirley Bassey (*Something*, EMI 1970); lazily seductive Peggy Lee (*Portrait of a Song Stylist*, Capitol 1990). Even Telly Savalas had a go (*Telly*, MCA 1974), and, amazing as it may seem, proved to be a rich, resonant bass. More important for the Beatles, perhaps, was that with 'Something' they realised their ambition to be covered by Frank Sinatra, who called it 'the greatest love song of the past 50 years'. On *Portrait of Sinatra* (Reprise 1977), he brings his customary finger-clicking warmth to the tune, backed by a big band which later lets loose like an explosion in a confetti factory. But Sinatra must take the blame for the version on Klaus Wunderlich's *A Tribute to Frank Sinatra* (Connoisseur 1991). It's one of those tortures you hear in cinemas before the lights go down: muzak strings, a Latin beat, and progressively more grating keyboard settings.

But 'Something' is also a jazzers' favourite. The Mike Westbrook Band go at it for eight and three-quarter minutes on *Off Abbey Road* (Tiptoe 1990; another song-by-song remake), Chet Baker is lonely and vulnerable on *Jazz en Verve Vol. Two* (Polygram 1987), and the flawless attack of Hammond-organ genius Charles Kynard (*Wa-Tu-Wa-Zu*, Prestige 1971) has so much life to its nine minutes 40 seconds you can forgive even the drum solo.

It's that openness again. After every sung line there is almost the same amount of 'dead' time again for the instruments to romp around in. On the sleeve notes to *Portrait of Sinatra*, orchestrator Nelson Riddle says of arranging for Sinatra's voice: 'When he's moving get the hell out of the way; when he's doing nothing, move in fast and establish something.' If this is a general rule for backing musicians, 'Something' provides the perfect framework within which a band can establish whatever it wants.

The Beatles supply the model: they take so many liberties that there are hardly any left. Their recording lasts a perfect-pop three minutes – though on an earlier edit a fade-out coda took it to seven minutes and 48 seconds – and they don't waste a second. On some listens you think that Paul McCartney provides a beautifully unfettered complement to Harrison's lyrical guitar; on other listens you wonder if he'd prefer the others just to shut up and let him get on with his bass solo. Either way, his playing is impersonated on dozens of other versions. Ringo Starr's ricochet from toms to high-hat triplets over the middle-eight is echoed by Johnny Johnson (*Soul Survivor*, EMI 1970) and Tanya Tucker (*America Salutes the Beatles*, Liberty 1995). The repeated staccato organ chords are borrowed by Bloodstone (*Natural High*, Decca 1988)

And so it goes. 'Something' is a kind of masterclass for any artist who wants to play others' material. There's your winsome melody, and see if you can match the finely woven intricacies of this arrangement. Lennon and McCartney named it as the best song on *Abbey Road* (Parlophone 1969), although that could have been partly to avoid nominating anything by each other. On Allen Klein's suggestion it became Harrison's first A-side, and it won him an Ivor Novello songwriting award. He would take further liberties with the song when, on tour in 1974, the first line became the more physical 'Something in the way she moves it'. That same year, Eric Clapton took away Harrison's muse. Patti Boyd/Harrison/Clapton had already been the woman behind 'Something' and 'Layla', and would go on to become the subject of 'Wonderful Tonight'. But that's another song.

Lives of the Great Songs, edited by Tim De Lisle, 1994

AS TIME GOES BY
By Derek Taylor

Derek Taylor, who died in 1997, was the Beatles' PR officer for a period in 1964, later returning to the fold as a director at Apple. He remained a close confidant of George Harrison throughout his life, and penned two highly entertaining sets of memoirs – the limited edition 50 Years Adrift *and* As Time Goes By.

I work for Apple. Apple is an ABKCO Managed Company, or so the advertisements for Apple tell us. Apple pays me, therefore ABKCO pays me. The head of ABKCO is Allen Klein of New York, New York. Allen Klein is a businessman. He has his dealings with a guy called Tony Calder who worked as a partner for Andrew Oldham. The three of them managed the affairs of the Rolling Stones. Oldham & Calder left the Stones scene, but Klein stayed. Oldham & Calder ran Immediate Records, which went bust. I know Calder and I like him. Calder sees me one morning, a year or so ago (he lives near me; I live in Sunningdale, he lives in the next village, which is Virginia Water), and he says he will give me a lift to work in his Morgan. I usually go to work by train, but I say, 'OK Tony,' and I travel to town in his two-seat Morgan with him and his wife. Clearly, there is one too many people in this car, but what the hell. Tony has something on his mind, that is why he is taking me to work in his Morgan.

He says: 'Allen Klein says you are in his way. Allen says you are blocking him from meeting the Beatles and doing business with them.'

I am amazed, I say, 'I never give Allen Klein a thought from one year to the next. What is the guy talking about, me being in his way?' Tony says, 'Allen couldn't accept that you don't give him a thought. His ego wouldn't stand it. He thinks he is on everybody's mind all the time.'

I say: 'Too bad.' Tony says: 'Allen thinks you are sore at him because he gave you a verbalising in his office in 1966.' I say: 'He is an asshole for thinking that.'

But true enough, Klein did give me 'a verbalising' in 1966. It happened like this. Andrew Oldham comes into the Gaiety Delicatessen on Sunset Strip where I did a lot of my business in 1966. He takes me from my table to a quieter table. He says: 'Would you like to handle the Stones' press?' I say, I would, because I am a sucker for saying 'Yes' in 1966. He says: 'OK. Come to NY, NY on Saturday and meet the fellers. Also you can meet Klein at the *Sullivan Show* the next day and do the deal. What will you want?'

I tell Oldham I'll ask for a thou a month. He looks very pi and I go to NY and I meet the Stones, one or two of whom I half know and we get on like a supermarket on fire. Next day I go to the *Sullivan Show* and there is this short fat man in a seersucker shirt and it is Allen Klein. He comes on very cool, like he knows all about me but he is not going to let it be any big thing. I know he knows I am always short of bread because everyone knows that. I know he knows that I am not short of friends, because everyone knows that, too. I also know that with Klein, bread/friendwise, it is exactly the other way round. I figure that either we will make it together or we will not. There will be no half measures.

We go to a restaurant and I have food and beer. He doesn't drink or smoke at all and he doesn't eat much either. He is not happy in the restaurant, but I am. It is Sunday afternoon. I am small-talking and he is drumming his fingers. He says: 'Hey, we can't talk here. Let's go to my office, I got a great office.' I don't think that I can think of anything less groovy than going to a Manhattan office on a Sunday afternoon, but it is no good arguing because he isn't going to do any deal in a café, and I have come 3,000 miles to do a deal so it is his call in his town. We go to his office and he sits me opposite him. He is in his big, important chair behind his big, important desk and I am dying of thirst. He is feeling very good, however, and he tells me all about where I should get myself re-motivated, start looking for the real bread, etcetera, why. I am wasting my life. I think maybe he is right, so I lay on him that I would like a thousand dollars a month to work the Stones and also I would like to know where is the water cooler. My mouth is dry from pills. I get some water and then some more. He tells me things about how to make money and what sort of a corporate set-up I should need and how he came from nowhere to be a big guy and by the time I leave and he leaves, I don't hear one word about whether I work for the Stones and the fee or any goddamn thing that I came to discuss but I think we–ell, maybe he feels better, and it was nice seeing the Stones and I will be home tomorrow so what's it matter apart from I had to leave Joan and the kids on the other side of the sub-continent (and Timothy had broken his arm a day or two before) to come to Allen Klein's 14,000th floor office in Manhattan.

A few months later he sent me some bread to cover my fare and I didn't give him another thought (didn't get the Stones either) till I was in this Morgan car with Tony Calder three years later, and one hell of a lifetime older and wiser.

So I tell Tony if Klein thinks I am in his way, and as I'm not in his way, I'd better show the guy I'm not, by moving out of the way anyone else who might be in his way.

I tell Tony to tell Klein I am (a) not in his way, and (b) if anyone else is, I will remove them. I tell Tony to tell Klein to call. I go into work at Apple and I see Peter Brown, Brian's old pal, mine, the Beatles', Apple's and so on. Peter knows many things. I say, 'Allen Klein wants to meet the Beatles.' 'Does he ever,' says Peter. I ask: 'Is there anyone in his way?' Peter says, 'Only the Beatles.'

He explains Brian didn't like Klein and the Beatles had never heard anything about him that attracted them either.

I ask him will he take a call from Klein (on account of he is the Beatles' personal assistant, the last filter – or was), and he says he will.

The way is clear and Klein places his call. He doesn't get through, nowhere near does he get, and he must have called Les Perrin who represented Klein because Les calls me and says: 'Klein says he can't reach Peter Brown.' I say I'll check and then I go into lunch with the Beatles in the room opposite Peter's, which is now Neil's, but was then the Beatles' own, born in a dream and left unfurnished – because a dream is just a wish you hope will come true and this one didn't. At lunch it is one of those days, it is like eating toast underwater. It is a real down time and they are still talking about how lousy Apple is and how we are a lot of time-serving fools, the usual stuff, you know. I say there is this guy Klein who badly wants to see them. John says yeah, Klein's been trying to reach him but he won't take the call. I do some hype for Klein and say he is a strange cat, hated by some of the people who met him and also by some of the people who have only heard of him. George says, 'he sounds really nice,' and I say that if they want someone to run their money scene then Klein may be the man.

I don't care what you think of Klein – call Klein something else, call him Epstein for now – and just consider the fact that three of us chose Epstein. Paul was the same with Brian in the beginning, if you must know. He used to sulk and God knows what. – *John Lennon*

But I also say they had better look at him very hard and ask around Jagger and Donovan and the others he handles. I mean *really* check Klein out. But see him too. See him face to face. John says OK, I'll see him and the others rhubarb a bit and that's the lunch over.

I call Les Perrin and tell him tell Klein call and Klein does and then he flies over really fast, like *yesterday*. He meets John, they talk all night and boy do they dig each other. John comes into the office and says, 'Don't care about the others, don't give a shit. . .but I'm having Klein, he can have all of my stuff and get it sorted out.'

John says there is too much fear around, everyone must stop being frightened, everything is going to be fantastic, like Klein is going to be the genie of the lamp.

Paul, George and Ringo get to meet Klein and he begins to act as if he is half-hired but maybe not. He says he will save Northern Songs from the wicked

Lew Grade. He says he will buy NEMS Enterprises. He says he will take EMI to the cleaners. In the end he doesn't save Northern Songs and he doesn't buy NEMS Enterprises, but takes EMI and Capitol to the cleaners and to hell and back, and it is Stanley Gortikov, a senior executive at Capitol, who says a lot later that year that OK, Capitol paid up, but did Klein have to be so hard about it? Capitol, says Gortikov, would have paid up anyway. Would they?

Klein tells George he will get him more money and he tells Ringo the same. He tells them all that there are four first-class Beatles, not two, and John doesn't mind being told this. Paul doesn't like any of it, none of it. He has a father-in-law who is also from New York and his name is Lee Eastman. Lee Eastman is also a toughie, but his manners are more formal than Klein's and some people like him. Paul would like Mr Eastman to be the Mr Big Apple needs. John wants Klein to be Mr Big. A year passes. It is 1970. Paul still doesn't like Klein but John digs him more than ever and George digs him more than that and Ringo doesn't mind him. Paul? He is so uptight about Klein he only leaves the Beatles, that's all.

Klein and me meet the press and TV and all that; together we sit on a sofa and talk about Paul. Mr Klein, why doesn't Paul like you? Mr Taylor, why doesn't Paul like Mr Klein? I don't know, don't ask me, man, don't ask me.

Paul releases his album and Klein releases the Beatles' album and they both make a million and Klein has had Phil Spector remix Paul's song 'The Long and Winding Road', adding a women's choir and some violins etc. Paul thinks this is the shittiest thing anyone has ever done to him and that is saying something, but Klein laughs up his silk sleeve and releases 'Long and Winding Road' as a single anyway and still with Phil's new arrangement. Up there in Scotland, Paul McCartney, one of the four owners of Apple, the company formed to give total freedom, artistic control, to struggling performers and writers, wonders what went wrong, when even *he* can't control his own work. I am wondering too. Everyone is wondering. But Klein isn't wondering. He knows, he knows.

Klein is now Mr Big and Apple is an ABKCO (Allen B. Klein & Co., get it?) Managed Company. Two dozen people have gone, maybe more. Some invited to go, others have resigned in despair, executives, accountants, beavers, squirrels, pluggers, musicians, gone, gone. There are no more hired cars, no more lunches, no more liquor for guests, workers sign in and out, the laughing is over, the wastage has been stopped, and as John Lennon has said, the circus has left town but the Beatles still own the site. Money is pouring into Apple so I guess you could say that Allen Klein straightened Apple out as the Beatles wanted it.

The only thing is. . . where is Apple and where are the Beatles? If you find out, please let me know, I haven't seen them in a long time.

As Times Goes By, Derek Taylor, 1973

LENNON
By Ray Coleman

An insightful account of the fractious circumstances surrounding the Beatles' final album release, Let It Be. *Originally planned as a spontaneous warts-and-all studio session, the documentary film of the same name would expose how things had started to go wrong.*

Let It Be had by this time . . . developed into a monster with three separate producers – George Martin, Glyn Johns, and Phil Spector – all trying to salvage something from the sessions at Twickenham and Apple studios . . .

Prior to the release of the *Let It Be* album, the eponymous single was released in March 1970. It was a Paul McCartney epic, although he publicly voiced his dissatisfaction with Spector's doctoring of the finished tapes. The B-side was a rarity – 'You Know My Name (Look Up the Number'. A throwaway number, written and recorded by Lennon in 1967, it features McCartney, the Beatles' road manager, Mal Evans, and saxophonist Brian Jones – the late member of the Rolling Stones, who was friendly with the Beatles. It is an enchanting, sleazy cabaret number, set in a mythical night-club – 'Slaggers' – with Lennon acting as MC and showman and McCartney crooning in his best put-on Vic Damone style.

The *Let It Be* album was finally released in May 1970. What had originally been intended as spontaneous proof of the Beatles' very existence and vitality comes across as a doctored valediction. 'It was hell,' recalled Lennon bitterly. 'Even the biggest Beatles fan couldn't have sat through those six weeks of misery.' The whole saga surrounding the 'finished' album was a sad reflection of how disillusioned the Beatles had become about their recording, their future, themselves, and, tragically, their music. The original intention was show the group 'warts and all', deliberately stripping away all the lavish production of their albums of the previous four years, to capture their spontaneity in the studio. The world was to eavesdrop on the Beatles in rehearsal and see them shape their songs for their next album. Over 30 hours of music are on tape somewhere; much has surfaced on sporadic bootlegs. You can listen to the undoctored versions of 'The Long and Winding Road', 'Let It Be', 'Across the Universe', the full version of 'Dig It', and great original material like the rockabilly 'Suzy Parker'. You can also hear the Beatles work out on songs of their youth, Hank Williams's 'You Win Again', Cliff Richard's 'Move It', Elvis's 'Good Rockin' Tonight', Chuck

Berry's 'Memphis, Tennessee', Lennon's ripe parody of 'House of the Rising Sun', and workouts on Dylan's 'Blowin' in the Wind' and 'All Along the Watchtower'. Ironically, John Lennon began collecting Beatles bootleg albums in 1974 when he could begin to enjoy re-living his past.

By the end of the film and recording sessions of January 1969 neither the Beatles nor George Martin could face wading through the miles of tapes. Given the original 'natural' idea of the project, Phil Spector was called in to edit and polish up the material and give the world the Beatles album it expected. Spector was a legend. He had virtually invented the idea of the record producer with his mini teen epics of the mid-1960s: 'Then He Kissed Me', 'River Deep, Mountain High', and 'You've Lost that Lovin' Feeling'. All were conceived and executed on a Wagnerian scale with Spector inventing the 'wall of sound', utilising multi-tracking, massed instrumentation, and laborious overdubbing. He was a genius, but like all geniuses, he could be difficult and unpredictable. Lennon recalled the *Let It Be* debacle: 'It was just a dreadful, dreadful feeling . . . We were going to let it out in really shitty condition. I didn't care. I had thought it would be good to let the shitty version out because it would break the Beatles myth. It would be just us, with no trousers on and no glossy paint over the cover, and no hype. "This is what we are like with our trousers off – would you please end the game now?"'

I'd like to say thank you on behalf of the group and ourselves and I hope we pass the audition. – *John Lennon, after the Apple rooftop performance recorded in the* Let It Be *film*

But the old magic did surface, even during those acrimonious final days. The album's opening track, 'Two of Us', was a McCartney song for Linda, but (in context) it becomes a moving requiem to two Liverpool kids, burning with ambition and talent: 'Two of us sending postcards, writing letters on my wall/You and me burning matches, lifting latches, on our way back home.' It is a memory of Liverpool as it was, when the world was open and bright for conquest, not shrouded in the acid connotations of 'Strawberry Fields'. At the dismal end, 'Two of Us' serves as a moving reminder of that bright beginning.

'Dig a Pony' celebrated Lennon's omniscience – 'You can celebrate anything you want . . . You can penetrate any place you go . . . You can radiate anything you are.' But as the refrain runs, 'I told you so, all I want is you.' That was definitely meant for Yoko. 'Across the Universe' was a song that infuriated Lennon at the time. He woke up one morning with the line 'Pools of sorrow, waves of joy' running through his head and proceeded to construct the song from it. The version on the album was 'subconscious sabotage' on his part, in the name of experimentation. One version ended up on a World Wildlife Fund charity album with two Beatles fans singing the 'Nothing's gonna change my world' chorus. 'The original track was a real piece of shit,' he recalled with some bitterness, 'I was singing out of tune and instead of getting a decent choir, we got fans from outside . . . Apple Scruffs or whatever you call them. They came in and were singing all off-key. Nobody was interested in doing the tune originally . . . Phil slowed the tape down, added the strings . . . He did a really special job.' The 'Jai Guru Deva OM' refrain harkens back to the days of gurus and avatars who could save the world. The song caught Lennon at a time when all his creativity and sexuality were being devoted to Yoko but when: 'Words are flowing out like endless rain into a paper cup . . . Thoughts meander like a restless wind.' Restless, the artist in him was beset by relentless images and a burning desire to create, while he wilfully stripped everything down for Yoko. 'Nothing's gonna change my world,' he sang. But it had.

'Dig It' was an example of the 'new-phase Beatles album' which the *Let It Be* album sleeve boasted. Distilled from a five-minute stream of consciousness rap, the existing 48-second track finds Lennon invoking Manchester United boss Matt Busby, Doris Day, and a series of acronyms, ending with the emphatic ' Whatever it is, whoever you are – just dig it!' Lennon's sardonic comments pepper the finished album – opening the album with 'I dig a pygmy by Charles Hawtrey,' prefacing the beautiful 'Let It Be' with the iconoclastic 'Now we'd like to do 'ark the Angels come,' digging up the traditional 'Maggie Mae', disembowelling 'Danny Boy', and pre-empting 'Get Back' with an improvised chorus of 'Sweet Loretta Fart/Thought she was a cleaner, but she was a frying pan.' It is only the tip of the iceberg, though, and unfortunately it is the poor-quality bootlegs which give a greater indication of the album's original concept.'I've Got a Feeling' was a Lennon-McCartney collaboration of sorts. The first half of the song is all Paul, while the 'Everybody had a hard year' section onwards is John. 'One after 909' was a genuine collaboration, written in 1959 in those dim and distant Liverpool days and disinterred for their last album together. Here was a joyous slice of Eddie Cochran-style rock, written by two teenagers with no real idea of that so-distant America, culled instead from images of contemporary rock'n'roll songs, with John and Paul singing enthusiastically together on the chorus. Sharply evocative of those earlier, sunnier, and simpler days, it seems now a glorious finale to the partnership of Lennon and McCartney; as the years passed and the acrimony between the two men subsided, their preferred memory was, indeed, of 'sagging off school' as Liverpool boys and writing songs in the back of the Beatles' van.

Lennon, Ray Coleman, 1984

APPLE TO THE CORE: THE UNMAKING OF THE BEATLES
By Pete McCabe

This extract describes the feud between Allen Klein – the Beatles' latter-day manager, appointed in 1969 against the wishes of Paul – and lawyer Lee Eastman. McCartney wanted Eastman, who was soon to become his father-in-law, to take over, and the dis-agreement was to hasten the already inevitable disbandment of the group.

Lee Eastman resorted to the lowest forms of animal life in order to describe Klein.

'I won't do business with him, he's a swine,' Eastman declared. 'When you go to bed with a louse, you get lousy.'

'We co-operated with Klein for about two weeks,' says his son, John. 'Do you know what he did? It was agreed that both of us [Eastman and Klein] would see all the Beatles' documents, but Klein took out all the important stuff and sent along a huge bundle of documents containing nothing of importance. Klein is impossible to deal with. I'm convinced that when he opens his mouth, he does-n't know what's going to come out.'

'He's right, I don't,' said Klein, rather ruefully, while Lennon exploded in hysterics. 'Yup, I ripped off those documents, damn right! But Eastman and McCartney had already gone behind our backs buying Northern Songs shares.'

'Lee Eastman has achieved a lot,' Klein concedes. 'I give credit where it's due. But you play to win, right? And if you lose, well, you don't try to kill everybody. That's what Eastman did. His attitude was, "If I can't get anything, I'm going to make it as difficult as possible for everybody else." Pure harassment!'

'Paul was too easily led by the Eastmans [Lee and John]. But he's not any-more. Now Paul's too easily led by Linda. She's leading him down the road. She even calls the sidemen for his album. "We'd like to audition you," she says. Paul is about two years behind John right now. John was just as heavily influenced by Yoko at one time, but that's not so any more. I pried John away from Yoko, artistically. There'll be no more John and Yoko twin albums.

'McCartney is an ideas man. You can't underestimate his talent, but it was Lennon who completed many of his ideas. The trouble with Paul's albums is that his ego won't allow him to use anyone good to bounce ideas off. George used

Phil Spector and Eric Clapton. With Ringo's single, I told George, "You've got to work with him, he needs help."

'I've done a lot for Ringo,' says Klein, getting into his stride and taking steadily larger gulps on his Coca-Cola. 'Do you know anyone who would have offered him a leading film part? I did, I didn't even send him the script. I said, "Meet the director and if that's okay, let me know." He went to Europe, met the guy and they got on really well. After half an hour, he said, "It's good, let's call Allen."'

Klein suddenly feels obliged to apologise for his lack of modesty.

'I used to play down my deals,' he says. 'I took a lot of shit from the English papers. The London *Sunday Times* really did a hatchet job on me. Later they wrote another piece about the way I was running Apple. It was almost an apology. Now I've decided to say what I think. John wanted to do his *Rolling Stone* interview for me, because I hadn't spoken up.'

A conversation with the ABKCO president can prove a mind-boggling experience. He proves each point by pulling thick files out of his drawer and shuffling through mounds of paper. Occasionally, he pulls an old envelope from his back pocket and does a rapid calculation to show how his brilliant deals worked out in his favour. He's impossible to pin down.

'Don't talk to me about management,' he says. 'Talk to me about net and gross.' His voice takes on a distinctly metallic edge, and that cherubic smile dances across his lips as he sees he's made his point.

'I made the boys lots of money,' he boasts, reverting to his favourite topic of conversation. '*Let It Be* made more money for them than all the other films put together. They wanted it for TV, but I told 'em that was stoopid.

'Before they met me, they were being fucked around by everybody. I did a great deal with Capitol and E.M.I. They knew they couldn't stop an artist recording. So up went the royalty rates. .We account for over 50 percent of Capitol Records' business. They're just our distributors. I did Capitol a great favour. I delivered them product. These boys want to work, but you have to motivate them. They won't work while they're bein' screwed by a record company. But when somebody gets rid of the bullshit, and they're getting a fair deal, they'll work.'

Klein's renegotiating of the Beatles' recording contract was unquestionably a big money-winner for them. He claims that even McCartney congratulated him on the deal. The industrious accountant is doubtless top man at bargaining with, or bullying, record companies. But he is a business manager, rather than an artists' manager.

'He made them lots of money, sure,' says one observer. 'But he alienated

McCartney and the Beatles broke up. Paul is a difficult bastard to deal with, but somehow Brian Epstein handled him.'

Klein still hasn't given up hope with McCartney.

'The Beatles could get together, but only if Paul matures and stops looking for all this middle-class bullshit,' he says.

No chance, say most other observers.

Klein might also have a problem getting John Lennon together with Paul.

The only thing that has prevented us from getting together again has been Klein's contractual hold over the Beatles' name. When he's out of the way, there is no real reason why we shouldn't get together again. – *Paul McCartney, on joining with Lennon and Harrison to litigate against Allen Klein, November 1973*

'It's a house we own together and there's no way of settling it, unless we all decide to live in it,' says Lennon. 'We only ever wrote together 'cause in the early days it was fun and later on convenient. But our best songs were always written alone. We'd been workin' apart ever since we'd been workin' together. It'll never happen, there's no use contemplating it. If I'm friends with him again, I'll never write with him again. There's no point. I might write with Yoko because she's in the same room as me. I was livin' with Paul, so I wrote with him. He writes with Linda, he's livin' with her. It's just natural. In five years, hell, you wake up.'

Klein still nurtures the hope that McCartney will come around. In the meantime, his defeat in the English courts gnaws at him.

'My friend, Johnny Eastman, won the first round,' he says bitingly. 'But it was a victory in PR. The trouble was the establishment was against us. The establishment, the fuckin' courts, the government, they can all exercise what's known as discretion, when they don't wanna face the facts.

'I knew the partnership would be dissolved. I know the English law. The only reason for opposing it was the horrendous tax consequences that could result. But that old judge, Stamp [Mr Justice Stamp appointed the receiver], he didn't understand what it was all about. He got lost. He got Beatlemania.'

Klein is once again rummaging through papers when George Harrison bursts into his office, just arrived from London and wearing an outrageous pair of Italian sunglasses. Klein drops everything he's doing, leaps up from his chair and gives George a big greeting. Immediately, he tries to interest him in business matters. George, however, is already immersed in conversation with Lennon, who is bubbling like a teenager over his new boots. The president of ABKCO Industries waves his arms in despair. Yoko is still screaming down the phone.

Eventually, George is ready to talk business, but not before he's avoided a concern of his own. He has a complaint about various groupies sitting outside the building that houses the ABKCO office.

'Allen, can't you get rid of those ABKCO scruffs?' he asks politely. 'They're bad for our image. They don't have the class of Apple scruffs.'
Allen Klein is stumped for words, a very rare occurrence.

Apple to the Core: the Unmaking of the Beatles, Pete McCabe, 1973

INTERVIEW WITH PAUL McCARTNEY
By Richard Meryman

An excellent first-person account of why McCartney took legal action against the other Beatles, in order to break up their corporate partnership.

'The whole Beatle thing – it's like it was all years ago – like going back a distance more than anything. And that's the whole point. The Beatles are really finished, over with, and it's just each of us alone now, living our lives the way we choose. I think while the Beatles were on – I can't really use any other word – while they were just on, there was no question of any of these normal hangups interfering with it because we just had an understanding. It's like a married couple. When we started off we were all aiming for pretty much the same thing. I think the troubles really began when we weren't aiming anymore for the same thing, which began, I think, when we stopped touring in 1966. During the making of the White Album, Ringo left the group saying he wasn't "getting through" to the rest of us. But he came back in two days. By the time we made *Abbey Road*, John and I were openly critical of each other's music and I felt John wasn't much interested in performing anything he hadn't written himself. When we made the *Let It Be* album, George walked out over a row about the performance of some songs – and said he was leaving the group. A few days later there was a meeting at Ringo's house, and he agreed to come back at least until the recording was finished.

'So I felt the split coming. And John kept saying we were musically standing still. One night – this was the autumn of '69 – Linda and I were lying there, talking about it, and I thought, "That's what I miss, and what they miss too – Playing." Because we hadn't actually played for anyone for a long time. And being an actual good musician requires this contact with people all the time. The human thing. So I came into the idea of going to village halls which hold a couple of hundred people. Have someone book the hall and put up posters saying, maybe, "Ricky and the Redstreaks, Saturday Night." And we'd just turn up there in a van and people would arrive and we'd be there. I thought that was great. John said, "You're daft."

'At this time John's thing was playing for 200,000 people because he'd been at a big festival or something. So he wanted to do that. And I can see now what he thought. I can see which way John sees progress. I see it sometimes another way.

'We were talking in the Apple offices. Ringo was there – he agreed – and maybe George wasn't there. So then John says, "Anyway, I'm leaving the group." He said, "I want a divorce." He literally said, "I want a divorce." And for the first time ever, he meant it. So that just hit everyone. All of us realised that this great thing that we'd been part of was no longer to be. This was the chop. That hits anyone, no matter what it is. It's like leaving school, and you love it then it hits like a chop. Or whatever your thing is. Our thing was the Beatles.

'The Beatle way of life was like a young kid entering the big world, entering it with friends and conquering it totally. And that was fantastic. An incredible experience. So when that idea really came that we should break up, I don't think any of us wanted to accept it. It was the end of the legend, even in our own minds. Marilyn Monroe gets to believe eventually that she's Marilyn Monroe. Now I feel that's how the Beatles got to be – I'm just speaking for me. You were very much a Beatle in your own eyes, and to an extent we all still are. Thinking back, I think it was great what John said. And he told us, "Look, everything sort of comes together right." And now I agree. We'd just made this album and it was to be called *Get Back* and on the cover was a photograph showing us in exactly the same position as in the first album we'd made – the whole lettering and the background was exactly reproduced. So John said, "It's a perfect circle, you know." I think what John did was tremendous from the point of view of "Okay, so we are actually going to go our own ways." You just can't be as tied together as we were for so long a period of time, unless you all live in the same house. From then onward it was to be a question of living your own life, which was the first real turn-on for me in a long time – and this coincided with my meeting Linda. So early in 1970 I phoned John and told him I was leaving the Beatles too. He said, "Good! That makes two of us who have accepted it mentally."

'I do think if it were just up to the four of us, if we were totally unencumbered, we would have had a dissolution – I hate these heavy terms – the day after John said he was leaving. We would have picked up our bags – these are my shoes, that's my ball, that's your ball – and gone. And I still maintain that's the only way, to actually go and do that, no matter what things are involved on a business level. But of course we aren't four fellows. We are part of a big business machine. Even though the Beatles have really stopped, the Beatle thing goes on – repackaging the albums, putting tracks together in different forms, and the video coming in. So that's why I've had to sue in the courts to dissolve the Beatles, to do on a business level what we should have done on a four-fellows level. I feel it just has to come. We used to get asked at press conferences, "What are you going to do when the bubble bursts?" When I talked to John just the other day, he said something about, "Well, the bubble's going to burst." And I said, "It has burst. That's the point. That's why I've had to do this, why I had to apply to the court. You don't think I really enjoy doing that kind of stuff? I had to do it because the bubble has burst – everywhere but on paper." That's the only place we're tied now.

'You see, there was a partnership contract put together years ago to hold us together as a group for ten years. Anything anybody wanted to do – put out a record, anything – he had to get the others' permission. Because of what we were then, none of us ever looked at it when we signed it. We signed it in '67 and discovered it last year. We discovered this contract that bound us for ten years. So it's "Oh gosh, Oh golly, Oh heck," you know. "Now, boys, can we tear it up, please?" But the trouble is, the other three have been advised not to tear it up. They've been advised that if they tear it up, there will be serious, bad consequences for them. The point, though, to me was that it began to look like a three-to-one vote, which is what in fact happened at a couple of business meetings. It was three to one. That's how Allen Klein got to be the manager of Apple, which I didn't want. But they didn't need my approval.

'Listen, it's not the boys. It's not the other three. The four of us, I think, still quite like each other. I don't think there is bad blood, not from my side anyway. I spoke to the others quite recently and there didn't sound like any from theirs. So it's a business thing. It's Allen Klein. Early in '69 John took him on as business manager and wanted the rest of us to do it too. That was just the irreconcilable difference between us.

'Klein is incredible. He's New York. He'll say "Waddaya want? I'll buy it for you." I guess there's a lot I really don't want to say about this, but it will come out because we had to sort of document the stuff for this case. We had to go and fight – which I didn't want, really. All summer long in Scotland I was fighting with myself as to whether I should do anything like that. It was murderous. I had a knot in my stomach all summer. I tried to think of a way to take Allen Klein to court, or to take a businessman to court. But the action had to be brought against the other three.

'I first said, "No, we can't do that. We'll live with it." But all those little things kept happening, such trivia compared to what has happened, but the kind of things that. . .well, for example, my record *McCartney* came out. Linda and I did it totally – the record, the cover the ads – everything presented to the record company. Then there started to appear these little advertisements. On the bottom was "On Apple Records," which was okay. But somebody had also come along and slapped on "An ABKCO-managed company." Now that is Klein's company and has nothing to do with my record. It's like Klein taking part of the credit for my record.

'Maybe that sounds petty, but I can go into other examples of this kind of thing. The build-up is the thing – All these things continuously happening making me feel like I'm a junior with the record company, like Klein is the boss and I'm nothing. Well, I'm a senior. I figure my opinion is as good as anyone's, especially when it's my thing. And it's emotional. You feel like you don't have any freedom. I figured I'd have to stand up for myself eventually or get pushed under. The income from the *McCartney* album is still being held by Apple, and Linda and I are the only ones on the record. John has a new record out with a song called "Power to the People". There's a line in it – sort of shouting to the government – "Give us what we own." And to me Apple's the government thing. Give me what I own.

Implicit in Paul's writings and interview statements are all sorts of thinly veiled recriminations and put downs, e.g., John's work 'doesn't give me any pleasure', and: 'Wish Ringo was here for this break?' 'No.' Remember, this is all stuff that Paul himself deliberately included . . . If one wanted to extend speculation on what it all means, the possibilities are endless. Why, for example, did Paul involve Linda in this album? Was it his vain attempt to do John and Yoko one better? – Rolling Stone *review of* **McCartney**

'So then we began to talk again about the suit, over and over. I just saw that I was not going to get out of it. From my last phone conversation with John, I think he sees it like that. He said, "Well, how do you get out?"

'My lawyer, John Eastman, he's a nice guy and he saw the position we were in, and he sympathised. We'd have these meetings on top of hills in Scotland, we'd go for long walks. I remember when we actually decided we had to go and file suit. We were standing on this big hill which overlooked a loch – it was quite a nice day, a bit chilly – and we'd been searching our souls. Was there any other way? And we eventually said, "Oh, we've got to do it." The only alternative was seven years with the partnership – going through those same channels for seven years.

'And I've changed. The funny thing about it is that I think a lot of my change has been helped by John Lennon. I sort of picked up on his lead. John had said, "Look, I don't want to be that anymore. I'm going to be this." And I thought, "That's great." I liked the fact he'd done it, and so I'll do it with my thing. He's given the okay. In England, if a partnership isn't rolling along and working – like a marriage that isn't working – then you have reasonable grounds to break it off. It's great! Good old British justice! But before I went into this, I had to check out in my mind, is there such a thing as justice? Like I throw myself into the courts I could easily get caught – tell the story, put it all in there, and then justice turns around and. . .I mean, these days people don't believe in justice. I really think the truth does win, but it's not a popular thought. But then all my life I've been in love with goodies, as against the baddies.

'You can read the other boys' side to find out I'm the stinker. I think I'm right. But don't we all! You couldn't believe it! It's a movie! Because I've had to take this action against the others, it looks like we can't stand each other. I can really only speak for myself, but I still like the other three. And maybe it's deeper than "like". But at the moment, I'm not stuck on them. I'm not pleased. We are not amused at the moment! I am not loving them. But I know when it's over I will really like them.

'People said, "It's a pity that such a nice thing had to come to such a sticky end." I think that too. It is a pity. I like fairy tales. I'd love it to have had the Beatles go up in a little cloud of smoke and the four of us just find ourselves in magic robes, each holding an envelope with our stuff in it. But you realise that you're in real life, and you don't split up a beautiful thing with a beautiful thing. I ignored John's [1971] interview in *Rolling Stone*. I looked at it and dug him for saying what he thought. But to me, short of getting it off his chest, I think he blows it with that kind of thing. I think it makes people wonder why John needs to do that.

'I did think there were an awful lot of inconsistencies, because on one page you find John talking about how Dylan changed his name from Zimmerman and how that's hypocritical. But John changed his name to John Ono Lennon. And people looking at that just begin to think, "Come on, what is this?"

'But the interview didn't bug me. It was so far out that I enjoyed it, actually. I know there are elements of truth in what he said. And this open hostility, that didn't hurt me. That's cool. That's John.

'I can't really describe what direction I'm going in musically, because it's ever-changing – and that's what it's all about. I have my personal influences, and they come from everywhere, from age nothing to today. Sounds I heard on the radio. Sounds I heard my father play on the piano. Sounds I found myself in rock and roll. Sounds that the group made. My music is all that – very personal – especially now that it's one person putting it down instead of four. I do what I feel. Make myself comfortable. It's a good job to have.

'Linda and I have been writing songs together – and my publishers are suing because they don't believe she wrote them with me. You know, suddenly she marries him and suddenly she's writing songs. "Oh, sure – wink, wink – Oh, sure, she's writing songs." But actually one day I just said to her, "I'm going to teach you how to write if I have to just strap you to the piano bench. I'm going to teach you the way I write music" – because I never write music anyway. I just write by ear. And I like to collaborate on songs. If I have to just go out in another room and write – it is too much like work – like doing your homework. If I can have Linda working with me, then it becomes like a game. It's fun. So we wrote about ten songs and then we discovered that it was becoming too much like work. We were getting serious about writing. And I've never been serious.

'When we decided to do the new album, we wanted to make it fun, because it isn't worth doing anything if you can't have fun doing it. The album will be out early in May, and then I'm thinking about getting a band together – another band – because I don't like to just sit around. I really like to play music.

'My musical direction – I'm trying for music that isn't too romantic, yet contains a romantic thing. I personally don't like things to be too cute – except babies. My music comes off best, I think, when there's hard and soft together.

'The best things are often the free bits, and that gets very tricky. I go out into the studio and I know I'm going to ad-lib. If I announce I'm going to ad-lib, I can't ad-lib because I'm no longer ad-libbing. So I've just got to go out there and improvise, and someone's got to be in there in the control room very cleverly thinking, "He's going to ad-lib now, I'd better tape it." It's very hard because good things get missed. Last night I was doing a real ad-lib and I was in a great mood and I was exploring what there was to be done – and they missed it. The next time around when they tried the tape, I wasn't exploring any longer. I was trying to repeat past glories, and that doesn't work. But there are compensations. Sometimes you don't want to share those moments. Okay, the record-buying public didn't hear it, but you and I did. That's beautiful. That's real. The moment was temporary like everything is. Nothing in life really stays. And it's beautiful that they go. They have to go in order for the next thing to come. You can almost add beauty to a thing by accepting that it's temporary.

'I suppose musically I'm competing with the other three, whether I like it or not. It's only human to compete. But I think it's good for us. I think George has shown recently that he was no dummy. I think we're really good, each one of us, individually. You know, there's like three periods in my life. There's the time when I was at school and just after leaving it. That was when I used to read a lot

– Dylan Thomas, paperbacks, a lot of plays, Tennessee Williams, things my literature master had turned me onto. I used to sit on the top level of buses, reading and smoking a pipe. Then there was the whole sort of Beatle thing. And just now again I feel I can do what I want. So it's like there was me, then the Beatles phase, and now I'm me again.

'It's rather serious – life. And you can't live as if you have nine lives. I find myself doing that often. I think everybody does, saying in his mind, "I'll get it tomorrow." But I can't do that anymore. Take One with the Beatles should have been like I said, with a puff of smoke and magic robes and envelopes. But we missed Take One, so now we do Take Two. And in the disappointment of Take Two – I feel I can always find something good in the bad – the good thing is that it really has made me come to terms more with my life. As a married couple, Linda and I've really become closer because of all those problems, all the decisions. It's been very real what I've been through – a breath of air, in a way – because of having been through very inhuman things.

'The Beatle thing was fantastic. I loved every minute of it. It was beautiful. But it was a very sheltered life. Why, somebody would even ring me up in the morning and say, "You've got to be at Apple in an hour." It got very nursemaidy. If you are a real human, you've got to wake yourself up. You've got to take on these tedious little things because out of the tedium comes the joy of life. I got fed up by Apple this year over Christmas trees. "Did we want one, because the office was buying Christmas trees for everyone?" I hated that. Actually we pinched one from a field in Scotland.

'I love my life now because I'm doing much more ordinary things, and to me that brings great joy. We're more ordinary than ordinary people sometimes.

'In New York, we go to Harlem on the subway – a great evening at the Apollo. We walk through Central Park after hours. You may find us murdered one day. Last time we went it was snowy like moonlight in Vermont – just fantastic. And I figure anyone who scares me, I scare him.

'We try never to organise our lives very much. We do things on the spur of the moment. We were in Scotland and we decided to take a trip to the Shetland Islands. So we piled in the Land Rover with the two kids, our English sheep dog, Martha, and a whole pile of stuff in the back with Mary's potty on the top. On the second day we get up to a little port called Scrabster at the top of Scotland. When we tried to get on the big car ferry, we got in queue but were two cars too late – missed it. So, don't despair. Okay, make the best of it. We really didn't want to go on that big liner, a mass-produced thing. So we thought, let's beat the liner. But we gave that up – it became a bit difficult with airplanes and such. "Let's try to get a ride in one of the little fishing boats, and how much should we offer?"

'So the romantic idea was that they'd rather have a salmon or a bottle of Scotch than the £30. I went to a bunch of boats but they weren't going to the Orkney Islands. So I went on this one and I went to this trapdoor sort of thing, and they were sleeping down below – the smell of sleep is coming up through the door. At first the skipper said no, and then I said there was 30 quid in it for him, and they say they'll take us. It was a fantastic little boat called the Enterprise and the captain named George, he's wearing a beautiful Shetland sweater. We brought all our stuff aboard and it was low tide, so we had to lower Martha in a big fishing net and a little crowd gathers and we wave our farewells. As we steam out, the skipper gives us some beer, and Linda, trying to be one of the boys takes a swig and passes it to me. Well, you shouldn't drink before a rough crossing to the Orkneys. The little one, Mary, throws up all over the wife, as usual. That was it. I was already feeling sick. I sort of gallant-ly walked to the front of the boat, hanging onto the mast. The skipper comes up and we're having light talk, light chit-chat. And I don't want it. So he gets the idea and points to the fishing baskets and says, "Do it in there!" So we were all sick, but we ended up in the Orkney Islands, and we took a plane to Shetland. It was great.

'We do things like that – do it sort of eccentric ordinary because we have got the money to do it eccentric. I always wondered what happened to those maharajahs who used to do things. But there never are really any of those peo-ple. So we try and do a bit of it in our own lives.

'People do recognise us sometimes, but they respect our privacy. It's a beau-tiful thing. If you come on as a star, you get star treatment and all the disadvan-tages. But often, when we dress in dungarees and sneakers – Last night we got turned out of two restaurants. The guy in an evening suit turns us out. But I quite like it when they chuck us out.

'I love to find that, even in this day of concrete, there are still alive horses and places where grass grows in unlimited quantities and sky has got clear air in it. Scotland has that. It's just there without anyone touching it. It just grows. I'm relieved to find that it isn't all pollution. It isn't all the Hudson. It's not all the drug problem. When we are in Scotland we plant stuff – vegetables – and we'll leave them there, and of their own volition they will push up. And not only will they push up and grow into something, but then they will be good to eat. To me that's an all-time thing. That's fantastic. How clever! Just that things push their own way up and they feed you. We don't eat meat because we've got lambs on the farm, and we just ate a piece of lamb one day and suddenly realised we were eating a bit of one of those things that was playing outside the window, gamboling peacefully. But we're not strict. I don't want to put a big sign on me,

"Thou Shalt Be Vegetarian." I like to allow myself. I like to give myself a lucky break. Give yourself a lucky break, son.

La la la la la lovely Linda
With the lovely flowers in her hair.
– Paul McCartney, 'The Lovely Linda'

'So I think you've got to live your own life. That sounds like one of those statements, but it is, in fact, just very necessary to realise that. And particularly necessary for me. Or else someone else is going to be living part of your life for you. But now I would like to stop talking and get up and get to work. I haven't done any today, and it's beginning to frustrate me. I've got that album to finish. We've got to get back to plant the seeds. Nature doesn't wait.'

Life, April 1971

INTRODUCTION TO THE BEATLES
By Leonard Bernstein

From the composer of West Side Story *and conductor of the New York Philharmonic –*
a glowing tribute to the Fab Four, which appeared as a foreword to a 1979 retrospective
book on the Beatles.

Once, a year ago (four years ago? last month?), I was asked by *Rolling Stone* to write a 5000-word introduction to a definitive volume on the Beatles – not the, but *The* Beatles. I instantly assented; but that was then, and today is fraught, and these several words must replace, inadequately, alas, what an introduction ought to do.

I fell in love with the Beatles' music (and simultaneously, of course, with their four faces-cum-personae) along with my children, two girls and a boy, in whom I discovered the frabjous falsetto shriek-cum-croon, the ineluctable beat, the flawless intonation, the utterly fresh lyrics, the Schubert-like flow of musical invention and the Fuck-You coolness of these Four Horsemen of Our Apocalypse, on *The Ed Sullivan Show* of 1964. Jamie was then twelve, Alexander nine, and Nina two. Together we saw it, the Vision, in our inevitably different ways (I was 46!), but we saw the same Vision, and heard the same Dawn-Bird, Elephant-Trump, Fanfare of the Future. What Future? Here we are, fifteen years later, and it's all gone. But for a decade or so, or even less, it remained the same Vision-Clarion, yet increasingly cogent, clear, bitter – and better.

Perhaps the clearest, bitterest (and maybe best) was an album called *Revolver* (*pace Sgt. Pepper, Abbey Road*, et al.). Of this album, perhaps the very best was a little-known ditty called 'She Said She Said', the very thought and memory of which recalls all the beauty of those Vietnamese Varicose Veins, The notes healed, the words teased; or perhaps it was vice versa. But *something* teased, and something healed, year after year, Rigby after Rigby, Paperback after Norwegian, perhaps ultimately signified in the gleaming, dreary truth of 'She's Leaving Home'.

Meanwhile, there was a slim volume of pure verbal genius by a new author called *John Lennon: In His Own Write*. If this weren't enough to rhapsodise upon, there were the notes (and the sylph-siren voice) of one McCartney. These two made a pair embodying a creativity mostly unmatched during that fateful decade. Ringo – a lovely performer. George – a mystical unrealised talent. But John and Paul, Saints John and Paul, were, and made, and aureoled and beatified and eternalised the concept that shall always be known, remembered and deeply loved as The Beatles.

And yet, the two were merely something, the four were It. The interdependence was astonishing, and in some ways appalling; do we really need all this to sustain us When We're 64? Well, today I am almost 64, and three bars of 'A Day in the Life' still sustain me, rejuvenate me, inflame my senses and sensibilities.

Nina, who was two way back then in '64, is now seventeen; and only last week we took out that thick, wretched Beatles volume of ill-printed sheet music and reminisced at the piano. We wept, we jumped with the joy of recognition ('She's a Woman') – just the two of us, for hours ('Ticket to Ride', 'A Hard Day's Night', 'I Saw Her Standing There'). . .

That was last week. The Beatles are no more. But this week I am still jumping, weeping, remembering a good epoch, a golden decade, a fine time, a fine time. . .

The Beatles, Geoffrey Stokes, 1980

INTERVIEW WITH GEORGE HARRISON
By Mitchell Glazer

The 'quiet Beatle' talks about his past. From a time when he was starting to concentrate less on music and more on the movie business – which may explain his mellowing attitude to potentially prickly subjects like the Maharishi, Let It Be, *and Eric Clapton's relationship with his ex-wife, Patti Boyd.*

Were you nervous before the Beatles' 1964 debut on The Ed Sullivan Show*?*
The Sullivan Show was funny because I didn't attend the rehearsal. I was sick somehow on the flight over on the first trip to the States. The band did play a lot of rehearsal for the sound people, they kept going into the control room and checking out the sound. And finally when they got a balance between the instruments and the vocals, they marked on the boards by the control, and then everybody broke for lunch. Then we came back to tape the show and the cleaners had been 'round and polished all the marks off the board. It was sort of a bit tacky in those days with the sound. People would put amplifiers off to the side of the stage so it didn't spoil the shot, you know.

I just always wondered if you felt the pressure.
Oh yeah, we did. But we knew we'd had sufficient success in Europe and Britain to have a bit of confidence. And we really needed a helluva lot of confidence for the States because it was such an important place. I mean, nobody'd ever made it, you know, British acts – apart from the odd singer like Lonnie Donegan.

But Ed Sullivan was, you know – Everybody had told us how he was really big. But again, we were pretty naive to certain things so that helped at the time. I remember them asking us did we know who Walter Cronkite was? And I said, 'I dunno, isn't he somebody on the television?' You know, things like that were good because they all had fun – the people asking questions and the press – us being naive and not seeming to care about that sort of thing.

Was there ever a tendency to still act naive after you wised up?
I dunno. But by that time we'd got into that whole sort of routine that we used

to have, you know, at press conferences. A lot of it was just nervous energy, just for jokes and stuff which everybody seemed to like. That was one of the big helps for the Beatles at the time – if anybody dried up in the press conferences there was always somebody else there with a smart answer. There was always a good balance, so nobody could ever really quite nail us.

The Sullivan Show was just the climax to the Beatles' whole America thing. In retrospect it probably wouldn't have mattered what we'd done on The Sullivan Show, it was like already established by the previous press that had gone before. But that was a long time ago. We'll get over the question, 'Are the Beatles getting together again?'

Fab – gear – long time ago when we was fab
Fab – but it's all over now Baby Blue.
George Harrison, 'When We Was Fab'

I won't even ask you.
. . .because the answer is just like going back to school again, really. The four of us are so tied up with our own lives, and it's been eight years since we split. And time goes so fast. It's not beyond the bounds of possibility, but we'd have to want to do it for the music's sake first. We wouldn't stick together because somebody had put an ad in the paper putting us on the spot.

Somebody in New York is saying the Beatles are getting back together to wrestle a Great White shark in Australia.
That was the other guy – he was gonna try and do the Beatles show, and then try and do the other one with somebody fighting a shark. I thought, 'If *he* fights the shark, the winner can be the promoter!'

It seemed that all four of you were locked into something larger than its parts.
It was. But none of us really thought about leaving until '67 or '68, which was after we stopped touring. I know the first time for me which was the most depressing was during 'The White Album'. It was a problem making a double album because it takes such a long time.

Why did you make a double?
I think it was because there were so many songs, but it was a period that had started a bit negative. It was a bit difficult and we got through it and it was fine. We finally got through the album and everybody was pleased because the tracks

were good. Then I worked on an album with Jackie Lomax on Apple records and I spent a long time in the States, and I had such a good time working with all these different musicians and different people. Then I hung out at Woodstock for Thanksgiving and, you know, I felt really good at that time. I got back to England for Christmas and then on January first we were to start on the thing which turned into *Let It Be*. And straight away, again, it was just weird vibes. You know, I found I was starting to be able to enjoy being a musician, but the moment I got back with the Beatles it was just too difficult. There were just too many limitations based upon our being together for so long. Everybody was sort of pigeon-holed. It was frustrating.

The problem was that John and Paul had written songs for so long it was difficult – first of all because they had such a lot of tunes and they automatically thought that theirs should be priority. So for me, I'd always have to wait through ten of their songs before they'd even listen to one of mine. That was why *All Things Must Pass* had so many songs, because it was like I'd been constipated. I had a little encouragement from time to time, but it was very little. It was like they were doing me a favour. I didn't have much confidence in writing songs because of that. Because they never said, 'Yeah that's a good song.' When we got into things like 'While My Guitar Gently Weeps', we recorded it one night and there was such a lack of enthusiasm. So I went home really disappointed because I knew the song was good.

The next day I brought Eric Clapton with me. He was really nervous. I was saying, 'Just come and play on the session, then I can sing and play acoustic guitar.' Because what happened when Eric was there on that day, and later on when Billy Preston. . .I pulled in Billy Preston on *Let It Be*. . .it helped, because the others would have to control themselves a bit more. John and Paul mainly because they had to, you know, act more handsomely. Eric was nervous saying, 'No, what will they say?' And I was saying, 'Fuck 'em, that's my song.' You know, he was the first non-Beatle person who'd ever played on anything.

It must have been terrifying. . .
And it was a good date. Paul would always help along when you'd done his ten songs – then when he got 'round to doing one of my songs, he would help. It was silly. It was very selfish, actually. Sometimes Paul would make us do these really fruity songs. I mean, my God, 'Maxwell's Silver Hammer' was so fruity. After a while we did a good job on it, but when Paul got an idea or an arrangement in his head. . .But Paul's really writing for a fourteen-year-old audience now anyhow. I missed his last tour, unfortunately.

'While My Guitar Gently Weeps' was such a personal song, I'd always wondered why Eric was there.
Well, I'd been through this sitar thing. I'd played sitar for three years. And I'd just listened to classical Indian music and practiced sitar – except for when we played dates, studio dates – and then I'd get the guitar out and just play, you know, learn a part for the record. But I'd really lost a lot of interest in the guitar. I remember I came from California and I shot this piece of film for the film on Ravi Shankar's life called *Raga* and I was carrying a sitar. And we stopped in New York and checked in a hotel, and Jimi Hendrix and Eric Clapton were both at the same hotel. And that was the last time I really played the sitar like that. We used to hang out such a lot at that period, and Eric gave me a fantastic Les Paul guitar, which is the one he plays on that date. So it worked out well. I liked the idea of other musicians contributing.

I helped Eric write 'Badge' you know. Each of them had to come up with a song for that *Goodbye Cream* album and Eric didn't have his written. We were working across from each other and I was writing the lyrics down and we came to the middle part so I wrote 'Bridge'. Eric read it upside down and cracked up laughing – 'What's *Badge*?' he said. After that Ringo walked in drunk and gave us that line about the swans living in the park.

I always thought your contributions guided the band's direction. Beatles '65 – the country influence. Or the Indian influence.
Well, Ringo as well, you know. We all gave as much as we could. The thing was, Paul and John wrote all the songs in the beginning. And they did write great songs, which made it more difficult to break in or get some action on the song-writing thing. But you know, we all did contribute such a lot to the Beatles. There was a period of time when people thought, 'Ringo doesn't play the drums.' I don't know what they thought of me, but they tended to think it was John and Paul for a period of time.

I helped out such a lot in all the arrangements. There were a lot of tracks though where I played bass. Paul played lead guitar on 'Taxman', and he played guitar – a good part – on 'Drive My Car'.

You played bass?
No, I didn't play – We laid the track because what Paul would do, if he's written a song, he'd learn all the parts for Paul and then come in the studio and say, 'Do this.' He'd never give you the opportunity to come out with something. But on 'Drive My Car' I just played the line, which is really like a lick off 'Respect', you know, the Otis Redding version – and I played that line on guitar and Paul

laid that with me on bass. We laid the track down like that. We played the lead part later on top of it. There were a lot of things. . .like on a couple of dates Paul wasn't on it at all, or John wasn't on it at all, or I wasn't on it at all. Probably only about five tunes altogether where one of us might not have been on.

Which of the Beatles albums do you still listen to?
I liked when we got into *Rubber Soul, Revolver.* Each album had something good about it and progressed. There were albums which weren't any good as far as I was concerned, like *Yellow Submarine.*

We put all the songs together into an album form – I'm talking about English albums now, because in the States we found later that for every two albums we had, they [Capitol] would make three. . .because we put fourteen tracks on an album, and we'd also have singles that weren't included on albums in those days. They'd put the singles on, take off a bunch of tracks, change all the running order, and then they'd make new packages like *Yesterday and Today*, just awful packages.

That entire era was so productive. Did it seem that way to you?
Yeah, it was good, it was enjoyable. We'd get into doing harmonies and this and that. Because in the early days we were only working on four-track tapes. So what we'd do would be work out most of the basic track on one track, get all the balance and everything set, all the instruments. Then we'd do all the vocals, or overdub. If there was guitar, lines would come in on the second verse and piano in the middle eight with shakers and tambourines. We'd line up and get all the sounds right and do it in a take, and then do all the vocal harmonies over.

Those old records weren't really stereo. They were mono records and they were rechannelled. Some of the stereo is terrible because you've got backing on one side. In fact, when we did the first two albums – at least the first album which was *Please Please Me*, we did it straight onto a two-track machine. So there wasn't any stereo as such, it was just the voices on one track and the backing on the other. *Sgt. Pepper* was only a four-track.

It's hard to believe.
Yup. Well, we had an orchestra on a separate four-track machine in 'Day in the Life'. We tried to sync them up. I remember – they kept going out of sync in playback, so we had to remix it.

Was the rest of the band difficult when you started getting into Indian music?
Not really. They weren't really as interested. When I'd first met Ravi [Shankar]

he played a private concert just at my house, and he came with Alla Rakha, and John and Ringo came to that. I know Ringo didn't want to know about tabla because it just seemed so far out to him.

He couldn't relate to it?
Well, he could relate to it as a percussion instrument, as drums. But how Rakha actually played it, he couldn't figure that out at all. But they liked it. They knew there was something great about it. But they weren't into it as I was. Then they all went to India and had those experiences in India, too. . .which, for anybody who goes to India, I think straight away you can relate much more to Indian music because it makes so much more sense having been there.

Indian culture unlocked this enormous big door in the back of my consciousness. – *George Harrison*

Was it intimidating to start out at age seventeen or eighteen, and be younger than the others?
No. There are around nine months between me and Paul. . .Nine months between Paul and John. In the early days when I was still at school, I was really small. I sort of grew in height when we were away in Hamburg. A few years before that we did a few parties at night – just silly things – John, Paul, and I. And there were a couple of other people who kept coming and going. John was in school, the College of Art, which was adjoining our school. Paul and I would sneak out of our school and go into his place, which was a bit more free, you know. Ours was still in school uniforms, and we could smoke in his place and do all that. I think he did feel a bit embarrassed about that because I was so tiny. I only looked about ten years old.

But in Hamburg, we were living right in the middle of St Pauli, which is right in the middle of the Reeperbahn district in Hamburg. All the club owners were like gangsters, and all the waiters had tear-gas guns, truncheons, knuckle-dusters. They were a heavy crew. Everybody around that district were homo-sexuals, pimps, hookers. You know, being in the middle of that when I was sev-enteen. (laughs) It was good fun. But when we moved into our second club we were becoming so popular with the crowd of regulars that we never got in any problems with all these gangster sort of people. They never tried to beat us up because they knew the Beatles. And you know, they'd say 'Pedels' [pronounced Peedles], that's German for prick.

The whole image of the Beatles got cleaned up and smoothed over, which is always attributed to Brian Epstein.

In the Hamburg days, we had to play so long and really rock it up and leap about and foam at the mouth and do whatever. We missed the whole period in England – Cliff Richard and the Shadows became the big thing. They all had matching ties and handkerchiefs and gray suits, but we were still doing Gene Vincent, Bo Diddley, you know, Ray Charles things. So when we got back to England that was the big thing. They didn't know us in Liverpool, and there was a big gig at the town hall or something, at a dance. There was an advertisement in the newspaper saying, 'Direct from Hamburg,' and so many people really dug the band, and they were coming up to us and saying, 'Oh, you speak good English!'

But a year or so after that, when Brian Epstein came on the scene, he said, 'You should smarten up because nobody wants to know you' – TV producers or record producers or whatever. We just looked too scruffy. In Germany they had a lot of leather stuff, like black leather trousers and jackets and boots.

Do you miss that Hamburg in your music?

I just had a good time just playing, you know. That's what I miss. Even when we sold records and started doing a lot of tours, it was a bit of a drag because we'd go on the road and we'd play the same tunes to different people, and then we'd drop a few and add the new ones all the time. It got stale. I felt stale, you know, because you play the same riffs. . . da-da-ding-ding-dow, you know. 'Twist and Shout' and things. By the time you came off the road, touring the world, I'd just want to not particularly. . .

. . .look at an instrument?

Yeah. . .for a while. And so we did get very stale, and that's a period when – I was saying about after being into the sitar – I got really friendly with Eric, and all the kids were playing guitars. I'd felt as though I'd missed so many years out.

You mean like Hendrix and Cream, and that whole era?

Yeah, and all the young kids coming up were all playing so good, and I hadn't been involved with it for so long, both being in the Beatles just playing the same old tunes, and playing Indian music. So I felt a long way behind. That was one reason why I had all the instruments. I suddenly realised, 'I don't like these guitars,' and Eric gave me this Les Paul which really got me back into it because it sounded so funky. That was one of the reasons I started playing slide, you know, because I felt so far behind in playing hot licks. With slide I didn't have any instruction, I just got one and started playing.

Do you feel self-conscious about your guitar playing?
I just had to force myself back. A lot of it was just confidence.

John said the best Beatle music happened before the group ever cut a record.
Mmm, well yes. I think some of the best stuff we did was when we stopped touring and spent a lot of time in the studio. You know, we lived in a studio, really. A lot of things which were innovations as far as recording went – I think *that* was some of the best music. But as far as playing live, I agree with what John says about the old days. We were really rocking. We had fun, you know. We really had fun.

Since you've gone solo, your signature musically is different from that now. Like when you did 'Wah-Wah'.
That was the song, when I left from the *Let It Be* movie, there's a scene where Paul and I are having an argument, and we're trying to cover it up. Then the next scene I'm not there and Yoko's just screaming, doing her screeching number. Well, that's where I'd left, and I went home to write 'Wah-Wah'. It had given me a wah-wah, like I had such a headache with that whole argument. It was such a headache.

When did you meet Eric for the first time?
We were in the Hammersmith Odeon, and the Yardbirds were sort of supporting a group on the bill, and I just met him then, but really didn't get to know him. I met him again when the [Lovin'] Spoonful were at the Marquee, and John and I went down and were just sort of hanging about backstage with them. We were going down to their hotel. . .I can remember just seeing Eric, 'I know him. I'm sure I know this guy, and he seems like, you know, really lonely.' I remember we went out and got in a car and went off to [John] Sebastian's hotel and I remembered thinking, 'We should've invited that guy 'cuz I'm sure we know him from somewhere and he just seemed, like, lonely.'

And then a couple of years, maybe a year or so later, the Bee Gees, the Cream, were all involved with Brian Epstein originally, so I started meeing Eric and hanging out with him then at Brian Epstein's house. We sort of went out quite a bit with Brian for dinner and stuff, and then the whole Cream thing started happening. Through that period he played 'Guitar Gently Weeps', and after that he just escaped out of London because some cop was after him. And he bought a house just a bit further out in the country from where I was, and we used to hang out.

'Savoy Truffle' on 'The White Album' was written for Eric. He's got this real sweet tooth and he'd just had his mouth worked on. His dentist said he was through with candy. So as a tribute I wrote, 'You'll have to have them all pulled out after the Savoy Truffle.' The truffle was some kind of sweet, just like all the rest – cream tangerine, ginger sling – just candy, to tease Eric.

I remember him saying he was dedicating 'Layla' to some mystery woman. Did you know what was happening?

Well yeah, sort of. The thing is, with Eric over the years, and you know we [George and Patti Harrison] both loved Eric. Still do. And there were a few funny things. I pulled his chick once. That's happened, and now you'd think he was trying to get his own back on me. (laughs) But much later, when all that thing was going on, when I split from Patti, you know. . .Patti and he got together after we'd really split. And actually we'd been splitting up for years. That was the funny thing, you know. I thought that was the best thing to do, for us to split, and we should've just done it much sooner. But I didn't have any problem about it – Eric had the problem. Every time I'd go and see him, and stuff, he'd be really hung up about it, and I was saying, 'Fuck it, man. Don't be apologising,' and he didn't believe me. I was saying, 'I don't care.'

You said All Things Must Pass *was like an explosion for you.*

Yeah. I had a lot from during the Beatles time and I was writing all the time, and I wrote a few while making the album as well.

Which was your favourite? 'My Sweet Lord?'

No, not particularly. I liked different songs for different reasons. I liked the first song that was on the album, 'I'd Have You Anytime', and particularly the recording of it, because Derek and the Dominoes played on most of the tracks and it was a really nice experience making that album – because I was really a bit paranoid, musically. Having this whole thing with the Beatles had left me really paranoid. I remember having those people in the studio and thinking, 'God, these songs are so fruity! I can't think of which song to do.' Slowly I realised, 'We can do this one,' and I'd play it to them and they'd say, 'Wow, yeah! Great song!' And I'd say, 'Really? Do you really like it?' I realised that it was okay. . .that they were sick of playing all that other stuff. It's great to have a tune, and I liked that song, 'I'd Have You Anytime', because of Bob Dylan.

I was with Bob and he'd gone through his broken neck period and was being very quiet, and he didn't have much confidence anyhow – that's the feeling I got with him in Woodstock. He hardly said a word for a couple of days. Anyway, we finally got the guitars out and it loosened things up a bit. It was really a nice time with all his kids around, and we were just playing. It was near Thanksgiving. He sang me that song and he was, like, very nervous and shy and he said, 'What do you think about this song?' And I'd felt very strongly about Bob when I'd been in India years before – the only record I took with me along with all my Indian records was *Blonde on Blonde*. I felt somehow very close to him or something, you know, because he was so great, so heavy and so observant about everything. And yet, to find him later very nervous and with no confidence. But the thing that he said on *Blonde on Blonde* about what price you have to pay to get out of going through all these things twice – 'Oh mama, can this really be the end?' So I was thinking, 'There is a way out of it all, really, in the end.'

He sang for me, 'Love is all you need/ Makes the world go 'round/ Love and only love can't be denied/ No matter what you think about it/ You're not going to be able to live without it/ Take a tip from one who's tried.' And I thought, 'Isn't it great, because I know people are going to think, "Shit, what's Dylan doing?"' But as far as I was concerned, it was great for him to realise his own peace, and it meant something. You know, he'd always been so hard. . .and I thought, 'A lot of people are not going to like this,' but I think it's fantastic because Bob has obviously had the experience. I was saying to him, 'You write incredible lyrics,' and he was saying, 'How do you write those tunes?' So I was just showing him chords like crazy. Chords, because he tended just to play a lot of basic chords and move *a capo* up and down. And I was saying, 'Come on, write me some words,' and he was scribbling words down. And it just killed me because he'd been doing all these sensational lyrics. And he wrote, 'All I have is yours/ All you see is mine/ And I'm glad to hold you in my arms/ I'd have you anytime.' The idea of Dylan writing something, like, so very simple.

Did you get any feedback from John or Ringo or anybody, saying, 'Congratulations'?
I remember John was really negative at the time, but I was away and he came 'round to my house, and there was a friend of mine living there who was a friend of John's. He saw the album cover and said, 'He must be fucking mad, putting three records out. And look at the picture on the front, he looks like an asthmatic Leon Russell,' there was a lot of negativity going down. You know. . .Ringo played on almost the whole album. I don't care about that. Fuck it – we've been through the thing. I felt that whatever happened, whether it was a flop or a success, I was gonna go on my own just to have a bit of peace of mind.

344

So you weren't apprehensive about how it would go over?
No. Not at all. I felt it was good music, whether people bought it or not. I was concerned that the musicians who played on it were concerned. It was good.

. . . I thought I'm not gonna just sing it myself, I've got Roy Orbison standing there. I'm gonna write a bit for Roy to sing. And then as it progressed . . . I just thought I might as well push it a bit and get Tom [Petty] and Bob [Dylan] to sing the bridge. – *George Harrison, on the 1980s formation of supergroup the Travelling Wilburys*

By the time it was finished, you were confident it was good?
Even before I started I knew I was gonna make a good album because I had so many songs and I had so much energy. For me to do my own album after all that – it was joyous. Dream of dreams.

Let's move ahead. On the new album I've never been able to figure out whether you're talking about Krishna or a woman.
That's good – I like that. I think individual love is just a little of universal love. The ultimate love, the universal love or love of God, is a basic goal. Each one of us must manifest our individual love, manfest the divinity which is in us. All individual love between one person loving another, or loving this, that or the other, is all small parts or small examples of that one universal love. It's all God, I mean if you can handle the word 'God'.

Ultimately the love can become so big that we can love the whole of creation instead of 'I love this but I don't like that.' Singing to the Lord or an individual is, in a way, the same. I've done that consciously in some songs.

I've had a lot of interest in different ways and one of the things I never liked was the whole bit in the late Sixties when everybody started getting into it. One thing I really disliked was this, 'My guru's better than your guru.' It's like little kids on the street – 'My dad's bigger than your dad.' The point is that there is only one God, he's got millions of names, but there's only one God. All Maharishi ever gave me was good advice and he gave me the technique of meditation which is really wonderful.

They say he was a. . .
Well you know, John went through a negative thing more so than I did with the Maharishi. I can see now much clearer what happened, and there was still just a

lot of ignorance that went down. Maharishi was fantastic and I admire him, like Prabhupada, for being able in spite of all the ridicule to just keep going. And there's more people now – especially in the United States – who are all doing it. And in the Sixties they were laughing at us, saying it was stupid. All of these people have influenced me and I've tried to get the best out of all of them without getting spiritual indigestion.

What about your albums like **Living in the Material World,** *the whole concept of maya. It's so ironic that you got caught up in it.*
Oh yeah. I'm living in it. But people interpret it to mean money, cars, that sort of thing – although those are part of the material world. The material world is like the physical world, as opposed to the spiritual. For me, living in the material world just meant being in this physical body with all the things that go along with it.

The litigation involved in the Concert for Bangladesh, didn't that depress you?
Yeah, that is sure enough to make you go crazy and commit suicide. The whole thing of being Beatles – it was very heavy on us four. It was like some people wrote saying, 'Well, the problem with the Beatles is that when we were all growing up they were just tooling 'round the world in limousines.' Actually it was the reverse. We were forced to grow up much faster. And what they call growing up was actually being stuck in a rut while we were transcending layer upon layer. So the heaviness of just the things we've been through, we either use it or rise above it or it pulls you down. For me, it's like it makes me have to call upon the inner me for the strength in order to rise above it, because that part is the maya. Whereas, if you just cop out, it doesn't do anybody any good.

Is it a priority to go 'round the world being a rock and roll star? That's what I'm saying. There's no time to lose, really, and there's gonna have to be a point where I've got to drag myself away and try and fulfil whatever I can.

There are a lot of people in the business that I love, friends, you know, who are really great but who don't have any desire for knowledge or realisation. It's good to boogie once in a while, but when you boogie all your life away it's just a waste of life and of what we've been given. I can get high like the rest of them, but it's actually low. The more dope you take, the lower you get, really. Having done that, I can say that from experience. Whatever it is – you just need more, and the more you take the worse you get.

I used to have an experience when I was a kid, which used to frighten me. I realised [years later] in meditation that I had the same experience. . .I'd feel really tiny, and at the same time I'd feel I was a whole thing as well. It was feeling like two different things at the same time. And this little thing with this feeling would vibrate right through me. . .and it would start getting bigger and bigger and faster and faster until it was going so far and getting so fast that it was mind-boggling, and I'd come out of it really scared.

I used to get that experience a lot when we were doing *Abbey Road*, recording. I'd go into this big empty studio and get into a soundbox inside of it and do my meditation inside of there, and I had a couple of indications of that same experience, which I realised was what I had when I was a kid.

Crawdaddy, February 1977

LENNON REMEMBERS (2)
By Jann S. Wenner

*By the time of Wenner's 1970 interview with Lennon, the former Beatle had become polit-
ically radicalised to the extent that he was now 'carrying pictures of Chairman Mao' himself.*

Why did you make 'Revolution'?
Which one?

Both.
Three of 'em. There's three.

Right. Starting with the single.
When George and Paul and all them were on holiday, I made 'Revolution',
which is on the LP, and 'Revolution Nine', I wanted to put it out as a single,
but they said it wasn't good enough. They came home, I had it all prepared and
they came back and said it wasn't good enough and we put out, what, 'Hello,
Goodbye' or some *shit*. No, we put – 'Hey Jude', sorry, which was worthy. But
we could have had both. I wanted to put out what I felt about revolution, I
thought it was about time we fuckin' spoke about it, the same as I thought it was
about time we stopped not answering about the Vietnamese war, on tour with
Brian. We had to tell him, 'We're going to talk about the war this time, we're
not going to just waffle.' And I wanted to say what I thought about revolution.
I'd been thinking about it up in the hills in India. And I still had this 'God will
save us' feeling about it. 'It's going to be alright.' But even now I'm saying,
'Hold on, John, it's going to be alright.' (1) Otherwise, I won't hold on. But
that's why I did it, I wanted to say my piece about revolution. I wanted to tell
you or whoever listens and communicate and say, 'What do *you* say? This is what
I say.' And that's why I say on one version, about violence, 'in or out?' because
I wasn't sure. But the version we put out said, 'Count me out,' I think. (2)
Because I don't fancy a violent revolution happening all over. I don't want to
die. But I'm beginning to think that what else can happen? It seems inevitable.

348

The violent revolution?

Yeah. And the 'Revolution Nine' was an unconscious picture of what I actually think will happen when it happens. That was just like a drawing of revolution. Because arbitrarily, I was making. . .all the thing was made with loops. I had about 30 loops going, I fed them onto one basic track. I was getting like Beethoven and I'd go upstairs, chopping it up and making it backwards and things like that to get sound effects. And one thing was an engineer's testing [tape], where they'd come on talking and say [*in a robotic voice*], 'This is EMI test series number nine.' So I just cut up whatever he said, and I had 'number nine.' 'Nine' is – I don't know, it turned out to be my birthday and me lucky number and everything, but I didn't realise it. It was just so funny, the voice went, 'number nine.' It was like a *joke*, bringing 'number nine' in all the time. That's all it was.

YOKO: It turns out to be the highest number in the, one, two, etc. up to nine.

JOHN: Nine, yeah, it's the. . .it's all. . .many symbolic things about it, but it just happened. It was an engineer's tape and I was just using all the bits to make a montage. But I really wanted that out. Never mind. So that's how I feel. And I know the Chairman Mao bit, I always feel a bit strange about 'cause I thought that if they're going to get hurt, the idea was, don't aggravate the pig by waving the red flag in his face. I really thought that – that love would save us all, but now I'm wearing a Chairman Mao badge, so that's where it's at. I'm just beginning to think he's doing a good job.

> **Politically we are very different, but I like the fact that he came out and said the Beatles were bigger than Jesus. I like that they considered him dangerous to the government and that they considered him a real threat. That's cool. – *Marilyn Manson***

YOKO: He is.

JOHN: He seems to be. I would never know until I went to China. I'm not going to be like that. I'm not like that. I just was always interested enough to sing about him. But I just wondered what the kids were doing that were actually Maoists. I wonder what their motive was or what was *really* going on. And I thought, if they wanted revolution, if they really want to be subtle, what's the point of saying, 'Well I'm a Maoist, and why don't you shoot me down?' I thought that was not a very clever way of getting what they wanted.

You don't really believe that we're headed for a violent revolution?
I don't know. I've got no more conception than you. I can't see − *eventually*, it'll happen. It *has* to happen. What else can happen? It might happen now, or it might happen in 50 or a hundred years, but it's like. . .

The problem is a violent revolution now would really just be the end of the world.
Not necessarily. They say that every time, but I don't really believe it. If it is, *okay.* I'm back to where I was when I was seventeen. At seventeen, I used to think, well, I wish a fuckin' earthquake or a revolution would happen, just to go out and steal and do what the blacks are doing now. If I was black, I'd be all for it. And if I was seventeen, I'd be all for it, too 'cause what have you got to lose? And now I've got nothing to lose. I don't want to die and I don't want to be hurt physically, but fuck, man, if they blow the world up, *fuck it!* We're all out of our pain then. *Forget it! No more problems!*

1. Referring to 'Hold On' on *John Lennon/Plastic Ono Band.*
2. Lyric is 'But when you talk about destruction/ Don't you know that you can count me out.'

Lennon Remembers, Jann S. Wenner, 2000

POWER TO THE PEOPLE
John Lennon and Yoko Ono talk to Robin Blackburn and Tariq Ali

The new radicalism that erupted in the left-wing student 'revolution' in Paris, May 1968, found its British voices in Ali, Blackburn and other contributors to the magazine Black Dwarf. *By the early Seventies, it had evolved into* Red Mole – *an appropriate platform for Lennon's mix of politics and agit-prop rock'n'roll sloganeering, which now seems rather more trendy than authentic.*

TA: *Your latest record and your recent public statements, especially the interviews in* **Rolling Stone** *magazine, suggest that your views are becoming increasingly radical and political. When did this start to happen?*

JOHN: I've always been politically minded, you know, and against the status quo. It's pretty basic when you're brought up, like I was, to hate and fear the police as a natural enemy and to despise the army as something that takes everybody away and leaves them dead somewhere. I mean, it's just a basic working class thing, though it begins to wear off when you get older, get a family and get swallowed up in the system. In my case I've never not been political, though religion tended to overshadow it in my acid days; that would be around '65 or '66. And that religion was directly the result of all that superstar shit – religion was an outlet for my repression. I thought, 'Well, there's something else to life, isn't there? This isn't it, surely?' But I was always political in a way, you know. In the two books I wrote, even though they were written in a sort of Joycean gobbledegook, there's many knocks at religion and there is a play about a worker and a capitalist. I've been satirising the system since my childhood. I used to write magazines in school and hand them around. I was very conscious of class, they would say with a chip on my shoulder, because I knew what happened to me and I knew about the class repression coming down on us – it was a fucking fact but in the hurricane Beatle world it got left out – I got farther away from reality for a time.

TA: *What did you think was the reason for the success of your sort of music?*

JOHN: Well, at the time it was thought that the workers had broken through, but I realise in retrospect that it's the same phoney deal they gave the blacks, it was just like they allowed blacks to be runners or boxers or entertainers. That's the choice they allow you – now the outlet is being a pop star, which is really what I'm saying on the album in 'Working Class Hero'. As I told *Rolling Stone*, it's the same people who have the power, the class system didn't change one little bit. Of course, there are a lot of people walking around with long hair now and some trendy middle class kids in pretty clothes. But nothing changed except that we all dressed up a bit, leaving the same bastards running everything.

RB: *Of course, class is something the American rock groups haven't tackled yet.*
JOHN: Because they're all middle class and bourgeois and they don't want to show it. They're scared of the workers, actually, because the workers seem mainly right-wing in America, clinging on to their goods. But if these middle class groups realise what's happening, and what the class system has done, it's up to them to repatriate the people and to get out of all that bourgeois shit.

TA: *When did you start breaking out of the role imposed on you as a Beatle?*
JOHN: Even during the Beatle heyday I tried to go against it, so did George. We went to America a few times and Epstein always tried to waffle on at us about saying nothing about Vietnam. So there came a time when George and I said, 'Listen, when they ask next time, we're going to say we don't like that war and we think they should get right out.' That's what we did. At that time this was a pretty radical thing to do, especially for the 'Fab Four'. It was the first opportunity I personally took to wave the flag a bit. But you've got to remember that I'd always felt repressed. We were all so pressurised that there was hardly any chance of expressing ourselves, especially working at that rate, touring continually and always kept in a cocoon of myths and dreams. It's pretty hard when you are Caesar and everyone is saying how wonderful you are and they are giving you all the goodies and the girls, it's pretty hard to break out of that, to say, 'Well, I don't want to be king, I want to be real.' So in its way the second political thing I did was to say, 'The Beatles are bigger than Jesus.' That really broke the scene, I nearly got shot in America for that. It was a big trauma for all the kids that were following us. Up to then there was this unspoken policy of not answering delicate questions, though I always read the papers, you know, the political bits. The continual awareness of what was going on made me feel ashamed I wasn't saying anything. I burst out because I could no longer play that game any more, it was just too much for me. Of course, going to America increased the build-up on me, especially as the war was going on there. In a way we'd turned out to be a Trojan horse. The 'Fab Four' moved right to the top

and then sang about drugs and sex and then I got into more and more heavy stuff and that's when they started dropping us.

RB: *Wasn't there a double charge to what you were doing right from the beginning?*
YOKO: You were always very direct.
JOHN: Yes, well, the first thing we did was to proclaim our Liverpoolness to the world, and say, 'It's all right to come from Liverpool and talk like this.' Before, anybody from Liverpool who made it, like Ted Ray, Tommy Handley, Arthur Askey, had to lose their accent to get on the BBC. They were only comedians but that's what came out of Liverpool before us. We refused to play that game. After the Beatles came on the scene everyone started putting on a Liverpudlian accent.

TA: *In a way you were even thinking about politics when you seemed to be knock-ing revolution?*
JOHN: Ah, sure, 'Revolution'. There were two versions of that song but the underground left only picked up on the one that said 'count me out'. The orig-inal version which ends up on the LP said 'count me in' too; I put in both because I wasn't sure. There was a third version that was just abstract, *musique concrete*, kind of loops and that, people screaming. I thought I was painting in sound a picture of revolution but I made a mistake, you know. The mistake was that it was anti-revolution. On the version released as a single I said, 'when you talk about destruction you can count me out.' I didn't want to get killed. I did-n't really know that much about the Maoists, but I just knew that they seemed to be so few and yet they painted themselves green and stood in front of the police waiting to get picked off. I just thought it was unsubtle, you know. I thought the original Communist revolutionaries coordinated themselves a bit better and didn't go around shouting about it. That was how I felt – I was real-ly asking a question. As someone from the working class I was always interested in Russia and China and everything that related to the working class, even though I was playing the capitalist game. At one time I was so much involved in the religious bullshit that I used to go around calling myself a Christian Communist, but as [Arthur] Janov says, religion is legalised madness. It was ther-apy that stripped away all that and made me feel my own pain.

RB: *This analyst you went to, what's his name?*
JOHN: Janov. . .

RB: *His ideas seem to have something in common with [R. D.] Laing in that he* *doesn't want to reconcile people to their misery, to adjust them to the world, but rather to make them face up to its causes?*

JOHN: Well, his thing is to feel the pain that's accumulated inside you ever since your childhood. I had to do it to really kill off all the religious myths. In the therapy you really feel every painful moment of your life – it's excruciating, you are forced to realise that your pain, the kind that makes you wake up afraid with your heart pounding, is really yours and not the result of somebody up in the sky. It's the result of your parents and your environment. As I realised this it all started to fall into place. This therapy forced me to have done with all the Godshit. All of us growing up have come to terms with too much pain. Although we repress it, it's still there. The worst pain is that of not being wanted, of realising your parents do not need you in the way you need them. When I was a child I experienced moments of not wanting to see the ugliness, not wanting to see not being wanted. This lack of love went into my eyes and into my mind. Janov doesn't just talk to you about this but makes you feel it – once you've allowed yourself to feel again, you do most of the work yourself. When you wake up and your heart is going like the clappers or your back feels strained, or you develop some other hang-up, you should let your mind go to the pain and the pain itself will regurgitate the memory which originally caused you to suppress it in your body. In this way the pain goes to the right channel instead of being repressed again, as it is if you take a pill or a bath, saying, 'Well, I'll get over it.' Most people channel their pain into God or masturbation or some dream of making it. The therapy is like a very slow acid trip which happens naturally in your body. It is hard to talk about, you know, because you feel 'I am pain' and it sounds sort of arbitrary, but pain to me now has a different meaning because of having physically felt all these extraordinary repressions. It was like taking gloves off, and feeling your own skin for the first time. It's a bit of a drag to say so, but I don't think you can understand this unless you've gone through it – though I try to put some of it over on the album. But for me at any rate it was all part of dissolving the Godtrip or father-figure trip. Facing up to reality instead of always looking for some kind of heaven.

God is a concept against which we measure our pain.
– *John Lennon*

RB: *Do you see the family in general as the source of these repressions?*
JOHN: Mine is an extreme case, you know. My father and mother split and I never saw my father until I was twenty, nor did I see much more of my mother. But Yoko had her parents there and it was the same.

YOKO: Perhaps one feels more pain when parents are there. It's like when you're hungry, you know, it's worse to get a symbol of a cheeseburger than no cheeseburger at all. It doesn't do you any good, you know. I often wish my mother had died so that at least I could get some people's sympathy. But there she was, a perfectly beautiful mother.

JOHN: And Yoko's family were middle-class Japanese but it's all the same repression. Though I think middle-class people have the biggest trauma if they have nice imagey parents, all smiling and dolled up. They are the ones who have the biggest struggle to say, 'Goodbye mummy, goodbye daddy.'

TA: *What relation to your music has all this got?*
JOHN: Art is only a way of expressing pain. I mean the reason Yoko does such far-out stuff is that it's a far-out kind of pain she went through.

RB: *A lot of Beatle songs used to be about childhood.*
JOHN: Yeah, that would mostly be me. . .

RB: *Though they were very good there was always a missing element. . .*
JOHN: That would be reality, that would be the missing element. Because I was never really wanted. The only reason I am a star is because of my repression. Nothing else would have driven me through all that if I was 'normal'. . .
YOKO: . . and happy.
JOHN: The only reason I went for that goal is that I wanted to say: 'Now, mummy-daddy, will you love me?'

TA: *But then you had success beyond most people's wildest dreams.*
JOHN: Oh, Jesus Christ, it was a complete oppression. I mean we had to go through humiliation upon humiliation with the middle classes and showbiz and Lord Mayors and all that. They were so condescending and stupid. Everybody trying to use us. It was a special humiliation for me because I could never keep my mouth shut and I'd always have to be drunk or pilled to counteract this pressure. It was really hell.
YOKO: It was depriving him of any real experience, you know.
JOHN: It was very miserable. I mean apart from the first flush of making it – the thrill of the first number one record, the first trip to America. At first we had some sort of objective like being as big as Elvis – moving forward was the great thing, but actually attaining it was the big let-down. I found I was having continually to please the sort of people I'd always hated when I was a child. This began to bring me back to reality. I began to realise that we are all oppressed which is why I

would like to do something about it, though I'm not sure where my place is.

RB: *Well, in any case, politics and culture are linked, aren't they? I mean, work-ers are repressed by culture not guns at the moment.*
JOHN: They're doped.

RB: *And the culture that's doping them is one the artist can make or break.*
JOHN: That's what I'm trying to do on my albums and in these interviews. What I'm trying to do is to influence all the people I can influence. All those who are still under the dream, and just put a big question mark in their mind. The acid dream is over, that is what I'm trying to tell them.

RB: *Even in the past, you know, people would use Beatle songs and give them new words. 'Yellow Submarine', for instance, had a number of versions. One that strikers used to sing began, 'We all live on bread and margarine'; at LSE we had a version that began, 'We all live in a Red LSE.'*
JOHN: I like that. And I enjoyed it when football crowds in the early days would sing 'All Together Now' – that was another one. I was also pleased when the movement in America took up 'Give Peace a Chance' because I had written it with that in mind really. I hoped that instead of singing 'We Shall Overcome' from 1800 or something, they would have something contemporary. I felt an obli-gation even then to write a song that people would sing in the pub or on a demon-stration. That is why I would like to compose songs for the revolution now.

RB: *We only have a few revolutionary songs and they were composed in the nine-teenth century. Do you find anything in our musical traditions which could be used for revolutionary songs?*
JOHN: When I started, rock and roll itself was the basic revolution to people of my age and situation. We needed something loud and clear to break through all the unfeeling and repression that had been coming down on us kids. We were a bit conscious to begin with of being imitation Americans. But we delved into the music and found that it was half white country and western and half black rhythm and blues. Most of the songs came from Europe and Africa and now they were coming back to us. Many of Dylan's best songs came from Scotland, Ireland or England. It was a sort of cultural exchange. Though I must say the more inter-esting songs to me were the black ones because they were more simple. They sort of said shake your arse, or your prick, which was an innovation really. And then there were the field songs mainly expressing the pain they were in. They couldn't express themselves intellectually so they had to say in a very few words

what was happening to them. And then there was the city blues and a lot of that was about sex and fighting. A lot of this was self-expression but only in the last few years have they expressed themselves completely with Black Power, like Edwin Starr making war records. Before that many black singers were still labouring under that problem of God; it was often 'God will save us.' But right through the blacks were singing directly and immediately about their pain and also about sex, which is why I like it.

They knock me for saying 'Power to the People' and say that no one section should have the power. Rubbish. The people aren't a section. The people means everyone. I think that everyone should own everything equally and that people should own part of the factories, and they should have some say in who is the boss and who does what. Students should be able to select teachers. – *John Lennon*

RB: *You say country and western music derived from European folk songs. Aren't these folk songs sometimes pretty dreadful stuff, all about losing and being defeated. . .?*

JOHN: As kids we were all opposed to folk songs because they were so middle-class. It was all college students with big scarfs and a pint of beer in their hands singing folk songs in what we call la-di-da voices – 'I worked in a mine in New-cast-le' and all that shit. There were very few real folk singers you know, though I liked Dominic Behan a bit and there was some good stuff to be heard in Liverpool. Just occasionally you hear very old records on the radio or TV of real workers in Ireland or somewhere singing these songs and the power of them is fantastic. But mostly folk music is people with fruity voices trying to keep alive something old and dead. It's all a bit boring, like ballet: a minority thing kept going by a minority group. Today's folk song is rock and roll. Although it happened to emanate from America, that's not really important in the end because we wrote our own music and that changed everything.

RB: *Your album, Yoko, seems to fuse* **avant-garde** *modern music with rock. I'd like to put an idea to you I got from listening to it. You integrate everyday sounds, like that of a train, into a musical pattern. This seems to demand an aesthetic measure of everyday life, to insist that art should not be imprisoned in the muse-ums and galleries, doesn't it?*

YOKO: Exactly. I want to incite people to loosen their oppression by giving them something to work with, to build on. They shouldn't be frightened of creating themselves – that's why I make things very open, with things for people to do, like in my book [*Grapefruit*]. Because basically there are two types of people in the world: people who are confident because they know they have the ability to create, and then people who have been demoralised, who have no confidence in themselves because they have been told they have no creative ability, but must just take orders. The Establishment likes people who take no responsibility and cannot respect themselves.

RB: *I suppose workers' control is about that. . .*
JOHN: Haven't they tried out something like that in Yugoslavia? They are free of the Russians; I'd like to go there and see how it works.

TA: *Well, they have; they did try to break with the Stalinist pattern. But instead of allowing uninhibited workers' control, they added a strong dose of political bureaucracy. It tended to smother the initiative of the workers and they also regulated the whole system by a market mechanism which bred new inequalities between one region and another.*
JOHN: It seems that all revolutions end up with a personality cult – even the Chinese seem to need a father-figure. I expect this happens in Cuba too, with Che and Fidel. . .In Western-style Communism we would have to create an almost imaginary workers' image of *themselves* as the father-figure.

RB: *That's a pretty cool idea – the Working Class becomes its own Hero. As long as it was not a new comforting illusion, as long as there was a real workers' power. If a capitalist or bureaucrat is running your life then you need to compensate with illusions.*
YOKO: The people have got to trust in themselves.

TA: *That's the vital point. The working class must be instilled with a feeling of confidence in itself. This can't be done just by propaganda – the workers must move, take over their own factories and tell the capitalists to bugger off. This is what began to happen in May 1968 in France. . .the workers began to feel their own strength.*
JOHN: But the Communist Party wasn't up to that, was it?

RB: *No, they weren't. With 10 million workers on strike they could have led one of those huge demonstrations that occurred in the centre of Paris into a massive* *occupation of all government buildings and installations, replacing de Gaulle with a new institution of popular power like the Commune or the original Soviets – that would have begun a real revolution but the French C.P. was scared of it. They preferred to deal at the top instead of encouraging the workers to take the initiative themselves.*

JOHN: Great. . .but there's a problem about that here you know. All the revolutions have happened when a Fidel or Marx or Lenin or whatever, who were intellectuals, were able to get through to the workers. They got a good pocket of people together and the workers seemed to understand that they were in a repressed state. They haven't woken up yet here, they still believe that cars and tellies are the answer. . .You should get these left-wing students out to talk with the workers, you should get the school-kids involved with *The Red Mole*.

TA: *You're quite right, we have been trying to do that and we should do more. This new Industrial Relations Bill the Government is trying to introduce is making more and more workers realise what is happening. . .*

JOHN: I don't think the bill can work, I don't think they can enforce it. I don't think the workers will co-operate with it. I thought the Wilson Government was a big let-down but this Heath lot are worse. The underground is being harrassed, the black militants can't even live in their own homes now, and they're selling more arms to the South Africans. Like Richard Neville said, there may only be an inch of difference between Wilson and Heath but it's in that inch that we live. . .

TA: *I don't know about that; Labour brought in racialist immigration policies, supported the Vietnam war and were hoping to bring in new leglislation against the unions.*

RB: *It may be true that we live in the inch of difference between Labour and Conservative but so long as we do we'll be impotent and unable to change anything. If Heath is forcing us out of that inch maybe he's doing us a good turn without meaning to. . .*

JOHN: Yes, I've thought about that, too. This putting us in a corner so we have to find out what is coming down on other people. I keep on reading the *Morning Star* [the Communist newspaper] to see if there's any hope, but it seems to be in the nineteenth century; it seems to be written for dropped-out, middle-aged liberals. We should be trying to reach the young workers because that's when you're most idealistic and have least fear. Somehow the revolutionaries must approach the workers because the workers won't approach them. But it's difficult to know where to start; we've all got a finger in the dam. The problem for me is that as I have become more real, I've grown away from most working-class people – you know what they like is Engelbert Humperdinck. It's the students who are buying us now, and that's the problem. Now the Beatles are four separate people, we don't have the impact we had when we were together. . .

RB: *Now you're trying to swim against the stream of bourgeois society, which is much more difficult. . .*
JOHN: Yes, they own all the newspapers and they control all distribution and promotion. When we came along there was only Decca, Philips and EMI who could really produce a record for you. You had to go through the whole bureaucracy to get into the recording studio. You were in such a humble position, you didn't have more than twelve hours to make a whole album, which is what we did in the early days. Even now it's the same; if you're an unknown artist you're lucky to get an hour in a studio – it's a hierarchy and if you don't have hits, you don't get recorded again. And they control distribution. We tried to change that with Apple but in the end we were defeated. They still control everything. EMI killed our album *Two Virgins* because they didn't like it. With the last record they've censored the words of the songs printed on the record sleeve. Fucking ridiculous and hypocritical – they have to let me sing it but they don't dare let you read it. Insanity.

RB: *Though you reach fewer people now, perhaps the effect can be more concentrated.*
JOHN: Yes, I think that could be true. To begin with, working class people reacted against our openness about sex. They are frightened of nudity, they're repressed in that way as well as others. Perhaps they thought, 'Paul is a good lad, he doesn't make trouble.' Also when Yoko and I got married, we got terrible racialist letters – you know, warning me that she would slit my throat. Those mainly came from army people living in Aldershot. Officers. Now workers are more friendly to us, so perhaps it's changing. It seems to me that the students are now half-awake enough to try and wake up their brother workers. If you don't pass on your own awareness then it closes down again. That is why the basic need is for the students to get in with the workers and convince them that they are not talking gobbledegook. And of course it's difficult to know what the workers are really thinking because the capitalist press always only quotes mouthpieces like Vic Feather [1908-76; General Secretary of the TUC, 1969-73] anyway. So the only thing is to talk to them directly, especially the young workers. We've got to start with them because they know they're up against it. That's why I talk about school on the album. I'd like to incite people to break the framework, to be disobedient in school, to stick their tongues out, to keep insulting authority.

YOKO: We are very lucky really, because we can create our own reality, John and me, but we know the important thing is to communicate with other people.
JOHN: The more reality we face, the more we realise that unreality is the main programme of the day. The more real we become, the more abuse we take, so it does radicalise us in a way, like being put in a corner. But it would be better if there were more of us.
YOKO: We mustn't be traditional in the way we communicate with people – especially with the Establishment. We should surprise people by saying new things in an entirely new way. Communication of that sort can have a fantastic power so long as you don't do only what they expect you to do.

RB: *Communication is vital for building a movement, but in the end it's power-less unless you also develop popular force.*
YOKO: I get very sad when I think about Vietnam where there seems to be no choice but violence. This violence goes on for centuries perpetuating itself. In the present age when communication is so rapid, we should create a different tra-dition, traditions are created everyday. Five years now is like 100 years before. We are living in a society that has no history. There's no precedent for this kind of society so we can break the old patterns.

TA: *No ruling class in the whole of history has given up power voluntarily and I don't see that changing.*
YOKO: But violence isn't just a conceptual thing, you know. I saw a pro-gramme about this kid who had come back from Vietnam – he'd lost his body from the waist down. He was just a lump of meat, and he said, 'Well, I guess it was a good experience.'
JOHN: He didn't want to face the truth, he didn't want to think it had all been a waste.
YOKO: But think of the violence, it could happen to your kids.

RB: *But Yoko, people who struggle against oppression find themselves attacked by those who have a vested interest in nothing changing, those who want to pro-tect their power and wealth. Look at the people in Bogside and Falls Road in Northern Ireland; they were mercilessly attacked by the special police because they began demonstrating for their rights. On one night in August 1969, seven people were shot and thousands driven from their homes. Didn't they have a right to defend themselves?*
YOKO: That's why one should try to tackle these problems before a situation like that happens.

JOHN: Yes, but what do you do when it does happen, what do you do?

RB: *Popular violence against their oppressors is always justified. It cannot be avoided.*

YOKO: But in a way the new music showed things could be transformed by new channels of communication.

JOHN: Yes, but as I said, nothing really changed.

YOKO: Well, something changed and it was for the better. All I'm saying is that perhaps we can make a revolution without violence.

JOHN: But you can't take power without a struggle.

The song 'Imagine', which says, 'Imagine that there was no religion, no more country, no more politics' is virtually the communist manifesto . . . Now 'Imagine' is a big hit almost everywhere – anti-religious, anti-conventional, anti-capitalist song, but because it's sugar-coated it's accepted. Now I understand what you have to do. – *John Lennon*

TA: *That's the crucial thing.*

JOHN: Because, when it comes to the nitty-gritty, they won't let the people have any power; they'll give all the rights to perform and to dance for them, but no real power.

YOKO: The thing is, even after the revolution, if people don't have any trust in themselves, they'll get new problems.

JOHN: After the revolution you have the problem of keeping things going, of sorting out all the different views. It's quite natural that revolutionaries should have different solutions, that they should split into different groups and then reform, that's the dialectic, isn't it – but at the same time they need to be united against the enemy, to solidify a new order. I don't know what the answer is; obviously Mao is aware of this problem and keeps the ball moving.

RB: *The danger is that once a revolutionary state has been created, a new conservative bureaucracy tends to form around it. This danger tends to increase if the revolution is isolated by imperialism and there is material scarcity.*

JOHN: Once the new power has taken over they have to establish a new status quo just to keep the factories and trains running.

RB: *Yes, but a repressive bureaucracy doesn't necessarily run the factories or trains any better than the workers could under a system of revolutionary democracy.*
JOHN: Yes, but we all have bourgeois instincts within us, we all get tired and feel the need to relax a bit. How do you keep everything going and keep up revolutionary fervour after you've achieved what you set out to achieve? Of course Mao has kept them up to it in China, but what happens after Mao goes? Also he uses a personality cult. Perhaps that's necessary; like I said, everybody seems to need a father-figure. But I've been reading *Khrushchev Remembers*. I know he's a bit of a lad himself – but he seemed to think that making a religion out of an individual was bad; that doesn't seem to be part of the basic Communist idea. Still people are people, that's the difficulty. If we took over Britain, then we'd have the job of cleaning up the bourgeoisie and keeping people in a revolutionary state of mind.

RB: *In Britain, unless we can create a new popular power – and here that would basically mean workers' power – really controlled by, and answerable to, the masses, then we couldn't make the revolution in the first place. Only a really deep-rooted workers' power could destroy the bourgeois state.*
YOKO: That's why it will be different when the younger generation takes over.
JOHN: I think it wouldn't take much to get the youth here really going. You'd have to give them free rein to attack the local councils or to destroy the school authorities, like the students who break up the repression in the universities. It's already happening, though people have got to get together more. And the women are very important too, we can't have a revolution that doesn't involve and liberate women. It's so subtle the way you're taught male superiority. It took me quite a long time to realise that my maleness was cutting off certain areas for Yoko. She's a red hot liberationist and was quick to show me where I was going wrong, even though it seemed to me that I was just acting naturally. That's why I'm always interested to know how people who claim to be radical treat women.

RB: *There's always been at least as much male chauvinism on the left as anywhere else – though the rise of women's liberation is helping to sort that out.*
JOHN: It's ridiculous. How can you talk about power to the people unless you realise the people is both sexes?
YOKO: You can't love someone unless you are in an equal position with them. A lot of women have to cling to men out of fear or insecurity, and that's not love – basically that's why women hate men. . .
JOHN:. . .and vice versa.
YOKO: So if you have a slave around the house how can you expect to make a revolution outside it? The problem for women is that if we try to be free, then

we naturally become lonely, because so many women are willing to become slaves, and men usually prefer that. So you always have to take the chance: 'Am I going to lose my man?' It's very sad.

JOHN: Of course, Yoko was well into liberation before I met her. She'd had to fight her way through a man's world – the art world is completely dominated by men – so she was full of revolutionary zeal when we met. There was never any question about it: we had to have a 50-50 relationship or there was no relationship, I was quick to learn. She did an article about women in *Nova* more than two years back in which she said, 'Woman is the nigger of the world.'

RB: *Of course we all live in an imperialist country that is exploiting the Third World, and even our culture is involved in this. There was a time when Beatle music was plugged on Voice of America. . .*
JOHN: The Russians put it out that we were capitalist robots, which we were I suppose.

RB: *They were pretty stupid not to see it was something different.*
YOKO: Let's face it, Beatles was twentieth-century folksong in the framework of capitalism; they couldn't do anything different if they wanted to communicate within that framework.

RB: *I was working in Cuba when* **Sgt. Pepper** *was released and that's when they first started playing rock music on the radio.*
JOHN: Well I hope they see that rock and roll is not the same as Coca-Cola. As we get beyond the dream this should be easier: that's why I'm putting out more heavy statements now and trying to shake off the teeny-bopper image. I want to get through to the right people, and I want to make what I have to say very simple and direct.

RB: *Your latest album sounds very simple to begin with, but the lyrics, tempo and melody build up into a complexity one only gradually becomes aware of. Like the track 'My Mummy's Dead' echoes the nursery song 'Three Blind Mice' and it's about a childhood trauma.*
JOHN: The tune does; it was that sort of feeling, almost like a Haiku poem. I recently got into Haiku in Japan and I just think it's fantastic. Obviously, when you get rid of a whole section of illusion in your mind you're left with great precision. Yoko was showing me some of these Haiku in the original. The difference between them and Longfellow is immense. Instead of a long flowery poem the Haiku would say, 'Yellow flower in white bowl on wooden table,' which

gives you the whole picture, really.

**Lennon swaddled himself in ('Imagine no . . .')
possessions; at the height of their swinishness, the
Ono-Lennons kept a whole apartment in the Dakota
building . . . for the exclusive occupation of their fur
coats – just to keep them at the right temperature.
Forget sex and drugs; that's probably the most
decadent, vile pop star antic I've ever come across in
my life. –** *Julie Burchill*

TA: *How do you think we can destroy the capitalist system here in Britain, John?*
JOHN: I think only by making the workers aware of the really unhappy position they are in, breaking the dream they are surrounded by. They think they are in a wonderful, free-speaking country. They've got cars and tellies and they don't want to think there's anything more to life. They are prepared to let the bosses run them, to see their children fucked up in school. They're dreaming someone else's dream, it's not even their own. They should realise that the blacks and the Irish are being harassed and repressed and that they will be next. As soon as they start being aware of all that, we can really begin to do something. The workers can start to take over. Like Marx said: 'To each according to his need.' I think that would work well here. But we'd also have to infiltrate the army too, because they are well trained to kill us all. We've got to start all this from where we ourselves are oppressed. I think it's false, shallow, to be giving to others when your own need is great. The idea is not to comfort people, not to make them feel better but to make them feel worse, to constantly put before them the degradations and humiliations they go through to get what they call a living wage.

Red Mole, 8-22 March 1971

WHEN THE MUSIC'S OVER
By Robin Denselow

Denselow's excellent analysis of the relationship between rock and protest politics includes this account of Lennon's early days in New York, as a born-again radical. His arrival had already been heralded at a meeting of the CIA and the FBI, when he was labelled a potentially dangerous subversive.

John Lennon arrived in the USA less than nine months after being secretly denounced at this extraordinary meeting. It was hardly surprising that Nixon treated this would-be American resident with suspicion verging on paranoia, and that Lennon was watched – especially when he teamed up with his natural allies, old Yippies like Jerry Rubin and the rest of the anti-Nixon, anti-war crowd. The American authorities tried to crush him, just as they had tried to crush Pete Seeger back in the fifties. The USA's musical Left were naturally delighted at his arrival: it was exactly the boost they needed. They were also just what Lennon needed: he was angry and bitter in the aftermath of the Beatles' break-up, and he found it easier to discuss politics with Rubin and his friends than with their counterparts back home.

Life in his new home seemed fun. He and Yoko could wander around New York without too much hassle, they could make friends with street-singers like David Peel (best-known for chanting 'The Pope Smokes Dope' and 'Have a Marijuana'), and they could talk politics for hours. Unknown to Lennon, there was another side to this; it seems he was bugged from the moment he arrived. He and Yoko had an apartment in Bank Street, Greenwich Village, where one of their neighbours was Ed Sanders. Sanders had been trying to get a phone installed in his loft, and was delighted when one was put in. He was less than delighted (and a little paranoid, having just written a book about Charles Manson) when he heard voices on the line.

'There was this English creep on the phone, and I was furious,' he remembers. 'But then I realised it was Lennon. We'd both been given the same phone!' Later, when Sanders managed to get hold of the FBI files, he found that he had been under surveillance during this period, 'so the police must have been bugging both Lennon and I.'

The authorities would have taken a great interest in what they heard. The

Imagine LP had been released, with its 'Give Me Some Truth' attack on Nixon, and within two months the Lennons were following up the sentiments with action, by appearing at a highly political benefit show, along with Jerry Rubin, Bobby Seale and others fresh from the Chicago Seven trial in a bill that also included Phil Ochs and Ed Sanders.

The 'Free John Sinclair' rally, held in the Chrysler Arena, Ann Arbor, Michigan, in December 1971, was hailed as a 'political Woodstock', and Yippies and pop stars came together to raise money for his legal fees. The show was a massive success, a 'typical, slick, well-oiled arena production,' according to Sanders, 'and a very noble evening.' He read part of his poem, 'The Entrapment of John Sinclair', and his friend Phil Ochs sang about Nixon.

Then there was an appearance from future superstar and local Michigan hero Bob Seger, who was born in Ann Arbor and had already been involved in musical anti-war activities (he had once recorded 'Ballad of the Yellow Beret' as an answer to Staff-Sergeant Barry Sadler's 'Ballad of the Green Berets'). Seger was followed by an already established superstar, Stevie Wonder, making a surprise appearance at an event that Rubin claimed was 'uniting music and revolutionary politics to build a revolution around the country'.

Today, Ed Sanders remembers Wonder's performance that night as the 'high point – he was terrific!' Wonder himself is slightly more cautious when talking about the support that he gave to the Yippies. Sitting in a London hotel room, fourteen years later, he said, 'I met them very briefly. We just did the show and ran, just performed and gave my musical support.' And what of the cause, and Sinclair being jailed for ten years because of a couple of joints? 'We joined in support for him being released. Ultimately, I don't know if I would say, "Everybody smoke grass," but alcohol for sure has killed more people, and people just accept it. . .'

Lennon came on last, and sang new protest songs about American issues, including 'John Sinclair' and 'Attica State', a song dealing with the prison massacre earlier in the year in which state troopers invaded a prison where hostages had been taken. It was his first concert in the USA since the Beatles days, and must have been as startling to the vast stadium crowd as the fact that John Sinclair, in prison, was able to speak to them by phone, his voice booming through the giant speaker system. It was an extraordinary event, and what's more, it was a success. Sinclair was set free just over two days later.

Lennon was excited, Rubin was excited, and new events were planned – after all, it was now nearly four years since Chicago, and Nixon would have to face a convention and an election during 1972. If Yippies and pop musicians could get Sinclair out of jail, what else could they achieve? After Ann Arbor, it was a thought that must have worried even Nixon. Lennon seemed as dangerous as Elvis Presley had warned. The Michigan show, and its consequences, certainly didn't go unnoticed, and Ed Sanders now says, 'I've always had a soft spot in my heart for John and Yoko for doing that, and taking that risk. It probably led to all of their troubles.'

If he had said, 'Bomb the White House tomorrow,' there would have been 10,000 people who would have done it. The pacifist revolutionaries are historically killed by the government . . . It was in the best interest of the United States to have my dad killed. And you know, that worked against them, because once he died, his power grew. – *Sean Lennon*

After Michigan, the Lennons kept campaigning. They played at a benefit for the families of the Attica prison victims, they introduced Rubin as their guest to attack Nixon and Vietnam on *The Mike Douglas TV Show*, and after the killings in Derry, Northern Ireland, on 'Bloody Sunday', 30 January 1972, they joined anti-British protests in New York. All these events were reflected in Lennon's most directly political LP, the experimental *Some Time in New York City*, which was released that summer. In a way, this was what Phil Ochs had been asking for: a great pop hero making revolutionary statements. It was a shame that this should be the worst album Lennon had made.

Some Time in New York City ought to have been remarkable, for it was a mixture of instant protest journalism and a gutsy rock'n'roll backing that both looked back to the fifties and hinted at the punk movement that was to come. But it was wrecked by the atrocious lyrics. The poet who could write 'Imagine', 'A Day in the Life', or 'Working Class Hero', now mouthed slogans that were as simple as 'All You Need Is Love', but seemed even more naïve because they dealt with real events. The attack on Attica had been appalling, but lines like 'Free the prisoners, free the judges, free all prisoners everywhere' seemed a pathetic response. The feminist songs like 'Woman Is the Nigger of the World' aligned the Lennons with one of the important issues of the seventies, but the heavyhanded lecturing technique was an embarrassment.

The songs about Ireland were even worse. 'If you had the luck of the Irish . . .you'd wish you was English instead' seemed downright insulting, while the suggestions at the end of 'Sunday Bloody Sunday' that the problem should be solved by shipping back to Britain the Protestants who had lived in Ulster for over 300 years was scandalous, naïve and even racist. Lines like 'You anglo pigs and scotties sent to colonise the North', 'Repatriate to Britain all of you who call it home', or (worst of all) 'Internment is no answer, it's those mothers' turn to burn' simply weren't worthy of Lennon, especially with his concern with racial problems, and his earlier avowed pacifism. Bloody Sunday had been horrific, but this was no way to reply – especially from New York.

Only two tracks on this unfortunate album succeeded, and they were the two written by Lennon, rather than in collaboration with Yoko. 'John Sinclair' drew neat parallels between the treatment of a man jailed for ten years for having two joints and the CIA's own alleged involvement in far more dangerous drugs activities (presumably a reference to the stories coming out of Vietnam), while 'New York City' was a jolly personal narrative in the style of 'The Ballad of John and Yoko'. It included yet another plug for David Peel.

If all the songs had been up to that standard, Lennon might have revived the political song as successfully as the far more poetic and imaginative young Bob Dylan had done back in the sixties. As it was, Lennon's first all-political LP was a flop, artistically and commercially. Why did he get it so wrong? Perhaps because he was away from Britain, and issues he had really investigated or understood, and perhaps because he was swept along by the new friends who surrounded him. Ed Sanders was deeply disappointed that Lennon should have been impressed with David Peel and 'stupid' songs like 'The Pope Smokes Dope'. 'Here was a world-class figure, possibly a genius, saddling himself with a lesser entity. . .it was embarrassing.'

Included in the *Some Time* packaging was a postcard, signed by Lennon, showing the Statue of Liberty. It was a symbol of a problem that obsessed him when the LP was released, and which was not fully resolved until July 1976. It was simply this: Lennon wanted to stay in the USA, and the Government wanted him thrown out. His appearance at the Free John Sinclair show had been noted, as had Rubin's plans for follow-up rock shows and a Chicago-style event when the Republicans met in San Diego. Lennon was under surveillance, the FBI had accumulated a hefty file on his activities and a report had been passed right up to the Attorney General. The Immigration and Naturalization Service noted the situation, and acted accordingly: Lennon's visa was revoked, and deportation proceedings started.

The resulting barrage of hearings, deportation orders, appeals, press conferences and legal briefings were enough to knock the political fight out of anyone. Lennon eventually won, against President Nixon's wishes, because of the public support he received, and because he dared to counter-attack the authorities. He was helped by the Mayor of New York, by a host of American art world celebrities, and by fellow performers like Bob Dylan and Stevie Wonder, who signed petitions asking for him to be allowed to stay. He was also helped by his own campaign of publicly accusing the authorities of tailing him and tapping his phone, and then actually suing the US Government for having done so.

But Lennon made one very major concession. Any plans he may have had for further concerts with Jerry Rubin, or for anti-Nixon political musical events in the period leading up to the Republican Convention, were firmly squashed. Lennon said he never intended to sponsor riots or revolution. He kept recording – for a while – but made no more LPs along the lines of *Some Time in New York City*, and began to back away from active political involvement. So, in a sense, Nixon had won after all. The Republican Convention went ahead, and the President was re-elected, only to be brought down not by Lennon, Rubin, the Yippies or the musical Left, but by Watergate.

Lennon got his green card, and having secured his place in the USA he eventually retreated into isolation in the Dakota building, New York, where he was shot in 1980. He quit the political pop scene after a classic farewell. In August 1972, just after the Republican Convention, Lennon appeared at a charity show for mentally handicapped children at Madison Square Garden, New York. He added new political lyrics to 'Come Together', paid homage to the early Elvis with 'Hound Dog' (without realising the irony of what he was doing), and he finished by joining up with Stevie Wonder for an extended, and (by all accounts) glorious and exhilarating version of 'Give Peace a Chance'. It was appropriate that John Lennon's last great fusion of music and politics should be in the company of a superstar who from the sixties to the eighties has managed to mix political and social comment with his hit dance songs and ballads.

When the Music's Over, Robin Denselow, 1989

BEATLEMANIACS NEVER DIE
(But They Sure Get Carried Away)
By Lilith Moon

This mid-Seventies look at the now-established Beatles' Convention illustrates how the group, with all their surrounding ephemera, remain a commodity. Also note the fans' hostile tone towards Yoko Ono, many obviously holding her responsible for the Beatles' disbandment.

It's the First Annual Beatles' Convention, Magical Mystery Tour, and I'm standing in the lobby of the Bradford Hotel, Boston. For the last hour I've been watching five teenage girls in black tee-shirts ('Bring Back the Beatles', 'The Beatles Forever') collecting signatures for a petition to keep John Lennon in the United States. In the center of the room, gaggles of lean boys wearing row on row of Beatles' buttons flash rare albums at each other and reach out to fondle LPs missing from their collections. A blind woman wearing a long, dayglo green dress with sparkling rhinestones spelling out 'JOHN GEORGE PAUL RINGO' is jauntily whisked through the lobby on the arms of a friend. No one notices.

Inside the hotel's cavernous ballroom this Saturday afternoon, twenty metal folding tables have been filled with Beatles' records and memorabilia. A thousand Beatle devotees, most of them under twenty, crush through each other or peer between bodies to get a better view of the merchandise. Money changes hands quickly and cheerfully.

Among the items: bubble gum cards with the Beatles ($1); the Polish poster for *A Hard Day's Night* ($3.50); tie tacks with individual Beatles' faces ($2); tie clasps shaped like a guitar with Beatle faces where the hole should be ($1.50); 1964 Beatles concert book, black with purple border and casual photos of all four Beatles inside ($20); foreign and domestic magazines with stories on the Beatles (80 cents to $20, including the 1964 *TV Guide* at $3), and more.

At one table the former president of the Beatles' New York fan club is selling promo photos, once free, for $2 to $4. She is only parting with her dupes, she says, as she keeps her eyes on the frenzy of hands flipping through her collection. 'I'll clear, let me see, $200 when it's over. Pretty good, since they didn't cost me anything, right?' She smiles and winks.

At another table, men and women are anxiously sifting through stacks of bootleg Beatles records at $4 each. At yet another table, I pick up a copy of the mimeographed Beatles' fanzine *Strawberry Fields Forever*, and brush up on my Liverpudlian slang. I also find that a letter writer, for reasons known only to himself, is looking for 'a list of George Harrison's childhood diseases'. Off in the corners of the auditorium, small groups of people pull out singles-carrying cases, bubble gum cards, press clippings, and start making individual trades.

Two hours of the Beatles singing, dancing, and following the bouncing ball – well, almost the Beatles. Just close your eyes and pretend. – *Internet ad for videos of the previously lost Beatles cartoon show*

Later in this weekend, there will be nine straight hours of Beatle films and promo clips (including *Magical Mystery Tour*, of which three prints, worth $50,000 each, exist), there will be a march on the State House to keep John Lennon in America, and there will be much admiring of each others' buttons. But right now, Joe Pope, 26-year-old organiser of the convention and publisher of *Strawberry Fields Forever*, is calling the room to order for an auction of rare Beatles' memorabilia. Among the items:

A lunch pail (without thermos) with the Beatles in bas relief and colour, is gobbled up by a New York publicist for $25. 'I'll use it as a pocket book,' she explains. 'It'll be just *great* at cocktail parties!'

A pair of Beatles sneakers (size seven-and-a-half, women's, the only sneakers at the convention) go for $25. *This Is Where It All Started*, a Metro LP of Tony Sheridan and the Beatles, is worth $20. A mobile display unit for record stores brings in $12.50.

'And now,' says Joe, 'what you've all been waiting for, and what most of you have never seen. You've heard about it. It's called "The Butcher". It's the original cover of *Yesterday and Today*. Only 100,000 were printed. Most were destroyed by Capitol. It was considered in bad taste. Some are under the new cover of the LP. But this copy is not steamed off, it's the original.'

Gasps go up from the crowd.

'We have a minimum of $200 on this item,' Joe says, 'and . here it is!'

He holds up a jacket with the four Beatles, grinning from ear to ear, dressed in white smocks and fondling decapitated dolls and sides of blood-red beef.

'You'll notice,' Joe says pointing to the cover, 'that there is no record with this. We collectors take out the record because it leaves a circle mark on the cover. The cover is the important thing. Now do I have a bid?'

The room grows silent, then one lone hand is raised. It belongs to an acned adolescent boy. He gets 'The Butcher' and the room erupts in applause. End of auction.

The seller of that last item is Wayne Rogers, jocular president of a bootleg company called Rock and Roll University. He looks dejected as he tells me, 'I didn't want to sell "The Butcher". My wife made me. I wanted to trade it for an Atco promo record, *Ain't She Sweet?*. There was one guy here who had it, but he didn't want to get rid of it. I make money from the bootlegs and the tapes. That's what my company does. Right now I'm collecting tapes from Dylan's tour. I trade to get them. But I also have a private collection and that "Butcher" was in perfect condition. I hung it on my wall.'

David Peel, sometime street singer and friends with John Lennon, shows me a demo tape of something called 'Marijuana', which he then proceeds to sing. 'Marijuana, marijuana, marijuana,' he yells. 'We want marijuana, BRING BACK THE BEATLES.' I tell him the song seems very appropriate.

The room is cleared and cleaned. Before long, it's filled up again, this time to hear Murray the K, once known as the fifth Beatle.

'I'm going to give you the bad news first. The Beatles will never, repeat, never, get together again.'

A groan, coupled with boos, goes up from the crowd. Murray, stuffed in khaki slacks and white cowboy shirt, waits for the noise to die down.

'Now that you have the bad news, let me fill you in on all the gossip. The biggest shocker I can lay on you is that Ringo and Maureen are going to be divorced.'

Murmurs from the crowd.

'George made sure, while Ringo was away, that Maureen wasn't lonely.'

More murmurs.

'And, John is seeing Yoko Ono.'

Boos.

'You know, I'd like to see a picture of Yoko Ono with a couple of lines that said, Rasputin in drag. All you Yoko Ono fans, well, all I can say to you is, Up Yours!'

Wild cheers.

'I'd just like to say one thing, there has never been nor will there ever be any-thing to rival the Beatles.'

Tumultuous applause.

Creem, November 1974

BOOTING THE BEATLES
By Charles P. Neises

An examination of the Beatles bootleg industry. We'll probably never know whether the 'Pakistanis' reference in the 'Get Back' outtake was knockabout satire, or simply reflected the populist racism of the time. The latter would knock a big hole into Adrian Mitchell's idea of the Beatles as ideological opponents to Enoch Powell – though it's also unlikely, given their cultural dalliance with the Indian sub-continent.

As Pablo Picasso created *Guernica*, the dramatic mural depicting the destruction of a Spanish town by German bombers during the Spanish Civil War, he allowed friend and photographer Dora Marr to photograph the work in progress. The first of her photographs only slightly resembles the finished work. Elements are removed and added as the series shows Picasso piecing together a puzzle of images relating to the catastrophe. The sketches on the canvas change as the days progress and as the artist refines his vision. The final photograph shows the great mural as we know it today.

In the business of recorded music, the artist rarely allows his product to be heard before it is finished. The Beatles were no different; their albums are generally considered great works of popular art. They did, however, allow the listener moments to hear the workings of the recording studio behind the record. Many groups start recording a song with a count-off (one, two, three, four!), which is later removed from the tape, but Beatles producer George Martin left in the count-off to 'I Saw Her Standing There' on their first album. False starts are dealt with in the same manner, but the LP *Rubber Soul* contains a false start in the song 'I'm Looking Through You'. At times, alternate versions of a single song are recorded, one to be released and the other to be discarded, but the Beatles released both fast and slow (not to mention politically decisive and indecisive) versions of 'Revolution'.

In fact, the Beatles planned the movie *Let It Be* to show how songs are written, practiced, refined and recorded in the studio. In one scene, Paul McCartney leads the band in a rehearsal of 'Maxwell's Silver Hammer', singing out the chord changes. In others, Ringo Starr plays the piano and sings a few early verses of 'Octopus's Garden', and George Harrison experiments with arrangements of 'I Me Mine'. As in the Dora Marr photographs, the pieces fall into place until the final scene, of the concert on a London rooftop, resembles the final product, the *Let It Be* album. *Let It Be* is like the Marr photos in yet another way: it was produced with the initial approval and cooperation of the artists involved. It was authorised.

Unauthorised recordings (bootlegs) of the *Let It Be* sessions do exist, but listening to them is a bit like peeking at the sketches that Picasso locked in his attic or burned after completing *Guernica*. It is not known if Picasso ever hid or destroyed sketches for his masterpiece; the reference was made for the sake of analogy, but tapes of the Beatles' unfinished songs and rehearsals were either locked in recording company vaults, pitched into recording company garbage cans or stolen, borrowed, or otherwise lifted to be copied and marketed. These bootlegs are not to be confused with counterfeit records, cheap copies manufactured to resemble actual releases and to trick unsuspecting buyers, but they are equally illegal.

The practice of selling unauthorised recordings of musical performances is as old as the recording industry itself. (1) Bootleg recordings of the Beatles, usually taken from concerts and live radio and television appearances, were available in the middle 1960s and now enjoy brisk sales at fan conventions, antique and memorabilia shows, and some record stores. Sold through mail-order catalogues by underground companies with unusual names and frequently-changed postal addresses, most bootlegs are priced comparably with authorised albums. But, recalling the difference between a bootleg and a counterfeit, the material contained on most bootlegs does not compete with that found on commercial releases.

Frequently bootlegged materials are concerts, interviews, and studio outtakes. Concert bootlegs are popular because the Beatles conducted three world tours in the mid-1960s and did not release a live album until 1977. Interviews are easily copied from radio and television appearances. In one famous and oft-bootlegged interview, John Lennon gives a preview of the song 'Don't Let Me Down' by strumming a guitar and shouting 'Don't let me down! Don't let me down! [clears his throat] Don't let me down! Don't let me down! Can't remember anymore. Don't let me down,' finally ending with an off-key rendition of 'Those Were the Days'. Studio outtakes are songs recorded in the studio but never released. Some are not released because of time limitations on albums, others are excluded because they are pitifully substandard.

Pitifully substandard is how many a bootleg sounds to the uninitiated. Sound levels can be uneven throughout a single disc, usually devoid of careful mixing. Some copies are several generations removed from the original tape and no sophisticated stereo can make them sound better. They are sometimes packaged only in white sleeves accompanied by photocopied liner notes which may or may not include an accurate list of song titles. Clearly, these records are not aimed at the mass market of normal record buyers. What normal record buyer would really want a recording of John Lennon clearing his throat and forgetting the words to 'Don't Let Me Down'? Some otherwise normal record buyers amass collections of every possible Beatles album and then set out to find material available only on bootlegs; these collectors are the counterparts of art enthusiasts who want to see pictures taken of a masterpiece before it was finished.

If we'd have had today's technology back then, it would sound like this because this is the noise we made in the studio. It's all exactly as it was in the room. You're right there now. – *Paul McCartney, on the 2003 CD release of* **Let It Be . . . Naked**

Bootleg recordings of studio outtakes can serve as valuable documentations of a recording artist's method of creating his work. As Picasso's creative process can be seen in the Man photographs, bootlegs of the *Let It Be* sessions provide insights not offered in the movie or the legitimate *Let It Be* album. One song, 'No Pakistanis', appears on several bootlegs of material from these sessions; the version discussed here is found on a record titled *Sweet Apple Trax*. 'No Pakistanis' is actually 'Get Back' sung with lyrics concerning the unpopular immigration of Puerto Ricans to the United States and Pakistanis to England. The second verse ends with the line, 'don't want no Pakistanis taking all the people's jobs.' Clearly anti-Pakistani, the exhortation 'get back! Get back to where you once belonged' is here not friendly advice to a man in California or to a transvestite named Loretta, as it is in the authorised version of 'Get Back', but a stinging attack on dark-skinned immigrants.

Several clues suggest that 'No Pakistanis' is an early version of 'Get Back': the arrangement is crude and the singer (Paul) mumbles the verses and improvises an instrumental solo by barking into the microphone. On the recording studio sketchpad of the tape machine, the group probably worked on the song, exercising enough good taste to omit the potentially offensive lyrics. What is left for the Beatles to perform on the authorised album is 'Get Back', stripped of its racial connotations, leaving only the Muslim name 'Jojo'. It is possible, however, that 'No Pakistanis' is a put-on, recorded as a satire on the already written 'Get Back'. But the Beatles were known to enter the recording studio with only a collection of incomplete songs. 'A Day in the Life' (from the LP *Sergeant Pepper's Lonely Hearts Club Band*) was created using a song with no middle section by John and a short ditty by Paul as the middle section. Also on *Sweet Apple Trax* are unreleased songs titled 'White Power' and 'Back to Commonwealth', both of which reflect the white-man's-burden tone of 'No Pakistanis'.

The use of bootlegs like *Sweet Apple Trax* in the study of the Beatles' music is apt to increase as the group itself grows in musical and historical nature. With the release of *Sergeant Pepper's Lonely Hearts Club Band*, the Beatles launched themselves into the world of serious music, or so it would seem from the material published in the 'serious' journals of the day. Their work was suddenly deemed suitable for discussion on the pages of *Partisan Review* and the *New York Review of Books*, and they became the subject of several Ph.D. dissertations. (2) The road to artistic immortality is long, but the Beatles are well on their way, as a new generation of young record buyers, to whom the group might have seemed as dated as Rudy Vallee and Al Jolson, are discovering anew *Abbey Road, Rubber Soul, Revolver* and other great Beatles albums.

If, as discussed above, the *Let It Be* movie, showing the Beatles at work on an album, is the recording industry's equivalent to Dora Marr's photographs of *Guernica*, then the studio outtake bootlegs (3) might someday take their places next to Leonardo DaVinci's notebooks. Like the outtakes, DaVinci's notebooks, with his mysterious code-like backward handwriting, were obviously intended for no audience but the artist himself. The surviving notebooks, however, are scrutinised by historians and are valued at millions of dollars each. Perhaps it is not presumptuous or pretentious to compare a rock-and-roll group with Picasso and DaVinci. Perhaps it is only premature.

1. *See You Can't Do That* (Pierian Press, 1981) by Charles Reinhart not only for its exhaustive index of Beatles bootlegs but for its appendix, an article ('Everything You Always Wanted to Know About Bootlegs, But Were Too Busy Collecting Them To Ask: A Treatise on the Wages of Sinning for Sound') by Tom Schultheiss detailing the history and present legal status of bootleg records.

2. Terence J. O'Grady (Ph.D., University of Wisconsin-Madison, 1975) used bootlegs of early live performances to prepare his dissertation *The Music of the Beatles from 1962 to Sergeant Pepper's Lonely Hearts Club Band*.

3. See Reinhart's bootleg discography for a complete list of titles.

The Beatles Reader, edited by Charles P. Neises, 1984

MAGICAL HISTORY TOUR
By Jerry Lazar

From Stan Freberg's 1950s takes on Elvis onwards, pop icons have been fair game for parody, not least the Beatles – the Rutles TV film being the most fully-rounded satire of the group.

Let's confess right up front here that when it comes to the Beatles a bigger sucker than me will not be found. Friends will flip through my albums, come to Harrison's *Wonderwall* or Lennon's *Two Virgins*. . .and you should see the looks. At least, I rationalise, I own only three of the twenty-odd virtually identical *Let It Be* bootlegs, and I never got duped into buying albums of Beatles songs by rip-off groups like the Liverpools. OK. OK. So I did shell out good money for *Best of the Beatles*, having been conned by the pre-Ringo shot of the group on the cover and a list of song titles that nobody had ever heard of. Talk about your first-on-the-block! As you probably know, the drummer in those days was a gent name of Pete Best. And this is his solo album. Get it? *Best of the Beatles*? I've since seen him on *What's My Line?*, where I was pleased to discover that he's become a baker in Liverpool. Good for you, Petey! I've hung onto your album, though; quite a little collector's item, isn't it? That and *Wonderwall*.

By now, of course, I've figured out where to draw the line on these matters. A fan, yes; a fanatic, no. For instance, you won't find me plunking down $15 to see this Broadway play(!) *Beatlemania*, or any other artificial imitation Beatle-flavoured product. Nonetheless, the show has found its market; it has just opened in Los Angeles and supposedly has plans to clone itself all over the place. Clive Davis' Arista Records has even brought out an $11.98 *Beatlemania* double album, which bears the warning: 'An incredible simulation.' (Look up the meaning of 'incredible' when you get a chance.) I haven't heard the album, but I'll bet anything it sounds quite a bit like the Liverpools, as I remember them. They, too, made my teeth itch.

No need to despair, though, for there are a few new Beatle bargains to be had. One is the complete *A Hard Day's Night* screenplay, recently published by Penguin Books ($6.95). I was overjoyed to see it – not for its shot-by-shot stills, not for its lengthy interview with director Richard Lester, but for its page 62. There, as I had been trying to tell everyone for years, is the scene, right near the beginning, in which Lennon is snorting a bottle of Coke. In 1964! How hip! How cool! How ahead! I was ecstatic.

Even bigger treats are to be found in the genre of revisionism. When I came across the book *Paperback Writer* last spring, I didn't realise at first it was a novel, because it was subtitled 'A New History of the Beatles'. But the author's disclaimer was the tip-off: 'Just because there'll never be another Beatles doesn't necessarily mean there can't be another Beatles' story.' Early in the first chapter we read the part about a young plumber named Brian Epstein who is called in late one night to repair a clogged pipe in the ladies room at the Cavern. From there we get a fairly funny account of the four rockers as we might have known and loved them. The plane of reality is tilted at odd angles:

Dylan instructs a worshipful Lennon and a cynical McCartney in the art of writing lyrics: 'Words and phrases. . .the first thing that comes to your mind. . .I don't even know what my songs mean.' The result of the trio's collaboration is 'Pneumonia Ceilings', typed on London Hilton stationery – except for the last line, which everyone is too stoned to remember.

Backstage at *The Sullivan Show*, George tries out a new song for Del Shannon, who wasn't even aware that George wrote any: 'Sounds to me like that song the Chiffons had out last year,' comments Shannon. 'Sounds just like it. Same changes.'

Mark Shipper, the author, is a 28-year-old assistant publisher of a weekly trade paper, *Radio and Records*. He tapped out *Paperback Writer* in six weeks and, investing his own savings, printed 500 copies, which he tried to sell by mail order for $5.95 a pop. One copy came to the attention of Fred Jordan, who now has his own imprint at Grosset & Dunlap. Jordan plans to publish it as a largeformat trade paperback in June. He's billing it as the first real rock novel ever written, but Shipper is more realistic. 'It's just meant to be fun,' he says.

Then we have the Rutles. You heard right: the Rutles. Ron Nasty, Dirk McQuickly, Stig O'Hara and Barry Wom – otherwise known as the Pre-fab Four. If you don't already know their tale – 'the legend that will last a lunchtime' – then you can tune in on March 22 to NBC's documentary , which was filmed last summer by Eric Idle and Gary Weis. *Saturday Night Live* and *Monty Python* meet the Beatles. Sort of.

Idle – who created, wrote and narrates the program – is Rutle bassist McQuickly. Neil Innes, of Bonzo Dog Band fame, wrote the lyrics and composed the Rutles tunes. (He's also Lennon sound-alike Ron Nasty.) Rikki Fataar, who once toured with the Beach Boys, is Stig. John Halsey, whom I never heard of before, is drummer Barry. A handful of the *Saturday Night* crew have cameo parts, and even Mick Jagger and Paul Simon were persuaded to come on camera to describe what effect the Rutles had on their careers.

Mark Shipper and Eric Idle have separately and independently recreated the Beatles era using roughly the same idiom, if not the same medium. Shipper puts his Beatles through episodes that, had this been an even zanier world, might have happened. He rewrites Beatles lyrics and titles. Idle goes one step further: he changes all the names; and Innes rewrites the music as well. It doesn't sound like a particularly funny concept (or even an original one; remember AM dee-jays cracking themselves up by singing 'I Wanna Hold My Nose'?), but it works. It works because of its underlying attitude: it's not analytical or imitative or grandiose. It's just meant to be fun.

It all dawned on me when we had the Bonzo Dog Band, about the time they were making *Revolver* . . . we actually met them in the corridor of Abbey Road. We were recording something called 'My Brother Makes the Noises for the Talkies' . . . [and] we heard George's track, 'I Want To Tell You'. I remember thinking at the time, 'Hmmm. That's really good. A lot better than "My Brother Makes the Noises for the Talkies".' – *Neil Innes (aka Ron Nasty of the Rutles)*

I find myself telling sceptical friends to be sure to catch this special, and I try to give them an idea of what makes the Rutles so good by singing one of their songs, like 'Get Up and Go' (the 'Get Back' take-off) or, better, 'OUCH!', the title cut of their second movie. ('Ouch! Please don't hurt me. Ouch! Don't desert me. Ouch!') Neil Innes has managed to capture the Beatles' sound as convincingly as Todd Rundgren did on his *Faithful* album, and with more purpose. Enriching the spoof of the Beatles (and of our collective reaction to them) is a marvellous send-up of the entire genre of television documentaries: their cost, language and camera techniques.

Watching the Rutles, one is struck by the number of Beatle images that have permanently implanted themselves in our brainpans and by how accurately they are recreated here. Film editor Aviva Slesin, who put in three months of four-teen-hour days on this project, has done a masterful job of capturing the mad-ness and bounciness of the original Richard Lester films; and the *Yellow Submarine* parody is indistinguishable from the real thing. Even the press con-ference sequences do justice to their prototypes. (Q: 'Did you feel better after seeing the Queen?' A: 'No. I feel better after seeing a doctor.')

Of course, it's tough to ridicule the inherently ridiculous. Sometimes real life can't be topped: Paul getting a hit single out of 'Mary Had a Little Lamb' or George getting convicted of plagiarism. How do you beat that? When the Rutles try to go real life one better, it doesn't always work. I mean, why show John and Yoko holding forth for peace in a shower? Wasn't a bed absurd enough?

Meanwhile, George and Ringo are teaming up for a TV special which is being touted as (good Christ!) a musical version of *The Prince and the Pauper*. I can't figure which is worse, this or the idea of a 1978 Beatles album with tunes like 'Disco Yoko', 'Disco Love Songs', 'My Sweet Disco' and Ringo's remake of 'Disco Duck'. I'm so glad the band packed it in when it did.

Now I'm a newly converted sucker for the Rutles. Their first (and last) album has just been released, and it's the genuine item. Where have these guys been all these years?

The Beatles Reader, edited by Charles P. Neises, 1984

PLAYBOY INTERVIEW WITH JOHN LENNON AND YOKO ONO
By David Sheff

This interview took place to coincide with the release of Double Fantasy — *Lennon's comeback record, and his most middle-of-the-road recording, though he himself remains characteristically pugnacious. Published in the January 1981 issue of* Playboy, *it was already on the stands in early December 1980, at the time of John's murder.*

PLAYBOY: *John . . . why is it so unthinkable that the Beatles might get back together to make some music?*

LENNON: Do you want to go back to high school? Why should I go back ten years to provide an illusion for you that I know does not exist? It cannot exist.

PLAYBOY: *. . . how did you feel about producer Lorne Michaels' generous offer of $3200 for appearing together on* **Saturday Night Live** *a few years ago?*

LENNON: Oh, yeah. Paul and I were together watching that show. He was visiting us at our place in the Dakota. We were watching it and almost went down to the studio, just as a gag. We nearly got into a cab, but we were actually too tired.

PLAYBOY: *How did you and Paul happen to be watching TV together?*

LENNON: That was a period when Paul just kept turning up at our door with a guitar. I would let him in, but finally I said to him, 'Please call before you come over. It's not 1956 and turning up at the door isn't the same anymore. You know, just give me a ring.' He was upset by that, but I didn't mean it badly. I just meant that I was taking care of a baby all day and some guy turns up at the door . . . But, anyway, back on that night, he and Linda walked in and he and I were just sitting there, watching the show, and we went, 'Ha-ha, wouldn't it be funny if we went down?' but we didn't.

PLAYBOY: *Was that the last time you saw Paul?*

LENNON: Yes, but I didn't mean it like that.

PLAYBOY: *. . . what do you think of Paul's work since he left the Beatles?*
LENNON: I kind of admire the way Paul started back from scratch, forming a new band and playing in small dance halls, because that's what he wanted to do with the Beatles – he wanted us to go back to the dance halls and experience that again. But I didn't . . . That was one of the problems, in a way, that he wanted to relive it all or something – I don't know what it was . . . But I kind of admire the way he got off his pedestal – now he's back on it again, but I mean, he did what he wanted to do. That's fine, but it's just not what I wanted to do.

PLAYBOY: *What about the music?*
LENNON: 'The Long and Winding Road' was the last gasp from him. Although I really haven't listened.

PLAYBOY: *. . . what did each of you contribute to the Lennon–McCartney songwriting team?*
LENNON: Well, you could say that he provided a lightness, an optimism, while I would always go for the sadness, the discords, a certain bluesy edge. There was a period when I thought I didn't write melodies, that Paul wrote those and I just wrote straight, shouting rock'n'roll. But, of course, when I think of some of my own songs – 'In My Life' – or some of the early stuff – 'This Boy' – I was writing melody with the best of them. Paul had a lot of training, could play a lot of instruments. He'd say, 'Well, why don't you change that there? You've done that note 50 times in the song.' You know, I'll grab a note and ram it home. Then again, I'd be the one to figure out where to go with a song – a story that Paul would start. In a lot of the songs, my stuff is the 'middle eight', the bridge.

PLAYBOY: *For example?*
LENNON: Take 'Michelle'. Paul and I were staying somewhere, and he walked in and hummed the first few bars, with the words, you know [sings verse of 'Michelle'], and he says, 'Where do I go from here?' I'd been listening to blues singer Nina Simone, who did something like 'I love you!' in one of her songs and that made me think of the middle eight for 'Michelle' [sings]: 'I love you, I love you, I l-o-ove you . . .'

PLAYBOY: *What was the difference in terms of lyrics?*
LENNON: I always had an easier time with lyrics, though Paul is quite a capable lyricist who doesn't think he is. So he doesn't go for it. Rather than face the problem, he would avoid it. 'Hey Jude' is a damn good set of lyrics. I made no contribution to the lyrics there. And a couple of lines he has come up with show

indications of a good lyricist. But he just hasn't taken it anywhere. Still, in the early days, we didn't care about lyrics as long as the song had some vague theme – she loves you, he loves him, they all love each other. It was the hook, line and sound we were going for. That's still my attitude, but I can't leave lyrics alone. I have to make them make sense apart from the songs.

PLAYBOY: *What's an example of a lyric you and Paul worked on together?*
LENNON: In 'We Can Work It Out', Paul did the first half, I did the middle eight. But you've got Paul writing, 'We can work it out/We can work it out' – real optimistic, y' know, and me, impatient: 'Life is very short and there's no time/For fussing and fighting, my friend . . .'

PLAYBOY: *. . . Haven't you said that you wrote most of your songs separately, despite putting both of your names on them?*
LENNON: Yeah, I was lying. [Laughs] It was when I felt resentful, so I felt that we did everything apart. But, actually, a lot of the songs we did eyeball to eyeball.

PLAYBOY: *But many of them were done apart, weren't they?*
LENNON: Yeah. *Sgt. Pepper* was Paul's idea, and I remember he worked on it a lot and suddenly called me to go into the studio, said it was time to write some songs. On *Pepper*, under the pressure of only ten days, I managed to come up with 'Lucy in the Sky' and 'Day in the Life'. We weren't communicating enough, you see. And later on, that's why I got resentful about all that stuff. But now I understand that it was just the same competitive game going on.

PLAYBOY: *But the competitive game was good for you, wasn't it?*
LENNON: In the early days. We'd make a record in twelve hours or something; they would want a single every three months and we'd have to write it in a hotel room or in a van. So the cooperation was functional as well as musical.

PLAYBOY: *Don't you think that cooperation, that magic between you, is something you've missed in your work since?*
LENNON: I never actually felt a loss. I don't want it to sound negative, like I didn't need Paul, because when he was there, obviously, it worked. But I can't – it's easier to say what I gave to him than what he gave to me. And he'd say the same.

PLAYBOY: *. . . while we're on the subject of lyrics and your resentment of Paul, what made you write 'How Do You Sleep?', which contains lyrics such as 'Those*

freaks was right when they said you was dead' and 'The only thing you done was yesterday/And since you've gone, you're just another day'?
LENNON: [Smiles] You know, I wasn't really feeling that vicious at the time. But I was using my resentment toward Paul to create a song, let's put it that way. He saw that it pointedly refers to him, and people kept hounding him about it. But, you know, there were a few digs on his album before mine. He's so obscure other people didn't notice them, but I heard them. I thought, Well, I'm not obscure, I just get right down to the nitty-gritty. So he'd done it his way and I did it mine. But as to the line you quoted, yeah, I think Paul died creatively, in a way.

PLAYBOY: *Let's move on to Ringo. What's your opinion of him musically?*
LENNON: Ringo was a star in his own right in Liverpool before we even met. He was a professional drummer who sang and performed and had Ringo Star-time and he was in one of the top groups in Britain but especially in Liverpool before we even had a drummer. So Ringo's talent would have come out one way or the other as something or other. I don't know what he would have ended up as, but whatever that spark is in Ringo that we all know but can't put our finger on — whether it is acting, drumming or singing I don't know — there is something in him that is projectable and he would have surfaced with or without the Beatles. Ringo is a damn good drummer. He is not technically good, but I think Ringo's drumming is underrated the same way Paul's bass playing is underrated. Paul was one of the most innovative bass players ever. And half the stuff that is going on now is directly ripped off from his Beatles period. He is an egomaniac about everything else about himself, but his bass playing he was always a bit coy about. I think Paul and Ringo stand up with any of the rock musicians. Not technically great — none of us are technical musicians. None of us could read music. None of us can write it. But as pure musicians, as inspired humans to make the noise, they are as good as anybody.

PLAYBOY: *How about George's solo music?*
LENNON: I think *All Things Must Pass* was all right. It just went on too long.

PLAYBOY: *You actually haven't mentioned George much in this interview.*
LENNON: Well, I was hurt by George's book, *I, Me, Mine* — so this message will go to him. He put a book out privately on his life that, by glaring omission, says that my influence on his life is absolutely zilch and nil. In his book, which is purportedly this clarity of vision of his influence on each song he wrote, he remembers every two-bit sax player or guitarist he met in subsequent years. I'm not in the book.

PLAYBOY: *Why?*

LENNON: Because George's relationship with me was one of young follower and older guy. He's three or four years younger than me. It's a love–hate relationship and I think George still bears resentment toward me for being a daddy who left home. He would not agree with this, but that's my feeling about it. I was just hurt. I was just left out, as if I didn't exist. I don't want to be that egomaniacal, but he was like a disciple of mine when we started. I was already an art student when Paul and George were still in grammar school [equivalent to high school in the US]. There is a vast difference between being in high school and being in college and I was already in college and already had sexual relationships, already drank and did a lot of things like that. When George was a kid, he used to follow me and my first girlfriend, Cynthia – who became my wife – around. We'd come out of art school and he'd be hovering around like those kids at the gate of the Dakota now. I remember the day he called to ask for help on 'Taxman', one of his bigger songs. I threw in a few one-liners to help the song along, because that's what he asked for. He came to me because he couldn't go to Paul, because Paul wouldn't have helped him at that period. I didn't want to do it. I thought, Oh, no, don't tell me I have to work on George's stuff. It's enough doing my own and Paul's. But because I loved him and I didn't want to hurt him when he called me that afternoon and said, 'Will you help me with this song?' I just sort of bit my tongue and said OK. It had been John and Paul so long, he'd been left out because he hadn't been a songwriter up until then. As a singer, we allowed him only one track on each album. If you listen to the Beatles' first albums, the English versions, he gets a single track. The songs he and Ringo sang at first were the songs that used to be part of my repertoire in the dance halls. I used to pick songs for them from my repertoire – the easier ones to sing. So I am slightly resentful of George's book. But don't get me wrong. I still love those guys. The Beatles are over, but John, Paul, George and Ringo go on.

PLAYBOY: *Do you have any interest in the pop historians analysing the Beatles as a cultural phenomenon?*

LENNON: It's all equally irrelevant. Mine is to do and other people's is to record, I suppose. Does it matter how many drugs were in Elvis' body? I mean, Brian Epstein's sex life will make a nice *Hollywood Babylon* someday, but it is irrelevant.

PLAYBOY: *What started the rumours about you and Epstein?*

LENNON: I went on holiday to Spain with Brian – which started all the rumours that he and I were having a love affair. Well, it was almost a love affair, but not quite. It was never consummated. But we did have a pretty intense relationship. And it was my first experience with someone I knew was a homosexual. He admitted it to me. We had this holiday together because Cyn was pregnant and we left her with the baby and went to Spain. Lots of funny stories, you know. We used to sit in cafes and Brian would look at all the boys and I would ask, 'Do you like that one? Do you like this one?' It was just the combination of our closeness and the trip that started the rumours.

And you were the one they backed up to the wall. All those years ago. You were the one who imagined it all . . . − *George Harrison, 'All Those Years Ago'*

PLAYBOY: *What memories are jogged by the song 'Help!'?*
LENNON: When 'Help!' came out in '65, I was actually crying out for help. Most people think it's just a fast rock'n'roll song. I didn't realise it at the time; I just wrote the song because I was commissioned to write it for the movie. But later, I knew I really was crying out for help. It was my fat Elvis period. You see the movie: He − I − is very fat, very insecure, and he's completely lost himself. And I am singing about when I was so much younger and all the rest, looking back at how easy it was. Now I may be very positive − yes, yes − but I also go through deep depressions where I would like to jump out the window, you know. It becomes easier to deal with as I get older; I don't know whether you learn control or, when you grow up, you calm down a little. Anyway, I was fat and depressed and I was crying out for help. In those days, when the Beatles were depressed, we had this little chant. I would yell out, 'Where are we going, fellows?' They would say, 'To the top, Johnny,' in pseudo-American voices. And I would say, 'Where is that, fellows?' And they would say, 'To the toppermost of the poppermost.' It was some dumb expression from a cheap movie − a la *Blackboard Jungle* − about Liverpool. Johnny was the leader of the gang.

PLAYBOY: *What were you depressed about during the 'Help!' period?*
LENNON: The Beatles thing had just gone beyond comprehension. We were smoking marijuana for breakfast. We were well into marijuana and nobody could communicate with us, because we were just all glazed eyes, giggling all the time. In our own world. That was the song, 'Help!'. I think everything that comes out of a song − even Paul's songs now, which are apparently about nothing − shows something about yourself.

PLAYBOY: *Was 'I'm a Loser' a similarly personal statement?*
LENNON: Part of me suspects that I'm a loser and the other part of me thinks I'm God Almighty.

PLAYBOY: *How about Paul's song 'Hey Jude?'*
LENNON: He said it was written about Julian. He knew I was splitting with Cyn and leaving Julian then. He was driving to see Julian to say hello. He had been like an uncle. And he came up with 'Hey Jude'. But I always heard it as a song to me. Now I'm sounding like one of those fans reading things into it. . . . Think about it: Yoko had just come into the picture. He is saying, 'Hey, Jude' – 'Hey, John.' Subconsciously, he was saying, Go ahead, leave me. On a conscious level, he didn't want me to go ahead. The angel in him was saying, 'Bless you.' The Devil in him didn't like it at all, because he didn't want to lose his partner.

PLAYBOY: . . .*[You say] the Beatles taught people how to swim?*
LENNON: If the Beatles or the Sixties had a message, it was to learn to swim. Period. And once you learn to swim, swim. The people who are hung up on the Beatles' and the Sixties' dream missed the whole point when the Beatles' and the Sixties' dream became the point. Carrying the Beatles' or the Sixties' dream around all your life is like carrying the Second World War and Glenn Miller around. That's not to say you can't enjoy Glenn Miller or the Beatles, but to live in that dream is the twilight zone. It's not living now. It's an illusion.

Playboy, January 1981
Copyright 1981 Playboy, for *Playboy Interview: John Lennon and Yoko Ono*.

NEW YORK CITY BLUES
For John Lennon By Adrian Henri

You do not cross the road
To step into immortality
An empty street is only the beginning

The words will still flow through you
Even on this cold pavement,
Are heard in some far place
Remote from flowers or flash-bulbs.

In that city, on Gothic railings
Dark against the snowy park
Still a dead flower, a faded letter,
Already one month old.

'Life is what happens to you
When you're busy making other plans,'
This empty street
Is only the beginning.

Here, in your other city,
Riot vans prowl the December dark,
Remember angry embers of summer,
Familiar ghost guitars echo from stucco terraces.

Meanwhile, in the Valley of Indecision,
We rehearse stale words, store up unexpected songs,
Celebrate sad anniversaries.
Flowers and flash-bulbs. Cold pavements.

You do not cross the road
To step into immortality
At the dark end of the street
Waits the inevitable stranger.

Collected Poems, Adrian Henri, 1986

THE ANDY WARHOL DIARIES

Warhol's minute-by-minute reaction to the murder of John Lennon — who he was well acquainted with — is almost strictly matter-of-fact. The details are extricated from Warhol's other, more trivial concerns of the week beginning 8 December, 1980.

Monday, December 8, 1980

Walked to Halston's. All his girls were there wearing all his clothes. There were three limos out front and we went to the Met Museum, to Diana Vreeland's opening-night Costume Institute dinner. It was the 650 people you know best. Someone who came in said John Lennon was shot and no one could believe it, so someone called the *Daily News* and they said it was true. It was scary, it was all anyone could talk about. He was shot outside his house.

When I got home I turned on the TV and they said he was murdered by somebody he gave an autograph to earlier in the evening.

Tuesday, December 9, 1980

The news was the same news that had been on all night, pictures of John and old film clips. Had to take Archie and Amos down to the office to be looked at by the Lewis Allen dummy people (cab $5). When I got there Howdy Doody was waiting for me. I'm doing his portrait, he's one of the Big Myths.

And Bob was feeling his oats because the collector's issue of the *Daily News* that had 'John Lennon Shot' headlines is the one that had the big story on him in it — 'The Man Behind Andy Warhol'. It was a long article, but it was boring.

I watched the John Lennon news and it's so scary. I mean, the other day, the kid named Michael who's been writing me letters for five years just walked in — somebody buzzed him in — and he walked over and handed me another letter and left. Where does he live? In institutions?

Wednesday, December 10, 1980

The papers still have the Lennon news. The one who killed him was a frustrated artist. They brought up the Dali poster he had on his wall. They always interview the janitors and the old schoolteachers and things. The kid said the devil made him do it. And John was so rich, they say he left a $235 million estate.

And the 'vigil' is still going on at the Dakota. It looked so strange, I don't know what those people think they're doing.

I don't intend to be a performing flea anymore. I was the dreamweaver, but although I'll be around I don't intend to be running at 20,000 miles an hour trying to prove myself. I don't want to die at 40. – *John Lennon*

Sunday, December 14, 1980

I was in a cab with a black driver during the minutes that were supposed to be silence to remember John and pray for his soul. He had a black station on and they had a ten-minute silence and the disc jockey said, 'We're up there with you, John,' and the driver laughed and said, 'Not me, baby, I'm stayin' right down here.' So he turned to another station and *that* station was (*laughs*) talking about the silence.

The Andy Warhol Diaries, edited by Pat Hackett, 1989

LET ME TAKE YOU DOWN
By Jack Jones

Jones, a journalist whose specialised subject is the US penal system, gained access to John Lennon's killer, Mark Chapman, in prison. Through a series of personal interviews, he produced the only in-depth analysis of what motivated the fateful events of the night of 8 December, 1980. In this extract, he discusses Chapman's obsession with J. D. Salinger's novel of adolescent alienation, The Catcher in the Rye, *and his identification with the book's central character, sixteen-year-old Holden Caulfield.*

Since John Lennon was just 'an image on a screen' in the mind of Mark David Chapman, the former Beatles fan found it relatively easy to incorporate the superstar into an intricate narrative that controlled his life. To justify the act of murder, Chapman also found it necessary to transform himself into the fictional character Holden Caulfield. According to the *Catcher* script as Chapman interpreted it, Lennon's blood would give him an identity as the Catcher in the Rye of his generation. His new identity would, in turn, lend an aura of literary dignity to the desperate and cowardly act of shooting a man in the back.

After firing the fatal shots, Chapman was dumbfounded when John Lennon failed to sprawl dead, as the gunman had envisioned, at his feet. Although mortally wounded, Lennon sprinted up a half-dozen stone steps and crashed through a glass door into the foyer of the Dakota building before he collapsed. Chapman had expected to curl into a foetal ball beside Lennon's bleeding body and flow at last into the inky world of the Catcher. At the anticipated moment of his rebirth, when the gun stopped firing in his fist, his greatest fear was that nothing had changed.

It would be another two months before the killer finally got his wish, of becoming the Catcher in the Rye of his generation. While awaiting trial in his cell at Rikers Island, Chapman became suddenly entangled in the deceptive web he had spun from the Catcher's message. After numerous extended sessions with defence lawyers and psychiatrists in preparation for 'the trial of the decade', Chapman collapsed finally into his own fictive persona as a bizarre mutation of Holden Caulfield. With an ironic touch of poetic justice, it was Holden himself who would destroy an elaborate insanity defence calculated to keep Mark David Chapman from being punished for the murder of John Lennon.

A verdict of insanity would have returned Chapman, a keenly intelligent and practiced sociopath, to the setting of a mental hospital where he already had proved himself able to manipulate psychiatrists and therapists. With his metamorphosis at last into Holden Caulfield, Chapman took the 'terrible kind of fall' described by Salinger into the web of his own self-delusion and deceit.

University of California psychologist Jay Martin is one of the foremost authorities on Holden Caulfield. In his book *Who Am I This Time? Uncovering the Fictive Personality*, Martin writes of Chapman and details the cases of several Holden Caulfields – along with several Elvis Presleys, Marilyn Monroes, Batmen, Supermen, and others the therapist has helped extricate from borderline worlds of dangerous fantasy.

To a person like Chapman, a person devoid of a personality of his own, 'a fictional character is unchangeable and safe. It gives a guarantee of a hold upon reality and has stories about it that can be imitated,' said Martin. *The Catcher in the Rye*, he says, is an especially appealing identity for depressed young adults who, like Chapman, suffered psychological trauma in childhood or adolescence that impairs their ability to function in the adult world.

'People who read *The Catcher in the Rye* twenty or 30 years ago don't tend to remember how depressed and psychically injured Holden Caulfield is. But if you go back and read the book, it's very apparent how wounded and how depressed he is,' Martin said.

Recalling the depression that drove Chapman to attempt suicide and that struck again on the eve of the Lennon killing, Martin suggests that it was easy for Chapman to imagine himself in the tortured adolescent disguise of Holden Caulfield. Fictive personalities, says Martin, 'become a substitute for a self that is threatened with annihilation' – the sort of self Chapman has described.

Chapman put on and discarded the personalities of friends with whom he sought to identify. In some cases, he says he virtually became the people that he admired. Until he became Holden Caulfield, the killer denies that he ever had a personality apart from 'the alter ego of whoever I was closest to at a given point in my life, usually a friend a few years older than myself. I was always somebody's sidekick. Anybody I was with, I became them. I had no personality of my own. Why didn't I have any substance to myself? What happened? Why was my personality always so fragmented?'

According to Martin, alter egos and fictive personalities are common features of a healthy personality – unless the fantasy overpowers the fantasiser.

'It is neither possible nor desirable to dispense with fictions,' the psychologist said. 'But to possess *only* fictions means to be possessed by them. However many roles we play for others, we must play as few as possible for ourselves.'

Separated from the melodic balance of the Beatles, Lennon's music became harsh and spiky, occasionally memorable and moving but more often strident and sloganising . . . What took him to America was a desire not just for (comparative) anonymity, but also for the teeming classlessness of New York. His murder was very typical of the city – flukey and meaningless. Deaths of this kind are what happens when the Warhol catchphrase – Everyone a Star – teams up with psychopathology . . . – *Martin Amis*

The line between reality and fiction has become further blurred in the aftermath of the John Lennon killing, a murder that itself has been transformed into the grist of pop culture and novels. The Lennon-Chapman tragedy, which inspired an outpouring of songs by superstar musicians like Elton John and David Gilmour, has also inspired books, including at least two recent works by Stephen King, the contemporary master of the literary horror genre. King's novel *The Dark Half*, based on preliminary psychological profiles that described the killer as Lennon's twisted alter ego, anchors itself in reality with repeated references to Chapman's cold-blooded act. King, himself an object of public adulation by virtue of his fame and success, alludes frequently in the novel to the phenomenon of celebrityhood and the fatal obsessions it inspires in fans on whose fascinations a celebrity's fame and fortunes depend. As the 'dark half' of John Lennon, Chapman is described by King as a 'crocodile hunter'. The writer explains the deadly sport of celebrity stalking as 'see-the-living-crocodile-syndrome. . .about the fellow who shot John Lennon and the one who tried to kill Ronald Reagan to impress Jodie Foster. They are out there. . .Look at Oswald. Look at Chapman.'

Let Me Take You Down, Jack Jones, 1992

IT WAS TWENTY YEARS
AGO TODAY

Keith Richards

I was downtown on Fifth Avenue in New York. The first bit of news I got, I thought: 'He'll make it. It's just a flesh wound.' And then, later on, the news really came. He wasn't just a mate of mine, he was a mate of everybody's, really. He was a funny guy. And you realise that you're stunned. You really don't believe it. And you think, 'God, why can't I do anything about it?' I got well drunk on it. And I had another one for John. Then there was the confusion, the phone calls, trying to find out if Yoko was OK.

There were the Beatles, and there was John. As a band, they were a great unit. But John, he was his own man. We got along very well. We didn't see each other very often, but he would sort of turn up at your hotel. Usually, if I was in the city, I'd stay at the Plaza. If John turned up, that meant he wanted to party. He didn't come there to discuss, you know, philosophy, although it would end up like that. I would just get into town, and there'd be a knock at the door: 'Hey, mon, what is going on around here?' We would get the guitars down and sing. And, in our spare time, discuss world domination.

He's rubbed off on me as much as anybody. A bit of me rubbed off on John, too, you know. He took it with him. My father just passed away, and he winked at me just before he died. I really feel a lot better about death now. I'm getting off on that wink. I'd give the wink to John.

Marianne Faithfull

I had just gotten into a minicab in London when the news came on, and then they played all John Lennon songs. The first was 'A Day in the Life'. I was completely shocked but, in a way, not that surprised.

The most amazing time I ever had with John is when we went to see the Maharishi, and that's when I really got closest to him. He was so funny. I was always a bit frightened of him because he was so incredibly clever. The weekend we went to Bangor where the Maharishi was delivering a lecture was very intense because we all went on the train there: the Beatles and me and Mick Jagger and the Maharishi. Then, over the weekend, we got the news that Brian Epstein had overdosed. John was devastated. I wish I'd gone on the retreat in India – not because I liked the Maharishi, because I didn't. Just to be there to hear Lennon's asides and to watch the whole thing unravel – because it did. I would have loved to be there for that.

Noel Gallagher

I was in my front-room in Manchester listening to a football match, and they interrupted it to say that John Lennon had been assassinated. It was like, 'Fuck,' it was just silence, really. Especially for my mum; she was a teenager in the Sixties and into the Beatles. Lennon dying had a more profound effect on her than on me, because at the time I was thirteen.

I didn't know what it meant until I dissected 'The White Album'. And then I thought: 'Fuck, this guy is not even around any more.' Lennon's legacy is absolutely 100 per cent his music. I'm not really interested in his politics or his bandwagon-jumping towards the end of his life.

His music is just completely timeless and unsurpassable. If it wasn't for John Lennon, I think that Paul McCartney would have had the Beatles writing 'Yesterday' right up until the day that they split up.

Ask any cutting-edge musicians in London, like the Chemical Brothers or Prodigy, if you trace all that music backwards, it all stops at 'Tomorrow Never Knows'. It was 1966 when Lennon wrote that song. All the other songs that were around, it was still all, 'You love me/ I love you/ Whoopie-doo.' Lennon wanted to sound like a thousand monks chanting on top of a hill. He's probably still twenty years ahead of his time.

Sting

I think the Police had just come offstage in Miami. I was told that he'd been shot, and I had the reaction that everybody had – disbelief, shock, horror. What happens when people like him die is that the landscape changes. You know, a mountain disappears, a river is gone. And I think his death was probably as significant as that. The Beatles were formative in my upbringing, my education. They came from a very similar background – the industrial towns in England, working class; they wrote their own songs, conquered the world. That was the blueprint for lots of other British kids to try to do the same. We all miss him, and I think about him every time I walk by that building.

Michael Douglas

I have a newborn son, so I've been listening a lot to 'Beautiful Boy'. John wrote it for Sean, and it's a lovely song to a child. It's been bringing back all of those times for me, in the Sixties and Seventies, when the Beatles and Lennon meant so much. And with the [2000 US presidential] election, I'm reminded of how politics today could really use John Lennon – his truthfulness. He's needed.

Ronnie Spector

I first met him in London in 1963. The Ronettes were the top group in England at the time. He saw us and got in touch with our manager, and there was this party and we danced all night with all the fellas, taught them the New York dances. He liked me for more than just my voice. As the party wound down, we started talking. I was just nineteen years old, and starting to make it big, and he knew things. He told me: 'It's all going to change, you're going to start riding in limousines.' I'm, like, 'You're kidding me!'

I met him in the street years later. He called my name: 'Ronnie!' and I turned around; it was so fucking cool. When he called my name, everyone turned around and saw him (and recognised him), and he didn't care. He got shot right after that.

When he was shot, I was so devastated, I stayed in bed for a week. I was in the studio when I heard; I just dropped the phone – it broke my heart. I always think of John Lennon every time I'm in the recording studio. I can't help it. He's my spirit talking to me, saying: 'Don't give up.'

Lenny Kravitz

I met Yoko Ono and Sean on my first tour. For my birthday one year, Yoko gave me one of John's shirts. It's black, one of those disco rollerskating shirts; he used to wear those tight, glittery shirts.

Today, I think John would be doing some cutting-edge hardcore music. His first solo record is one of the most hardcore pieces of music ever recorded. And at the end of 'Mother', when he's saying, 'Mama, don't go, Daddy, come home,' his soul is just spilling out; it's so hardcore.

Sinead O'Connor

It was my twelfth birthday and I was walking home from school. I guess I would have been young enough to not see death as being entirely disastrous. The nature of my own personality is that I don't see death as a disastrous thing. It's just a door that opens, and somebody goes somewhere else.

Lennon had a sense of everybody's right to stir shit. He was very brave and vulnerable, and saw that it was brave to show one's vulnerability.

He would probably love the rap movement. In a lot of ways, rap is where his voice can still be heard. People underestimate the subliminal impact of not just his music but the things he was doing publicly, like the shit-stirring. All of that had a huge influence on rap, and on little, bold, big-mouthed Irish singers. You almost forget how sexy he was. Plus, he was wonderful and gorgeous.

Sheryl Crow

I was watching Monday night football at the University of Missouri and Howard Cosell announced Lennon's death. He basically denounced the importance of the game and proclaimed that one of this generation's icons had been killed.

In the band that most influenced music and, moreover, culture, he represented the rock'n'roll attitude of rebellion, dissatisfaction and social consciousness, the idea that we as people can expand our minds, grow, live together and love in peace. He tried to incorporate those ideals in his music and his life. His influence is everywhere – in every rock'n'roll singer-songwriter.

Tom Petty

I was in Cherokee Recording Studios in Hollywood when I heard. I was working with producer Jimmy Iovine, who knew John and had worked with him quite a bit. Someone called the studio from New York and said that John had been shot. We thought it was a gag and we kept working. Then someone called and said: 'John's dead.' It just stopped the session. I went home and on the way I could see people sitting in their cars at traffic lights just crying. It was a hard thing to believe. I still have trouble believing it.

John Lennon meant everything. His influence was immeasurable when I started to play in the mid-Sixties. He was probably one of the two or three great rock singers ever, and what can you really say about his songwriting? He was just. . . transcendental. And his rhythm-guitar playing – I really studied it quite a bit. If you ever want to see some great rhythm guitar, check out in *A Hard Day's Night* when they do 'And I Love Her'. He could really make a band just kind of surge and jump.

To me, Lennon's legacy is honesty. When I was young and seeing the Beatles performing on TV, they were the first ones who weren't just saying pat, show-biz banter. They'd actually say something. He was a great role model for my whole generation, because you knew when John suffered and you knew when John was happy, but it all somehow came out OK.

Shirley Manson

I was fourteen, and I was in my first class of the day and some girls in the class who knew I was a freak about the Beatles started teasing me, saying: 'Oh, you know John Lennon, he's dead.' Then our teacher told us the news, and there were other girls in that class who loved the Beatles like I did, and we all cried and cried. Nobody has been able to encompass his humanity, his humility and his humour, his wit and his intelligence quite the same way he has done – like the perfect rock star.

The best dream I ever had was that I was sitting next to him in an airplane. I was his wife, but I was me. Nothing happened in the dream except that I could hear the drone of the airplane. And I said nothing, but I could feel the connection between us. When I woke up in the morning, I don't think I've ever felt so deeply contented.

John Travolta

I blocked out where I was when I heard – I kind of just travelled in my mind to where it happened. I was so familiar with that spot, because I had lived in the building next door. There was a building that Carly Simon and James Taylor, the Beatles and Mick Jagger had lived in at various times, and it was right around the block.

I imagined how safe he must have felt going in and out of there, because I know I did. Even though it had been years since I had lived there, it was kind of like finding out that it had happened to somebody on your block.

The Beatles meant everything to me growing up, and John was part of that. I loved Lennon's persona. He knew who he was and he knew what he represented to a worldwide public. John knew he had the floor; he knew he had to parlay that into something. I think he incited and inspired a whole group of youth to speak out and say what they felt.

Drew Barrymore

When he died I was only five. I just remember when I discovered the Beatles, feeling sad because the one that I loved so much wasn't here. It was the early Eighties, and then I didn't listen to the Beatles for a few years after that.

I really got into them again when I was sixteen, and it's been all I've listened to since then. That's when I really started falling in love with John Lennon. Every song he sings, I freak. I feel like I can't speak eloquently enough. Anything in life, whatever your question is for the universe, if you put on a John Lennon song, he will answer you.

I think 'Watching the Wheels' is the song I love the most, because it is so true. I completely feel like that song. I feel like sometimes he's saying that the people he's talking about are himself – himself looking at himself. And just how perfect a song it is for how we feel inside our own minds: We're trying to go on these paths that feel right and good to us, but we're always questioning how it's affecting others along the way.

He gave everyone great music to be sad to and make love to and laugh to and drive to, and every sort of thing that you live for in the world. If you put his music on to anything that you're doing in life, it fits right alongside of it.

Peter Fonda

I was ploughing the snow from my driveway in Montana in the morning, and I went inside and heard on the news that he had been shot the night before.

I couldn't imagine why somebody would want to shoot someone who had done so much explaining of our lives through his art.

I met the Beatles individually in 1965, then spent a couple of days with them. We took LSD at my house. I knew John was having trouble with me. We put on a movie of Jane's, and he was upset. There was too much Fonda going on: my dad, myself, my sister. But as the trip wore on, he became easier with me. I was right there with him the whole time. We ended up in the bathroom, in a big sunken tub – fortunately not filled with water – playing electric guitars that were amplified by the room, singing songs.

Out of that experience came 'She Said, She Said'. John said in *Rolling Stone* that I had something to do with that song. I thought it was so far out that he had made something of it. He used the exact words I said to George [Harrison], who thought he was dying during the acid trip. I had said: 'I know what it's like to be dead.'

John and George are sitting at the table with me, and John says: 'How do you know what it's like to be dead?' And I said: 'I shot myself when I was a boy. But by accident. Everything was all right in my mind.' Of course, it wasn't. Then I hear the song: 'When I was a boy/ Everything was right.'

I see Lennon's influence in my children. They think of 'Imagine' as an anthem. There's a generational zap there. The Beatles wrote these crowd-pleasing dance songs, which evolved into songs of our moments on this planet.

Thank God we had him, that his essence didn't float by us to some other place. We got lucky.

Steven Tyler

I remember going to write alone up in New Hampshire – to get in touch with my insides. Then, when I heard the news, it was almost too much for my insides to handle. It ripped out a piece of me – I don't know how to say it any other way. I was so angry for so long – I was physically angry for years after that fucker shot him. It felt good to have a cry because I was so fuckin' pissed off.

As a kid, I used to go down to Greenwich Village all the time and fantasise I was going to bump into one of the Beatles or Stones. I never got to meet John, but I always felt like I knew him anyway. The Beatles taught us to fly, and John taught us to freefall back to earth. All songwriters ever want to do is crawl inside other people's souls and psyches, and somehow change everything. Jesus, what part of John or the Beatles did not get inside every one of us?

Wyclef Jean

When I heard that John Lennon had died, I was in my grandmother's house in Brooklyn. I was like: 'That's fucked up.' I was mad, young. I got that same butterfly feeling in my stomach when Marvin Gaye died. It was completely unexplainable. I didn't even know the guy.

Lennon was just a great songwriter. The simplicity with which he wrote songs. . .it's something even a child can understand. But it's not easy to write a simple song. And every one of Lennon's songs had a dope hook.

He wrote about what was going on, and he always encouraged world peace. Like Bob Marley and even Sting, he transcended his border to make a difference. He came to New York and sang about the Vietnam war. Although he never saw world peace, I think he changed a lot of people's minds.

Graham Nash

I was lying on my bed watching Monday night football – it was Miami and the New England Patriots – when I heard the news. Howard Cosell broke the news. Apart from being very, very upset by the loss of someone whom I had met many times, the first thing that occurred to me was wondering how many songs we were never going to get to hear, that were working around in his head.

I'd been acquainted with John since about 1958, before the Beatles. The first time I actually met him was at the Cavern in Liverpool in 1962, when the Hollies were playing on the same bill as the Beatles. John was always on the front edge – it's very much the same as what Neil Young does. All those incredible people are always on the front edge. And sometimes they fall, and sometimes they fly. John's legacy is that he gave as much dignity to the common man as he could. He stood for dignity and respect and songs that had a reason for being.

David Crosby

I don't remember where I was at the time. I just remember being very depressed, because I loved him very deeply. We were friends. I found him to be smart, acerbic, shrewd, witty and a good guy. He and the other Beatles were all very kind to us when we came over to England as the Byrds. They kind of took us under their wing, and from that point forward, we saw each other a lot. Whenever they came to the United States, I would go to the gigs and hang out with them.

For me, John Lennon's legacy is his songs – all those brilliant, beautiful, incredible pieces of work. John was a very fierce guy – he wasn't a shy little human being. He was a guy with strong opinions, and he had no problem expressing them.

Art Garfunkel

I remember the day John Lennon died. I was recording at Criteria Studios in Miami, making my *Scissors Cut* album. I was doing vocals that night, and the second engineer interrupted and said: 'I have terrible news to tell you.' I took a long pause, and I tried to carry on, and I failed, and I came into the control room, and I said: 'That's it for tonight; I can't work. I can't speak, I don't know what to say.'

I knew him a little bit, and he was unbelievably engaging. At the Dakota once, after dinner, he pulls me into the bedroom, so I'm sitting on the end of his bed, and he says: 'I want you to tell me about your work with Paul Simon, because I understand you just recorded in Nashville together.' We had just done 'My Little Town'. 'I'm getting calls from my Paul,' he said, 'who's doing an Allen Toussaint project. And he wants to know if I'm available for the recording. What should I do?' Can you imagine how I felt? John Lennon asking me for my advice? I could have pinched myself at that moment, because it made me realise in a flash: no wonder he captivated the whole goddamned world – he's so commercial.

He knew what to say to me that was connected and human and real and grounded and fascinating. And that's what he did with the whole planet earth. He was a hit record – his very being was like a hit. And I said to him: 'John, I would do it – put all personality aside and go with the fun of the blend. Make music with somebody you have made a sound with. A great pleasure is the thing to stick with.' He didn't take my advice.

Joe Strummer

I can't remember where I read this, but it struck me, so I'll repeat it: the Beatles were from the first generation of working-class kids in Britain, after the war and rationing and all, who were asked to think about their feelings – and to express themselves in an artistic way. Obviously, Lennon was a one-off, but it's amazing to think of what might have been wasted in other generations. Part of his legacy is opening the door to people who'd never been allowed to dream of such things. We'll compare our new geniuses against that one forever.

Johnny Marr

I was still at school. I remember the news being on the radio and television; the whole country seemed to be in shock, it was all anyone could talk about.

The Beatles stuff has always seemed to be there, the sound of Lennon and McCartney's voices together is a part of British culture. I can remember reruns of *A Hard Day's Night* and *Help!* and my earliest memory is of seeing him playing harmonica on 'Love Me Do'. His legacy has transcended that of the pop star; he's now a political symbol, a modern mystic.

Mike Myers

I was watching Monday night football. My father referred to it as an 'assassination'. That's how much impact his death had in our house.

My parents are from Liverpool. So you can imagine, he was a god in our house. To say we were intensely proud would be an understatement. I even went through a time when I actually thought I was related to him because he had the same accent as my mum and dad. What I admired most about John was that he was faithfully his own man, and he let his heart dictate his actions.

Hunter Davies

My diary tells me I had a very poorly leg that day; that's the sort of dopey stuff I record. I'd got injured playing football and was hobbling around. And moaning around. I see I was also doing a children's book, proceeds to charity, and my editor was chasing me for copy. So I woke up that morning, groaning at the day ahead.

It was the Jimmy Young programme which informed me. I did a chat with Jim, and then the phone never stopped. Once you do one, they all want you. Since doing my biog in 1968, I'd tried to keep out of Beatles stuff, feeling a fraud, my knowledge so out of date. The day turned into chaos, so my diary says. The full horror of it didn't strike me for several weeks.

Neil Harrison, aka John Lennon in the Bootleg Beatles

I was in the Bootlegs when he died. We'd been going since about March of that year and we'd just played Keele University. We woke up on the ninth and the landlady of the digs we were staying at said that John Lennon had been shot in New York. She didn't say shot dead. Then we switched on the news and found out he was dead. We drove back to London and we couldn't say a word. We were dumbstruck.

Some of these interviews first appeared in *Rolling Stone*. Others are by Kim Bunce and Chloe Diski.

The Observer, 3 December 2000

PLAYBOY INTERVIEW WITH PAUL AND LINDA MCCARTNEY

Paul looks back on his relationship with John, before, during and after the Beatles.

PLAYBOY: *Paul, it's been nearly four years since John Lennon died and you haven't really talked about your partnership and what his death meant to you. Can you talk about it now?*
PAUL: It's . . . it's just too difficult . . . I feel that if I said anything about John, I would have to sit here for five days and say it all. Or I don't want to say anything.
LINDA: I'm like that.
PAUL: I know George and Ringo can't really talk about it.

PLAYBOY: *Yet the only thing you were quoted as saying after John's assassination was, 'Well, it's a drag.'*
PAUL: What happened was we heard the news that morning and, strangely enough, all of us . . . the three Beatles, friends of John's . . . all of us reacted in the same way. Separately. Everyone just went to work that day. All of us. Nobody could stay home with that news. We all had to go to work and be with people we knew. Couldn't bear it. We just had to keep going. So I went in and did a day's work in a kind of shock. And as I was coming out of the studio later, there was a reporter, and as we were driving away, he just stuck the microphone in the window and shouted, 'What do you think about John's death?' I had just finished a whole day in shock and I said, 'It's a drag.' I meant drag in the heaviest sense of the word, you know: 'It's a – DRAG.' But, you know, when you look at that in print, it says, 'Yes, it's a drag.' Matter of fact.

PLAYBOY: *Do you remember your last conversation with John?*
PAUL: Yes. That is a nice thing, a consoling factor for me, because I do feel it was sad that we never actually sat down and straightened our differences out. But fortunately for me, the last phone conversation I ever had with him was really great, and we didn't have any kind of blowup. It could have easily been one of the other phone calls, when we blew up at each other and slammed the phone down.

PLAYBOY: *Do you remember what you talked about?*

PAUL: It was just a very happy conversation about his family, my family. Enjoying his life very much; Sean was a very big part of it. And thinking about getting on with his career. I remember he said, 'Oh, God, I'm like Aunt Mimi, padding round here in me dressing gown' . . . robe, as he called it, cuz he was picking up the American vernacular . . . 'feeding the cats in me robe and cooking and putting a cup of tea on. This housewife wants a career!' It was that time for him. He was about to launch *Double Fantasy*.

PLAYBOY: *But getting back to you and your flipness over John's death, isn't that characteristic of you . . . to show little emotion on the outside, to keep it all internalised?*
LINDA: You're right. That's true.
PAUL: True. My mum died when I was fourteen. That is a kind of strange age to lose a mother . . . cuz you know, you're dealing with puberty . . . Actually, that was one of the things that brought John and me very close together: He lost his mum when he was seventeen. Our way of facing it at that age was to laugh at it . . . not in our hearts but on the surface. It was sort of a wink thing between us. When someone would say, 'And how's your mother?' John would say, 'She died.' We'd know that that person would become incredibly embarrassed and we'd almost have a joke with it. After a few years, the pain subsided a bit. It was a bond between us, actually; quite a big one, as I recall. We came together professionally afterward. And as we became a writing team, I think it helped our intimacy and our trust in each other. Eventually, we were pretty good mates – until the Beatles started to split up and Yoko came into it.

PLAYBOY: *And that's when all the feuding and name-calling began. What started it? Did you feel hurt by John?*
PAUL: You couldn't think of it as hurt. It was more like old army buddies splitting up on account of wedding bells. You know . . .[sings] 'Those wedding bells are breaking up that old gang of mine.' He'd fallen in love, and none of us was stupid enough to say, 'Oh, you shouldn't love her.' We could recognise that, but that didn't diminish the hurt we were feeling by being pushed aside. Later on, I remember saying, 'Clear the decks, give him his time with Yoko.' I wanted him to have his child and move to New York, to do all the things he'd wanted to do, to learn Japanese, to expand himself.

PLAYBOY: *But you didn't understand it at the time?*
PAUL: No, at the time, we tried to understand. but what should happen was, if we were the least bit bitchy, that would be very hurtful to them in this . . .

wild thing they were in. I was looking at my second solo album, *Ram*, the other day and I remember there was one tiny little reference to John in the whole thing. He'd been doing a lot of preaching, and it got up my nose a little bit. In one song, I wrote, 'Too many people preaching practices,' I think is the line. I mean, that was a little dig at John and Yoko. There wasn't anything else on it that was about them. Oh, there was 'You took your lucky break and broke it in two.'

LINDA: Same song. They got the message.

PAUL: But I think they took it further . . .

LINDA: They thought the whole album was about them. And then they got very upset.

PAUL: Yeah, that was the kind of thing that would happen. They'd take one small dig out of proportion and then come back at us in their next album. Then we'd say, 'Hey, we only did two percent, they did 200 percent' and we'd go through all of that insanity.

(Paul leaves to take a telephone call)

LINDA: I was just going to say that I think if John had lived, he might still be saying, 'Oh, I'm much happier now . . .'

I was lucky to have Linda, because she did ground me. There were certain things I was going off on that she could pull me back from. Linda would say, 'Are you sure you want to do that tonight?' And I'd go, 'Oh, there's an alternative?' She reminded me there was this real life there that I liked a lot. – *Paul McCartney*

PLAYBOY: *And you don't believe it?*

LINDA: The sad thing is that John and Paul both had problems and they loved each other and, boy, could they have helped each other! If they had only communicated! It frustrates me to no end, because I was just some chick from New York when I walked into all of that. God, if I'd known what I know now . . . All I could do was sit there watching them play these games.

PLAYBOY: *But wasn't it clear that John wanted only to work with Yoko?*

LINDA: No. I know that Paul was desperate to write with John again. And I know John was desperate to write. Desperate. People thought, Well, he's taking care of Sean, he's a househusband and all that, but he wasn't happy. He couldn't write and it drove him crazy. And Paul could have helped him . . . easily. (Paul returns)

PLAYBOY: *How much did John's praise mean to you when he was alive?*

PAUL: A lot, but I hardly ever remember it, actually. There wasn't a lot of it flying about! I remember one time when we were making *Help!* in Austria. We'd been out skiing all day for the film and so we were all tired. I usually shared a room with George. But on this particular occasion, I was in with John. We were taking our huge skiing boots off and getting ready for the evening and stuff, and we had one of our cassettes. It was one of the albums, probably *Revolver* or *Rubber Soul* . . . I'm a bit hazy about which one. It may have been the one that had my song, 'Here, There and Everywhere'. There were three of my songs and three of John's songs on the side we were listening to. And for the first time ever, he just tossed it off, without saying anything definite, 'Oh, I probably like your songs better than mine.' And that was it! That was the height of praise I ever got off him, [mumbles] 'I probably like your songs better than mine.' Whoops! There was no one looking, so he could say it. But, yeah, I definitely did look up to John. We all looked up to John. He was older and he was very much the leader; he was the quickest wit and the smartest and all that kind of thing. So whenever he did praise any of us, it was great praise, indeed, because he didn't dish it out much. If ever you got a speck of it, a crumb of it, you were quite grateful. With 'Come Together' for instance, he wanted a piano lick to be very swampy and smoky, and I played it that way and he liked that a lot. I was quite pleased with that. He also liked it when I sang like Little Richard – 'Tutti-Frutti' and all that. All my screaming songs, the early Beatles screaming stuff . . . that's me doing Little Richard. It requires a great deal of nerve to just jump up and scream like an idiot, you know? Anyway, I would often fall a little bit short, not have that little kick, that soul, and it would be John who would go, 'Come on! You can sing it better than that, man! Come on, come on! Really throw it!' All right, John, OK . . . He was certainly the one I looked up to, most definitely.

PLAYBOY: *. . . is there a part of you that's still looking for a new partner – someone you can write with the way you did with John?*

PAUL: I like collaboration, but the collaboration I had with John . . . it's difficult to imagine anyone else coming up to that standard. Because he was no slouch, that boy. He was pretty hot stuff, you know. I mean, I can't imagine anybody being there when I go, [sings] 'It's getting better all the time.' I just can't imagine anybody who could chime in, [sings] 'It couldn't get much worse.'

Playboy, April 1984

Copyright 1984 for *Playboy Interview: Paul & Linda McCartney*.

GEORGE HARRISON
By Dave Laing and Penny Valentine

By the time the Beatles released their first No 1 hit, 'Please Please Me', in February 1963 – and made their first appearance on ITV's *Thank Your Lucky Stars* – it was apparent that three members of the group had clearly defined personalities. John Lennon was the most acerbic, Ringo Starr was the joker in the pack, and Paul McCartney, smoothing ruffled feathers, was the public relations man.

Perhaps because of the way he had joined the group, George Harrison, who has died of cancer aged 58, was always the quietest Beatle, and the least easy to pigeonhole – although he would occasionally surprise journalists with a sudden, pithy, off-the-wall remark. He was, however, unquestionably the best looking, and certainly the most dapper, with those little collarless jackets, *á la* Pierre Cardin, sitting comfortably on his shoulders, not a button under pressure.

Harrison's isolation was most noticeable on stage. The Beatles gravitated from church halls and Hamburg's red light district to a global fame greater than any British performers since Charlie Chaplin, but it was Lennon and McCartney who dominated. The early line-up saw McCartney, Lennon and Harrison strung out stage front, with Starr flailing his drumkit at the back. That style superseded the daft foot movements of the Shadows, and became *de rigeur* for British Sixties groups, but it started to fracture as the Beatles grew more successful.

From 1963, McCartney and Lennon wrote more of the songs, and it became more usual to see their two heads crowding round a single mike, providing lead vocal and back-up or chorus. Harrison, even when he was adding his voice to the mix, seemed stranded at the far side of the stage, even if he was the best musician and the motor of the band.

For the Beatles, he designed breaks and riffs. But for himself, he lacked – or rarely took – the opportunity to cut loose in the rockabilly style of his American hero, Carl Perkins. And with, and without, the Beatles, he was also an underrated songwriter. 'Something' (1969) was a great song – even the Beatles' antithesis, Frank Sinatra, picked up on it – and 'My Sweet Lord' (1970), while unconsciously plagiarised from Ronnie Mack's 'He's So Fine', justifiably sold in its millions.

In 1971 came his New York concert for Bangladesh. That new country had been devastated by war and floods, and the event launched the vogue for celebrity rock fund-raising. It also resulted in a three-volume album, featuring Harrison with Ringo Starr, Bob Dylan, Eric Clapton and Ravi Shankar, and put the stamp on Harrison's relationship with the Indian sub-continent that had begun when he effectively introduced the sitar to the Beatles in the mid-1960s.

The formula with the Beatles was that Harrison got to sing at least one number on each album, beginning with the Lennon and McCartney song 'Do You Want To Know A Secret?' on the group's debut album, *Please Please Me*. Gradually, his own work began to feature. There was 'Within You Without You', on *Sgt. Pepper's Lonely Hearts Club Band* (1967), 'Here Comes the Sun' and 'Something', on *Abbey Road* (1969), and 'While My Guitar Gently Weeps,' on 'The White Album' (1968).

I am devastated and very, very sad. He was a lovely guy and a very brave man and had a wonderful sense of humour. He is really just my baby brother.
– *Paul McCartney*

The youngest Beatle, Harrison was born in Wavertree, Liverpool, eight months after McCartney, two years after Lennon and three years after Starr. He experienced his rock'n'roll epiphany in 1956, when, on the verge of his teens, he cycled past an open window out of which was wafting Elvis Presley's 'Heartbreak Hotel'.

The son of a bus driver, he was educated at Dovedale primary school, where the young Lennon had gone, and, after passing the eleven-plus, was awarded a place at the Liverpool Institute, one of the city's leading grammar schools. He met McCartney – also at the institute – on the bus to school. The pair became close friends. When, in 1957, McCartney linked up with Lennon in the Quarrymen skiffle group, he tried to persuade them to invite Harrison along. At first, Lennon resisted – he didn't want a fourteen-year-old in the band – but then relented after hearing Harrison play Bill Justis's rock instrumental, 'Raunchy'.

Lennon realised that having someone who could play guitar solos – and Harrison was already a more competent musician than McCartney or himself – would expand the group's ability to handle rock'n'roll. The disapproval with which Lennon's guardian, his Auntie Mimi, greeted the new boy's teddy-boy style and thick Scouse accent may also have helped to change his mind.

Harrison's absorption into music took its toll on his school career, and he left the Liverpool Institute in 1959 with only one O-level, in art. By then, the Quarrymen had metamorphosed into the Silver Beatles. The following year, and by now the Beatles, they were booked to play for four months in a club on Hamburg's Reeperbahn. The trip was cut short when the seventeen-year-old

Harrison was discovered to be under age, but the quintet (as it then was, with Pete Best on drums and Stuart Sutcliffe on guitar) had gelled into an arresting, idiosyncratic unit.

By 1962, and now managed by Brian Epstein, the Beatles had signed their recording contract with EMI. In those simple times, when the group was almost a proto-teeny bop band, fan sheets listed Harrison's pet likes as 'hamburgers, the colour purple and friendly girls'. When their record producer George Martin asked if there was anything they were unhappy with, Harrison managed: 'Yes, I don't like your tie.'

Although Harrison was a fine lead guitarist – and his understated work was influential on many later players – his most important influence on the Beatles was always concerned with the new sound textures he introduced. Chief among these was the sitar.

He had first heard the instrument during the filming of *Help!* (1965), the second Beatles movie. He was intrigued, and the instrument was to feature on the *Rubber Soul* album, being recorded at the Abbey Road studios. A string had broken on Harrison's sitar, and the Indian embassy had put him on to the Hampstead-based Asian Music Circle, where the Beatles were introduced to Ravi Shankar at the home of the circle's co-founder Patricia Angadi. Harrison briefly studied with Shankar in order to use the sitar in Beatle music. The two remained close friends, touring the United States together in 1974, and Shankar's recordings appeared on Dark Horse, the record label Harrison started in 1976.

Between 1967 and 1968, Harrison's interest in Indian music led to the group's entanglement with transcendental meditation, via the Maharishi Mahesh Yogi. When they headed east, Harrison was with his then wife Patti Boyd – whom he had met on the set of the first Beatles film *A Hard Day's Night* (1964), and married in 1966, with Paul McCartney as best man. But the Indian trip was not a success, and, although Lennon and Yoko Ono used chanting Hare Krishna followers on their recording of 'Give Peace a Chance', it was Harrison alone who remained faithful to the Vedic tradition. He observed that one of his greatest thrills was seeing members of the London Hare Krishna Temple on *Top of the Pops*, chanting the record he had produced with them.

He donated a Hertfordshire mansion – renamed Bhaktivedanta Manor – for use as a Hindu centre, and played concerts in support of that curious political manifestation, the Natural Law Party. He did, however, turn down the Maharishi's request that he, McCartney and Starr should stand in Liverpool in the 1992 general election.

By 1968, the Beatles were on a downward path. McCartney and Lennon were drifting apart, and both had antagonised Harrison, who walked off the set of their documentary, *Let It Be* (relased in 1970), after an argument with McCartney. In March 1969, during a Fleet Street and police media blitz on drugs, youth, politics and rock stars, Harrison and Boyd were fined for possessing cannabis. That August, the group were in the recording studios for the last time together, to complete tracks for *Abbey Road*.

Harrison was the first Beatle to succeed as a solo artist. He had made two instrumental albums – *Wonderwall Music* and *Electronic Sound* (both 1969) – while the group was still together. Then, in 1970, he co-produced the double album, *All Things Must Pass*. It sold three million copies, and was his most commercially successful record, although a plagiarism suit over the song 'My Sweet Lord' cost him almost $600,000 in the American courts.

He continued to write and record at a fast pace for the next few years, releasing the hit, 'Give Me Love: Give Me Peace On Earth' (1973), and the albums, *Living in the Material World* (1973) and *Extra Texture* (1975). By the end of the 1970s, the Beatles partnership had been officially dissolved. Harrison's spiritual soft rock, meanwhile, had gone out of fashion and, for much of the next decade, he concentrated on a new career as a producer with Handmade Films, the company he had formed in 1979 with Denis O'Brien.

Their first success was Monty Python's *The Life of Brian* (1979), which they took on after EMI decided it might incur charges of blasphemy. In 1980, there was *The Long Good Friday*, followed by *Time Bandits* (1981), *A Private Function* (1985), *Mona Lisa* (1986) and *Withnail And I* (1987). The failure of the appalling Madonna–Sean Penn vehicle, *Shanghai Surprise* (1986), heralded a downturn in the company's fortunes, and it was eventually wound up in acrimony, with Harrison winning an $11 million lawsuit against his former partner.

> **George was a best friend of mine. I loved him very much, and I will miss him greatly . . . for his sense of love, his sense of music and his sense of laughter.**
> **– Ringo Starr**

After John Lennon's murder in 1980, Harrison composed a tribute song of his own, 'All Those Years Ago', but his own recording career was not effectively rekindled until 1987. Then, he and Jeff Lynne, of the Electric Light Orchestra, co-produced the album *Cloud Nine*, which included two singles, 'Got My Mind Set On You' and 'When We Was Fab'.

With Lynne, he also formed the Traveling Wilburys, with Bob Dylan, Roy Orbison and Tom Petty. In 1992, the success of two of the group's albums encouraged Harrison to undertake his first international tour for eighteen years. In the 1980s and 1990s, he appeared in public infrequently, usually on Beatle-related occasions. He lived quietly in his restored nineteenth century mansion at Friars Park, Henley on-Thames, with his second wife, Olivia, whom he married in 1978, and their son, Dhani, an idyllic life shaken only when a schizophrenic Beatles fan, Michael Abram, broke in in December 1999, and badly injured Harrison. He is survived by Olivia and Dhani.

George Harrison, guitarist, singer, songwriter, born February 25 1943; died November 29 2001.

The Guardian, 1 December 2001

GEORGE HARRISON 1943-2001
Youngest Beatle Loses Fight Against Cancer
By Richard Williams

George Harrison was the youngest and prettiest of the Beatles and, although it may sound improbable now, thinking of latter-day images of a crusty grey-haired chap supervising an army of gardeners behind the electrified fence guarding a vast estate near Henley-on-Thames, in the beginning he was the one the girls fancied and the boys instinctively wanted to become.

At first sight, Paul McCartney displayed a hint of puppy fat and an ingratiating air, while John Lennon seemed curiously and inappropriately grown-up: there was no innocence in that thin, sarcastic grin. Ringo Starr alone presented himself as exactly the man he would turn out to be. George was only nineteen but he was born with the kind of lost-angel looks – hooded eyes, good cheekbones – that all rock stars should have. And he had the best hair, which was supremely important just then: he had the first perfect Beatle cut.

So for a while – between, say, 'Love Me Do' in late 1962 and 'From Me To You' the following spring – he gave the impression of being the face of the Beatles, possibly even the leader. And he was, after all, the lead guitarist, a role which has its own glamour.

It took a while to work out that what made the Beatles different from everything that had preceded them was coming from the puppyish one and the sarcastic one. After all, beat groups had not contained their own songwriters before. As that recognition sharpened the outlines of their characters, so the young guitarist receded into a supporting role, greatly to his frustration.

It would be some years before the true George Harrison emerged – if, indeed, he ever did, at least in public. He was, it turned out, the shy one. And then, after a further interval, the prickly one. No doubt these characteristics were connected to each other, the product of the eternal resentment of the youngest child. For so long he had been overshadowed by the enormous public acclaim for Lennon and McCartney, whose first group, the Quarry men, had been going for almost a year when he joined them in March 1958 as a skiffle-crazed fifteen-year-old.

And now he has become the second member of the group to die. With

John, the world lost the Beatle who engineered the death of deference, taking a certain tendency within English humour and turning it into a weapons-grade wit that was sometimes delicately sardonic – 'the rest of you can rattle your jewellery' – and at others cruelly sarcastic.

George's demise removes the impressionable enthusiast whose inquisitive nature guided the Beatles beyond the frontiers which had hitherto constrained the attitudes and behaviour of four-piece beat groups from the industrial cities of the north. He may not have written the songs for which they will be remembered, but without his gift for discovery the group might have taken quite a different course and possibly a much less interesting and productive one.

It was George who, in Paris in the early weeks of 1964, during a nineteen-night season at the Olympia music hall, bought the copy of Bob Dylan's *Freewheelin'* that was to change the way the Beatles thought about songwriting. Brought up on the work of Chuck Berry and professional songwriters such as Carole King and Gerry Goffin, their horizons limited by pop song conventions inherited from Tin Pan Alley, they seized on Dylan's example to help them make the giant leap, in both content and form, from 'She Loves You' and 'I Want To Hold Your Hand' to 'Norwegian Wood' and 'Strawberry Fields Forever'.

If Harrison's enthusiasm had generated the breakthrough, his colleagues were the immediate beneficiaries. The lead guitarist's contribution as a songwriter had begun with 'Don't Bother Me' on their second album, *With the Beatles*, in 1963, but his output was restricted and overshadowed by the blossoming genius of Lennon and McCartney. By the time of *Rubber Soul* two years later he was demonstrating, in 'If I Needed Someone' and 'Think for Yourself', his ability to write a good mainstream rock song, but not until the appearance of *Abbey Road* in 1969, when the Beatles were already in the throes of divorce, did he produce a song, the glowing ballad 'Something', worth much more than a footnote in their discography. And then, as if to make up in hyperbole for what he had lost in time, no less an authority than Frank Sinatra was to describe it as 'the greatest love song of the last 50 years'.

In some respects Harrison resembled a conventional pop star. As the Beatles accumulated fame and fortune, he developed a taste for fast cars, married blonde model Patti Boyd, whom he met on the set of *A Hard Day's Night*, became a backer of Sibylla's, a West End nightclub, and lived in a bungalow on National Trust land near Esher, Surrey.

On his 21st birthday he received 60 sacks of mail containing an estimated 30,000 cards and presents. After he told an interviewer of his liking for jelly babies, he found himself subjected to showers of the sweets during concerts. A sign of affection from the girls in the front stalls, it interfered with his playing and, like the incessant screaming which obliterated the sound of the music, soon became tiresome.

So did life on his stockbroker belt estate, and on June 1 1966, four nights after joining Lennon in a box at the Albert Hall for a concert by Dylan, Harrison returned alone to the same venue to see Ravi Shankar, the Indian classical sitar virtuoso. A few days later Harrison met Shankar, who turned out to be barely aware of his existence. 'He told me how impressed he was with the sitar and my playing,' Shankar recalled. 'I asked him if he would show me what he had learned on the sitar, and he very humbly told me it was "not very much". I was struck both by his sincerity and his deep humility.'

There was one sitar lesson from the master at the Esher bungalow, followed by an invitation to India. Shankar, now fully apprised of Harrison's celebrity, told his pupil it might be advisable to grow a moustache to help preserve his anonymity during the journey. And so in mid-September, a fortnight after the Beatles had played their final concert, George and Patti Harrison flew to Bombay, where they checked into the Taj Mahal hotel under assumed names. When their presence was discovered midway through their five-week stay, they attempted to lift the siege of their hotel by giving a press conference at which they announced they were in India to study yoga and the sitar, and to get some peace and quiet. When they returned to Heathrow airport, on October 22, George was seen to be wearing a moustache. When he returned to the airport to meet Shankar four days later, he was wearing Indian clothes.

If the Harrisons were not the first westerners to fall in love with the culture of the east, they were certainly the most famous and influential. Their Indian adventure became a significant catalyst in a mass shift of thought and taste that ranged from the adoption of non-violent resistance in the counter-culture to the desire for a purer, simpler, more natural way of life symbolised by the popularity of organic food and loose-fitting clothes.

Within a year, indeed, the Harrisons were leading John, Paul and Ringo – all with moustaches, soon to be emulated by most western males under 30 – and their kaftan-clad partners on a trip back to India, to learn meditation techniques from the Maharishi Mahesh Yogi, a journey that kickstarted the personal-growth industry.

Of the four, Harrison was probably the most enthusiastic about the prospects for Apple, the cooperative company they set up in 1968 to manage their affairs and develop their interests after the death of Brian Epstein. His utopianism produced mixed results when he invited the Hare Krishna people and a party of Hell's Angels from California to stay in Apple's headquarters, an elegant town house at No. 3 Savile Row, where good intentions were gradually soured by competing egos.

> **He was a giant, a great, great soul, with all of the humanity, all of the wit and humour, all the wisdom, the spirituality, the common sense of a man and compassion for people. He inspired love and had the strength of a hundred men . . . . The world is a profoundly emptier place without him.** – *Bob Dylan*

But the occasional disillusionment never removed his capacity for turning those utopian impulses into constructive action. In 1971, with the wreckage of the Beatles still smoking, he corralled Dylan, Eric Clapton, Leon Russell and Billy Preston into playing the Concert for Bangladesh at Madison Square Garden in New York, a charity event which established the template for Live Aid and all the many similar star-studded charity concerts up to the televised benefit for the families of the World Trade Centre victims at Madison Square Garden in October, featuring McCartney, Clapton, Mick Jagger and the Who. For, curiously enough, the shy, suspicious one had also turned out to be the most successfully gregarious. Where McCartney gathered the surrogate family of Wings around him, and Lennon flitted from the street musician David Peel to the superstar David Bowie, Harrison's friendships with fellow musicians were built to last, probably to compensate for the feeling of being excluded from the creative centre of the Beatles.

He and fellow guitarist Eric Clapton played on each other's records, their bond even surviving the upheaval when Patti Harrison completed rock's most celebrated eternal triangle by leaving George, who had written 'Something' for her, to move in with Clapton, who had wooed her with 'Layla' and was to serenade her with 'Wonderful Tonight'.

He and Clapton toured with Delaney and Bonnie, a US duo, and in 1988 George co-founded the Travelling Wilburys, a sort of half-joking anti-supergroup, with Dylan, Tom Petty, Jeff Lynne and Roy Orbison.

He was, in short, a 'muso' – a term derisively applied in the post-punk era to a musician who was proud of his craft and strove to improve his instrumental technique in order to broaden his expressive range.

Harrison was thirteen when he discovered rock and roll and the study of the guitar as an alternative to academic education. He had used the instrument as a channel into which he could pour every ounce of the single-minded intensity that characterised his nature. He grew to love the company of other musicians, but he loathed the demands (while accepting the rewards) of the sort of immoderate fame that was the Beatles' reward for their gift.

He despised the music business, too, and no wonder. The Beatles were surrounded by sycophants, incompetents and thieves. Even Epstein could not protect them, lacking the experience to stay away from the elephant traps set by those who wished to market Beatle wigs, Beatle guitars, Beatle boots, Beatle mugs and a thousand other gewgaws.

He continued to act on his beliefs, taking part in demonstrations against nuclear energy and against the demolition of the old Regal cinema in his home town, Henley. He maintained his long-standing interest in motor racing, frequently turning up in the paddock at grand prix meetings, and used his company, Handmade Films, to back a series of British films, including Monty Python's *Life of Brian*, *Time Bandits* and *The Long Good Friday*. A mellowing of his attitude to his own history could be detected when he released a single called 'When We Was Fab', an amusing, poignant pastiche of *Revolver*-era Beatles, complete with layered sitars and tape-reversed drums.

Of the four, he was always the least comfortable with the demands of fame. 'I am not really Beatle George,' he said in 1995. 'Beatle George is like a suit or a shirt that I once wore on occasion, and until the end of my life people may see that shirt and mistake it for me.'

Sometimes he had harsher things to say about life as a Beatle and about the people who expected him to be fab forever. From 'Don't Bother Me' to 'Taxman' and 'Piggies', his songs sometimes seemed to be the product of irritation. It would be fairer to conclude that what occasionally sounded like ingratitude and sanctimoniousness was simply the reaction of a sensitive but uneducated boy confronted by unimaginable fame and wealth, and trying to find a satisfactory response.

The Guardian, 1 December 2001

THEY SOUGHT WITHOUT FINDING
By R. D. Laing

This brief cultural retrospective ran in Rolling Stone's *'twenty years on' commemoration of* The Ed Sullivan Show. *Laing was a Scottish psychiatric guru, whose controversial theory — that what society calls insanity is merely a defence mechanism against tensions created by the nuclear family — was fashionable in the late Sixties and Seventies.*

They performed 'All You Need Is Love' on the first live world-wide-TV hook-up, before an estimated 400 million people, in 1967. The times fitted them like a glove.

Everyone was getting the feel of the world as a global village — as us, as one species. The whole human race was becoming unified under the shadow of death. We knew we were one, because we could now commit suicide together. For some years, we had been able to kill ourselves by poison and plagues, and now we had nuclear devices. Short of complete suicide, we could and did inflict terrible havoc on ourselves. And it seemed it could break out anywhere. We were unified, but terrified of being united. We feared ourselves maybe no more than before, but in a new way.

That was the dark side. There was, and is, a God-given bright side. One of the most heartening things about the Beatles was that they gave expression to a shared sense of celebration around the world, a sense of the same sensibility. We loved what we heard, and it was great that hundreds of millions loved it at exactly the same time.

As classical music had never done, as the most popular music of any other country or race, even jazz, or any individual — Bing Crosby, Elvis Presley, Frank Sinatra — had never done, the Beatles' music flew through young and old, rich and poor, the snobs and the anything-goes brigade.

I remember being startled to see the Beatles exhibited next to Bach in a very highbrow music store that would not have dreamt of stocking any 'popular music' and had never heard of Scott Joplin. Even George Gershwin was barely on the right side of the tracks.

The Beatles were just in time for my company. They played and sang just how we wanted to feel more often, and, with a little help from our friends and them, we often did. They cheered us up. As all music threatens to do. Only music that comes from God, according to Bach, is music.

Their music is now taught in schools, imitated in concert halls and sung in cathedrals. They sang for all the lonely people they sang about. Even the old began to realise that they were not trying to do them in. They embraced R&B, Broadway and English pop. There was nothing you could hold against them. They came from the underprivileged classes, they were definitely white, yet they were not singing against or for any class or sectarian interest. They were not so poor that they had to bore the rich by singing about poverty. They came out of the fibrillating heartland of capitalism, yet they were not chanting the dirges of desolation or disappearing in puffs of smoke through their transcendental arseholes.

I knew that the Beatles were going to be a lasting phenomenon when I saw my then three-year-old sister playing with Beatles images and talking to them as if they were real. – *Camille Paglia*

They were beyond in more than they knew. You would not seek me if you had not already found me, goes an old saying. They sought and did not find, and in so doing, millions found in them the expression of their seeking.

For a few years, they combined the lowest common denominator with the highest common factor. They were the first group to send out sounds that reverberated and resonated within, and thereby united, so many hearts at the same time.

A.S. Neill, a pioneer of 'free education', a pupil and friend of Wilhelm Reich, told me, when he was over 80, that the greatest compliment of his life was that at the end of World War II he was refused entry into the USA and the USSR at the same time. The Beatles expressed the same theories as Reich and Neill. And in England, the story goes that they were lucky to get out of America on their last tour there because John Lennon had declared they were more popular than Jesus Christ. That's the sort of statement they lived for, and he died for.

> *We strung our tears among the stars*
> *And laughed with the light of the moon*
> *They sang for the divas*
> *And the divas sang for them*
> *The infinity of om.*

419

However, in case this sounds too much of a eulogy, the Beatles never caught right into my lead belly and gutted me out. But they were not too young to love or to console an old, tired 30-year-old heart like mine, and they kept up a whistle on the long, long way to Tipperary.

Rolling Stone, 16 February 1984

FIGHTING THE FAB
By Philip Larkin

Curmudgeonly poet Larkin was, perhaps surprisingly, one of the older cultural commentators who took the Beatles seriously. Here he writes in his other capacity, as a newspaper music (mainly jazz) critic.

. . .Only of course they were not altogether ordinary young men. The music that made them famous was an enchanting and intoxicating hybrid of Negro rock and roll with their own adolescent romanticism. The Lennon-McCartney collaboration produced a series of love songs that appealed to the highest in the land as directly as to the Liverpool typists in the Cavern at lunchtime, in a manner that constituted the first advance in popular music since the war. This cannot be gainsaid.

. . .At the same time, they remained individuals. Instead of riding their early successes on ever-more-deafening tours, they defiantly 'went private' to concentrate on doing their own thing, or Lennon and McCartney's own things, in the recording studio. 'Please please me' was displaced by surreal lyrics, mystic orientalia, peace messages and anti–American outbursts. The trouble was that as surrealists, mystics or political thinkers the Beatles were rather ordinary young men again. Their fans stayed with them, and the nuttier intelligentsia, but they lost the typists in the Cavern.

. . .The decade from their break-up in 1970 until the murder of Lennon in 1980 makes a sorry, fragmentary story. . .All four Beatles continued to make records, but never has a whole been greater than its parts.

. . .So gigantic a success as theirs seems like the tapping of some unsuspected socio-emotional pressure that when released swept them completely away from their natural artistic context to perish in the rarefied atmosphere of hagiolatry. The four tiny figures, jerking and gesticulating inaudibly at the centre of larger and larger stadiums of screaming, were destroyed (in Lennon's case literally) by their own legend.

When you get to the top, there is nowhere to go but down, but the Beatles could not get down. There they remain, unreachable, frozen, fabulous.

The Observer, 9 October 1983

THE SOUND OF THE SIXTIES
By Blake Morrison

This insightful, posthumous overview of the Beatles' career, by Northern English poet and novelist Morrison, appeared within a few months of John Lennon's death.

The question is not, as it used to be, 'Why did the Beatles break up so quickly?' but 'How did they keep going for as long as they did?' Ten years is a long time in rock music, and the Beatles not only spanned the 1960s, but managed to become peculiarly identified with them: for many people, as we're frequently told, the spirit of the decade was to be found in their music, and still is, as in no other cultural form. Yet the irony is that the Beatles saw less of the decade than most of us, or, rather, saw it in what was literally an artificial light: through the smoked windscreens of security vehicles; in cellars, nightclubs, recording studios and floodlit stadia; from hotel rooms they didn't dare leave. Little wonder that their music should have hankered for a fine and private place out of reach of their admirers – 'A place where I can go', 'a place to hide away.' And yet it was precisely their ability to stay imaginatively in the open, to stay responsive to other people's worlds, whether those of Radio Luxemburg listeners, Swinging Londoners, hippy travellers, university history men, not to mention the ordinary millions who didn't conform to these clichéd 1960s types, that gave them their success. They may not have been exceptionally original; but a combination of astute management, an instinct for keeping always one step ahead of current trends, and an energy and inventiveness fostered by a tough apprenticeship in Hamburg, enabled them to survive the 1960s and to give the decade an image of itself it was prepared to accept.

Looking back at the Beatles' early songs, one would have to admit that they augured very little. They belong, fairly routinely, to that Petrarchan tradition – the democratic version of Courtly Love – that has always dominated popular music. Accusations of cruel treatment and inconstancy ('now today I find/ you have changed your mind'), proclamations of pain and suffering ('the world is treating me bad, misery'), proprietorial admonitions ('It's the second time I caught you talking to him/ Do I have to tell you one more time I think it's a sin'), importuning of the love-me-do variety: there is nothing very distinctive here. Phones ring out in empty rooms; fickle girls buy tickets to elsewhere; and above all there are the letters home, the male itinerant forbidding mourning and assuring his mistress of undying love ('I'll be coming home again to you love/ Until the day I do love/ PS I love you', 'While I'm away/ I'll write home every day/ And I'll send all my loving to you'). Many of these songs were written during the Beatles' apprenticeship in Hamburg, when John Lennon was separated from his fianceé (and later wife) Cynthia and the other Beatles from their families and girlfriends, which may explain the occasionally authentic note of loneliness and self-pity. But there was mostly a bland familiarity about these songs, in keeping with the group's reassuring moptop image. At a time, the early 1960s, when the sexual morals of teenagers were under intense public scrutiny, here was a music you could trust your daughter with: it wanted to hold her hand and nothing more.

Or so it seemed. In fact this was a music with its fingers well above the stocking top. The opening words of the Beatles' first LP were a nudge in the ribs and a knowing leer – 'Well she was just seventeen/ You know what I mean.' 'Please Please Me', their first Number One single, had strong suggestions, for those who cared to notice, of heavy petting, its singer a frustrated male who can't get his girlfriend to do back to him what he's doing to her. When Peter Sellers did a comic spoken version of 'A Hard Day's Night', with smutty pauses ('When I'm home, feeling you. . .'), he wasn't traducing the original but drawing out a sexuality already there. The Beatles rather enjoyed the gap between what they were actually getting up to and what Brian Epstein, with his promotion of the lovable Fab Four, pretended they were. In the middle eight of 'Girl' they sang 'tit-tit-tit-tit' in the background; the 'big teaser' of printed versions of 'Day Tripper', was in fact a 'prick teaser'; and there was the 'finger pie' of 'Penny Lane', an obscenity they got away with because it wasn't widely known in the South.

The Beatles thrived on such deception: it corresponded to the difference between their role-playing at press conferences, all wholesome wisecracking, and the reality backstage. John Lennon later compared that reality to the *Satyricon* – 'We were the Caesars. . .the kings of the jungle.' And it was as much a matter of violence as of sex. A sixteen-year-old was booted to death during one of their concerts in 1960; in Hamburg bouncers patrolled the stage with coshes and knuckledusters; once, on the South Coast, the then-famous Fab Four set on an elderly journalist, breaking one of his toes. It was Hamburg which first licensed their licence: they had the kind of rampaging disrespect for abroad and its customs that English football supporters still feel today. On Sundays John Lennon would taunt local churchgoers from a balcony, on one occasion urinating on the heads of three nuns. It was the first of many anti-

Christian gestures on Lennon's part, and in it he resembled those seventeenth-century Court Wits prosecuted for gathering on a balcony to expose themselves and throw wine bottles down into the crowd.

Despite these anarchic elements in the Beatles' lives, and with the exception of the genuine feeling behind Lennon's song 'Help!', it was not until the middle albums of 1965–66, *Revolver* and *Rubber Soul*, that their songs began to move beyond the bittersweet round of boy-girl relations. These were the years of 'Swinging London', and part of the reason London was swinging lay in the fact that the Beatles had moved there or thereabouts: Paul to St John's Wood and the other three to the Surrey stockbroker belt. It was the stuff of fiction, specifically English fiction of the previous decade, with its tales of upward and Southward mobility. The new songs began to reflect the Beatles' working-boys-made-good success, contemplating what wealth made possible ('Baby you can drive my car/ Yes I'm gonna be a star'), and what it did not ('I don't care too much for money/ Money can't buy me love'). The love songs were more self-assured, even cynical: 'Norwegian Wood', for example, was a disguised account by Lennon of an affair he'd had, the inspired title simultaneously mocking current trends in interior design and playing with popular myths about Scandinavian sexual promiscuity. Above all there was an edge of comedy and satire. 'Paperback Writer', with its convincingly wheedling persona ('I can make it longer if you like the style') was in part a joke about the literary ambitions behind Lennon's *In His Own Write*, 1964, a book praised in the *TLS* as 'remarkable'. It was also, no doubt, aimed at the growing number of journalists offering to write the Beatles' story. 'Taxman' expressed the group's resentment at its squandered fortune (punitive business deals and the Inland Revenue had by then already deprived the Beatles of millions) but transformed it into more populist anti-bureaucratic sentiment. 'Nowhere Man', an Auden-like smack at the bored, unimportant dork of popular mythology, also had its anti-bureaucratic elements, but qualified the attack by asking, rhetorically, 'Isn't he a bit like you and me?' and through a soft-hearted la-la-la chorus. If there was little bite to all this, even that seemed the right, topical note, in keeping with the accommodating ethos of the newly-elected Labour government. An establishment itself enamoured of the Beatles (several MPs and members of the Royal Family confessed to being fans) wasn't to be subjected to anything very threatening.

Some of this mutual tolerance disappeared in 1967 with the release of the *Sergeant Pepper* album and the Beatles' admission that they had recently 'experimented' with LSD. This was what you said you did with the drug in those days: it sounded more edifying than merely 'taking' it. But in fact the Beatles had always taken drugs, for various purposes and of various kinds: uppers, downers; purple hearts, black bombers, yellow submarines; and marijuana. In Hamburg, John Lennon had once consumed so many pills that he came on stage naked, foaming at the mouth and with a lavatory seat round his neck. But only now was the drug-taking officially in the open and reflected in their songs. The subsequent talk of the brave new hallucinogenic world opened up by *Sergeant Pepper* was almost wholly misplaced. For the Beatles' psychedelic landscape was more Lewis Carroll than William Burroughs; all that they'd done was to re-open the nursery door. 'Marmalade skies', 'newspaper taxis', 'rocking horse people', 'kaleidoscope eyes', 'marshmallow pies': it wasn't a cleansing of per-ception but a visit to toytown. Even the less childlike songs turn out to have had humdrum origins. 'Being for the Benefit of Mr Kite' were words found on a poster; 'Strawberry Fields' was the name of a Liverpool orphanage; the 4000 holes in Blackburn, Lancashire (from 'A Day in the Life') were thought by many to have been caused by heroin needles, but had actually appeared in a newspaper report. For all their supposed expansion into dream worlds, the Beatles remained securely down-to-earth.

The Beatles planted the seeds of rebellion against what was expected of you. And that you could come from a little neighbourhood and take over the world. – *Bono*

The same Scouse nous soon asserted itself in their dealings with the Maharishi Mahesh Yogi, with whom they were briefly infatuated in late 1967 and early 1968, Worshipped themselves to the point where cripples and epilep-tics used to be brought backstage after concerts to be given their healing touch, they were ripe for a flirtation with higher powers. At the height of their mate-rial success, they were taught by the Maharishi to doubt the existence of the material world: that 'nothing is real' was for a time one of their dominant themes. But for three of the group disaffection came quickly: after a spell in India, where they renounced the world and competed with each other to see who could meditate longest, Ringo Starr returned complaining of the spicy food, and Lennon and McCartney soon followed, John denouncing the Maharishi as a fraud and lecher. Later the group paid him back by casting him in the ludicrous guise of 'Sexy Sadie' – 'you made a fool of everyone.'

The Beatles' songs had always been full of such covert allusions, and by now it was becoming respectable to treat them seriously. As early as 1963 William Mann had detected 'chains of pandiatonic clusters' in one song and 'an Aeolian cadence' in another; then Tony Palmer compared the gifts of Lennon and

McCartney to those of Schubert; later Wilfrid Mellers was to subject their music to a full-length book study, *Twilight of the Gods*, arguing that 'the basic Beatles song is Edenic'. The lyrics, too, were granted the status of poetry. American campus courses with titles like 'The Poetry of Relevance' ranked the Beatles, Bob Dylan and Leonard Cohen with Blake and Shelley. In Britain, Karl Miller's 1968 anthology *Writing in England Today: The Last Fifteen Years* included the Beatles' 'Eleanor Rigby' and the Pink Floyd's 'Arnold Layne' alongside Golding, Osborne and Larkin. 'She's Leaving Home', with its intriguing 'man from the motor trade' (actually Terry Doran, one of the Beatles' entourage) might have been an equally plausible candidate, for both these Lennon-McCartney songs touched on the sadness of ordinary life – 'all the lonely people' – in a way that Larkin's poetry had also done (it was no surprise, either, that 'the Beatles' first LP' should later make an appearance in Larkin's poem 'Annus Mirabilis').

John and I sat down on 295 occasions. On every occasion we sat down, we only spent about three hours and we never ever came out without a song. It is very lucky but we were good and it was a passion. We loved doing it and it sure beat working.
– *Paul McCartney, 2001*

The Beatles themselves remained relatively unmoved by this intellectual acclaim, as they also were by the Foyles launches of Lennon's books and by a dinner given in their honour at Brasenose College, Oxford. They were anti-academic (just before his death John Lennon was still talking of 'intellectual artsy-fartsies') and they rather resented ingenious interpretations of their songs. Lennon's track 'Glass Onion' on 'The White Album' teased the interpreters ('Here's another clue for you all/ The Walrus was Paul'), but even this trick backfired, initiating the famous rumour that Paul McCartney was dead and that proof of the fact could be gleaned from Beatles' songs and album covers.

This last phase of their career as a group coincided with political unrest throughout Europe and in the United States and the Beatles were put under pressure to declare their allegiances. Up until now, and long before Lennon released his track 'Working Class Hero', a tag which he incidentally had the least claim to (the home he grew up in, his Aunt Mimi's, was a solid semi-detached in a respectable suburb), the Beatles had been closely identified with the Labour government, whose leader had his constituency in Huyton and whose party slogan – 'Let's Go With Labour' – was aimed at pop fans. After 1967, however, they liked to be seen as embracing radical ideals outside the party system. Their business venture, Apple, its name inspired by Paul McCartney's enthusiasm for a Magritte painting, was in large part simply a means of exerting control over their own finances, which had been chaotic for too long; but they saw it also, more ambitiously, as what McCartney described as 'a controlled weirdness. . .a kind of Western Communism' and what Lennon called an attempt to wrest capital from 'the men in suits'. Lennon also became a popular campaigning figure, supporting James Hanratty's parents, American Indians and (more dubiously) Michael X. Such was his political charisma that *Rolling Stone* in 1970 named Lennon its 'Man of the Year' and suggested 'a five hour talk between John Lennon and Richard Nixon would be more significant than any Geneva Summit Conference between the USA and Russia.' The success of 'All You Need Is Love' – a single on which 'She Loves You' can at one point be heard playing in the background, as if to indicate the group's development from songs of teenage coupledom to ones of universal togetherness – encouraged the Beatles to try their hand at sloganising. But such songs had a habit of slipping from under them. 'Come Together', as Lennon admitted, 'was intended as a campaign song but it never turned out that way.' 'Get Back' ('to where you once belonged') tried to send up Powell-like racism, but Yoko Ono – by now Lennon's constant companion, even, to the chagrin of the others, at recording sessions – wondered whether it wasn't aimed at her. 'Give Peace a Chance' became a favourite of American protest marchers, but in Britain soccer supporters reclaimed it for the terraces ('All we are saying/ Is give us a goal'). Most symptomatic of all was 'Revolution', from 'The White Album'. In one version Lennon sang, 'count me in,' in a second, 'count me out.' Finally the 'out' seemed to weigh more heavily:

> But if you want money for people with minds that hate
> All I can tell you is brother you have to wait. . .

The story of the Beatles' lives and lyrics seems to suggest that their secret was to be all things to all men. If their music gave pleasure, that was partly because people could find in it what they wanted to find, could go to it for a confirmation of their own attitudes, however contradictory these might be. Many people in the 1960s, certainly those in their teens and twenties, were tempted to believe that the Beatles in some way acted, spoke and sang on their behalf. The truth seems to be that the group stood for very little at all, merely clarified the options. Sexual freedom, experimentation with drugs, political commitment, transcendental religion, counter-cultural activity of all kinds: their songs simultaneously incited us to try these things, and warned that we'd in the end be disappointed, as they had been, The ambivalence was the appeal.

Times Literary Supplement, 15 May 1981

AFTERWORD

What resonates most throughout this anthology is the shared sense of surprise: the surprise of the pop music industry as the Beatles first stormed the charts; the multiple surprises that accompanied the release of each new Beatles album; the surprise of critics and intellectuals that rock'n'roll might be of some value, after all.

My own experience on first hearing the Beatles was no exception. Back in 1962, I was what Lennon would have regarded as a jazz snob. Rock'n'roll for me had finished in the late Fifties; Buddy Holly was dead; Elvis was never the same after he went into the Army; Top 20 hits by Fats Domino, Little Richard and Jerry Lee Lewis were a thing of the past. In a world where pop had come to mean pap, jazz and R&B were the hip religion, Ray Charles and Charles Mingus its high priests.

So it was with some reluctance that I allowed a girlfriend to drag me to the Cavern, to hear a pop group with an awful pun for a name. I was stunned – first of all by the volume (nobody played that loud in those days), by their sheer energy, their riveting charisma, but most of all by their unique interpretation of what had seemed to be unrepeatable rock'n'roll classics.

When, a couple of months later, I took the same girl to a Little Richard concert (she didn't have to be dragged there – 'the boys' were fourth on the bill), her reaction afterwards was that the headliner, who she'd never heard of before, was great – because 'he sang all Beatles songs'!

From there on in, they never ceased to surprise all of us, with their consistently inventive songwriting, their wit, their lack of pretension, and their innovations in the recording studio. But, most surprisingly of all, as all of the writings in this book testify, they changed our lives.

Mike Evans, 2004

CONTRIBUTORS

Alan Aldridge is an artist and illustrator. His famous 1969 anthology, *The Beatles Illustrated Lyrics*, variously showed the influences of pop art, comic books and LSD.

Tariq Ali was born in Lahore and educated at Oxford, where he joined the anti-Vietnam war movement. As a writer-broadcaster, his interests are politics and Islamic history.

Glenn A. Baker is an Australian rock journalist and disc jockey. He is also the author of *Monkeemania*, a study of American TV's ersatz Beatles, published by Plexus.

Nicholas Barber writes for *The Guardian, The Scotsman, Esquire, The Independent* and *The Independent on Sunday*. He was the latter's pop critic from 1994 to 2000, and is now a film critic.

Carol Bedford was an American teenager when the Beatles 'invaded' in 1964. Her memoir of the era, *Waiting for the Beatles*, captures the hysteria of Beatlemania.

Carl Belz is editor-in-chief of Art New England and Director Emeritus of the Rose Art Museum at Brandeis University, MA. In the late 1960s, he wrote *The Story of Rock*.

Leonard Bernstein was a musical polymath: director of the New York Philharmonic Orchestra, composer of orchestral symphonies, and of hit musicals like *West Side Story*.

Pete Best was the original full-time drummer of the Beatles until his sacking in 1962. He currently plays in his Merseybeat revival outfit, the Pete Best Band.

Robin Blackburn is Professor of Sociology at the University of Essex. He has written studies of capitalism and the slave trade, and is consulting editor at *Verso* with Tariq Ali.

John Blake is a former UK pop journalist for the *London Evening Standard* and *The Sun*. In the early 1990s, he founded the tabloid-oriented John Blake Publishing.

Michael Braun wrote the first serious book on the Beatles, who reputedly wrote 'Paperback Writer' about him. He later had a career in film and theatre, and died in 1997.

Peter Brown was the director of the Apple Corporation, representing the Beatles' business interests. He now lives in New York where he is the director of a PR company.

William F. Buckley is a US columnist and author. He founded the conservative journal *National Review*, and can be seen every week on the PBS TV show *Firing Line*.

Abram Chasins is a classical pianist, composer and author. He has written several books on his chosen field, and is married to acclaimed concert pianist Constance Keene.

Robert Christgau is acclaimed as 'the Dean of American Rock Critics'. He has written for New York's *Village Voice* since 1969 and authored a number of books on rock music.

Maureen Cleave was the first journalist outside of Liverpool to write about the Beatles, for London's *Evening Standard*.

Nik Cohn is an English author living in the US. His writings on pop culture include 'Tribal Rites of the New Saturday Night', the article that inspired *Saturday Night Fever*.

Ray Coleman edited UK music paper *Melody Maker* for many years. His *Lennon* won the co-operation of Yoko Ono, and he also wrote biographies of McCartney and Epstein.

Ray Connolly is a veteran UK newspaper journalist and novelist. He also wrote the screenplays for cult rock movies *That'll Be the Day* (featuring Ringo Starr) and *Stardust*.

Jonathan Cott is an author and longtime contributing editor to *Rolling Stone*. His music interviews, collected in *Back to a Shadow in the Night*, range from Lennon to Bernstein.

Noel Coward was an eminent British actor/playwright. From *enfant terrible* to star of musical theatre, he courted controversy.

Hunter Davies is a UK journalist who has worked for the *Sunday Times* and *Punch*. His books include the authorised Beatles biography and a history of Tottenham Hotspur FC.

Robin Denselow has been a rock writer for *The Guardian* and a political reporter for BBC1's *Panorama*. He is currently international correspondent for BBC2's *Newsnight*.

Richard Dilello was the house hippie at the Apple Corporation.

Peter Doggett is the former editor of *Record Collector*. His books include *Let It Be/Abbey Road*, on the final Beatles albums, and *Growing Up in Public*, about Lou Reed.

Patrick Doncaster was a British tabloid journalist. He was Pete Best's collaborator on his autobiography, but died in 1984 before the book's completion.

Brian Epstein was the Beatles' manager for six years. He was integral in their transformation into a cultural phenomenon. Epstein was found dead from a prescription drug overdose on 27 August 1967, aged 32.

Mike Evans was a 1960s Liverpool poet, and saxophonist in the Liverpool Scene music-poetry ensemble. As a rock writer, his works include *The Art of the Beatles* and *Elvis: A Celebration*.

Simon Frith wrote regularly for the 1970s music press. He is Professor of Film and Media at the University of Stirling and chairman of the Mercury Music Prize committee.

John Gabree is a US journalist and a reviewer for *New York Newsday*. His books include *World of Rock*, *Gangsters from Little Caesar to The Godfather* and *Surviving the City*.

Charlie Gillett is an innovative UK radio broadcaster and author of *The Sound of the City*, a rock'n'roll history. His record company, Oval, released a series of tie-in albums.

Mitchell Glazer was a 1970s rock writer on *Crawdaddy* magazine. His 1977 cover feature on comedian John Belushi was followed by a book on *The Blues Brothers*.

Leonard Gross was the European editor of *Look* magazine in the 1960s and 70s, whose interviewees included Prince Charles. His books include *The Last Jews in Berlin*.

Adrian Henri was a prolific painter and poet, and a performer in the Liverpool Scene. He died in December 2000, after he was awarded the Freedom of the City of Liverpool.

Howard Horne was Professor of Sociology at the University of Warwick. He is the co-author, with Simon Frith, of *Welcome to Bohemia!*, a doctoral thesis, and *Art into Pop*.

Chris Hutchins is a veteran UK tabloid journalist. He has written popular biographies of such prominent figures as Princess Diana, Sir James Goldsmith and the Onassis family.

Paul Johnson was the editor of the left-wing *New Statesman*, before defecting to Thatcherism in the 1970s. As a historian, his works include the acclaimed *Modern Times*.

Phil Johnson writes about music and the arts for *The Independent* and *The Independent on Sunday*. He is also the author of *Straight Outta Bristol*, a book about the Bristol music scene.

Jack Jones has won awards for his writings on the US penal system. He conducted interviews with the 'Son of Sam', and the killer of John Lennon, in Attica state prison.

Pauline Kael was the doyenne of film critics from 1968-1991, while writing for the *New Yorker*. Her opinionated reviews are reprinted in titles such as *5001 Nights at the Movies*.

Dave Laing has written about rock from a sociological or Marxian perspective. He is the co-author of books such as *The Faber Companion* to *Twentieth Century Popular Music*.

R. D. Laing was renowned for his controversial psychiatric theories. His works include *The Divided Self*, *Knots*, and an album of verse and music entitled *Life Before Death*.

Philip Larkin was Britain's poet of everyday life, musing on its disappointments. He also worked as a librarian, reviewed jazz, and declined the post of poet laureate.

Jerry Lazar is a journalist specialising in popular culture, largely films and TV. He has written for a range of publications including *Vogue*, *Film Comment* and *US*.

Cynthia Lennon attended Liverpool College of Art with John Lennon, and later became his first wife. She is the mother of his eldest son, Julian.

John Lennon was born on 9 October 1940. As the founder of the Beatles, his partnership with Paul McCartney became the most famous songwriting team in the world. He died on 8 December 1980, murdered by a deranged fan.

Bernard Levin began writing for the UK broadsheet newspapers in 1953. Noted for his wit, he has been a book, TV and theatre critic, and chief columnist of the *London Times*.

Mark Lewisohn is a former contributor to *Beatles Monthly* and the author of two books, *The Complete Beatles Recording Sessions* and *The Complete Beatles Chronicle*.

William Mann was the music correspondent of the *London Times*. His locating of 'pandiatonic clusters' helped legitimise the Beatles' music for intellectuals.

Charles Marowitz has directed and written West End and Broadway plays. He has written extensively on the theatre, and was the drama critic of the *LA Herald Examiner*.

George Martin was the director of Parlophone, an EMI records subsidiary, when he signed the Beatles. His skilled arrangements and experimentalism as a producer earned a knighthood for services to the British record industry.

Pete McCabe was born in Liverpool and educated at Cambridge. He worked at Reuters before becoming a contributing editor to *Rolling Stone*, *Penthouse* and *Harpers*.

George Melly has been a surrealist art collector, jazz and blues singer, and film/TV critic. In his eighth decade, he is currently preparing his latest volume of autobiography.

Richard Meryman was an interviewer for *Life* magazine before becoming a freelance writer. His works include a study of alcoholism and a memoir of marital bereavement.

Barry Miles co-founded *International Times* in 1960s London. He has written books on the Beat poets, and the best-selling biography *Paul McCartney: Many Years from Now*.

Adrian Mitchell is a performance poet and playwright. Since his lyrics for the 1966 anti-war show *US*, his populist style has combined humour and song with apocalyptic satire.

Lilith Moon is a pseudonym popularly used by Wiccan witches and eco-feminists. In the mid-1970s it was adopted by an unidentified contributor to *Creem*.

Blake Morrison is a Yorkshire-born poet. His books include *The Ballad of the Yorkshire Ripper* and the factual work *As If* – about the Bulger murder that traumatised Liverpool.

Charles P. Neises edited *The Beatles Reader: A Selection of Contemporary Views, News and Reviews of the Beatles in Their Heyday*, published in 1984.

Philip Norman is a former *Sunday Times* journalist who conducted a series of interviews with the Beatles. He has written biographies of the Beatles, the Stones, and Buddy Holly.

Jeff Nuttall emerged from the 1960s British underground as a painter and co-founder of the People Show theatrical troupe. His book *Bomb Culture* was debated in Parliament.

Vance Packard was a US pop-sociologist. His best-selling study of advertising, *The Hidden Persuaders*, set the tone for gently alarmist books about consumer society.

Tony Palmer is a film and theatrical director. His 1960s/70s pop music documentaries, *All My Loving* and *All You Need Is Love*, pay titular homage to the Beatles.

John Piccarella was a rock journalist from 1976-1991, for the *Village Voice*, *Rolling Stone*, *New York Rocker* and the *Boston Phoenix*.

Stanley Reynolds was an expatriate American journalist who regularly contributed to the *Manchester Guardian*.

Robert Sandall is chief rock critic for the *Sunday Times*, and the director of publicity for Virgin Records in London.

Ed Sanders is a lifelong member of the counterculture, and founder of 1960s New York anarcho-folk band the Fugs. His writings include *The Family* and *Tales of Beatnik Glory*.

Jon Savage became a music journalist during the punk era. He wrote *England's Dreaming*, a history of that period, and an award-winning documentary on Brian Epstein.

Jean Shepherd was a US talk-radio innovator, weaving fictitious autobiography and surrealism into his night-time show. He wrote for the *Village Voice*, *Mad* and *Playboy*.

Giles Smith is the former keyboard player of the Cleaners from Venus. Their failure to 'go global' pushed him into journalism and prompted his first book, *Lost in Music*.

Gloria Steinem is a founding mother of modern feminism. A lifelong campaigner for equal rights for all, as a journalist she co-founded *Ms.* and *New York* magazines.

Alistair Taylor was first employed by Brian Epstein in 1960. He later became a personal assistant to the Beatles until his sacking by their new manager, Allen Klein, in 1969.

Derek Taylor was the Beatles' PR agent, and later a director of Apple. He maintained lifelong links, contributing to the Anthology CD/book/TV series before his death in 1997.

Paul Theroux is an American travel writer and novelist, whose notable fiction includes *The Mosquito Coast*. He is the father of British TV personality Louis Theroux.

Peter Thompson is the co-author, with Chris Hutchins, of *Elvis Meets the Beatles*, plus biographies of Princess Diana, Lady Sarah Ferguson and the Onassis family.

Steve Turner is a veteran rock interviewer who has written for *NME*, *Q* and *Rolling Stone*. His books include *A Hard Day's Write* and *Conversations with Eric Clapton*.

Kenneth Tynan was *The Observer*'s esteemed theatre critic, 1950–63. He collaborated in founding the British National Theatre, and created the erotic revue *Oh! Calcutta!*

Penny Valentine was the first noted British woman rock journalist, co-founder of *City Limits* magazine, and authorial collaborator on Dusty Springfield's autobiography. She died in early 2003.

Andy Warhol was the most successful pop artist, and the enigmatic founder of a multi-million dollar empire. He survived a near-fatal 1968 shooting, but died from illness in 1987.

Jann S. Wenner launched *Rolling Stone* at age twenty. He introduced writers such as Hunter S. Thompson and P. J. O'Rourke, and now presides over Wenner Media Inc.

Jon Wiener is an academic and a left-wing journalist for *The Nation* and *The New Republic*. His words of dissent are anthologised in *Professors, Politics and Pop*.

Richard Williams is former editor of the UK's *Melody Maker* and *Time Out*, now chief sports writer for *The Guardian*. He is also the biographer of Phil Spector and Bob Dylan.

Michael Wood is the head of the English department at Princeton University. Born in England and educated at Cambridge, he is the author of *America in the Movies*.

Andrew Yule is an entertainment biographer and a native of Scotland. His subjects include Richard Lester, Sean Connery, and Scottish comedian Chic Murray.

INDEX

ACKNOWLEDGEMENTS

Colin Webb is responsible for the idea behind this book, which came about in a discussion one evening at the Frankfurt Book Fair. We salute him. Our aim was to present a collection containing some of the best writing on the Beatles of the last 40 years, spanning the whole of their career and beyond. It sounded a good idea at the time, but nothing could have prepared us for the enormity of the job. We were lucky to find Mike Evans, with his extraordinary knowledge of the Beatles and the era that they dominated, who was able to track down an amazing range of materials; we are also indebted to Paul Woods, who was dogged in clearing permissions, assisting Mike in his selections, and choosing the quotations that run throughout.

Many people helped to bring this anthology together and special thanks are due to: the *Playboy* corporation, John Blake, Tony Palmer, Harvey Weinig, Tim Hailstone, Steve Turner, Robin Denselow, Jeff Nuttall, Ray Connolly, Robert Sandall, Simon Frith and Howard Horne, Pete Best, Tariq Ali and Robin Blackburn, Jonathan Cott, Robert Christgau and John Piccarella, Adrian Mitchell, the estate of Derek Taylor, the estate of Leonard Bernstein, Mark Lewisohn, Carl Belz, Tim De Lisle, Peter Doggett and Alan Aldridge.

We must also acknowledge Elizabeth Thomson and David Gutman's anthology *The Lennon Companion*, Macmillan, 1987; *The Beatles Reader*, edited by Charles P. Neises, Popular Culture, Ink, 1984, 1991; *The Age of Rock*, edited by Jonathan Eisen, Vintage Books, 1969. Much time was spent at the British Library and the National Sound Archive. Our thanks to their staff.

It has not been possible to trace the copyright owners of every piece included here, and we would be pleased to hear from any unacknowledged copyright holders.

Acknowledgement is hereby made to the following for permission:
John Lennon 1940–1980, Ray Connolly, Fontana Paperbacks, 1981. By permission of the author.
A Twist of Lennon, Cynthia Lennon, Virgin Books, 1978.
'The Arty Teddy Boy', Mike Evans, *The Lennon Companion* edited by Elizabeth Thompson and David Gutman, Macmillan, 1987. By permission of the author.

Art into Pop, Simon Frith and Howard Horne, Routledge, 1987. By permission of the authors.
A Cellarful of Noise, Brian Epstein, Souvenir Press, 1964. By permission of the publisher.
Beatle! The Pete Best Story, Pete Best and Patrick Doncaster, Plexus, 1985. By permission of the publisher.
'Why the Beatles Create All That Frenzy', Maureen Cleave, *Evening Standard*, 2 February 1963.
The Sound of the City, Charlie Gillett, Souvenir Press, 1970. Reprinted by permission of the publisher.
'Twist and Shout', Phil Johnson, *Lives of the Great Songs*, edited by Tim De Lisle, Pavilion, 1994. Reprinted by permission of the author and editor.
'Big Time', Stanley Reynolds, *The Guardian*, 3 June 1963. Reprinted by permission.
The Love You Make, Peter Brown, Macmillan, 1983.
Love Me Do: The Beatles' Progress, Michael Braun, Penguin, 1964. Reprinted by kind permission of Jonathon Clowes Ltd, London. Copyright © 1964 The Estate of Michael Braun.
A Secret History, Alistair Taylor, John Blake Publishing, 2001. Reprinted by permission.
Shout! The True Story of The Beatles, Philip Norman, Hamish Hamilton/Penguin, 1981. Reprinted by permission.
'Building the Beatle Image', Vance Packard, *Saturday Evening Post,* 1964. Reprinted by permission.
'Why We Loved the Beatles', Paul Theroux, *Rolling Stone*, 16 February 1984. Reprinted by permission.
Waiting For The Beatles: *An Apple Scruff's Story*, Carol Bedford, Blandford/Cassell, 1984.
Beatles Down Under: 1964 Australian and New Zealand Tour, Glenn A. Baker, Pierian Press, 1986.
The Man Who Framed the Beatles, Andrew Yule, Donald I. Fine, Inc., 1994.
'Beatle with a Future', Gloria Steinem, *Cosmopolitan*, 1964. Reprinted by permission of the author.
'Neville Club', John Lennon, *In His Own Write*, Jonathan Cape, 1964. Reprinted by permission of The Random House Group Ltd.
'*Playboy* Interview with the Beatles', Jean Shepherd, *Playboy Magazine,* February 1965. Copyright © 1965; 1993 by *Playboy*. Reprinted with permission. All rights reserved.

'The Menace of Beatlism', Paul Johnson, *New Statesman*, 28 February 1964. Reprinted by permission.

'Joint Honours', Robert Sandall, *Mojo*, February 2002. Reprinted by permission of the author.

The Noel Coward Diaries, edited by Graham Payn and Sheridan Morley, Weidenfeld and Nicolson, 1982. Reprinted by permission of the publisher.

'Yesterday', Giles Smith, *Lives of the Great Songs*, edited by Tim De Lisle, Pavilion, 1994. Reprinted by permission of the author and editor.

'John Lennon's School Days', Michael Wood, *New Society*, 27 June 1968. Reprinted by permission.

'*Help!*' Kenneth Tynan, *Tynan Right and Left*, Kenneth Tynan, Longman, 1967.

'High-Brows vs No-Brows', Abram Chasins, *McCall's Magazine*, September 1965.

'Elvis Meets the Beatles: Uncensored', Chris Hutchins and Peter Thompson, *Elvis Meets the Beatles* Chris Hutchins, Smith Gryphon Ltd/Blake Publishing, 1994. Reprinted by permission of the publisher.

'High Times', Mark Lewisohn, *Mojo*, February 2002. Reprinted by permission.

'How Does a Beatle Live? John Lennon Lives Like This', Maureen Cleave, *Evening Standard*, 4 March 1966.

'First Steps Toward Radical Politics: The 1966 Tour', Jon Wiener, *Come Together: John Lennon in His Time*, Jon Wiener, Faber and Faber Ltd, 1984. Reprinted by permission of the publisher.

Revolt into Style, George Melly, Allen Lane, 1970. Reprinted by permission of A. M. Heath & Co. Ltd. Copyright © 1972 by George Melly.

'Eleanor Rigby', Steve Turner, *A Hard Day's Write*, Steve Turner, Carlton Publishing, 1994. Reprinted by kind permission of the author and publisher.

Bomb Culture, Jeff Nuttall, McGibbon and Kee, 1968. Reprinted by kind permission of the authors.

'Portrait of the Artist as a Rock & Roll Star', Robert Christgau and John Piccarella, *The Ballad of John and Yoko*, the Editors of *Rolling Stone*, Doubleday/Dolphin/Rolling Stone, 1982. Reprinted by permission of the authors.

'Interview with John Lennon', Leonard Gross, *Look Magazine*, 13 December 1966.

'Private on Parade', Jon Savage, *Mojo,* February 2002. Reprinted by permission.

'Going Underground', Barry Miles, *Mojo*, February 2002. Reprinted by permission.

All You Need Is Ears, George Martin, Macmillan, 1979. Reprinted by permission of Curtis Brown Ltd, London on behalf of George Martin. Copyright © 1979 by Maria Coffey.

'Beatles Not All That Turned On', Alan Aldridge, *Washington Post*, 1969. Reprinted by permission.

Awopbopaloobop Alopbamboom, Nik Cohn, Weidenfeld and Nicolson, 1969. Reprinted by permission of the author and his agent.

Yesterday: The Beatles Remembered, Alistair Taylor, Sidgwick and Jackson, 1988. Reprinted by permission.

'Sgt. Pepper and Flower Power', Jon Wiener, *Come Together: John Lennon in His Time*, Jon Wiener, Faber and Faber Ltd, 1984. Reprinted by permission of the publisher.

Lennon Remembers, Jann S. Wenner, Verso, 2000. Reprinted by permission of Verso.

'The Beatles and the Guru', William F. Buckley, *National Review*, 12 March 1968. Reprinted by permission.

'The Beatles in Perspective', John Gabree, *Down Beat*, 1967. Reprinted by permission.

'The Beatles' Home Movie', Charles Marowitz, *Village Voice*, 4 January 1968.

'Metamorphosis of the Beatles', Pauline Kael, *The New Yorker*, 30 November 1968. Reprinted by permission.

'Beatles', Adrian Mitchell, *The Listener*, 3 October 1968. By permission of the author.

The Beatles, Hunter Davies, Jonathan Cape, 1968/ Weidenfeld and Nicolson, 2000. Reprinted by permission of the publisher.

Born Under a Bad Sign, Tony Palmer, William Kimber, 1970. Reprinted by permission of the author.

The Longest Cocktail Party, Richard Dilello, Mojo Books, 1972/2000. Reprinted by permission of Curtis Brown. Copyright © Richard Dilello 1972, 2000.

'Interview with John Lennon', Jonathan Cott, *Rolling Stone*, 23 November 1968. Reprinted by permission of the author.

'Rock and Fine Art', Carl Belz, *The Story of Rock*, Oxford University Press, 1969. Reprinted by permission of the author.

The Pendulum Years – Britain and the Sixties, Bernard Levin, Jonathan Cape, 1971. Reprinted by permission of Curtis Brown. Copyright © 1971 by Bernard Levin.

'1969: Helter Skelter', Ed Sanders, *The Family*, Ed Sanders, Hart Davies, 1971. Reprinted by permission of the author.

All You Needed Was Love, John Blake, Hamlyn, 1981. Reprinted by permission of the author.

Classic Rock Albums: Let It Be/Abbey Road, Peter Doggett, Schirmer, 1998. Reprinted by permission of the author.

'Those Inventive Beatles', William Mann, *The Times*, 5 December 1969. Reprinted by permission.

'Something', Nicholas Barber, *Lives of the Great Songs*, edited by Tim De Lisle, Pavilion, 1994.

Reprinted by permission of the author and editor.
As Time Goes By, Derek Taylor, Davies Poynter, 1973. Reprinted by permission of the Estate of Derek Taylor.
Lennon, Ray Coleman, Pan Macmillan, 1984. Reprinted by permission.
Apple to the Core: The Unmaking of the Beatles, Pete McCabe, Sphere, 1973.
'Interview with Paul McCartney', Richard Meryman, *Life*, April 1971. Reprinted by permission. Copyright © 1997 Time Inc.
'Introduction to *The Beatles*', Leonard Bernstein, *The Beatles*, Geoffrey Stokes, Time Books, 1980. Reprinted by permission of the Estate of Leonard Bernstein.
'Interview with George Harrison', Mitchell Glazer, *Crawdaddy*, February 1977.
'Power to the People', Robin Blackburn and Tariq Ali, *Red Mole*, 8–22 March 1971. Reprinted by permission of the authors.
When the Music's Over, Robin Denselow, Faber and Faber, 1989. Reprinted by permission of the author.
'Beatlemaniacs Never Die (But They Sure Get Carried Away)', Lilith Moon, *Creem*, November 1974. Reprinted by permission.
'Booting the Beatles', Charles P. Neises, *The Beatles Reader*, edited by Charles P. Neises, Popular Culture Ink, 1984.
'Magical History Tour', Jerry Lazar, *The Beatles Reader*, edited by Charles P. Neises, Popular Culture Ink, 1984.
'*Playboy* Interview with John Lennon and Yoko Ono', David Sheff, *Playboy Magazine*, January 1981. Copyright © 1980 by *Playboy*. Reprinted with permission. All rights reserved.
'New York City Blues', Adrian Henri, *Collected Poems* by Adrian Henri, Allison & Busby, 1986. Reprinted by permission of the author. Copyright © 1986 by Adrian Henri.
The Andy Warhol Diaries, edited by Pat Hackett, Warner Books, 1989.
Let Me Take You Down, Jack Jones, Virgin Books, 1992. Reprinted by permission.
'It Was Twenty Years Ago Today', Various interviewees, *The Observer*, 3 December 2000. Reprinted by permission.
'*Playboy* Interview with Paul and Linda McCartney', *Playboy Magazine*, April 1984. Copyright © 1984 by *Playboy*. Reprinted with permission. All rights reserved.
'George Harrison', Dave Laing and Penny Valentine, *The Guardian*, 1 December 2001. Reprinted by permission of the publisher.
'George Harrison 1943–2001: Youngest Beatle Loses Fight Against Cancer', Richard Williams, *The Guardian*, 1 December 2001. Reprinted by permission of the publisher.
'They Sought Without Finding', R. D. Laing, *Rolling Stone*, 16 February 1984. Reprinted by permission.
'Fighting the Fab', Philip Larkin, *The Observer*, 9 October 1983. Reprinted by permission.
'The Sound of the Sixties', Blake Morrison, *Times Literary Supplement*, 15 May 1981. Reprinted by permission.